a unified theory *of*
happiness

a unified theory *of*
happiness

An East-Meets-West Approach
to Fully Loving Your Life

Andrea F. Polard, PsyD

sounds true
BOULDER, COLORADO

Sounds True, Inc.
Boulder, CO 80306

Published 2012
Cover and book design by Rachael Murray
Photos on cover © Minerva Studio and Cbenjasuwan from Shutterstock.com
Illustrations © Lack-O'Keen, KoboldArt, W7, Christopher Jones, MedusArt
Printed in Canada

Library of Congress Cataloging-in-Publication Data

Polard, Andrea F.

A unified theory of happiness : an East-meets-West approach to fully loving your life /
by Andrea F. Polard.

    p. cm.

Includes bibliographical references and index.

ISBN 978-1-60407-788-9

1. Happiness. 2. Confidence. 3. East and West. I. Title.

BF575.H27P65 2012

158—dc23

                              2011039317

eBook ISBN: 978-1-60407-818-3

10 9 8 7 6 5 4 3 2 1

To the love of my life, the ever-caring father, the humanist,
the last lion, the man who sees God in nature,
the inspired gardener and artist, Steven Gregory Floren Polard.

He who binds to himself a joy
Does the winged life destroy;
But he who kisses the joy as it flies
Lives in eternity's sun rise.
WILLIAM BLAKE, "ETERNITY"

Contents

Part 3

THE SUPREME MODE

Foreword

I'm not a Buddhist or a psychologist—not even a person likely to open a self-improvement or spiritual book—but rather a professor of political science and an expert on China. And yet, I found myself surprisingly and deeply moved by this remarkable book. Pondering what was so different about *A Unified Theory of Happiness*, I concluded that it accomplishes something unique and transformative: it unifies not merely Western and Eastern concepts (thus satisfying the reader's thinking mind), but also provides something non-conceptual, something beyond words and worldviews, speaking to and transforming the reader's physical and spiritual mind.

In part it is Dr. Andrea Polard's style of language that elicits such a complete human response. The prose is not pragmatic, especially not for the research-based, scientifically sound study that it is. It is carefully crafted language with a poetic rhythm. The author refers to poetry with frequency, arousing aesthetic sensibilities in the reader. Interspersing the written language with graphics, images, a questionnaire, and exercises, the book engages the reader visually and personally. All of this makes the medicine—the many practical skills, exercises, building blocks, strategies, and Eastern techniques and paths—go down with ease and pleasure, opening the mind on many different levels simultaneously.

Beyond style, *A Unified Theory of Happiness* unites Western and Eastern approaches to happiness into one theory that Dr. Polard calls the Theory of Elastic Consciousness. It is not derived by finding commonalities in the causes of happiness, but rather by examining experiences of happiness—experiences that at first seem too diverse to cohere. Experiences of success, for example, are very different from experiences of love for people; experiences of love for people are very different from experiences of love for humanity or for life itself. Dr. Polard identifies what unites all of these experiences: namely a form of vibrancy, a stream or flow of consciousness, and a certain life quality, either generated in an active mode of consciousness or realized in a non-active mode of consciousness. The book's beauty is greatest when the reader begins to fathom that these two modes are already unified within consciousness, and that all that is left to do is to give attention to that whole.

Happiness has evaded far too many people. People have been seen as either happy or not—as if happiness is something one is born with or stumbles upon by luck. Fractions of happiness have been addressed in other books. *A Unified Theory of Happiness* is different—it makes the whole of happiness accessible to all. In a world too often filled with unhappiness, fear, materialism, and greed, this book shines. Do yourself a favor and read it; it will help you find happiness—or help happiness find you.

—Teresa Wright, PhD
Chair and Professor, Department of Political Science,
California State University, Long Beach
Author of *Accepting Authoritarianism: State-Society Relations in China's Reform Era* and *The Perils of Protest: State Repression and Student Activism in China and Taiwan*

Acknowledgments

This book would not be in your hands right now if it were not for my visionary publisher Tami Simon; the one and only Jennifer Y. Brown who "found" me; my masterful editor Florence Wetzel; copyeditor Elisabeth Rinaldi; and the whole spirited team of Sounds True. Thank you all.

Would I be at this juncture without the recommendation and encouragement of Rick Hanson, author of *Buddha's Brain,* and Howard Gardner, author of *Multiple Intelligences,* and his latest work *Truth, Beauty, and Goodness Reframed?* I will never know for sure. What I do know for sure is that they have touched my heart and caused me to believe in kindness even more. Thank you both.

I want to acknowledge all those who have inspired and enriched me with their ideas, but the list would be too long and, I'm afraid, incomplete. I am very grateful to all of you.

To my family and friends, thank you for being there during the last twelve years of writing this book, especially Sabina Floren and my mother, Elisabeth Floren; my beloved buddy Margo Gladjie; beloved Uncle Matthias Beltinger; and one bright star under the intellectual firmament: Sean Kearney. Also, thank you Teresa Wright for writing such a beautiful foreword.

Special thanks to the former head of the Zen Center of Los Angeles, my Zen teacher Bernard Silvers: your wisdom, compassion, and humility have greatly strengthened my experience of the all to which I belong.

To my children: Sophia, Tristan, and Karla, you have contributed so fundamentally to my happiness, you made me a real expert in that field. I am so grateful you are in my life.

Finally I wish to acknowledge and thank my beloved husband, Steven, who stood by me firmly, year after year, trusting I would grow as a writer in a foreign language, trusting I was following my bliss, and trusting that this would be beneficial not only to me, but to the wider community. Thank you for being my greatest critic and my best friend.

Introduction

L ife cannot be reduced to a single variable, and neither can happiness. Happiness is not a single type of positive human experience such as pleasure, control, surrender, compassion, or even love. Life is multifaceted, and so is happiness. If we wish our lives to be happy, we need to accept life's complexity and respond to it with our full human potential. We have to learn to relate to all facets of life.

Many popular psychology books center on only one or two aspects of happiness and are therefore destined to be ineffective. This book, written for seekers of true happiness, takes into consideration the whole of life and the necessity to reflect upon its dynamic complexity.

For nearly two decades I have explored happiness. I have found that once our primary needs are met, happiness depends entirely on the development of our consciousness. The development I refer to pertains to the ability of consciousness to change its focus and to skillfully relate to what it focuses upon. First, such a consciousness can narrow its attention and engage with other beings and external goals. Second, such a consciousness can broaden its engagement with life itself. It can thus slide in and out of two types of mental modes, namely the Basic Mode and the Supreme Mode. In the Basic Mode, we relate to "who" and "what" we perceive as distinct from ourselves. In the Supreme Mode, we relate to the plain Being that lies within us all. These two modes can work as harmoniously as the wings of a bird. I refer to this union as the Two Wings of Happiness.[1]

To obtain this harmony, we must examine both wings. Western thought is best suited to the Basic Mode. In the Basic Mode, we apply tools that help us function with deep satisfaction in various areas of life. I will elaborate on the Supreme Mode mostly from the Eastern perspective. The Supreme Mode stresses the realization of Being and the multitude of paths toward it. I integrate Eastern ideas into our Western way of thinking because focusing on Being gives us enormous peace and strength. This is deeply fulfilling, and it also makes us fit for action in the Basic Mode. Together the Basic Mode and the Supreme Mode make it possible to relate to all levels of life and achieve full life participation.

In order to develop our consciousness, we must find out how to access and utilize both modes. In part 1, I will begin by discussing both modes in depth, and follow up with the Two Wings of Happiness questionnaire for easy self-assessment. In parts 2 and 3, I will offer tools and paths to help you learn how to skillfully use and access both modes of consciousness. Each chapter ends with concrete suggestions and practical exercises. This book thus becomes a personalized guide for the transformation of consciousness that allows for your happiness to flourish.

You might be convinced that happiness is impossible for you, perhaps because pain and unhappiness currently dominate your life. I full-heartedly encourage you to treat your unhappiness. It is possible to get help, because there is much knowledge available about how to heal and manage yourself. However, do not expect that happiness will automatically follow from treating your unhappiness. It rarely does. Happiness needs special attention, because it relies on distinct knowledge and skills. No matter how long and well you treat your unhappiness, you need to focus on your happiness to make the quantum leap.[2]

As a psychologist and former victim of childhood abuse, I was tempted to focus only on unhappiness. Yet I was always looking for more—more than a mere "piece of sky." [3] My longing took me beyond psychotherapy and into meditation, comparative religion, philosophy, and the new science of happiness. Eventually, and with the help of personal relationships, I learned to soar. I learned that we can all make happiness a high priority. Happiness is well within our reach, and in some ways, it is already within us.

I invite you to learn how to master your life in the Basic Mode as well as how to become still, deeply touched, and nurtured by the experience of life in the Supreme Mode. In my conclusion, I will introduce the Theory of Elastic Consciousness, which shows the link and potential harmony between the two modes.

Let us now turn to the Two Wings of Happiness. Let us make them work for us. Let our wings spread, and let us fly above and beyond that which keeps us struggling and pinned to the ground.

HAPPINESS REFERENCE CHART	
BASIC MODE	**SUPREME MODE**
Confidence (chapter 7) Authenticity Self-Support Recognizing and Nurturing Existing Strengths Perseverance	**Receptivity** (chapter 9) Loosen Rigidities Skepticism Wonder versus Analysis Meditation Gratitude
Connection (chapter 6) The Importance of Connectedness Ten Building Blocks of Connections Connecting in Today's Society Feeling Disconnected	**Tranquility** (chapter 10) The Value of Tranquility Creating External Tranquility Understanding Our Buddha-Nature Trance and Tranquility The Practice of Humility
Competence (chapter 5) The Joy and Role of Competence Can We Afford to Develop Our Competence? Competence-Building Strategies	**Reliance** (chapter 11) Control versus Reliance What Not to Rely On Relying on Effort, Compassion, and Virtues Relying on Indefinable Being
Ambition (chapter 4) What Constitutes Good Goals? How Do I Discover Good Goals? Playing the Game Well	**Lightheartedness** (chapter 12) The Nature of Lightheartedness On Becoming an Adult Rediscovering the Nature of Lightheartedness via Eight Qualities
Mind/Body Fitness	
Nutrition	Exercise
Commitment to Happiness	
Definition of Happiness	
Differentiation from Survival Feeling Fully Engaged: Happiness as Full-Life Participation	The Confluence of Western and Eastern Thought
Surviving Well	
Psychological Health (Treating Unhappiness) Pleasure	Opportunities Competitiveness in the Workplace
Surviving	
Fulfillment of Basic Needs Peace Global Nuclear Disarmament Green Energy (Reverse Global Warming)	Healthcare Law, Order, Regulations Protection of Ecosystems

Part I

Happiness and the Two Modes of Consciousness

There are only two lasting bequests we can hope to give our children. One of these is roots, the other, wings.
HODDING CARTER

The Two Wings of Happiness

By drawing on wisdom that is balanced—ancient and new,
Eastern and Western, even liberal and conservative—
we can choose directions in life that will lead to satisfaction,
happiness, and a sense of meaning.

JONATHAN HAIDT

As long as we do not chase happiness the way dogs chase their tails, happiness is a superior way of being, inviting creativity, increasing a sense of efficacy, and attracting and motivating others. As the ground-breaking research of Barbara Frederickson demonstrates, positive emotions broaden our resources, from the intellectual to the social.[1] Because of all these advantages, happiness may even help us live longer.[2] With happiness being such a good thing, Thomas Jefferson included it in the Declaration of Independence, making it a "'self-evident' objective" and an inalienable right to pursue.[3]

Happiness is good for us, but primarily, it just *feels* good. Some happy people attribute their happiness to luck, some others to the fact that they appear younger and more beautiful than their unhappy counterparts. The physical attractiveness of happy people has its origin in their smiles and laughter, expressions that put people's best face forward.[4] Most people want to be happy, appear happy, and share their happy experience with their peers.

There is no doubt: happiness is good, feels good, and does a lot of good. The desire for happiness is so strong that the ancient Greek philosopher Aristotle (384–322 BC) concluded that we are born to be happy, and everything we do is an attempt to achieve happiness.[5]

Based on these observations and highly regarded philosophical input, it only seems logical to assume that Mother Nature would provide happiness-seekers with a little help, such as a genetic program that sets us on our way and protects us from major mistakes. After all, we have pretty good instincts about our survival; that is, the survival of our genes. Left alone, these instincts can guide us like an automatic pilot through the jungle of life. In other words, we have good reason to expect that happiness is easily accessible and easy to come by. It is understandable that we expect happiness to be easily accessible, especially because the flourishing "happiness industry" in the West reinforces this belief: we are bombarded with products and ideas that promise to work like jumper cables, turning something inside of us on, instantly, simply, and reliably.

Current Western thinking only encourages these expectations. Cognitive psychology, for example, seems to suggest that our entire well-being is the result of positive thinking, according to the mottos "Think happy and you are happy" or "Think positive, and everything will turn out positive." Serious scientists in the field of Positive Psychology, such as trailblazers Martin Seligman and Mihaly Csikszentmihalyi (who we will discuss in subsequent chapters),[6] know that human behavior cannot be traced back to a single aspect or a single thought. This, unfortunately, does not stop popular writers from propagating "*the* secret of happiness."

Eastern thinking—at least the way it is frequently packaged and sold—also encourages our expectations for quick fixes and easy happiness. We only have to be compassionate to be happy (Tibetan Buddhists), or to let go of preconceived notions to be happy (Zen Buddhists), or to feel "the energy" to be happy (Hindus). Although, once again, serious practitioners regret the trivialization of these deep wisdom traditions, plenty of enthusiastic well-wishers keep popularizing "the moment," within which lies the power to become rich tomorrow and remain young forever.

We need to ask ourselves how reality fits into our expectations. Even though some slogans and products can be helpful, none ever work the way they promise. The truth is, happiness does not come easily. Despite society's calls to happiness, most people feel left behind. Instead of being keyed to the goal of happiness, we seem keyed to the survival of our genes, seeking our advantage even when we *clearly* impair our happiness. Against our better judgment, we stress ourselves and our children to assure the best possible spot in the hierarchy of our group. Not the positive, but the negative, more stressful, fear-driven strategies, such as fighting and fleeing, come easily to us, which is why they, and not the happy ones, are so ubiquitous.

There are no quick fixes for one reason: there is nothing much to fix. We have no biological program, no automatic pilot, and no strong instinct to guide us toward happiness. It is time and—as will soon become apparent—advantageous to confront Aristotle and his premise that our ultimate goal is happiness. Mother Nature, or the entirety of what we refer to as "biological nature," wants nothing more than that her children's genes live on. Aristotle neither had knowledge of the evolutionary process nor of our genes. Without this knowledge, even the best thinkers are bound to mistake *a* wish for happiness with *the* wish of all wishes: the automatic, ultimate goal for all human beings at all times and in all cultures.

The fact that there is little in our biological nature that compels us to aim for happiness might dampen our enthusiasm. Yet we can also make several good and encouraging claims about happiness. The first one is that happiness and survival must not be mutually exclusive. Indeed, they often overlap: that which is good for our happiness can be good for our survival. Because of this overlap, there is a slight pressure in our culture to improve the conditions in which happiness can thrive. It is very encouraging to see the resulting slow movement toward happiness, as people increasingly want more than just to "do well" or "do better." Also, Mother Nature allows us to be aware of her and make conscious choices. This means we are free to guide her. After acknowledging that she is limited in what she can do for us in regard to happiness, we can begin to see the good in her. I find it wonderful that we are free to see Mother Nature for who she is, in relation and in contrast to ourselves. Mother Nature permits us to be conscious, permits us to see her in the midst of herself, and, ultimately, permits us be guided by something other than the goal to survive. These degrees of freedom are part of our human potential, and that's good news.

9

AN INVITATION TO HAPPINESS

I've stated that it is advantageous to confront the premise that human beings automatically pursue happiness. Why? Because doing so opens our eyes to reality so we can make an informed decision about the direction we want to take in life. We can decide to give happiness the necessary importance. Also, by consciously ranking happiness as high as—or even higher than—our survival, we are in a much better position to learn new skills. Knowing that happiness rests upon a conscious decision implies the recognition that happiness can be learned. As we choose a goal, we become more motivated to learn and apply ourselves toward that goal. Now that too is good news when it comes to happiness.

Indeed, deciding to live not merely for survival but for happiness sets us on a promising path. It is a path that is more complicated than the path of survival, where we either try to win or prevent others from winning. It is a path on which we engage in adventures of love, creativity, passion, and peace. It is definitely the road less traveled, scattered with numerous unforeseeable risks.[7] Doors may be opened to places we have never visited before, where it is unclear who wins and who loses. Our views may change as our horizon broadens, threatening our very identity. Although exciting, facing the unknown is not always pleasant, and it is sometimes difficult. Choosing happiness as our road less traveled, the high road so to speak, reminds us of that and of why such a choice is necessary, preparing us for the uncertainties along the way and helping us to stay the course.

If we do not choose happiness as our goal, we are left with several options. Unless we have been blessed with an outstanding education from happiness-practicing parents, we are likely to live mostly for our survival. This option is good and necessary when we live under horrid circumstances. Comparative studies by psychologist Ed Diener show that if we cannot take care of our basic needs, we are, with few exceptions, simply too *un*happy to be happy.[8] Accordingly, the poorest people in the world report lower levels of happiness than the more prosperous ones.[9] Yet unless we are in dire need, there is no significant correlation between material success and happiness. Should we live exclusively or primarily for the former, progress comes at the price of depression and anxiety.

Not choosing happiness as a priority can also leave us stranded, lost, and empty, especially in Western societies where many people have lost their religious bearings. We know that human beings do not live on bread alone, that we need food for our souls too, nourishment that is traditionally provided by religion. As religion incrementally loses its influence, many people end up spiritually starved.[10] At the first sign of trouble or at any crossroad with the sign "survival" pointing in one direction and the sign "happiness" in the other, we choose the familiar direction, hoping to find soul food in more empty calories. To even know the difference between the two directions, happiness has to be a serious agenda for us.

In a society in which happiness is growing on people, there is yet another option for those who do not like to commit to happiness and whose main interest is survival. As the talk of the town becomes more often "happiness," and as our culture speaks more frequently of our human potential, we begin to feel the pain of not participating in this conversation and of not fulfilling that potential.[11] I am not referring to the ever-pervasive peer pressure that urges us to smile when we don't want to, but to a changing consciousness, a new Zeitgeist that is putting out an open invitation, saying something like:

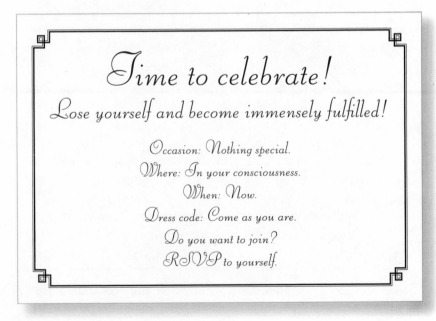

Time to celebrate!

Lose yourself and become immensely fulfilled!

Occasion: Nothing special.
Where: In your consciousness.
When: Now.
Dress code: Come as you are.
Do you want to join?
RSVP to yourself.

If we ignore this invitation, maybe out of fear, maybe out of contempt, maybe for no reason whatsoever, we will eventually feel the pain of missing out. Anybody who loves life wants to celebrate it. As more and more people are in the position to love life because their primary needs are fulfilled, not wanting to celebrate it is akin to self-inflicting pain. We need to sing hymns to life, dance with its music, speak up, speak out, do it, feel it, and be it.

When we decide for happiness and accept the invitation, our attitude will help us become ready to adopt a variety of different skills to cultivate happiness. Some of these skills will come from the West, others from the East. When we ignore or reject the invitation, life will eventually feel painful, as it does whenever we settle for less without good cause. As writer Anaïs Nin puts it: "There came a time when the risk to remain tight in the bud was more painful than the risk it took to blossom."[12]

So make that decision! Do not leave your fate up to your biological nature. Instead, pledge yourself wholeheartedly to happiness. Everything that follows in this book will come much easier if you have prepared by making this important decision. It is your RSVP for the invitation to celebrate life:

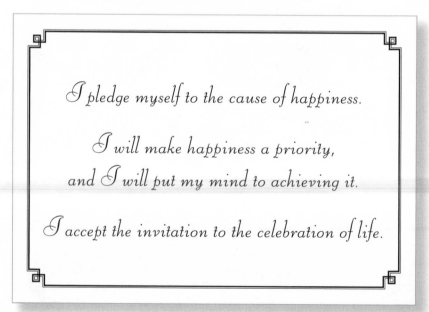

I pledge myself to the cause of happiness.

I will make happiness a priority,
and I will put my mind to achieving it.

I accept the invitation to the celebration of life.

Although we are largely genetically unprepared to celebrate life, we are born to make decisions. Even though we cannot choose to rid ourselves of Mother Nature, who is part of our greater human nature, we can choose to keep her at bay when necessary, work with her harmoniously when possible, refuse the seductive methods she uses to contribute to the goal of survival—such as greed, hatred, and fear—and instead utilize other tools to reach our goal of happiness.

Much can be achieved when we put our mind to it. For example, we are not exactly genetically predisposed to read and write, yet look how far we have come with plain and technical texts, playful prose and poetry, all of which inform, connect, and inspire people across the globe. Who needs genes when we have been bestowed with the gift of mind?

WHAT IS HAPPINESS?

Having chosen not just to live, but to live with happiness, being determined not to obey blindly the command "Survive at all cost!," and to follow goals and other inherent virtues that may or may not be in alignment with this command, we should wonder what happiness is exactly. A surprising number of researchers skip over this point. Many view happiness as something too personal and elusive to define. Consequently, the subjects of their respective studies are left to rate themselves on scales that contain terms that are only loosely associated with happiness. The implicit idea behind this omission is that everybody already knows intuitively what happiness is.

Besides leaving us to wonder if people who participate in research projects think of happiness as something that is socially desirable, and whether they equate happiness with pleasure, meaning, goodness, luck, the love of God, contentment, big breasts, or self-induced rushes of adrenaline, it is a fallacy to believe that we all know intuitively what happiness is. Within human history, happiness is a very young subject of study.[13] Few people have had the luxury to ponder the question of happiness, a luxury of which even fewer people approved.

It was not too long ago that mentioning Paul Watzlawick's "guidelines for unhappiness" triggered instant admiration among my fellow psychologists, while mentioning the subject of happiness raised serious eyebrows.[14] To think about happiness was considered a waste of time; to want happiness a sign of superficiality; and to experience happiness a sign of neurotic evasiveness.

Because of these biases and the relative novelty of the subject, it is a challenge to define happiness, requiring not only the use of empirical research, but first and foremost a systematic deduction and careful synthesis of that which was deduced. I took on this challenge with the hope that the results might be helpful and will be improved upon by future happiness scholars. I'd like to share my process with you in the hopes that you will find it helpful to understanding my views on happiness.

First I accumulated diverse thoughts about happiness with the help of a purposive sample—an intentionally chosen group most likely to represent a subject matter. The sample consisted of (1) descriptions of happiness by fiction and nonfiction writers, and (2) descriptions of happiness by approximately one hundred interviewees who had expressed interest in the subject of happiness. The latter group was given an informal interview, leading with the question: "What is happiness in your opinion?" and proceeding with follow-up questions for clarification purposes.

To begin with, it is worthwhile noting that both writers and interviewees frequently explain happiness by pointing out what it is not. After giving it some thought, most people believe that happiness is not related to "having," as in having certain characteristics, positions, goods, or money. Indeed, a surprising number of people contest that happiness cannot be bought. Also, for most people, happiness is not a final outcome, such as something we can possess, but rather something that must be regenerated because "you get used to everything," "things may not turn out to be as you had thought," and "things change throughout our lifetime."

Early in the process, I realized that in many descriptions of happiness, there was a need to distinguish between causes for happiness and the experience of happiness. There are as many causes of happiness as there are people, a fact that probably contributes to researchers' hesitation to define happiness. Yet when people speak or write about the experience of happiness, words

14

and patterns begin to repeat themselves, suggesting commonalities between individual experiences and pointing to overarching themes. Not surprisingly, the experience does lend itself to the use of "being" statements: being in the flow of things, being elevated, being fulfilled, being overwhelmed, being taken by experiences—experiences described as flying, floating, swimming, and dancing. In other words, people think of happiness as a dynamic state of well-being, a state in which we are advantageously and energetically engaged.

Keeping the term "dynamic" in mind will help us shape a definition of happiness, and it can also point to the importance of good nutrition and exercise. Both are needed for dynamic states. A balanced diet of low-sugar, low-salt whole foods, little or no red meat, possibly fish, and lots of fruits and vegetables, as well as exercise, stimulates the production of neurotransmitters, hormones, and neurotrophic proteins.[15] All of the above contribute to good brain chemistry. Exercise especially leads to healthy and even new brain cells that rid themselves of toxins and communicate well with each other. As a result of exercise and good nutrition, we become inoculated against stress, feel energized, and stay younger, healthier, and more focused. While in this context I can only hint at mind-body fitness, it is surely part of the foundation of our well-being.

So far we can ascertain that for most people, happiness is not so much connected with "having" as with "being" and that it is a dynamic process, requiring energy and thus mind-body fitness. When I examined the explications on happiness further, I noticed that they frequently contradicted each other, not unlike biblical texts, causing confusion, if not schisms, among believers.

For example, some accounts of happiness stress the importance of taking initiative and control: "You are the maker of your own happiness," while others warn against such intrusion: "The more you look for happiness, the less likely you will find it." Companionship seems just as essential to some people as solitude is to others. The list of contradicting accounts on happiness is endless. Let me share just a few:

"My greatest happiness consists precisely in doing nothing whatever that is calculated to obtain happiness. . . . Contentment and well-being become possible the moment you cease to act with them in view." —Chuang Tzu Chuang	versus	"One is happy as a result of one's own efforts, once one knows the necessary ingredients of happiness—simple tastes, a certain degree of courage, self-denial to a point, love of work, and above all, a clear conscience. Happiness is no vague dream, of that I now feel certain." —George Sand
"I find it wholesome to be alone the greater part of the time. To be in company, even with the best, is soon wearisome and dissipating. I love to be alone. I never found the companion that was so companionable as solitude." —Henry David Thoreau	versus	"Happiness is in the comfortable companionship of friends." —Pam Brown "All who joy would win must share it—happiness was born a twin." —Lord Byron
"Happiness is as a butterfly, which, when pursued, is always just beyond our grasp, but which, if you will sit down quietly, may alight upon you." —Nathaniel Hawthorne	versus	"Far away there in the sunshine are my highest aspirations. I may not reach them, but I can look up to see their beauty, believe in them, and try to follow where they lead." —Louisa May Alcott
"Contentment is the philosopher's stone, that turns all it toucheth into gold; the poor man is rich with it, the rich man is poor without it." —Proverb	versus	"Create all the happiness you are able to create: Remove all the misery you are able to remove." —Jeremy Bentham
"The sense of existence is the greatest happiness." —Benjamin Disraeli	versus	"Existence is a strange bargain. Life owes us little; we owe it everything. The only true happiness comes from squandering ourselves for a purpose." —William Cowper

We may look at these contradictions as two sides of the same coin—the coin being happiness. This conclusion is likely because these contradictions have something essential in common: they all point to the good and full life, a life in which we are positively and dynamically engaged.

HAPPINESS AND THE STREAM OF LIFE

All explications of happiness are about the experience of engagement with or participation in life. When we understand happiness as such, namely as the experience of participating in life, negative experiences become part of it. People who ponder happiness know this and often include the entire spectrum of bad feelings. Just think of parenting. Kids can be a real pain: robbing parents of their sleep, creating havoc in the house, forcing parents to relearn schoolwork they may have disliked the first time around, and stressing parents' relationship. And yet . . . and yet: could there be anything greater than watching kids play, giggle, and throw themselves into our arms? Yes, displeasure, sadness, and anger *can* and sometimes *must* be part of happiness. But as long as we experience ourselves overwhelmingly as participants in life, we can consider ourselves happy.

Accordingly, the opposite of happiness is the overwhelming experience of static disengagement, of standing by life, as if separated by impenetrable glass through which we observe the lives of others, like spies. And really, the greatest pain is feeling a single feeling statically and repeatedly, or feeling nothing at all, as often happens with clinical depression.

It does therefore not come as a surprise that researchers find that the inability to participate in valued life activities is a major hallmark of depression. Cantor and Sanderson, for example, describe depression as typically associated with alienation from both activities and relationships.[16] Nothing important seems to happen when we feel this alienated. When we become aware of other people participating in life while we do not, our unhappiness knows no bounds. Life seems in our grasp, and yet it feels like a play on a stage that we cannot join. We envy the ones on stage even when they cry, because at least they are alive, while our heart just keeps ticking and ticking, with neither emotional

17

highs nor lows, without rhyme or reason, without consequence or meaning.

The acceptance that timely unhappy feelings are part of happiness is a quintessential step, because from then on our hearts and minds are more open, wider, allowing us to take in more of the world with which we wish to feel connected. For example, if we cannot mourn after the death of a loved one, we are closed off from life in some significant way. Not feeling sad or disappointed in a relationship on occasion is a sign of disengagement, of an inability to be intimate with self and other. Even more charged feelings, such as fear and anger, have a place in the happy life, however civilized and contained they must be. This is not saying that we must always act on what we feel or become overwhelmed by our feelings. We must, however, accept that which we feel or at least notice that which we feel.

Because of the bad reputation negative feelings have acquired in both the West and the East, we are frequently warned against these monsters lurking in the dark, ready to attack and to plague us mindlessly. However, clinging to happy feelings, chasing after the light while running away from uncomfortable truths, can bring on bigger monsters, self-deception being one of them. If we want to be part of the stream of life, we must accept changes in the stream. Changes are inevitable, and our feelings alert us to these changes and thus contribute to the full life. They only cause problems and impair the good life when they erupt without a purpose and awareness, when they linger and control our actions, or when they are all we have to lean on.

So, happiness is not just one experience or the accumulation of only good experiences. Nor is happiness the whole spectrum of experiences all at once, without emphasis, order, or direction. Common sense suggests that happiness has to do with harmony, not chaos. What orders our experiences is a multitude of functional relationships with the world, relationships that are based on skill and focused attention. As a result of these functional relationships, we get to experience who we are besides ego, namely a creative partaker in life. Happiness depends, in other words, on our ability to relate, a dynamic experience par excellence.

HAPPINESS AND ACTION

With these thoughts in mind, I took another look at the contradictions that I had found in people's explications of happiness. I noticed that the contradictions were pointing at two different types of relationships with the world: (1) being *active;* that is, taking part or making ourselves a part of life, and (2) being *non-active;* that is, realizing how we are already taken in by life as one of its parts. Happiness, I concluded, had to be the result of relating to life both ways.

Let us explore the active way of participating in life first. We make ourselves predominantly a part of life by way of relating to other people: our parents, siblings, life partner, children, friends, neighbors, coworkers, dogs, cats—in short, to our fellow creatures. This is why we find endless references to love, compassion, and friendship in spoken and written accounts of happiness. Being the social animals that we are, nothing cuts us off from life quite as much as social isolation. To Aristotle—the most influential proponent of the active way of happiness—friends were so important that he considered a life without them not worth living.[17] While this may seem an extreme position, there is overwhelming support that personal relationships are the most important ingredient to happiness (see chapter 6).

We also make ourselves a part of life when we work toward realizing our dreams. The pursuit of definable goals can be considered a relationship when we receive feedback about our work in progress. Mihaly Csikszentmihalyi has written extensively about this type of relationship with life, emphasizing the focused pursuit of attainable and individualized, suitable goals.[18] In doing so, we would create a harmoniously ordered consciousness that generates an experience often described as *flow.* Csikszentmihalyi writes that flow experiences "add up to a sense of mastery—or perhaps better, a sense of participation in determining the content of life—that comes as close to what is usually meant by happiness as anything else we can conceivably imagine."[19]

The idea of happiness as active participation dominates Western thought. We tend to believe that happiness is the result of active interactions with the world of form or mental formations, including other living beings and external goals. Our interactions are supposed to empower us and, when applicable, empower others as well. We believe that work, play, and love lead to happiness—which is true, at least in part.

HAPPINESS AND NONACTION

Active life participation is not the whole story of happiness, not even in the West. When we look at our most influential book, the Old Testament or Torah, we see that it begins with the ulti-mate story of active participation: God pursued an immense—but for him suitable and attainable goal—namely the creation of the entire world in less than a week. Humans were supposed to dom-inate the earth and thus parallel in some way the divine activity.

Yet, regardless of how pleased God was with his creation, it was not the six days of work that he sanctified, but the day after. We learn one of the reasons for this sanctification was that he had spent that day resting:

> And on the seventh day God ended his work which he had made; and he rested on the seventh day from all his work which he had made. And God blessed the seventh day, and sanctified it: because that in it he had rested from all his work which God created and made.[20]

In the New Testament, we find another poignant example of happiness being something other than just active participation. In the Gospel of Matthew, Jesus advises us that we should not spend all our time working for and worrying about our livelihood. He insists that things fall into place when we have faith in God:

> Consider the lilies of the field, how they grow; they toil not, nei-ther do they spin: And yet I say unto you, That even Solomon in all his glory was not arrayed like one of these. Wherefore, if God so clothe the grass of the field, which to-day is, and to-morrow is cast into the oven, shall he not much more clothe you, O ye of little faith?[21]

Therefore, besides active life participation being happiness, there is the complementary way. It isn't an inactive way; passivity can hardly be associated with happiness. Instead, it is a nonactive way. When we realize that we are already a part of life or existence—which is by definition the one and only, and thus perfect in its own right—we refrain from struggling and striving, from hustling and bustling, meddling and molding. At times of heightened awareness of existence, we no longer have the urge to do and to interfere. Instead, we notice what is being done, to us, for us, and through us. Doing subsides when we notice Being; everything slows down, we relax and enjoy.

Much of Eastern thought is devoted to this nonactive way of life participation. Lao-tzu, the legendary founder of the Chinese philosophy of Taoism, wrote:

> The way to use life is to do nothing through acting,
> The way to use life is to do everything through being.[22]

The same lines in another translation begin with the word *Tao*, which may be translated as "the Way," "movement," or "essence of nature":

> Tao never makes any ado,
> And yet it does everything.[23]

So, the nonactive way of life participation is not the doing of nothing, but the awareness of life in and around us as it does everything so wonderfully and so completely. In other words, nonactive participation is realizing our relatedness to the great stream of life. We can see the stream when we do something or when we do nothing, but we do need to keep our eyes open for it.

The active way makes us get our hands dirty, plant the seeds, harvest the fruit, and share it with friends and family. The nonactive way is seeing the interplay of hands and dirt, plant and seeds, sun and fruit, friends and family. Neither way is enough by itself: Action without awareness makes time fly and life short; awareness without action uproots us, making us think we fly, while really we are just out of touch with Earth.

Western writer Hermann Hesse, who was heavily influenced by Eastern thought, wrote about happiness from the nonactive perspective. On one occasion, he described the happiest moment of his life. I paraphrase:

> It happened on a Sunday morning when I was just a young boy. Almost asleep, lying on my bed, I was staring through a window at the sky and the roof of my home. Suddenly I felt in complete alignment with the world. While looking at the different shades of blues and browns of the sky and the roof, the colors seemed to play with each other. They made sense to me. They belonged together as a unit. I was wide awake, all while I felt independent from time; I neither feared nor hoped for anything.[24]

To feel such happiness, the young Hesse had to have had a heightened sense of his participation in this unity at that moment in time. This sense is a reoccurring theme in much of Eastern thought. Buddhists, for example, contemplate or meditate in order to sense their oneness with the world.[25] No feeling about the past or present, no thought, no tangible goal should bind the mind if we want to sense our partaking in this oneness to its full extent.

Grounded in Eastern thought and based on these kinds of experiences, Hesse defines happiness as follows:

> The participation in timeless being, in the eternal music of the world, in what others have called the harmony of the spheres or the smile of God. . . . To breathe with the perfect now, to sing with the choir of the spheres, to dance in the round dance of the world, that is how we take part in happiness.[26]

Without focusing on the moment, the young Hesse could not have heard the "eternal music of the world." Indeed, both the active and nonactive way of life participation depend on the ability to focus our attention. When we focus strongly on a distinct entity or a goal on one hand, or when we focus on Being on the other hand, everything else disappears into the background, including our sense of possession, time, ego, and even our feelings. A weight is lifted when matter (form) or ideas (mental formations) about matter lose power, causing us to feel less burdened, more free, and alive.

22

Unfortunately, the defenders of the active way of life participation often do not see the value of the nonactive way, and vice versa. Thus most people understand, appreciate, and practice consciously only half of the skills of happiness, always missing something of the complementary side, never feeling completely fulfilled or confidently on the right track.

People limit their happiness without realizing it. The Persian Shah Nasreddin is a historic example of this one-sidedness. When he traveled through Europe in 1873, the Shah was puzzled by the action-oriented ways of people he expected to be happy. He simply could not fathom why one emperor, for instance, "slaved away" even though many competent people surrounded him. When the Shah was invited to dance, he felt almost repulsed because in his world only slaves engaged in such "tiresome activity." He was much relieved when his host spared him from participating in the ball.[27]

Then again, the makers and shakers of modern societies are, at best, limited to the active way of life participation, practically condemning nonactivity that is simply Being. Appreciating life the way it is, marveling at existence, enjoying Being without rushing to action, seems like a waste of time to a great many people. Besides, nonaction is all too easily mistaken for laziness, the devil in productive or capitalistic societies. We look suspiciously upon stillness, leisure, and even sleep. The philosopher Alan Watts observed: "Despite the immense hubbub and nervous strain, we are convinced that sleep is a waste of valuable time and continue to chase these fantasies far into the night."[28] Westerners especially steal time from the night. Deprived of rest, we often end up worrying too much about the future, never being fully in the present moment. This tendency contributes to the spiritual void in our highly productive times. In the long run, doing without connecting with Being, without stillness and rest, leaves us empty, even when we can generate flow experiences and good personal connections.

Happiness is therefore not possible when we limit ourselves to either creating relationships (striving), or to realizing our existing relationships (serenity). To be happy we need a balance between these two main ways of experiencing our participation in life. They are two sides of one coin.

BALANCING ACTION WITH NONACTION

But how do we strike a balance between these two ways of participating in life? Since experiences are created in our consciousness, it is our consciousness that must somehow find its way, and that must somehow know what to focus on in any given moment.

Each way of participating in life requires particular skills, particular know-how, and particular focus. Our consciousness must access particular states or modes, one which I call "basic" and one which I call "supreme." When we actively relate to the so-called objective world, we are in a Basic Mode—not to be mistaken with the survival mode in which we relate to form. When we focus on Being, we are in a Supreme Mode—not to be mistaken for inactivity or passivity.

While one mode tends to facilitate the other, they are still very different from one another. The distinction between the two modes of consciousness helps us sort through seemingly contradicting ideas and experiences of happiness. Together the Basic Mode and the Supreme Mode are what I refer to as the Two Wings of Happiness. Following this line of thinking, we arrive at this definition of happiness:

> Happiness is when we habitually experience both active and nonactive participation in life. The experience of active participation is generated in the Basic Mode of consciousness, in which we focus on and actively relate to distinct other beings and external goals in the so-called objective world. The experience of nonactive participation is generated in the Supreme Mode of consciousness, in which we focus on and relate to non-distinct Being.

I know this definition is a mouthful, and that it is simplicity that we crave. But simplicity does not apply when it comes to happiness. By walking mindfully along the road of happiness, without short-cuts and empty promises, we learn to identify and pick the treats that grow along the road less traveled. Happiness is a complex path that becomes easy only as we walk it.

INTRODUCING THE TWO MODES
OF CONSCIOUSNESS

Let me begin this introduction by pointing out what the two modes of consciousness have in common. As noted, both modes depend upon our ability to focus. Whether we look to the West or to the East, happiness escapes the unfocused mind. Left alone, our consciousness wobbles like an amoeba, bumping indiscriminately into things, engulfing whatever it can use, surviving at all costs. Unfocused, we live below capacity, without choice, direction, and fulfillment. Leaving our consciousness to its own devices saps our vitality.

In contrast, focusing our consciousness helps us absorb information, grow, and possibly change the very information on which we focus. Because focused attention facilitates interchanges with our environment, it is instrumental in our ability to partake in life, and is thus instrumental to our happiness.

Furthermore, it is not only important that we focus, but it's important what we focus on. A murderer focuses on killing his victim, but is not happy. A good thief is watchful while stealing a car, and a good liar is vigilant while concealing the truth, but they are not happy, at least not in the long run. Not only do we need focus, but we also need to focus on good goals, good people, and on the good life that is Being.

An engineer who focuses on good goals is not happy when he goes home to an empty, cold house. A workaholic does not have the time to relate to anybody or to Being long enough to benefit, however full and warm her house. Regardless of how much enjoyment we get out of our focused mind, nothing should ever separate us from human connection and from Being in general. It is essential to our happiness that our focused attention never impinges on our general sense of relatedness, but instead enhances it.

We must strike a careful balance in our relationships with and within life. We must focus on good goals, good people, and on Being, without neglecting any one of these three variables. The problem is that the right balance is highly personal and that it changes throughout our lifetime. No teacher or book can tell us with certainty how exactly to weigh and fill in the variables. It is our job to learn about ourselves, about how we relate and do not relate when in the two modes of consciousness, namely the Basic Mode and the Supreme Mode. Taking a closer look at each mode and identifying their distinctive characteristics is part of learning more about ourselves.

BASIC MODE

Focusing on a goal and focusing on a person in the Basic Mode have in common that the focal point is outside our consciousness. When we focus on a definable, external goal, we feel a relationship with it. The relationship is between us (the "Self") and an "Other." If we pursue the Other ambitiously, competently, and confidently, the relationship becomes filled with life, as opposed to the individual self only. We experience this relationship as an energetic flow, a tension, an interchange between us and the goal.

When we relate to another sentient being, we also experience an energetic flow, a flow that is socially if not erotically charged. A sustainable flow rises when the focus shifts from two separate selves to a mutually empowering relationship, which requires work and effort, similar to the pursuit of good goals. Let us imagine our consciousness in the Basic Mode as something that is stretching between us on the one side and a distinct being or goal on the other side:

Basic Mode

In the Basic Mode, our consciousness focuses on external
focal points that are capable of giving feedback. This
creates an energetic flow between Self and Other.

To cause an energetic flow, our consciousness must be extended. In other words we must keep some distance from the Other. While the relationship makes us feel part of life, in the Basic Mode we can neither merge with a goal or another being entirely, nor can we allow ourselves to become cut off from it, her, or him. When we are too close to a problem, for example, we won't see all of the issues and will therefore get side-tracked. On the other hand, if we are too far from a problem, we lose touch with its reality and miss the issues altogether. In both instances, the process of solving the problem won't make us feel alive.

The same goes for personal relationships. Except on rare occasions, namely when we cross over to the Supreme Mode in a balanced way, it is counterproductive to feel ourselves as "one" with the Other. We need to maintain and even enhance a separate sense of self by developing our unique potential. On the other hand, we should not lose sight of the relationship. It is extremely important to share ourselves, as well as continuously take an active interest or delight in the other. Without the right distance between us and the other, our relationship will become lame and lifeless.

In order to make our relationships with goals or people good and fulfilling, we have to focus on one at a time. Our consciousness can only be extended to one Other when we want to feel invigorated and alive. As necessary and exciting as multitasking may be, it overstimulates us. Of course we can and should have many goals and friends in our life. Yet, each needs spotlight attention in order to uphold the energetic relationship. If we do not know how or are unable to set priorities, we become flustered and, in the long run, unhappy.

When we focus on one goal or on one person at a time, we often do and have good reason to expect success. Accordingly, in the Basic Mode we want to feel that something is within our reach. Keeping our eyes on the ball enables us to score points, solve problems, and build skills. Expectations rise—and sometimes should rise—when we pursue something or someone. Beware of expecting nothing, because this will likely turn into getting nothing. Think of personal relationships. Women especially were—and sometimes are still—being told that they should not have any expectations about their significant other, that woman should only give and act devoted, self-forgetting, and self-denying, preferably with a smile on their faces. However, while certain or too many expectations can obstruct happiness in our pursuits, having no expectations definitely obstructs happiness.

Let us now summarize the distinctive characteristics of the Basic Mode:

- spotlight/single-pointed attention
- tension between Self and Other
- distance between Self and Other
- expectation of a successful pursuit of an external goal or of a distinct other being
- effort

Because pursuing relationships with goals and people takes effort, our experiences in the Basic Mode are not always optimal. Even with a lot of practice, we constantly have to adjust our skills and expectations. It is an enormous challenge for people with multiple responsibilities to allocate ample time for any pursuit other than making a living. Sometimes we are just too tired or too distracted to give and receive feedback. Outside information or support may be needed but hard to come by. Interpersonal relationships are especially vulnerable, because we are "moving targets" for each other, meaning that the flow between two people can easily become interrupted.

SUPREME MODE

Even when all the criteria for a perfect experience are met, we cannot intensely concentrate onto an external goal or another being forever. The tension takes its toll. While our relationships with an Other cause us to feel alive and empowered, this can also become too much of a good thing. For all these reasons, our consciousness eventually withdraws its attention, and the boundaries we experience between the world of form and ourselves become blurry. Our consciousness turns on itself. If this happens with awareness, we access the Supreme Mode of consciousness in which we feel our all Being.

Instead of the single-pointed attention that we need in the Basic Mode, we need "floodlight" or general attention for the experience of Being in the Supreme Mode. Being does not just entail our own mind-body, but everything that exists. Still, we begin and end all experiences of Being in our own mind, that is, in the Supreme Mode of consciousness. Congruency between what is on our mind and our mind itself, between Self and Other, is like a rubber band contracting to a point. Perfect congruency is what is known as enlightenment in Eastern thought. It is the mind in extreme awareness of itself. It is the tranquil mind that has let go of any desire or particular object, that has no expectation, and is entirely emerged in the present.

Supreme Mode

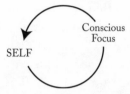

In the Supreme Mode, our consciousness focuses onto itself and experiences no distinction between Self and Other, only the energetic flow within consciousness that is Being or nonduality.

Aware of our consciousness, we are both relaxed and alert, which allows us to experience the spontaneity of life. The focus is no longer on controlling action but on action as it arises, that is, on nonaction or on Being. To notice Being is to notice how filled we are with life. Instead of creating relationships for ourselves as we do in the Basic Mode, in the Supreme Mode we need only realize our relationship to Being.

When we realize our existing relationship with Being—consciously, for the first time—some people feel bliss while others feel exactly as they always do, except perhaps lighter, as if they are held up or cradled by natural or supernatural forces. Usually we get to this point gradually, but if it happens suddenly, it is like a rubber band snapping. Either way, we become overwhelmed with contentment as we awaken to being filled up by life, and as we feel our participation in life and our happiness.

Here are the characteristics of the Supreme Mode. They are the mirror image of the characteristics of the Basic Mode:
- floodlight/general attention
- relaxed ego or I-experiences; letting go

- experience of oneness; nonduality
- feeling of "being there"
- spontaneity

EXPLORING THE TWO MODES

I began with the characterization of the Basic Mode because the active way of life participation is more familiar to us Westerners. Some of us also need more grounding in concrete relationships before focusing on something as intangible as Being.

Yet we can approach happiness the other way around, too. Especially when we are feeling a lot of pressure, beginning our journey with the nonactive way of life participation is most beneficial. Sometimes we need to relax all effort and plunge right into the great stream of life in which there is no need for distinction, no inside and no outside, indeed no separation of any sides, any parts, or any events. Also, since all of us started out in the womb without perceiving a separate outside, exploring and expanding the Supreme Mode first may be the more natural choice.

The remainder of the book is designed so you can either start learning about the Basic Mode first (part 2) or the Supreme Mode first (part 3). Do what feels best to you. To help you personalize your quest, the following chapter includes a happiness questionnaire. It lists the basic tools (ambition, competence, connection, and confidence) and the supreme mental skills or paths (receptivity, tranquility, reliance, and lightheartedness). You may also wish to refer to the illustration of the Happiness Reference Chart (page 4) that summarizes what happiness is based upon. Please enjoy both.

The Happiness Questionnaire

Although finding new ways to participate can present
a challenge for individuals, it also presents new opportunities
for experiencing well-being.
NANCY CANTOR and CATHERINE A. SANDERSON

I n order for you to learn about how you can personally access the two mental modes that we have defined as the Basic Mode and the Supreme Mode, I have designed the Happiness Questionnaire. Make sure that you only compare your scores with the maximum scores. Comparing yourself to others is not helpful, because your answers are like a fingerprint: they are completely unique to you.

The Happiness Questionnaire has turned out to be a valuable tool for many. Because the questionnaire helps us turn inward and offers feedback, it can increase our awareness and point us in the right direction. Please keep in mind that it is not a test.

A group of above-average happy individuals was used to design the questions for the questionnaire's validity. I did not attempt to scientifically weigh the questions—that is, I did not find out which questions correlated more strongly or less strongly with the underlying concept—except that there are more questions related to the themes of connection and lightheartedness since most people rate these domains as most important to their happiness. Not all questions will weigh equally on your happiness. This means that no particular question is likely to be more important to your happiness than another, even though the scores evenly range from 1 to 5. Only you can know the significance of one question versus another. For example, when you rate yourself high in almost all but a few questions, you may attribute more weight to this finding than the numeric score suggests.

To benefit the most from the Happiness Questionnaire, allocate some quiet time to complete it. Don't overthink the questions, but trust your initial instinct. If you are not comfortable with a question, you can leave it unanswered and come back to it at a later time. If a question seems ambivalent, only respond to the part of the question that speaks loudest to you.

After having finished the questionnaire, you can tailor your approach to happiness to your personal needs via the feedback section. If you prefer, you can also fill out the questionnaire with automatic tallying on my website: andreapolard.com.

QUESTIONS RELATED TO THE BASIC MODE

Let me begin with questions about the four main domains of the Basic Mode that relate to happiness: ambition, competence, connection, and confidence. Answer all questions without regard to what the "right" answer may be. Choose the best, personal answer, and circle the number next to it.

Read the following statements, and answer based on how much they reflect your internal views.

Ambition

1. "I don't know what I want in life."
   Very much like me   1
   Like me   2
   Neutral   3
   Unlike me   4
   Very much unlike me   5

2. "I like to pursue realistic goals."
   Very much like me   5
   Like me   4
   Neutral   3
   Unlike me   2
   Very much unlike me   1

3. "I go after what is important to me."
   Very much like me   5
   Like me   4•
   Neutral   3
   Unlike me   2
   Very much unlike me   1

4. "Venturing out and trying out new things is too uncomfortable."
   Very much like me   1
   Like me   2
   Neutral   3
   Unlike me   4
   Very much unlike me   5•

5. "Rules are there to be broken. I am not afraid to do things my own way."
   Very much like me   1
   Like me   2
   Neutral   3•
   Unlike me   4
   Very much unlike me   5

Competence

1. "There is magic in all beginnings."
   Very much like me   5 ~
   Like me   4
   Neutral   3
   Unlike me   2
   Very much unlike me   1

2. "I don't know why I should have to update my skills when others don't."
   Very much like me   1
   Like me   2
   Neutral   3
   Unlike me   4
   Very much unlike me   5 ~

3. "Becoming my best self is more important than what others do or want from me."
   Very much like me   5 ➤
   Like me   4
   Neutral   3
   Unlike me   2
   Very much unlike me   1

4. "A working adult has no time for learning new skills."
   Very much like me   1
   Like me   2
   Neutral   3
   Unlike me   4
   Very much unlike me   5 ➤

5. "I am satisfied with taking small steps before I do nothing or do too much."
   Very much like me   5
   Like me   4 ➤
   Neutral   3
   Unlike me   2
   Very much unlike me   1

Connection

1. "I have a lot in common with my closest friend/partner."
   Very much like me   5
   Like me   4
   Neutral   3
   Unlike me   2 ➤
   Very much unlike me   1

2. "I don't connect with people other than with my immediate family."
   Very much like me   1
   Like me   2
   Neutral   3
   Unlike me   4 ➤
   Very much unlike me   5

3. "I have no time to socialize."

Very much like me	1
Like me	2
Neutral	3
Unlike me	4—
Very much unlike me	5

4. "I am in an intimate relationship."

Very much like me	5
Like me	4
Neutral	3
Unlike me	2—
Very much unlike me	1

5. "My relationships give me strength."

Very much like me	5
Like me	4
Neutral	3
Unlike me	2—
Very much unlike me	1

6. "I am very self-critical."

Very much like me	1—
Like me	2
Neutral	3
Unlike me	4
Very much unlike me	5

7. "The harder I try to connect, the less it seems to work."

Very much like me	1
Like me	2—
Neutral	3
Unlike me	4
Very much unlike me	5

8. "I view my friends' and partner's flaws as 'part of the package.'"

Very much like me	5⌐
Like me	4
Neutral	3
Unlike me	2
Very much unlike me	1

Confidence

1. "I basically accept who I am."

Very much like me	5
Like me	4⌐
Neutral	3
Unlike me	2
Very much unlike me	1

2. "I wish it were possible to cut out the bad parts of me and exchange them for better ones."

Very much like me	1
Like me	2
Neutral	3⌐
Unlike me	4
Very much unlike me	5

3. "I am prepared to deal with setbacks."

Very much like me	5
Like me	4⌐
Neutral	3
Unlike me	2
Very much unlike me	1

4. "I have difficulty enjoying what I do."

Very much like me	1
Like me	2
Neutral	3⌐
Unlike me	4
Very much unlike me	5

5. "Discipline is a positive force in me."
   Very much like me   5
   Like me   4 ⬅
   Neutral   3
   Unlike me   2
   Very much unlike me   1

QUESTIONS RELATED TO THE SUPREME MODE

I will now ask questions about the four domains or paths to the Supreme Mode: receptivity, tranquility, reliance, and lightheartedness. Read the following statements, and answer based on how much they reflect your internal views. Once again, instead of trying to choose the "right" answer, choose the best, personal answer.

Receptivity

1. "I can discuss my most precious beliefs without aggression."
   Very much like me   5
   Like me   4
   Neutral   3 ⬅
   Unlike me   2
   Very much unlike me   1

2. "I feel I have to 'know' before I can relax."
   Very much like me   1
   Like me   2 ⬅
   Neutral   3
   Unlike me   4
   Very much unlike me   5

3. "Living is a joy even when life hurts."
   Very much like me   5
   Like me   4
   Neutral   3 ⬅
   Unlike me   2
   Very much unlike me   1

4. "Compliments make me feel uncomfortable."
   Very much like me   1
   Like me   2
   Neutral   3~
   Unlike me   4
   Very much unlike me   5

5. "I am a giving person, but it does not come easy."
   Very much like me   1
   Like me   2
   Neutral   3
   Unlike me   4
   Very much unlike me   5~

Tranquility

1. "I live in a relatively peaceful and quiet environment."
   Very much like me   5
   Like me   4
   Neutral   3
   Unlike me   2~
   Very much unlike me   1

2. "I have a very hard time accepting death and pain as part of life."
   Very much like me   1
   Like me   2~
   Neutral   3
   Unlike me   4
   Very much unlike me   5

3. "When people ask me how I am, I want to say 'busy.'"
   Very much like me   1
   Like me   2
   Neutral   3
   Unlike me   4~
   Very much unlike me   5

4. "Imagination is a powerful relaxant."
   Very much like me   5
   Like me   4
   Neutral   3
   Unlike me   2
   Very much unlike me   1

5. "I hate interruptions."
   Very much like me   1
   Like me   2
   Neutral   3
   Unlike me   4
   Very much unlike me   5

Reliance

1. "I believe that many things tend to work themselves out."
   Very much like me   5
   Like me   4
   Neutral   3
   Unlike me   2
   Very much unlike me   1

2. "I practice authentic kindness, even when the 'other' is strange to or different from me."
   Very much like me   5
   Like me   4
   Neutral   3
   Unlike me   2
   Very much unlike me   1

3. "There is nothing inherently good in our nature."
   Very much like me   1
   Like me   2
   Neutral   3
   Unlike me   4
   Very much unlike me   5

4. "I rely on a God, a good force, or higher purpose."

Very much like me	5
Like me	4
Neutral	3
Unlike me	2
Very much unlike me	1

5. "One cannot rely on anything or anybody but oneself."

Very much like me	1
Like me	2
Neutral	3
Unlike me	4
Very much unlike me	5

Lightheartedness

1. "I'd rather not exercise."

Very much like me	1
Like me	2
Neutral	3
Unlike me	4
Very much unlike me	5

2. "I depend on my intuitive sense."

Very much like me	5
Like me	4
Neutral	3
Unlike me	2
Very much unlike me	1

3. "I like to feel 'in the know'; too many questions are unsettling."

Very much like me	1
Like me	2
Neutral	3
Unlike me	4
Very much unlike me	5

4. "I take things with humor."
   Very much like me   5
   Like me   4
   Neutral   3
   Unlike me   2
   Very much unlike me   1

5. "I tend to worry too much."
   Very much like me   1
   Like me   2
   Neutral   3
   Unlike me   4
   Very much unlike me   5

6. "I like to sing, hum, or whistle."
   Very much like me   5
   Like me   4
   Neutral   3
   Unlike me   2
   Very much unlike me   1

7. "Life is serious business."
   Very much like me   1
   Like me   2
   Neutral   3
   Unlike me   4
   Very much unlike me   5

8. "I laugh at my own lapses, my vanity, and rigidities!"
   Very much like me   5
   Like me   4
   Neutral   3
   Unlike me   2
   Very much unlike me   1

Tallying Your Score

After completing the entire questionnaire, add up your scores in each domain. Then write them in the following tables.

BASIC MODE SCORES		
Domain	Your Scores	Maximum Scores
Ambition	19	25
Competence	24	25
Connection	22	40
Confidence	18	25
Total Score: Basic Mode	77	115

SUPREME MODE SCORES		
Domain	Your Scores	Maximum Scores
Receptivity	16	25
Tranquility	13	25
Reliance	21	25
Lightheartedness	34	40
Total Score: Supreme Mode	81	115

WHAT DO MY SCORES MEAN?

Your scores can give you valuable feedback about the areas in which you would like to grow the most. While you should not over-interpret numeric feedback about the workings of your mind, you can use the feedback as a gentle pointer for your growth.

Basic Mode Scores

Total Basic Mode Score

In order to be happy, we need to be active and make ourselves feel part of the world. We accomplish this by focusing on and pursuing connections with a partner, friends, and family, as well as by focusing on and pursuing positive goals at work or at play. Making ourselves active participants is a basic requirement for the happy life, which is why I call our state of mind during such pursuits the Basic Mode. The higher the score you have in the mode, the more likely it is that you have good access to this state of mind. A lower score may suggest that you need to learn:

- some essential skills and strategies that help you be more focused in your pursuits
- how to distinguish between "surviving well" and "happiness," so that you can use these skills and strategies wisely
- to understand this side of happiness better

(Recommended reading: chapter 1 and part 2)

Ambition Score

Scoring low in this area may mean that you are unsure of:
- what constitutes good goals
- how to discover good goals
- how to play the game while striving toward your goals

(Recommended reading: chapter 4)

Competence Score

Scoring low here may mean that you:
- need to retrieve the joy of competence you once had
- feel overwhelmed by life and think you cannot afford to build competence
- need a competence-building strategy

(Recommended reading: chapter 5)

Connection Score

Scoring low here may mean that you:
- isolate yourself without understanding the urgency of connecting
- lack an essential building block in your connections
- need tools for how to connect in today's society
- feel disconnected despite your "know-how"

(Recommended reading: chapter 6)

Confidence Score

Scoring low here may mean that you:
- have difficulty being yourself and developing authentically
- indulge in wishful thinking while leaving your inner reality unsupported
- are focused on your deficits rather than on your strengths
- lack perseverance

(Recommended reading: chapter 7)

Supreme Mode Scores

Total Supreme Mode Score
In addition to making ourselves actively feel part of life, living a happy life also means being aware of our participation. This nonactive approach to happiness is not to be confused with inactivity. Instead it is the skill of our consciousness to turn its focus upon itself, that is, upon Being. When we realize Being, we are in what I call the Supreme Mode. In Eastern thought this is often referred to as the natural mind, or awareness, which allows us to notice our relationship to "nothing in particular," emptiness, or the All to which we belong. The higher your score in this mode, the more likely it is that you have good access to the Supreme Mode. A lower score may suggest that you need to:
- learn to enjoy Being by relaxing some of the intellectualizing that obstructs your experience of the All
- unlearn the compulsion to dissect the world
- understand this flip-side of happiness better
(Recommended reading: chapter 1 and part 3)

Receptivity Score
Scoring low here may mean that you need to learn to:
- loosen rigidities (impenetrable beliefs, habits, identifications)
- enjoy not-knowing via the method of skepticism
- wonder instead of trying to understand everything with your intellect
- meditate
- become aware of what is good in your life and foster natural gratitude

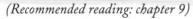

(Recommended reading: chapter 9)

Tranquility Score
Scoring low here may mean that you need to learn about:
- the value of tranquility
- creating tranquility in your external life
- your Buddha-nature (your mind's ability to see the forest and not just the trees)

- surrendering to the flow of things
- trance (leaving your thinking mind for a while)
- the practice of humility

(Recommended reading: chapter 10)

Reliance Score

Scoring low here may mean that you:
- do not see when taking control is futile
- rely on people, things, and constructs when you should not
- rely solely on your own individual power
- need to rely on higher powers and principles (on effort, compassion, and virtues)
- overlook your existing reliance on indefinable Being

(Recommended reading: chapter 11)

Lightheartedness Score

Scoring low here may mean that you need to:
- remember the nature of lightheartedness you once had as a child
- understand why you have forgotten it
- rediscover the nature of lightheartedness

(Recommended reading: chapter 12)

Uneven Basic Mode Scores and Supreme Mode Scores

When you score unevenly in the two mental modes, you may have difficulty balancing between them. In this case, happiness eludes you despite your ability to actively participate in life and realize your existing participation. You may find a balance between the two mental modes by:
- deeply understanding the connection between each mode and the reality of life
- learning about the synthesis of Western and Eastern thought

(Recommended reading: chapter 3, chapter 8, and conclusion)

Part 2

The Basic Mode

You have to be somebody before you can be nobody.

JACK ENGLER

The Fragility of Life

One is happy as a result of one's own efforts . . .
Happiness is no vague dream, of that I now feel certain.
GEORGE SAND

We are as fragile as our world. Death, disease, accidents, all kinds of misfortune are part of everyone's life, but still we usually forget how fragile we are. We struggle so hard to stay and look young and strong. Despite our efforts, we bend like sunflowers that eventually droop to the ground. Youth is no protection either. Although resilient, youngsters need adults to protect them as they are even more oblivious of their fragility while less capable. We are all in the process of "falling."

German poet Rainer Maria Rilke found the words for this fragility:

> The leaves are falling, falling as if from far up,
> as if orchards were dying high in space.
> Each leaf falls as if it were motioning "no." . . .
>
> We're all falling. This hand here is falling.
> And look at the other one . . . . It's in them all.[1]

American poet Robert Frost also describes the fragility of life in his poem "Nothing Gold Can Stay," using the changing colors of tree leaves as a metaphor for the ultimate fate: death. Leaves replace buds in the shortest of all times that is youth; new leaves swiftly replace those early and now-old leaves; precious green turns brown as "Eden sank to grief."[2] Frost opens our eyes to the beauty of nature's gold so that we can also see the inevitable loss of that beauty—the morbidity written into the promise of new life—a fact we might find hard to bear but that awaits us with absolute certainty.

"Falling" is built into life. When I traveled through eastern Africa, I became keenly aware of life's fragility. In the wilderness, the smallest mistake, a fraction of time or distance, defines life or death. I observed warthogs mingling with lions in the savannah. Warthogs usually outrun lions and dare to come astonishingly close to them, but sometimes they forget or miscalculate the distance. Suddenly, the mistake reverses the odds in favor to the lion that quickly catches up with the warthog.

We need not travel that far to acknowledge life's fragility. We all know about local catastrophes such as earthquakes and hurricanes. Whole species die out due to small but consequential changes in their ecosystem. Our own habitat harbors plenty of hazards. As soon as we drive into traffic or enter any aspect of public life, we are at risk. The modern lifestyle supports the denial of life's fragility. Our unconscious mind, however, cannot afford such luxury. It can relax, but it won't be fooled. It knows that it has to protect our body from "falling," even when our conscious mind does not.

THE I-EXPERIENCE

Our unconscious mind also protects our sense of self, what I call our I-experience. It is a precious human survival tool. Many of us pretend that this sense of self is as invulnerable as our body, and that it cannot be hurt. Yet anybody who is capable of and willing to engage in personal love is vulnerable. When we feel betrayed or abandoned by our life partner or a dear friend, we feel crushed. Anybody who loves her career is vulnerable to the feeling of failure. Only people with a severe psychological disorder remain untouched by harsh, ongoing criticism. Children are especially vulnerable to attacks on their I-experience. They become terribly hurt when others, especially their parents, treat them unkindly.

We do not want to face the fragility of life because it terrifies us. The result is that we rigidify our body (especially our back muscles) and its experiences (our I-experience). Before we let ourselves be aware of life's fragility, we would rather neglect and abuse our body, as well as exploit everything that seems in the way of "I." As a consequence we take from Mother Earth as if there were no tomorrow.

We lock up sick people in hospitals and avoid looking at the dead, even when we loved them. When someone gets a divorce, we are likely to end our friendship with them. Children, especially boys, learn from us at an early age to hide their fears and other psychological pain.[3] We want nothing to do with the weak and are eager to point out how we differ from them. Some of us have rigidified and hardened our hearts so much that we tease and attack those who merely appear fragile. Hate crimes are based on the fear that we might sink as low as those we presume to be inferior to us. To protect ourselves, these people must remain at what we perceive to be the bottom. All this because we are afraid of life's fragility.

Surely, the fear of life's fragility does not lead to a happy interchange with life, but to isolation and anxiety. Instead of putting our head in the sand, we must learn to deal with this fragility. We'd be much better off if we understood that life cannot just be strong, but must also be fragile. Fragility is a necessary part of reality. Only when we can accept this part can we work with it, instead of against it. In the long run, we should not treat the fragility of life as an enemy that we must fear, but as an opportunity for becoming a mature human being. We must not defy it or feel that we are its victim, but instead we need to build skills and develop a sense of mastery. Instead of trying to change the things we cannot change, we should try to change the things we can.[4]

In order to take charge of life, we look at it from a distance. Although woven right into the fabric of life, our I-experience suggests that we are distinct from our environment. Humans are the only species capable of this trick—of feeling entirely distinct and different. If all we want is survival, we use this trick to dominate as much as we can. Yet, if we desire more and wish to invite happiness into our lives, we will acknowledge our experience of separateness that we ouselves generate, abstain from dominance, and learn to relate skillfully to the Other. We cannot become masters of a life that is inherently fragile, but we can become masters of how we relate to this life.

FRAGILITY AND ACTIVE LIFE PARTICIPATION

Because active life participation is linked to the fragility of life, it becomes apparent why we need to exert ourselves in the Basic Mode. Focusing on a distant Other, such as other beings or external goals, takes energy. We might not know it, but our consciousness works hard to distinguish between surrounding forms in order to determine what is useful to us. If our consciousness did not analyze and structure these other forms, which I often refer to as "Others," we could not handle our complex human relations. We would not even be able to handle ourselves, because we too are a distinguishable form. Without the many distinct skills we learn, some general (such as communication skills, functioning in daily life), some tailored to our person (such as interacting with a particular person in a particular circumstance or with a particular task), we would not be capable of complex interactions.

Anytime we are about to exert ourselves, we need motivation. It is no different with our activities. Adults should not have to be told what to pursue, but should instead be intrinsically motivated. Stephen Covey calls "desire," along with knowledge and skills, a necessary ingredient to develop a habit.[5] We need to be ambitious to make active participation a persistent factor in our life. This is why ambition is the beginning of practicing happiness in the Basic Mode.

The subsequent chapters will all contribute to essential skill-building in the Basic Mode. In a wide sense, ambition, competence, connection, and confidence are all basic tools that enable us to relate to the world of distinguishable form. I will describe them mostly with the aid of Western thought.

Just by reading about the four basic tools, we strengthen our relationship to the fragile world that is part of who we are. Living with the acceptance of the fragile world can be frightening, unless we know how to live in it. By becoming familiar with the tools and beginning to use them, we become more actively engaged with the whole of life, which, inevitably, will invite happiness into our lives more often.

Ambition

Keep away from people who try to belittle your ambitions.
Small people always do that, but the really great make you feel
that you, too, can become great.

MARK TWAIN

All ambitious people set goals for themselves. However, not all who do so are happy. There are many reasons for this, but there is one so fundamental that we should learn about it first. Unhappy ambitious people often feel haunted by life's fragility or are driven to defy it. As a consequence, goals are likely to be chosen for the wrong reasons. Many people want to vindicate themselves. An heir might feel pressure to make his or her own fortune; a loser to become powerful; a misfit to become the center of attention.

For us to be happy *and* ambitious, we must reconcile with weakness, imagined or real. It is the only way to leave the survival mode and access the Basic Mode instead. To do so, we should begin by examining whether our striving's primary purpose is avoidance. Coming to terms with personal weakness—and fragility in general—is quintessential to assuring that we are not getting lost in survival issues, but are ready to plunge into the Basic Mode through which we actively engage with life.

GOALS THAT LEAD TO HAPPINESS

If we choose our goals freely and for the right reasons, our engagements begin to have inherent worth. We discover that, in case of failure, we can never lose as much as we gain. For example, if we pursue marriage because we should, we may not find happiness in it. On the other hand, if we see marriage as the best ground for love and growth, we are more likely to enjoy the commitment. Because we aim for something good, we will live up to it. While there will be disappointments, we find ourselves actively participating in life. Even when there are losses, we will have loved, and become better people for it.[1]

This is similar to pursuing athletic or professional goals. As long as we do not pursue them out of spite or a sense of competitiveness, but out of love for the activity, we will reap benefits. Our achievements will be meaningful and cause for celebration. Even when we fail—which we all do—we will not have wasted our time. The fact that we will have given it our best, and felt ourselves change and grow with the challenge, means we have lived the good and full life. Nobody can ever take that away from us.

It is not possible to dream our way to our goals. Some people think they can be happy without being ambitious. While degrees of ambition vary significantly, all happy people need it. It is the first step in reaching out to the world.

The congenial centenarian Marge Jetton, interviewed by Dan Buettner, was still engaged in volunteer work at the age of 100. Every stranger looked like a potential friend to her, although, she knew, some could care less. She shared her wisdom: "I realized a long time ago that I need to go out to the world . . . The world was not going to come to me."[2]

Still, even if we agree with Marge, it is not easy to know what parts of the world we should go out to. We have to choose our direction well and determine what goals are actually good for us. Few goals are obviously good, like making sure that we can function in this life. There is no way around the basics. We have to earn some money, handle it right, and take care of ourselves. Also, we should do our best to abolish unnecessary suffering and stand up for good and fair living conditions. Composer Franz Liszt said: "Man can only be happy when he ends the harmful conditions that otherwise end him."[3]

Despite the obvious importance of these goals, most books on happiness refrain from mentioning them. I am the first to admit that we need to go beyond issues of survival. However, we cannot skip over the basics either, if for no other reason than to preserve credibility. As one skeptic friend of mine remarked while conversing with me over the subject of happiness: "Everybody says 'Money does not make one happy,' but everybody is going for it." Even monks and nuns take care of themselves. If their monastic order does not encourage working for a living, they ask for donations or beg for food.

PRIORITIZING OUR GOALS

While maintaining the foundation for happiness by pursuing our basic functioning and good conditions, we can set much higher and fulfilling goals for ourselves. Since this choice is highly subjective, I won't attempt to list common concrete goals. Instead, I will share what researchers have found about the general characteristics of good goals.

Let me begin with psychologist Ed Diener. He suggests that all of our goals have to be congruent with each another. If they are not, we become the battlefield of this conflict and suffer. Only when our goals are in relative harmony with each other can we feel in harmony with ourselves. We must carefully examine our goals, set priorities, and, if necessary, let go of the ones that do not fit into our life.[4]

My friend Robert faced such a choice. All his life he aspired to a political career. However, from a certain age on, he also wanted to have a family. Soon Robert realized that his goals were clashing. He wanted to feel close to his wife and kids on a daily basis. Since his particular job meant spending much of his time away from home, having a family and being a politician became incongruent goals.

Robert had to make a choice. To him, family came first, and politics second. For the time being, he had to give up his second goal. While he no longer pursues a political career, he decided to stay involved in politics as much as he could.

Prioritizing goals requires maturity. We must take an honest look at our life, think about the consequences of our goals, weigh them, compromise where we can, and let go of some goals without regret.

To gain this maturity, it is helpful to rate our goals in terms of their importance on a scale from 1 to 10. Writing about each goal's consequences and how we plan to reconcile them may also help us mature. Above all, we need to come to understand what happiness is (see chapter 1) and remember that some pain cannot be avoided in life, including in a happy life. Only people who go solely after power succumb to their greed of "wanting it all."

Here is another example of prioritizing and letting go. Helena came to see me because she was feeling anxious and overwhelmed much of the time. Although she had her professional life under control, she felt rundown from taking care of her two little kids and herself.

I asked her what exactly she wanted to accomplish for her kids and herself, and how she defined being a good mother and being a good friend to herself. We made a list of ten "good goals," and in doing so Helena realized right away that some of her pursuits were only culturally imposed, such as offering her children a scheduled activity every single afternoon.

Then Helena rated the remaining "good goals." She realized that physical exercise, healthy food, reading to her children, and seeing her girlfriend were high on her list (1–4), while swimming lessons, a clean home, and piano lessons were in the middle (5–7), and her drawing lessons, sleepovers for her children, and having three mini-vacations per year came last (8–10).

Subsequently Helena made a plan for how she would make sure not to sacrifice the top goals, reduce but not eliminate the effort for the middle goals, and drop the drawing lessons (this was hard but felt necessary, at least for the time being), have bi-weekly playdates instead of weekly sleepovers (the kids would surely protest), and travel slightly longer, but only once a year (however much she would miss the novelty of new places in the coming years). Although Helena would miss some of her old life, the anticipated life of new priorities felt saner to her immediately.

MAKING OUR GOALS FIT OUR STRENGTHS

The second characteristic of good goals is personality congruency, which means that our goals must fit our personal strengths and virtues. Only such goals can bring what Martin Seligman calls "authentic happiness."[5] Once we have found our individual strengths, we can apply them to our activities. When we force goals upon ourselves, we often feel inadequate or like frauds. On the other hand, when we set goals that we feel naturally inclined to pursue, we end up feeling in alignment with ourselves. We must come to a point at which we do what we are. Congruency between goals and personality makes for an enjoyable, gratifying, and meaningful life.

Gail Evans, executive vice president of the CNN Newsgroup, thoroughly enjoys the business world. Her natural inclination helps her pursue high career goals. She advises us to preserve our integrity for the sake of our happiness. Since the business world is still mostly a men's world, she specifically addresses women in her book: "[Integrity] means being true to yourself and being your true self everywhere you go, including the office. . . . No amount of hiding or pretending will change a person's inner self. A woman who constantly recreates herself, who tries to be something other than who she is, will never be comfortable inside her own skin—or anywhere else."[6]

MAKING OUR GOALS CORRESPOND TO OUR SKILL LEVEL

The third criterion of good goals is that they have to correspond to our skill level. Although activities that fall below our skill level may be relaxing, they do not create the optimal experience of active life participation that Mihaly Csikszentmihalyi describes as "flow."[7] However, if our activities are above our skill level, they make us feel inadequate. If we have the right amount of skills for particular activities, we feel adequately challenged and thoroughly alive when we pursue them. Each activity contains a "bundle of opportunities" that, given a matching level of skill, gets our juices flowing.[8]

This too means that our good goals should be challenging and attainable. A goal out of our reach can create frustration and, over time, even agony. Anthony Robbins is one of the most vocal proponents of the "take control of your life" approach to happiness, but even he admonishes against trying to control the uncontrollable: "As long as we structure our lives in a way where our happiness is dependent upon something we cannot control, then we will experience pain," he writes.[9]

For example, in schools where A grades cannot be attained, students feel unmotivated and frustrated. On the other hand, if As are attained too easily, students become arrogant, bored, and feel empty.

In addition, good goals must be clear to us. We must be able to define or at least describe them. Only then can they serve as focal points in the Basic Mode. Without a good sense of what we want to accomplish, we will lack determination. This is not to say that we must be able to perfectly picture our goals. Too clear a picture might rigidify us and hamper our creativity. Therefore, instead of waiting for the perfect image, let us begin our pursuits with a good and sound idea. Often, we have to adjust our vision during the creative process. The closer we come to the goal, the sharper our understanding of it should be.

It is similar when we search for a life partner. It is wise to know what we are looking for. Picturing a body type, as especially young people do, is not enough. On the contrary, it might divert our attention from the characteristics that matter most to us. To find *the* special person, we must know what we need to have in common with that person and how we should differ from them. Besides thinking about what we like and dislike, we must think of what actually fits. The ultimate goal isn't a particular type of man or woman, but a particular type of connection that we want to experience (see chapter 6). Here too we mustn't become rigid, but must remain open to the moment with a real human being.

At some point in our lives, we should also be clear about our career goals. It is neither enough to know the amount of money we aspire to make nor the kind of job we want to hold. We have to become much more specific about our goals. For example, many people aspire to become actors, but few care to know what this job entails, such as the endless rehearsals of scenes. Instead, fantastic ideas dictate our ambition.

We ought to learn as much as we can about the reality of a job. Visiting a workplace, interning with a company, interviewing other employees, and reading reports may all help us obtain a clear picture. Besides, we need to distinguish between short- and long-term goals. It is very helpful to know what lies ahead in order to remain confident and persevere (chapter 7).

GETTING FEEDBACK ABOUT OUR PROGRESS

The clearer we can be about our goals, the easier it is to obtain accurate feedback about our progress.[10] This may be the most important aspect of good goals, because this is how we can relate to the Other. When we define a height we want to jump, we know something specific about our actual athletic performance. In one way or the other, we have to make the Other talk to us.

If feedback can't be automatically obtained, we need to find other ways of evaluating our progress. For example, a writer must seek out experts, and not just friends, about the quality of his or her work. As painful as an objective evaluation may be, it helps us adjust or improve so that our pursuit becomes more enjoyable in the long run.

WHAT IS OUR PURPOSE IN LIFE?

As with many others concerned with happiness, I suggest that we benefit greatly from having a purpose in life, an overarching goal that gives direction to the entirety of our life. It is true that a higher goal in life helps us stay the course. A purpose that also entails giving back to the community makes us feel less self-absorbed and more grateful. All these characteristics are known to have a positive effect on our happiness.

Yet finding and staying with a good purpose is a challenge in itself. Therefore I suggest that we apply the same criteria to our purpose as to all our goals. Our purpose should:
- be congruent with our other goals
- be congruent with our personality
- be a good fit with our level of skill
- be challenging, but attainable
- be clear
- provide us with feedback over our progress

These general guidelines might protect us from becoming unnecessarily frustrated. Susan, a former patient of mine, used to feel inadequate because she felt she could do so little to improve the world. Such was her purpose. However, she needed to first clarify that purpose and explain exactly how she wanted to see the world improved. Then, she could begin to distinguish between attainable and unattainable, short- and long-term goals.

Her purpose became less of an overwhelming task as Susan became clearer about it. She ended up focusing on helping to end hunger, in connection with a particular organization, in a particular region in Africa. As a result of specifying her purpose, she also became more methodical in her approach in how to go about fulfilling it. Although a purpose should be attainable, we may never see its full attainment personally. While our ambition may bring us happiness, the ultimate goal is often only reached by future generations, as was the case for Martin Luther King, Jr. We need to use our imagination and "have a dream."

Obtaining feedback in regard to pursuing a purpose provides one of the greatest difficulties. Susan should not expect to hear from the entire world about her progress, but she could expect to hear from the specific organization she collaborated with. Sometimes we may find feedback by joining a group of like-minded peers. Many charitable organizations provide feedback about what becomes of donations. If we cannot obtain real data, we must become creative, turning to our own conscience, listening to Mother Nature, or speaking with God.

Sometimes all I can do to keep going forward is use my imagination. I envision the peak and my progress toward it, which keeps me going amid the thickest fog. For example, while I was researching and writing this book for twelve long years, I was often isolated in my office. During the breaks I took, walking quietly in the garden and listening to the wind rustling the drying leaves, I interrupted my silence and started talking out loud to Mother Nature. Pretending my book was done and read by many people who could benefit from it, I imagined the drying leaves were little hands applauding my effort, the wind whispering that my loneliness was worth it.

Admittedly, these were moments of grandiosity, but they really did energize me. They made me feel as if I had picked and eaten sweet dates in an oasis that sustained me while crossing the Sahara desert.

DISCOVERING OUR GOALS

Even though we now know in theory what good goals are, discovering our own can be problematic. To begin with, we often have difficulty knowing what we want. This is, in part, due to a lack of the right encouragement. Parents often project their wishes or anxiety onto their children. Hence, we end up fulfilling their dreams or becoming too afraid of pursuing any at all. If our friends have no ambitions, they often deliberately or inadvertently discourage ours. It is easy to forget about our dreams when others do not respond favorably to them. In addition to our family and friends, our culture pushes its particular goals, which often have nothing to do with us.

Yet for the most part, we do not know what we want because we confuse ourselves. We either fly too high, indulging in fantasy, or we fly too low, being hyper self-critical. Neither approach is grounded in reality. As to the former, we try to imagine ourselves as successful and pretend we are there, or at least *should* be there, when in fact we are far from it. This way we can never verify if the goals we pursue are commensurate with who we are. For example, some people call themselves actors, without ever having had a role in a play or a film.

We can imagine a particular life to enhance or comfort ourselves. But only the actual pursuit leads to clarity. We may try to avoid a potentially painful reality. However, when we dare to wake up and face reality, we begin to learn about ourselves. We learn more about our true skills, our true joys, and our true expectations. This reality check is essential for discovering authentic goals. While it is hard to give up fantasy, once we do, we will have the chance of finding happiness. Instead of escaping reality, we learn to participate in it in a most fulfilling way.

When we are too self-critical, our eyes are often blind to what is good for us. We punish ourselves for mistakes, feel bad, and thus divert our attention from anything positive, including potentially rewarding goals. Much of what we could succeed in escapes our attention. When someone suggests that we have potential for achieving in a particular area, we act surprised: "Why would anybody believe this about me?" Self-critical people often do not wish to be bothered with compliments, so they discourage them.

In our culture, it is popular knowledge that in order to foster ambition, we should "applaud successes and go easy on failures."[11] Yet, we rarely know how hard we are on ourselves. We are oblivious of our internal reality, because self-punishment is our habit. Additionally, we often mistake self-punishment for self-discipline, and think it necessary for our success. Eventually, or so we hope, we will make no more mistakes and will be deserving of love, money, and attention. We do not seem to grasp that nobody is perfect. What distinguishes successful from unsuccessful people is how quickly the former get over their mistakes, learn from them, and move on (see chapter 7). Our negative distortions and misperceptions of reality keep us apart from success. Thus it is very difficult to discover authentic good goals and make ourselves part of this reality.

Yet, even when we ground ourselves in reality and receive encouragement, finding the right pursuits for ourselves does not automatically follow. Psychologist Dean Simonton cites the case of Franklin D. Roosevelt. If Roosevelt had not learned valuable lessons about patience and tenacity from his disabling polio, he might not have been the same president or even become president at all.[12]

Often, after having gone through traumatic or near-death experiences, people suddenly see what matters to them and strive toward it. I do not mean to suggest that we should provoke such misfortune. Yet, we cannot expect to be hit by a sudden flash of insight by being couch potatoes. Somehow, we must take charge and see to it that we too learn valuable lessons that reveal what is worth striving for. What we need are tangible learning opportunities that help us stumble into or recognize good goals.

GETTING INTO DISCOVERY MODE

Joseph Campbell used to encourage people with the expression: "Follow your bliss,"[13] which we may take to mean as "Follow your true passion in life." We can only do that, however, if we get ourselves into a discovery mode.

Instead of remaining in our own personal cocoon, we must venture out and open up to a much broader world. There, we will be confronted with unpredictable events, gain fresh knowledge, and be forced to experiment with it all. In the end we will find aspects within ourselves that we did not know existed. In Campbell's words, "It's inevitable that a person with any sense of openness to new experience will say to himself, 'Now, this won't do, the way we are living.' So, one goes out for one's self to find a broader base, a broader relationship."[14] Willingness to learn and experiment is essential for following our bliss and discovering goals for which we want to strive.

There are various ways of venturing out. Some of us need to venture out through travel. The German poet Johann Wolfgang von Goethe, for example, was a frequent traveler. When he took his trip throughout Italy, he wrote to a friend that he was a changed person because of traveling and that no other experience could compare to it.[15]

Even though Goethe had already discovered that his main passion was writing, there was plenty left to discover and create. As he gained knowledge about classicism, he wrote the play *Iphigenie of Tauris*. He also began to work on *Faust*, the tragedy that brought him international fame.

Experiencing the ambiance of a distant place, being struck by its culture and beauty, getting to know its people, being pressed to find solutions to problems we did not know existed, we discover all kinds of things. But we have to step out of the familiar. In one way or another, we have to "leave mother and father" and follow our bliss.[16]

We also venture out of our limited circle of experience when we observe, read about, and listen to other people's experiences. As long as it touches us, vicarious traveling can be very powerful. In addition, we can learn by doing something outlandish and new. We might take up Chinese. We might learn to play an instrument, attend lectures, or do research on new subjects. If we have never been nice, we can make that a new habit. Without stimulating our mind, there cannot be a new vision. Without experimenting, we cannot discover a passion. We must subject ourselves to a new world that will renew us.

When we venture forth, we must not simply accumulate new information. We must learn from it in a personal and meaningful manner, integrating, questioning, wrestling with, or rejecting it. What counts is that we not remain passive, but learn about ourselves while learning from it. If there is a way to apply our new knowledge, we should do so. For example, having read about gardening, we should plant something. Having taken a class about creativity, we should do something creative. If psychology interests us, we should try to understand people from the perspective of the mind. Collecting cookbooks alone cannot make us happy, but cooking can.

Sometimes this process is completely unpredictable. After having been completely in the dark about what to do with his life, Stewart, my friend's adolescent son, found his love for marine biology during a presumably boring boat trip. He was just as surprised as his parents by this sudden discovery.

When we immerse ourselves in a variety of new experiences, we will eventually find something that gets our blood flowing. To involve our emotions is the key to ambition, finding our purpose, and setting goals. Robert Cloninger's research suggests that people who score high in persistence also have the highest activity level in the limbic system—the region of the brain linked to emotions and habits.[17] While there are innate inter-individual differences, there is some passion, a small fire, if only a spark within all of us. Venturing out, we will eventually discover what will make us *want* to exert ourselves. With the discovery of authentic goals, almost everybody who desires happiness can become fired up.

GOOD GOALS ARE NOT ENOUGH

So far I have made the case for *why* pursuing authentic goals contributes greatly to our happiness. Yet, *how* we pursue them is of equal importance. In order to enhance our experience of active life participation, *having* good goals is not enough. We too have to be good. If all we want is to achieve our goals in life, we might as well join the rat race and do whatever it takes to win: cheating, bullying, and cutting corners so that we get ahead while others fall by the wayside. This is no way to be happy! We must apply moral and psychological rules to our game, even when nobody is looking.[18]

It is amazing how many of us feel an urgent need to yawn when particularly moral rules are brought to our attention. Dusty books; old, bearded men preaching while waggling their index fingers; or broken records come to mind. We probably have heard enough threats of the kind, "Behave, or else . . . " What we have not heard enough is how rules are linked to our happiness, and

how we can actually benefit from them. The ability to begrudg-
ingly follow rules is not the same as deeply understanding and
accepting them. Evidence of this difference is that so many
alleged morally upright and psychologically savvy people break
rules when an opportunity arises. Until then, they were good citi-
zens as authority dictated.

We have to understand that without rules, ambitious pursuits are little fun and do not enhance experiences of active life
participation. Cheating and elbowing our way to the top will certainly bring us something. Yet, in doing so, we won't enjoy any
real pride. Adhering to the rules gives us a chance to feel good
about our own and other people's efforts. We learn to enjoy the
process itself and become relatively independent from reaching
the goal per se. Instead of focusing on the goal here or the action
there, we thus become free to focus on the interaction that is the
energetic flow between us and the goal. Striving honorably and
constructively makes us *feel* honorable and constructive. Our positive contribution to the good life reveals the best and not the
worst of us and others. Eventually, in every challenge we will feel
important, and in every struggle we will feel valuable. Life just
feels better when we play by the rules.

If we unleash our ambition without restraint, we are not in the
right frame of mind to enjoy our pursuit. We either lack the time
or the leisure to focus on it. Greedy for success and fearful of failure, we do not become energized by our activity, but exhausted.
High stress and burn-out are often the consequences.

Anthropologist Peter Demerath's research on high-achieving
high-school students gives examples of such consequences. Seventy
percent of these adolescents report feeling stressed "frequently" or
"all the time." Their extracurricular activities and homework are
extensive, and they spend very little time talking with their parents
at home. Besides lacking hours of serenity and family connection,
they are also engaged in unethical behavior. The majority of these
driven students seem to cheat to advance themselves.[19]

When we cheat, we immediately and strongly link a feeling
of competitiveness to our ambition. While some competitiveness
can be enjoyable, there is no reason why we should have to feel it
compulsively. Demerath warns: "While competition will always

be present in American schools and society, data from the study suggest that student (and parent) preoccupations with 'getting ahead' can interfere with their learning, result in a loss of civility, and have deleterious effects on their well-being."[20]

WIN-WIN

In order to be happy, we must maintain the psychological flexibility to stop comparing ourselves with others and turn our attention back onto our own activity. If we are rigidly focused on others, we lose ourselves in them instead of in our interaction with them. In the moment we cheat, we push the world aside and can no longer genuinely reach out to it. When Peter Demerath visited Papua New Guinea, he found that the students there were much more collaborative in their efforts. Cheaters appear vain to the New Guineans, a vice that their community-oriented society strongly discourages. It is understood that one cannot succeed at the expense of the group.[21]

Since our personal happiness is interwoven with the happiness of others, we should try to set up our pursuit as a win-win situation. Often in nature, one person wins because another person loses. Because the results cancel each other out, such an interaction is called a "zero-game" in game theory, which is a method to determine which available strategies are likely to maximize one's gain or to minimize one's loss in a particular situation. Author Robert Wright points out that we all have the potential to engage in "non-zero-games" as we become "embedded in larger and richer webs of interdependence."[22] We can decide to adhere to a game plan that is beneficial to us *and* to others. When we go for "non-zero games," we will not harm others with our ambition, but rather we will attempt to strengthen our connection, assure mutual advancement, as well as foster love and peace.

I have already talked about the importance of having a purpose in life. Although I cannot suggest a specific purpose for anyone, I think that aspiring to create win-win situations should be part of it. Examining the habits of highly effective people, Stephen Covey advised us to have a higher purpose and to subordinate our smaller goals to this purpose.[23] This rule should not only help us with delaying gratification and cultivating perseverance (see chapter 7), but also with curbing and limiting our ambition. We should always remember why we began pursuing a particular goal. Sometimes when we are too ambitious, we lose that perspective and thus impair our own and other people's happiness.

We ought not to delay *the pursuit* of our dreams any longer. Many people have great dreams, but never do anything about them. Our dreams must become more important and move into the "urgent" category, as Stephen Covey suggests.[24] Life is now, and now is the time to move to discover personal good goals and endeavor in stride and with honor. True, even healthy striving in the Basic Mode takes effort. Eventually though, such striving will also give us power as we relate to our goals and avoid the pitfalls of striving in a mere survival mode. The pursuit in the Basic Mode is not fear-driven and is well worth it. Let's go!

BASIC MODE EXERCISES—AMBITION
The following exercises address many skill levels to open up your mind and make it more flexible.

Something to Think About
What is your general attitude about ambition? How do you envision your future in five, ten, and fifteen years? What do you need to do in order to discover your personal goals in life? Do you have a game plan? Do you know the rules?

Imagine This
- Close your eyes and imagine yourself on stage. People around you are applauding you for following your dream. What are they applauding you for?
- Imagine yourself taking the first step toward your goal. What advice would you give your daughter or son if they were in your position? Do the same exercise for all steps toward your goal and write down your plan and a time table.

Reach Out to Others
- Talk to other people about your ambition. Ask and learn from others how they discovered their goals. Ask others

for what you need in terms of "following your bliss." For example, you might need some concrete encouragement to take the first step toward your goal.

- Consider finding yourself a coach, mentor, therapist, teacher, or likeminded "buddy."
- It is perfectly fine and psychologically sound to talk to your mother/father about your ambition. (Some of us are overly worried about reaching out to our parents for advice).

Explore Your Feelings

1. Sit quietly, alone or with another person. Speak about the rules that you follow out of fear as well as the rules you deeply believe in. Remember a time when you broke a rule and you regretted it. Then remember a time when you achieved something and were proud of it. What feelings arise?
2. How were you supported in following your dreams?
3. Talk about what happened to your childhood, adolescent, or young-adulthood dreams. Can you realize them now in a mature way? If not, is there anything similar you could do instead?

Things You Can Do

- Watch the movies *Seabiscuit, The Rookie, The Contender, Defending Your Life, Working Girl, Spartacus, Black Stallion,* and *Slumdog Millionaire.*
- Hang your certificates or trophies on a wall for everybody to see. (Don't hide your successes out of modesty). Talk about what you already have accomplished. Make ambition part of conversations.
- On occasion, leave your circle of security. Take a trip, read a book in a new field, join a class if you usually learn by yourself, seek time alone if you are enmeshed with others. Do not merely expand your existing knowledge, but gain entirely new knowledge.
- Become serious about your dreams and treat them as "urgent" matters. Do not put off what you can do today, even if you can only do a small part or a first step. For example,

if your goal is to look better, do not wait until you have lost that weight. You can take care of your hair and put on fashionable clothes today. Doing little things can jump-start your ambition.

• Follow through with your ideas. For example, write the poem that you have started in your head. Try to publish the book you have written. Pick up the guitar you have bought. Decide whether or not to continue with a certain pursuit only after you have given it a good try.

• Read biographies of people who have done what you secretly desire. Let yourself be inspired. Reading fiction is also a wonderful source for inspiration. Personally, I was very inspired by the early books of Rita Mae Brown. Ask for recommendations in your bookstore.

• Set three good goals according to the criteria listed in this chapter. Write down what kind of rules you have to follow in order to succeed with honor. Begin working toward them immediately.

• Read Michael Carroll's books *Awake at Work* and *The Mindful Leader* to live mindfully while practicing ambition. To learn more about setting and committing to goals read Sonja Lyubomirsky's *The How of Happiness*.

Spiritual Growth

• When you follow your passion, you might inadvertently cause others to be jealous. There is not much that can be done about other people's feelings. How will you deal with other people's jealousy?

• Contemplate on—pray about, meditate about, or be quite with—the image of pursuing your goals as a "citizen of the world."

• Make a list of positive beliefs as they relate to success. For example: I believe that I am worthy of success. I believe that I *will* feel worthy of success. I believe in my potential. I believe in *having* a potential.

Competence

Most gulls don't bother to learn more than the simplest facts
of flight—how to get from shore to food and back again. For
most gulls, it is not flying that matters, but eating. For this gull,
though, it was not eating that mattered, but flight. More than
anything else, Jonathan Livingston Seagull loved to fly.

RICHARD BACH

L ife's fragility necessitates striving for definable goals, and
to do so with relative competence. Faced with potentially
threatening situations, we have no choice but to learn how
to swim if we do not wish to sink. Survival demands competence.

Yet should we seek happiness, we need to take nature's demand
a step further. Swimming to just "stay afloat" will not do. When
an activity is important to us, we should develop it, usually with
hard work, and do well if not our best. This is because we feel
alive to the degree that our mind is growing. Learning stimulates
our brain cells and growth. As we take ourselves to depths and
elevations never experienced before, we grow new connections
between already existing brain cells.[1] Striving for competence is
essential for enhancing the experience of life participation in the
Basic Mode.

THE JOY OF COMPETENCE

Just like Jonathan Livingston Seagull, healthy children take tremendous joy in building competence. Toddlers, who are naturally
ambitious, do not become tired of learning how to walk. They
take a few steps, fall, and get up, again and again. Once they have
learned anything, they radiate with pride and are unstoppable in
their enthusiasm. As children gain competence they realize that
they have an effect on the world. Overjoyed by their efficacy, they

are known to express themselves uninhibitedly: "Look at me, look at what I can do! I am the best!" While first-time activities impress us the most, learning in general engages us. Life is exciting when we realize that we can make a difference.

The older we grow, the more our competencies with which we increasingly affect the world become sophisticated and specialized. When happiness is a high priority, we most likely have a strong desire to contribute to the world by utilizing our potential. If we fail to do so, we feel that we have let ourselves, our parents, and maybe even the world down. Doing our best also satisfies a deep human need. Our accomplishments may bring tears to our eyes, especially when we imagine our parents or others who have contributed to our potential.

For most of us, the joy is not caused by mere achievements, but is about doing the work. It is not so much the goal that makes us happy, but the process of working with our potential. Intuitively we recognize that we must do as life does and never stop the process of becoming.

To parallel this natural process, the poet and novelist Hermann Hesse encourages us to abandon old ways of being in order to thrive and grow. Letting go of the past with our eyes focused on our ever-changing life in progress are often themes in his writing. Rainbows, soap bubbles, sand, wind, rivers, the seasons, flickering lights, and shadows in the forest are recurring symbols. In Hesse's poem "Stages," he urges us to leave our old habits for the sake of inner freedom and love of our natural, unfolding life. It is not easy for us to change when the status quo feels comfortable, but according to Hesse, reminding ourselves of the magic inherent in all beginnings prepares us for departure and change. The driving force of nature can lift us "stage by stage to wider spaces," which is the opposite of stagnation. The price for stagnation is high because it means that we keep ourselves chained to the past—or, in Hesse's words, that we "remain slaves of permanence."[2]

COMPETENCE IS CRUCIAL

It only makes good sense to aspire to grow more competent as we grow older. The crucial role of competence is scientifically expressed in the self-determination theory by R. M. Ryan and E. L.

Deci.[3] According to the researchers, we need to fulfill three related human needs to optimize our well-being and social development: the need for competence, belongingness, and autonomy. Lately, this originally humanistic idea of fulfillment of our potential has been adopted by academic psychologists who now believe that fulfillment can, after all, be researched systematically.[4]

Although developing competence is such an important ingredient of the good and full life, few adults sincerely aspire to it. The joys of developing knowledge and skill seem to become lost after childhood, and we are left to wonder if and how we can retrieve them.

According to developmental psychologist Gisela Ulmann, children develop as long as they (1) have a reason to, and (2) have the means to do so.[5] When we observe teens become indifferent about learning after they had earlier come to a "sense of competence,"[6] they either find it harder to find reasons to develop or do not have the means to develop.

As for having the means to develop, young people need to identify opportunities and the resources to pursue them. The culture needs to support young people so that they have and are able to recognize the resources they need to grow. If we were deprived of such support as children, it is up to us as adults to find the means to reignite the fire. It could take anything from seeking out information, fueling the mind-body with exercise and good nutrition, to pursuing cultural and educational opportunities offered by our community, including virtual communities. By spending a little bit of time, anybody can find such resources, online, in libraries, museums, churches, and community colleges.

Mostly we lose the joy of competence because we find it more difficult to discover good reasons to develop. Good reasons to develop are usually plentiful and evident when we are young. There are plenty of rewards, as well as independence, awaiting us. Yet as we grow older, we often become spoiled. Why should one work hard when everything is already provided, and everything has become as easy as spelling using a word processing program? Even when we are not spoiled to the point of indifference, good reasons are no longer evident in the adult world. As a result, people often retire from learning after childhood.

FROM GENES TO CONSCIOUSNESS

There are several more noteworthy factors that make it harder to identify good reasons to develop competency throughout our lives. If we wish to renew our joy in competence, we should understand and address them.

The greatest factor may well be biological. Nature assists us capably in the acquisition of basic skills, such as walking and talking, but is less helpful with more sophisticated ones. There is not much in our biological nature that guides us toward physics, computer technology, foreign languages, or any complicated skill. If we do not employ conscious tools, conscious motivation, and conscious choice, we may lose the right motivation to do well, to learn, and to grow.

Clearly, we increasingly depend on our consciousness to find good reasons to develop. When we lack motivation, we need to engage in a careful analysis of our specific cultural environment and evaluate our situation in it, with or without the help of a professional counselor. Based on this analysis, we can devise a new and powerful plan. A plan or new vision must deliver compelling reasons why continued learning is in our best interest, and what task skills match the demand (specific goals) that we have chosen for ourselves. The plan should lay out what we can gain in the short-term and the long-term from exertion in a specific field.

Composing such a plan is not easy. Indeed, it is comparable to finding a purpose for our lives. If, however, we want to go back to experiencing the "magic" of a new beginning and take delight in the development of new competencies, we must outline such a plan. Hence, after determining our goals and understanding how continuous learning contributes to our happiness, we must become clear about all the various skills that we need in order to accomplish our goals. While some skills are apparently necessary, many are not. It is up to us to find out about all of them. It is not sufficient to simply go by official, institutional requirements of schools or to pass exams.

Let me give you an example. Many students of psychology come to the field without understanding why they have chosen it or what it entails. Some aspire to receive a higher academic degree or add a doctorate to their names to increase their status. A fellow

I knew named Andreas, a very bright young man, confided in me that he hoped to meet a lot of women in this female-dominated field. Needless to say, people with such limited visions see no point in working hard or experience no joy when they do.

Others begin to study psychology because of one specific aspect of psychology, such as a favorite theory or treatment (with which they may hope to cure themselves). When asked to learn about statistics, tests and test theory, alternative theories and treatments, neurology, philosophy, physical illness, or medication, they show little or no interest.

Upon understanding what our culture offers, what it supports, and what it needs, and upon matching this information with our personal qualities, we need to concoct a concrete vision for ourselves. In the example of psychology, we ought to take into account the whole field and the whole mind. Our vision must not serve the purpose of proving a point or reaching a narrow goal. If we want to enjoy pursuing our goals and become lost in the process of our activities, we must support our goals with a greater vision for our lives. In short, our consciousness must kick in when genes fail to give clear directions. We must excite ourselves with grand dreams founded in reality.

THE ROAD OF LEAST RESISTANCE LEADS TO MEDIOCRITY

Another factor that makes it harder to find reasons to develop is our changing perception of reality. As we grow older, we cannot help but discover that success is not necessarily rooted only in competence. We correctly begin to perceive that often it is not competence that decides our success, but luck (for example parental, monetary, and cultural support; being the "right" race or sex; timing; physical attributes), connections, and shrewdness.

Upon waking up to the reality of adulthood, our efforts and sense of efficacy may now seem foolish. When we determine from a simple cost/benefit analysis that we exert ourselves more than our neighbors and perhaps more than absolutely necessary, we readily retreat—which leads to mediocrity.[7]

Thinking things through, however, we can see that this analysis is erroneous if our goal is to lead outstanding, happy lives.

Mediocre lives can do away with growing competencies. Most of the time, great success and happiness depend on hard work. Luck is merely a good starting point. Competence remains a great asset for the especially unlucky and unconnected. A sense of mastery can lift us up and overcome just about everything. Being able to pursue exciting goals capably is fulfilling.

The mere thought of being able to answer life's challenges provoked happiness in an older man with health problems who I am proud to call my father-in-law, Arthur. He had always been a doer: not only did he build up his own business, he also volunteered as a fireman and a Boy Scout leader, accepted engagements in several charities and organizations, and started a golf-cart business after his official retirement. Responding to challenges with ever-growing management skills helped him even with his last challenge, his death. Instead of focusing on his pain, he focused on what he was still capable of doing: he took care of some house projects to assure his wife's quality of life and applied himself the best he could up to his last conscious breath, all without a hint of self-pity. We should take into account that happiness is indeed work, so that we can choose more accurately how to spend our precious energy. If we strive toward happiness, it is secondary that luck and connections play a role in society. Nothing should deter us from the joy that comes with learning and the excitement of positive control.

MISPERCEPTIONS AND FOOLISHNESS

As we grow older, we are also more able to fool ourselves. Besides acting out grandiose ideas based on fantasy (see chapter 4), we tend to think of ourselves as competent by owning tools we never use or devices that have no real merit. Equipped with the latest gadgets and being accessible 24/7, we make ourselves (look) busy and exhausted.

Ironically, when we are hooked up and stressed out, we accomplish little. Falling into this trap, and sustained by our own fear and greed, we mistake *having* for *being*. Stress is not a sign of mastery, but of maladjustment and of circumstances that beg to be changed! At least we should not take pride in mere possessions when their main purpose is distraction.

Owning and making more and more money tend to compromise us. Not that wanting money or the power it buys is altogether wrong; we all need at least some to experience self-efficacy. Yet, as Tolkien's story (*The Lord of the Rings*) about a precious ring that causes all who come close to it to become power obsessed suggests, money easily stirs up greed, and with greed comes the illusion that money can buy happiness. Only growth of what is living has that kind of power, be it in us, be it in people with whom we feel connected, or be it in trees. Dead things cannot make us feel alive, unless we mistake transient excitement for life.[8]

There are other foolish ideas in our culture, one of which is to consider "parenting" a skill at which we can become competent. There is, of course, no truly competent parent, but only a good-enough parent with countless skills, patience, faith, and love.

The remedy here is self-evident: some ideas have to be dropped and others seriously examined. If we wish to retrieve the joy of competence, we need to wake up from the mass trance that culture induces. Things and stress tend to obstruct the process of becoming, while good, hard work supports it.

FINDING POSITIVE FEEDBACK LOOPS

The last factor that makes it harder to find good reasons to develop is that it is difficult to define what "good" is. Pursuing goals early in life, such as taking our first steps, engages us easily. We can feel our little but steady progress in a direct manner. Even falling is fun. And when we can walk, it is quite apparent.

Now think of the adult world. The feedback loop can be long and arduous, sometimes resulting only in symbolic feedback. For example, when we learn a language, it may be fun to learn the first few words and simple sentences. Yet to become proficient, it takes years of study and practice. Making mistakes is no fun at all, because critical teachers and others throw negative feedback our way.

Also, progress is usually conveyed to us indirectly via tests and test scores. And no matter what the scores are, it is unclear when we really are proficient in a language. Indeed, as we grow up, it is quite difficult to realize or become part of a positive feedback loop.

It is also interesting to note that boys especially become beaten down in the current system and receive way too much criticism. Indeed, it is established that parents and teachers scold and punish boys more severely than girls.[9]

To retrieve the joy of competence, we have to think of ways to make the whole pursuit more enjoyable and more tangible. As far as languages go, for example, we ought to be praised and spurred on with challenging games. Instead of grading only, we should measure success by speaking occasionally with a native speaker, by solving a real-life problem, by using a variety of media, or by taking a trip. All activities ought to be as interactive and tangible as possible so that we can *feel* that learning is good, as opposed to being told that it is so.

Nevertheless, many activities require us to transition from direct feedback to the symbolic feedback of grades, trophies, and money. To maintain the perception of that being positive and prevent habituation (yes, even making money becomes boring with time), we need to add real human contact and attention to the experience. Anonymity is a killer, but a sense of connectedness a real asset when we learn anything. Anytime we take a class, we ought to shake the teacher's hand, engage with classmates, or form a study group.

Research supports that it is not sufficient to be good at anything, but that we must believe that we are good or becoming so. Todd Kashdan writes:

> Events that cause individuals to believe they can interact effectively with the environment (perceived competence) or desire to interact effectively (competence valuation) tend to enhance curiosity and predict achievement gains. . . . Strong abilities are not sufficient, as competency beliefs appear to be the primary mechanism for experiencing high task curiosity and persistence, increasing the likelihood of achievement success.[10]

We all have to make certain that we "get it" when we make progress in developing skills. Our levels of connectedness and confidence will affect whether or not we are receptive to positive feedback (see chapters 6 and 7). We ought to view failures as further opportunities to learn, to learn to have fun with failures, to "roll with the punches," and to celebrate progress. As a Snoopy poster I saw thirty years ago stated: "There is always a reason to celebrate."

CAN WE AFFORD TO DEVELOP OUR COMPETENCE?

Acquiring skills and practicing them takes time, focus, and devotion. Many people feel that they cannot afford such an investment in themselves. Yet it really is the other way around: in increasingly more circumstances, we cannot even make a good living without continuously building new competencies.

In the old days, we could more or less depend on our original training to carry us through until retirement. Nowadays companies adapt quickly to new, international market demands. Our highly competitive economy demands our willingness to constantly update our knowledge and enhance our competence. Robert Reich, former secretary of labor and current professor of social and economic policies at University of California, Berkley concludes:

> Even if you're doing well, you've got to continue to hustle. The
> market is changing quickly, customers are being offered a lot of
> alternatives to which they can switch easily, and competition is
> intense. There is no relaxing, no cruise control, no resting on
> your laurels or seniority. Today's great idea might not last more
> than a few days or weeks, because rivals will be quick to copy it
> or try to come up with something even better.[11]

Reich continues to say that we grow more afraid as we see the gap between the rich and the poor widening. Whoever is effective is easily detected and rewarded, while the less effective are punished. This adds to the already-existing sorting mechanisms of race, sex, and class. We work longer hours and worry more than we did just a few decades ago.

The fact that, for the sake of survival, we cannot afford to be incompetent may cause us to doubt whether competence itself really is an ingredient to happiness. Advocating perpetual self-growth and self-improvement seems to play into the hands of anxiety-driven, purely consumption-oriented societies. Books on happiness, so the skeptic may think, should lead us away from popular culture and to the cultivation of peace and contentment only.

In part, I must agree with the skeptic. Being compelled to search, to change, and to do is a narrow path. This is why I place as much weight on the experience of Being in the Supreme Mode as I do on action in the Basic Mode.

But the Supreme Mode, however more refined and noble, is only half of what we need. Life without struggling brings about complacency, not contentment. We must make things happen, to interfere and take part in the world. Otherwise we become unfit for the dance of life. It is a dance that requires us to learn the steps, while at the same time enjoying them as we dance. So although striving for competence harbors the risk of overdoing it, we must still commit to it.

Investing in our competence will not cause anxiety when we also have access to the Supreme Mode in which we become nurtured (see part 3). It is true that we need to invest in ourselves for the sake of our survival, but also for the sake of our happiness. Unless we experience self-efficacy or a sense of mastery, happiness evades us. Our potential is so great and our life so long that a mere or unhappy existence is increasingly unacceptable. As fewer and fewer people see suffering as caused by God as an opportunity to make themselves worthy of God, or as a method of purification, we are probably unhappier about unhappiness than ever before.

As long as we do not mistake happiness for perpetually happy and pleasurable feelings, this is a good development. Happiness as a result of full life participation elevates not only the individual, but the whole community to a more humanistic level.

COMPETENCE-BUILDING STRATEGIES

"Be the best you can in whatever you do" is common advice. Of course, if we applied ourselves 100 percent in all activities, we would be overwhelmed. Nobody can afford to be outstanding in everything. There are not enough hours in a day to fulfill such a demand, and it is not prudent to try. We are "average" in most areas of lives, which is adequate and beneficial to our overall health. Picking goals, choosing carefully the areas in which we want to excel, and forming a grand vision for ourselves are therefore important steps. It is also helpful to become aware of intelligent, competence-building strategies. The following insights will help us go beyond what competencies we should develop and more into how to go about developing them.

Become Curious

To begin with, we need to understand the connection between competence and curiosity. It is curiosity that propels us to learn. It is curiosity that creates and sustains the wish to gain and refine skills. I am talking about the kind of curiosity that helps us uphold our attention on a specific point, a subject, goal, or person in the Basic Mode. (Curiosity that utilizes floodlight attention in the Supreme Mode will be discussed in a later chapter.)

Todd Kashdan believes that our curiosity in the world is the foundation for our need for mastery. He writes: "Curiosity and interest are sometimes used interchangeably. When individuals experience these positive emotional-motivational states, they initiate and sustain goal-oriented behaviors in response to incentive cues."[12]

Kashdan goes on to explain how we can increase curiosity, and he suggests:
- building up our awareness of what we know and what we do not know
- making sure that we feel free to explore and learn (facilitate autonomy and competence experiences)
- setting up mentor relationships in fields that have personal meaning
- engaging in open-ended learning experiences[13]

As always, it is wise to examine our motivation for becoming competent. If all we want is to become rich and increase our status, we will not find joy in being curious or competent, at least not for too long. After a graduation or a promotion, our mood is likely to become elevated. It is exciting to apply newly acquired skills and the subsequent increase of responsibility. Yet once the novelty wears off, we will go back to the baseline and begin the treadmill again.

Instead, we ought to seek competence and employ curiosity for their own sake. Curiosity must become part of our lifestyle. We must learn to love learning and growing for as long as we live. Unlike anything else, this love propels us to become an active part of life.

Prioritize

Besides reawakening our curiosity, we need to decide carefully what we want and in what context we want to build our competence. Taking the criteria for good goals into account (see chapter 4), we must pick and choose wisely. Focusing on concrete goals, while setting others aside, is extremely important. Being unfocused makes us dilettantes, an invitation to diversified mediocrity.

Instead of spreading ourselves too thin by taking up too many activities, we can dive into one or two particular activities, and thus give ourselves an opportunity to become really good at what we do. To become really good at writing, for example, we must become devout readers, take lots of courses, and practice writing for many, many, many years. There is hardly anything more gratifying than becoming masterful in our chosen subject. And because life is long, we can do this with new subjects several times over.

In order to make things happen for ourselves, we must be ready to sustain our interest, which brings us to the subject of commitment.

Make a Commitment

Commitment has never been as outdated in the West as it is now. Just try to take a nonmandatory course in school: toward the end of the course, so many people have dropped out of the class that it might even face cancellation. Noncommittal behavior is practically taught by many parents who allow their children to choose and switch around classes as they please. Many parents take pride in their children's noncommittal behavior, as if it proves the children's autonomy. Even teachers recommend endless "exposure" as opposed to expertise. In reality, less is more when it comes to building competence. It helps us confront difficulties and tolerate boredom until we hit a new level of mastery.

Commitment to a chosen activity or area is the difference between dating and meaningful relationships. Dating is fun and a necessary time of play and exploration. But once we have found the one love and said "yes" to this love, we enter a common reality, the naked truth of who we are in ordinary life, with the potential of deep personal growth in this connection. Giving one person or one activity special attention is not just a virtue, but a chance to discover and develop parts of ourselves.

When I was young, I used to be leery of commitment for many reasons, one of which was the fear of feeling trapped or limited. I did not want to be pinned down and reduce my chances of becoming a master in a great many things. What I did not understand was that it was this very fear that prevented me from spending enough time with any one thing long enough to become a master in anything at all. Once I let go of becoming "everything," I could become "something," namely a clinical psychologist. This meant a whole lot more to me than a title or a way of positive identification, because I was responding to and partially fulfilling my human potential.

As a result of this decision, I became challenged in deeper emotional and intellectual ways than I could have foreseen, preparing me also for subsequent activities, such as writing about psychology. Thus, my commitment to psychology helped me become a passionate and, I dare say, competent psychologist. Making a commitment that reflects a part of who you are makes that part bigger and contributes to a greater, more competent, more engaged you.

Gather the Right Support

When we have the right support for our endeavors, our willingness and ability to commit are likely to increase. Some people work well in groups, while others do not. Allegedly, many boys thrive on competitive performance, while many girls thrive on cooperative teamwork. One-on-one consultations help us stay focused and motivated. The role of the loving parent and the supportive life-partner cannot be overestimated. Because we are social animals, we rely on other people cheering us on and taking an active interest in our activities.

Teachers and mentors can be very important as part of our support. They come in many shapes and colors; in person or online; in books, films, or audiotapes. We may surprise ourselves at how well we can learn once we have found the support that suits us. Only gradually do we reach a level at which we become our own best support and teacher, relying mostly on lone experience and the good old trial-and-error method. While we should always seek feedback with others, becoming our own best support is a sign of maturity.

Don't Work Too Hard

Some of us work hard and have great skills, but we neglect to watch over ourselves. Smart competence entails smart judgment about when and how much of it we want to employ. Our competence will not make us feel happy when we overdo it. Women are especially prone to working too hard. We try to advance ourselves by approximating perfection, while leaving our other needs unfulfilled. Many of us feel guilty picking up a book or meeting up with a friend because we think we ought to spend all our time in one area, be it at-home parenting or at work improving our business.

Edward Hirt's study shows that women pride themselves on being hard workers and have little tolerance for people who lack motivation.[14] Hard work can be good, but we need to keep in mind what we want to accomplish with it. Often, too much of a good thing does not become rewarded, but taken for granted. Meanwhile we wear ourselves out. Ultimately this could diminish the quality of our work. In other words, hard work is not synonymous with competence and may be counterproductive. Some may even take it as a sign of incompetence.

Instead of being too accommodating, we need to learn how to leave some work undone. Also, we must involve others, make requests, or delegate some work entirely. A better strategy than working too hard is speaking out, speaking up, and tooting our own horn as executive Gail Evans suggests.[15] She had witnessed that people, including herself, had much greater success and a much better time when they asserted themselves. It is important to let our superiors know what we are capable of, pin our certificates to the wall, and avoid chores and tasks that should be or could be handled by someone else. I would rather do a great job in an area of my expertise than a mediocre job in an area others can handle.

Don't work yourself to the ground! Less is often more.

Take Subfields into Account

Skills that seem only loosely connected to our goals can be crucial to our overall competence. For example, some people think they can accomplish their goals without social skills. I know several talented people who refuse to acknowledge the need to foster their social skills. They do not want to dress professionally, make small talk, validate others, or even smile.

Yet much of what we want to accomplish involves other people. We are better off admitting to ourselves that people function better in a friendly environment, especially if we personally have difficulties communicating or suffer from a social phobia. There is no escaping the fact that we all affect each other. Students learn better when the professor is cordial and enthusiastic. A political speechmaker needs charisma to convince potential voters. With the right demeanor, an attorney may sway a judge.

Keep in mind that smart competence encompasses many subfields that we should know about in advance. If we do not like the subfields or rules of a game, maybe the game is not for us. Our rejection of the game's rules is likely to spoil everybody's fun.

When to Hide and When to Show Competence

If our position is not high and our earnings are small, watching over ourselves is even more important. Resources should not be wasted in vain. Barbara Ehrenreich, the author of *Nickel and Dimed: On (Not) Getting By in America*, writes:

> Similarly, at Wal-Mart, a coworker once advised me that, although I had a lot to learn, it was also important not to "know too much," or at least never to reveal one's full abilities to management, because "the more they think you can do, the more they use you and abuse you." My mentors in these matters were not lazy; they just understood that there are few or no rewards for heroic performance. The trick lies in figuring out how to budget your energy, so there'll be some left over for the next time.[16]

However, hiding our competence is often a sign that we lack generosity or feel a general insecurity. Frequently we hide our competence because we simply lack confidence or a willingness to exert ourselves. As discussed above, it is often necessary to show off our knowledge and skills in order to become acknowledged and appreciated by others. It is only smart to make it very clear to key people in key moments that we have what it takes. If we miss such key moments, we could seriously hurt ourselves.

Of course we should not make a nuisance of ourselves. The point is not to be a show-off, but a person ready to remind others of one's accomplishments and true competence. One way of doing so is to display items such as certificates or trophies, which women especially prefer to hide. If we have missed an opportunity to show off our qualifications, hopefully we make up for it soon thereafter. As with all skills, practice showing your light ahead of time and practice it often.

Pace the Learning Process

Lastly, I would like to discuss the pace of building competence. Going too fast or expecting too much are major reasons to spoil the joy of learning. We can observe this in children. When someone puts pressure on them, they lose joy. Sometimes they even do this to themselves. My son, for example, used to love building high towers with blocks. When he attempted to do better than his dexterity or gravity allowed, his face turned red and he gave up in utter frustration. Demolition soon followed.

As mature adults, we should anticipate a realistic learning curve. Occasionally there will be growth spurts. However, by and large, we have to grow slowly and steadily, just as a strong tree does. The rings of its trunk grow one after the other. We cannot get ahead of ourselves.

Of course the most ambitious of us will want to increase the speed of learning. If we do this, we ought to be smart about how we go about it. Occasionally we may overdo it—working through the night, for example—but we should never allow ourselves to reach the point of burnout. The price of exhaustion is simply too high, especially as we grow older.

Remember that quick achievements are often followed by regressions, as we see in extreme dieting behavior. The faster we lose the pounds, the quicker we gain them back and more. Overly zealous people are prone to crash suddenly, and they may become passive for extended periods of time. Our minds and bodies ache to be in balance and often overcompensate after having been abused or deprived. We should commit to learning slowly and steadily, and to making that a permanent part of our lives.

Building up our competence allows us to move from the satisfaction of surviving well to happiness in the Basic Mode when we feel ourselves grow. A pursuit must not only be experienced as making progress, but also as a process of becoming. Finding good and conscious reasons to engage in this process means shifting our attention away from success to personal fulfillment, away from fantasy to a realistic vision, away from being on "top of the food-chain" to being on "top of our game" for the love of the game, for the love of life.

There are so many strategies we can use to become joyfully competent in the Basic Mode, such as becoming aware of what we do not know and of open-ended opportunities in order to increase our natural curiosity. It also helps to prioritize, to commit to a field that mixes well with our personality, to gather support for our endeavors, to apply expertise and avoid doing it all, to build upon an expertise by including subfields, to skillfully hide and show off ability, and to grow steadily and slowly, without pressure. Ultimately, retrieving the joy of competence means you take a more active part in your life and assure greater happiness in the Basic Mode.

BASIC MODE EXERCISES—COMPETENCE

Something to Think About
Once I lamented to my husband how hard I had to work to be successful. I demanded a break from destiny and said: "Can't I have it easy too for a change?" I felt truly sorry for myself. My loving husband put his arms around me and said: "Well, I hope you too will soon be successful without deserving it."

What do *you* want for your life?

Draw a personal competency chart: write down two or three of the most important fields in which you have at least some competency (for example, business). Next, write down all the important subfields as they pertain to you (for example, accounting). Then, add the adjacent fields (for example, marketing). Think about the "extra" skills you need to become an expert in your main field or a subfield (for example, social skills—verbal and nonverbal communication skills, teamwork, the art of small talk and making a good first impression—public speaking skills, writing skills, rhetoric skills, computer skills).

Main Field: _____
Subfield 1: _____   Subfield 2: _____
Subfield 3: _____   Subfield 4: _____
Subfield 5: _____   Subfield 6: _____
Adjacent Fields: _____
Extra Skills: _____

Main Field: _____
Subfield 1: _____   Subfield 2: _____
Subfield 3: _____   Subfield 4: _____
Subfield 5: _____   Subfield 6: _____
Adjacent Fields: _____
Extra Skills: _____

Main Field: _____
Subfield 1: _____   Subfield 2: _____
Subfield 3: _____   Subfield 4: _____
Subfield 5: _____   Subfield 6: _____
Adjacent Fields:_____
Extra Skills:_____

Imagine This
Close your eyes and imagine standing in the middle of a long stairway. When you look down, see yourself on different steps. First as a baby, then as a toddler, child, teenager, young adult, up until now.

On each step, see how you were building different strengths. Slowly look up until you arrive at your current step. What are you learning right now? Take a few minutes to simply look inside yourself. How does learning feel to you today? Looking farther up: Where would you like to go from here? What do you like to learn?

Reach Out to Others

You might have to ask a variety of people for feedback to help you see more clearly which areas in your life need improvement. Engage in dialogues and weigh the various inputs carefully. Decide on how you want to improve yourself and grow. Maybe you need to accept help from others. Don't shy away from expert consultations. After you have decided, make a commitment and stay focused.

Explore Your Feelings

If you feel easily pressured when thinking about increasing your level of competency, chances are you are asking too much of yourself. Before you can grow healthily, you need to improve your relationship with your imperfections. Consider that imperfection is the natural state of all individuals, while perfection or something close to perfection lies in the energetic flow between individuals or individuals and goals, the interplay of "Self" and "Other." The best you can do in life is to *play* your part.

Have fun with yourself, and take pride in who you are. Tell another person five of your strengths and then say out loud: "And I am proud of these strengths." Let yourself feel good about yourself.

Things You Can Do

- For inspiration, watch the movies *Yentl; Billy Elliot; Dangerous Beauty; Dead Poets Society; The Emperor's Club;* and *Crouching Tiger, Hidden Dragon.*
- Sign up for something you would like to enhance your competence in. During this month fill out an application, make an appointment, and acquire the relevant material.
- Focus your energy. Frantic behavior is not going to make you more competent. Be deliberate in what you do.
- Allow yourself to work at your natural rhythm. Your rhythm cannot be found when you rush or delay. Start working on a specific skill, and then observe yourself. If you need to plunge into "doing," plunge. If you need to approach it

slowly and consistently, do that. There is no one way for how to start—only your way.

Spiritual Growth

Let your innermost longing for happiness and your dream for becoming the greatest person you can be carry you. Remember Dr. Martin Luther King, Jr.'s "I Have a Dream" speech. Write your own dream speech. Let the dream grow on you by reading it out loud over the next days and weeks until it is fully integrated.

Connection

Most of us, we believe, would develop more capacities for action,
and ways to be active, if we had optimal mutual relationships.

JEAN MILLER AND IRENE STIVER

When we grow with our skills, and are able but not compelled to compete, a good life is in sight. Yet, if we
cannot connect with other people, we won't reach it. Our
connectedness within the world we are part of, and which is part of
us, is of fundamental importance. Connectedness is included in the
Basic Mode, as we actively have to reach out to someone outside of
ourselves, which takes effort. As we will see later, good relationships
are also sources of strength and are part of the Supreme Mode.

THE IMPORTANCE OF CONNECTION
Life's fragility is never as apparent to us as when we are alone,
especially in fearful situations. When my brother Matthias was
four years old, he fell headfirst from a slide onto concrete blocks,
which left him in critical condition for more than twenty-four
hours. I sat in the back of the ambulance that took him to the
emergency room, and my mother sat in front. A paramedic cried
out: "Six breaths a minute!" I couldn't do anything, not even hold
his hand. My tears felt cold. Although we were rushing through
the streets, time stood still. "Four breaths a minute!" the voice
squeaked. My eyes pierced through the window of the ambulance and I saw pedestrians who were going about their business.
Nobody could see us. Nobody cared. Nobody.

Although my brother survived, I was haunted for years by
the aloneness that I had felt. An even more poignant example

is given in the film *Touching the Void*.[1] Mountain climbers Joe Simpson and Simon Yates were the first to climb the west face of Siula Grande, an Andean peak in Peru. Simpson broke his leg on the way back down the peak, and Yates bravely began a rescue mission. The mission failed, and Simpson vanished into an icy crevasse. He was believed dead. Yates continued on alone through a dangerous blizzard, completely devastated by the loss.

Yet Simpson miraculously survived because he had landed on a small bridge of ice. "There he lay, in a dark, eerily silent hole, more alone than he ever thought possible," write the authors of an article about the ordeal. "'I cried like a baby,' says Simpson, who remarkably suffered no additional injuries in the fall. . . . Unable to climb up and with a limited supply of rope, he could only crawl deeper into the void."[2]

Eventually Simpson found his way out, which is when the most horrific part of his ordeal began. Even though suffering terrible pain, with no food and only ice around him, he began a seemingly endless descent, crawling, hopping, and falling. Insanely lonely and delirious at times, he inched himself forward. Motivated solely by the desire to die in the company of others, he managed to return to their camp. There, his companion Yates, still in shock himself, was able to complete the rescue mission. Although both men have moved on with their lives, Simpson experienced the sort of shattering emptiness only human abandonment can bring about.

While perhaps less dramatic, we can probably all recall a time when we felt entirely disconnected. The feeling can be so devastating that the body slows down and reduces its sensory input. After an involuntary separation from a loved one, for example, we are vulnerable to depression. Also, it is well documented among the elderly that after a spouse's death, the surviving spouse is at risk of dying of a "broken heart" shortly thereafter. Even the hospitalization of a spouse can increase the risk of death.[3] After a divorce or separation, men tend to want to combat negative feelings with alcohol,[4] while women are prone to simply become overwhelmed by those feelings.[5] Many studies have shown that prolonged isolation bears health risks and, if experienced over one's lifetime, shortens the lifetime significantly.[6]

Just as being disconnected can strike us down, being connected has the opposite effect. In fact, nothing can lift the spirits quite the way close relations can. Connection is thus the most powerful tool and the most important ingredient to happiness in the active mode, that is, in the Basic Mode.[7]

Other people are crucial to our survival because they help us pursue individual and common goals.[8] Yet even when we have no goals in mind, relating to others brings us happiness. It is true that relationships cost us plenty of energy and other resources. In fact, there are days when relationships cause more negative than positive feelings. This is especially so with parenthood which does not correlate to happiness.[9] Yet when the aim is the good and full life and not just positive feelings, even and especially our little trouble-makers contribute to our happiness. Good relationships enrich us so much because we become thoroughly engaged and often greatly empowered by them.

As mentioned in chapter 1, the importance of connection was already known to Aristotle, the ancient Greek philosopher who went so far as to state that a life without friends is not worth living. Aristotle's opinion is remarkable because he subscribed to a rather sophisticated understanding of happiness, which he defined as "the good life." One of his theories of the good life is the "active life," in which we strive for excellence and the fulfillment of our potential. The other one is the "contemplative life," in which we reflect and examine ourselves.[10] Conversing with friends is not a necessary component in either of these theories. Still, Aristotle placed such great value on the people with whom we feel ourselves connected because they facilitate learning—and thus the process of becoming a better person.

Aristotle's link between connection and happiness is confirmed by modern research. For example, Ed Diener and Martin Seligman found that people who consider themselves "very happy" are much more likely to be social, are infrequently alone, and have strong relationships with friends, family, and romantic partners.[11] In addition, there is strong support for the hypothesis that engaging people are overall happier people. There is a positive correlation between extroversion and happiness. According to William Fleesen's research, even just acting extroverted spurs positive feelings.[12]

When we connect with others, we do more than just chit-chat and are more than just entertained. Connecting is an interchange. We are no longer the same person after an interchange because we really do *change* as a result of it, in whatever minute psycho-physiological way. Jean Baker Miller and Irene Pierce Stiver point out that women in particular tend to engage in mutual empathy leading to "mutual empowerment."[13] As a result of such a connection, we feel more zest, are more prone to act, gain knowledge about ourselves and others, increase our sense of worth, and are open to new connections.

Men benefit from empathy just as much, but they tend to have a different approach to it. Man-to-man empathy often expresses itself in common interests. When men find themselves mirrored in other men's actions, they feel—as my male clients have often shared with me—reassured and strengthened. These observations reveal mere tendencies and do not take sexual orientation into account. Both sexes have the potential to connect via verbal communication and action.

As discussed in chapter 1, people who cannot take care of their basic needs due to poverty will experience less happiness than people who can.[14] Yet let me tell you how much happiness I saw expressed in the faces of poor people in the African countries of Tanzania and Kenya. In many areas that I traveled through, barefoot people in torn clothes walked miles and miles along dirt roads under a furiously burning sun. Nevertheless most people were smiling and laughing while greeting each other, walking and talking side by side. While poverty hurts, being connected is an invaluable asset; an asset that the wealthy hemisphere of the world is in the process of losing.[15]

WE NEED EACH OTHER

In the beginning of our lives, we were symbiotically connected with our mothers. The navel, located almost in the center of our body, is a metaphorical reminder that we cannot exist without others. Because we needed others so completely when we were infants, and because this dependency changed only gradually over a long period of time, we may not like to think of needing others now. Besides, our needs reveal weaknesses and vulnerabilities of which we may not be proud. Others could try to take advantage of us when they realize our soft spots and could try to damage us in one way or the other.

While we must self-protect, we inflict great damage on ourselves if we conceal our needs completely and close ourselves off from the world. Our soft spots are openings through which we reach out and receive. They make human interchange necessary. No matter how old we are, we will always need others to touch us, literally and figuratively. If we wish to be happy, we need another person to stimulate, see, understand, and accept us until our dying day.

It's not only individuals who resist this idea. Our culture glorifies independence as well, while connection falls by the wayside. Millions of people feel lonely and remain isolated at home and at work. Depression is on the rise. While we manage to be active from dawn to dusk, fewer and fewer of us enjoy *active* friendships that go beyond Hallmark-card advice or text messages. Too much is invested in work, entertainment, and organized activities. People we call "friends" today are often just strangers with e-mail addresses. This means we stay somewhat disengaged, unchanged, if not indifferent.

I consider the loss of friendship a drastic societal change with unknown consequences. It certainly hampers our happiness. Friends are close, yet not as close as the nuclear family. This unique distance is a platform for extraordinary interchanges. We are bestowed with positive feelings when we spend time with friends. After all, there is no need to worry about dirty diapers or other duties when we are away with friends. This and the fact that meeting with friends breaks up our routine, make us pay more attention to our interchanges. According to Daniel Kahneman, our focused attention causes us to feel engaged or, as discussed in chapter 1, to experience ourselves as true participants in life.[16]

In contrast to what I have seen in Africa, people in Western countries gather without real opportunities to meet one another. Even if we do leave the house, we join the masses of cars on the highway—we are literally encapsulated: when we sing, we sing along with a recorded voice. When we talk, we talk on the phone. Usually, we do not speak on cell phones to share personal thoughts and feelings, but to exchange information. Unless there is a client on the other end of the line, there is no need to listen attentively. Everybody understands: we are in the car.

Wherever we go, there is noisy chatter in which lies the kind of silence that leaves us cold and empty. There is nothing more isolating than being among others without being able to connect. While we should be able to enjoy solitude and need moments to ourselves, isolation causes meaningless suffering. There is nothing good about feeling like we are "living in a bubble," "behind a curtain," or "one step removed."

MAKING OURSELVES AVAILABLE

When we seek happiness, we must lift the curtain in order to make ourselves available for true connections. This is not to say that we have to sell our cars and throw out our cell phones. Yet we must make sure that we also meet people face to face. We should not fool ourselves into thinking that mediated contact can substitute for direct contact. Furthermore, we need to make time for others even when we can only connect via the telephone. Taking other calls or letting ourselves become otherwise distracted when we are with others should be unacceptable. We must put others on hold, not the one with whom we speak.

Technology is no excuse for inattentiveness. We must be present and sensitive when we want to connect with others. We must see to it that our words affect the other in the way intended. Sending off hasty e-mails, leaving frantic messages, or interrupting too often can be perceived as a slap in the face. Connection depends on our ability to choose our words sensitively, at the right time, and with the right person. As Harriet Lerner puts it: "Through our speech and our silence, we diminish or enhance the other person, and we narrow or expand the possibilities between us. How we use our voice determines the quality of our relationships, who we are in the world, and what the world can be and might become. Clearly, a lot is at stake here."[17]

Connections help us broaden our personalities, and this can only happen when we come to a deep sense of understanding and appreciation of the other. John A. Sanford, the author of *Between People*, stresses that such a sense causes us to become more complete,[18] which helps tremendously in becoming full-life participants.

TEN BUILDING BLOCKS OF CONNECTION

Upon realizing the importance of deep connections and by making wise use of technologies that often keep connections shallow, we have already taken an important step. Next lies the task of building connections, which is increasingly difficult in an era of complex relationships in which gender roles are no longer outlined by our culture. Yet the task is by no means insurmountable. Nobody has to be alone or feel disconnected. We are meant to live with others, and thus we all have what it takes to acquire the necessary "know-how." To facilitate acquiring this skill, I have identified the ten most important building blocks of connection.

All of us have relationships. To make them work, much of what we do is spontaneous and without much thought. When everything goes well, this is of course, a good thing. However, when things go wrong, our thoughtlessness makes it difficult to see what exactly caused the problem, what skill we have been lacking, and what skill we need to refine. Many of us prefer to remain oblivious to avoid changing the way we are, which is the only way that feels natural to us. The danger here is that by overlooking just one building block or a mere part of one, we might not be able to connect at all. Once we give more thought to how connections work, the remedy is often simple.

The first eight building blocks pertain to friendships, and the last two pertain especially to intimate connections:
- selectivity
- expressivity
- recognition
- validation
- taking care of the other
- appreciation
- having fun
- bearing pain together
- falling in love
- saying "yes" to each other

1. Selectivity

The first building block, selectivity, is one of contention, because it says that in order to connect, we have to choose our friends and partners wisely and be selective. This is quite the opposite from what we have been hearing from many contemporary spiritual leaders, who say something to the effect that we need to be able to connect with everybody. All beings have so much in common that there is no need to hone in on the differences. The Dalai Lama, for example, shares himself willingly and openly with every person he meets.[19]

It is true that we are happier people for interacting openly and kindly with people. However, this chapter is not geared toward everyday connections, but ongoing, deeper ones. While these two types of connection overlap, they are also very different from each other. It is also true that life is so much richer when we begin to see the essence of people. We should realize that we are all bound by life. This is the spiritual dimension of connectedness, which we will discuss in part 3.

Whether we are aware of them or not, there are biological strategies at work in order to find the "right" friend or mate for ourselves. We are steered toward that which has the greatest advantage possible to increase our fitness, the survival of our genetic material. I speak about these inconvenient biological truths because only when we have gained knowledge about these strategies can we make wise choices when it comes to happiness.

The fact is that it is easy to be drawn to attractive and resourceful people; the former is true more so for men, the latter is true more so for women.[20] Attractive people signal health, the ability to work hard, to support a family, and to reproduce. When at our side, they also increase our status, which is especially, but not exclusively, important to men.[21] On the other hand, resourceful people signal that they are able to take care of a community such as a family. Given the high cost of rearing a child, this is especially, but not exclusively, in the best interest of women. Resourcefulness is not just limited to money; it includes personal qualities such as dependability, emotional stability, industriousness, ambition, and intelligence.[22]

Whether or not we are fond of these biological strategies, they are strong and pervasive across all cultures.[23] They even include friends, as they too assist us in our survival. The question is if these strategies help us make lasting connections or stand in the way of them. Apparently, when we are entirely dominated by our biology, it gets in the way of our happiness. For example, we might not find or be found by the right person because we are chasing beauty and resources. As so many of us know from experience, people cheat and leave their partners for this reason. We could end up with a highly desirable person at our side but not be able to communicate with him or her. The beauty or the prince may turn out to be a beast or a bore. We might feel so much pressure to fit a certain profile that feeling good about ourselves becomes difficult. As it is, there are too many people suffering from anorexia nervosa and anxiety disorders.

On the other hand, it is fairly unappealing to deny or revolt against the dictates of our biology. My friends and I did just that when we were young. The ones who protested loudest about not being interested in the "superficial" often surprised, if not shocked, me with their ultimate choice of friends and mates. No matter what they had *said,* half of them clearly bonded with the prettiest female or highest earning male in their league. Those who blamed society and never nature for imposed standards, dressed and behaved "aggressively asexual,"[24] that is, deliberately unappealing. Needless to say, they often found themselves dissatisfied with their lives. Some who were more "at odds with" as opposed to "belligerent toward" nature, advanced themselves with self-deprecating criticalness. None of us accepted nature, but rejected her with a vengeance.

There must be something in between succumbing entirely to Mother Nature and rebelling aggressively against her. Nuns and monks choose celibacy, which can be a highly rewarding alternative. Yet if we wish our species to continue, we will not hope for more than a minority to walk down this remarkable path. Sigmund Freud believed the only alternative was living with awareness, which would help us contain the dark forces of nature.[25] While Freud referred to the unconscious part of our psyche, namely the id, we might include our unconscious genetic dispositions in the dark forces of nature. Awareness is more than just knowing and recognizing. As we learn more about our biological strategies, we can choose to act or not to act on them. In other words, just because we realize an attraction, we do not *have* to act on it. We can focus on whatever we see fit. It is not necessary to train ourselves to dislike beauty or wealth, which can be great fun and comforting. Yet, these qualities are insufficient for good connections. We must dig deeper to find more essential qualities. Beauty and wealth are but cherries on the cake—nothing more and nothing less.

Therefore, after humbly acknowledging our biology, we need to clarify what we must have and what we can live without in friendships and intimate relationships. We have to know what we need, like, and love, as well as what we like to give, dislike, and hate. These qualities change dramatically during youth. It is safe to assume that the younger we are, the more time we should take to determine whether a potential friend or partner has a chance of passing the test of time. It took me a long time to find out my essential needs. While I like completely independent, attractive, strong, handy, family men, I absolutely need creative intellectualism, artistic expression, laughter, and love of nature. Only when I had my priorities straight did I find the love of my life.

First and foremost, however, we need to be compatible with friends and life partners. This may mean that we have complementary traits. Yet I contend that for societies that move toward emancipation, connections work best when we have a lot in common. As opposed to completing ourselves with someone who is what we want to be or who has what we lack, we should try to find someone with whom we can share common ground.

This does not mean that we have to like the same ice-cream flavor or share the same color of skin. If we only conversed with people who are like us, we would be boring and egotistical. Democrats are stimulated by Republicans, and vice versa. Christians become inspired by Jews, and Jews by Muslims. We all benefit from the creative juices cooked in the melting pot of diverse cultures. Broad categories keep apart what otherwise would blend together well, and we might well feel most connected to people in the "other" category.

What matters in the long-term is: (1) the same age bracket to ensure similar interests and energy levels, (2) maturity, (3) intelligence and education (for balance in problem solving and conversation), (4) social behavior (i.e. agreeableness, manners, traditions, cleanliness), (5) values and how they manifest (i.e. in rituals, worshipping, charity), and (6) personality traits such as extraversion or introversion, and conscientiousness.[26]

Here differences often lead to conflicts between friends and partners that prevent us from pursuing common goals and enjoying each other's presence. Zick Rubin and a team of researchers followed up on 202 dating couples over several years. They observed that 103 couples who split up differed in values, attitudes, romanticism, and religious beliefs, while 99 couples who stayed together were more alike.[27]

Common ground is essential to friendships. Since there is no need to share the household or a budget with friends, we can allow for more differences. Still, our friendships ought not to be riddled with conflict. Only when we are roughly on the same level with a friend can we exchange advice and other forms of help, enjoy activities, and find mutual understanding.

To share values with friends, such as honesty, is especially important because "friends can hurt you in ways no enemy can."[28] They can do so because they know our strengths and weaknesses the best. Not choosing our friends wisely can lead to deception and even to "mate poaching." David Buss explains: "True friends enrich life. Without them, existence would probably seem empty. But friends are in the position to betray us. And when a friend deceives you and poaches your mate, you experience the double cost of deception—you risk losing a friend and a romantic partner with a single stroke."[29] Being similar facilitates lasting connections that are—from the perspective of happiness and, to a degree, survival—in all of our best interests.[30]

If we desire happiness, we must find common ground beyond matching superficial biological traits and get to know the other's spiritual, emotional, and intellectual makeup. We must ask a lot of questions, listen attentively, observe, and be as honest with ourselves as we can when we see incompatible traits. Taking the time to explore the other and possibly breaking up a friendship or partnership means that we honor who we are and what we need in a relationship. It takes time and courage to be selective, but it is well worth it, and it provides the foundation of everything else that follows in our connections.

2. Expressivity

Once we are in a relationship with a friend or life partner, we have to make it work, which takes strength and effort. Remember that we must exert ourselves in the Basic Mode. Even the best matches in our important connections require our prolonged attention and skill. Part of that is the need for expressivity.

Regardless of whether or not we are naturally extroverted or introverted, we all need to be good communicators. Some people, especially males, still make themselves unavailable at the first sign of conflict with statements such as: "I don't want to talk about this" in partnerships or by cracking jokes in friendships. Others, especially females, are adamant about imposing the "silent treatment" in partnerships when sad or angry, or harboring resentment toward a friend. Both men and women have the propensity to engage in indirect communication and to speak instead to a third party as opposed to the one they should be talking to. Strategies like these are only constructive when they are short detours that encourage us to either drop the subject or address it directly.

This does not mean we ought to share every detail or passing thought that we have. There is no good reason to burden our partner when we find someone else attractive. And there is no reason to bore our friends with unnecessary details, to brag, or to rub in success when they lack it or are going through a difficult time. When, however, something is important enough to even just potentially preoccupy or put a wedge between us, it is time to talk about what is on our mind. This includes when we are making repeated contact with someone we are attracted to. Not telling may either lead to keeping many secrets, which are detrimental to connections, or to causing diversions from the relationship that could be changed for the better. We must not sweep anything of significance under the carpet; we must openly share our insights, dreams, worries, strong emotions, future plans, and important decisions. When my girlfriend and I decide to talk about something that "came up," and we do so out of care for our relationship, we most definitely improve it.

It is possible to be and stay together without expressing ourselves. Many people act as if they were two completely separate beings in a friendship or partnership, instead of an interactive whole. They function as independent entities that have no needs. More often than not independent people have only loose, superficial friendships or end up separating from partnerships, while *inter*dependent people rely on open interchanges and grow closer together.

Expressivity is also the key to keeping any type of relationship interesting because we deepen what otherwise would remain shallow. It is commonly believed that letting uncomfortable issues go for the sake of peace is in the best interest of a relationship. Unfortunately this is frequently what causes the most damage. It is true, straightforwardness can awaken the sleeping lion, and who wants one of those in the backyard? Yet, it is better to tackle a problem as opposed to being tackled by it. Besides stirring up things, expressivity brings us learning and growth opportunities that make us feel alive. Also, we ought not to forget that expressivity entails not only important negative experiences, but also important positive ones. Women tend to express both their positive and negative emotions with their friends and partners more than men, and, maybe as a consequence, *feel* more happy and unhappy than men.[31] Women are often more connected than men, as they share both the burden and the joy of emotions, which results in social support. Maybe we will eventually discover that it is this support that causes women to live longer than men. While lamenting does not have positive effects on our well-being,[32] expressing ourselves for the purpose of insight adds to the good and full life. Remember though, that since our ordinary life mostly takes place between the negative and the positive, expressing and validating (see "validation" later in this chapter) the subjectively important, but ordinary, is also part of a good connection. Couples experience sharing of the ordinary as love, and friends experience it as having a "really good old time."

All that being said, it amazes me how many of my clients hold back important information from their friends and partners. "She will be too upset if I tell her what bothers me," "It won't do our relationship any good if I tell him how I really feel," "I don't want to hurt his feelings," are just some of the excuses we use to remain silent. A lot of us even hold back the good, such as expressions of love, compliments, and tender feelings. In order to avoid unnecessary pain for the other, we need to know how and when to speak to the other. Blurting everything out without taking the other person and the situation into account does not accomplish anything for the connection. Aristotle, who did not even have the benefit of psychology as we know it, said this about anger: "Anybody can become angry—that is easy; but to be angry with the right person, and to the right degree, and at the right time, and for the right purpose, and in the right way—that is not within everybody's power and is not easy."[33]

Expressivity is only a valuable part of connection-building when we make it a skill. Only people humble enough to take the other's sensitivities into account can learn it. Most importantly, we need to learn from the other how and when he or she can hear us. I have witnessed friends and couples fighting very comfortably in public, while others become visibly humiliated by such a display. Some people can talk best about personal conflicts sitting side by side, others across from each other. Most of us can only take in criticism when it is "sandwiched" by something positive, or introduced by something that takes our feelings into account. If the other needs us to use or avoid a certain language or tone, we should be willing to deliver the message in the requested form.

In order to learn from the other person, it is often insufficient to observe their reactions; in addition, we must ask for instructions and feedback. I have asked my girlfriend about how she wants me to bring up conflict and learned a lot. If we have further difficulties, we ought not to hesitate to read books on the subject or consult with a licensed psychotherapist. The measures suggested in this section reflect the importance of this skill.

3. Recognition

Expressivity goes hand in hand with recognition. We must see and understand the other person. While others carry the responsibility for revealing themselves to us, we need to be willing and able to recognize them.

Here, nothing is more important than focusing on the other, with emphasis on "other." As opposed to the Supreme Mode, connectedness in the Basic Mode demands that we look at the other as different from us. Some of us are too self-absorbed to see anything but a reflection of who we are. A sign of such self-absorption is when we have unreasonably high expectations in regard to our friends' and partner's attentiveness. While we want the other to be a perfect mirror for us, however, we cannot reciprocate and anxiously await our turn.

A subtle and unconscious form of self-absorption is projection. Almost all of us do it at least occasionally. I know I do, after the fact, as projections are unconscious and can only be recognized as such in hindsight. When I react strongly, I observe myself and consider the possibility of projection. The more practice we have in realizing our projections, the less likely we are to use them in the future. For example, I used to be easily convinced that others were angry when in reality I was angry, a fact I could not accept at the time. In response, I felt afraid of the projected anger in the other, which often extended to the entire world. By owning my projections, they could not do as much damage, and eventually they vanished altogether.

We project that which we do not like or care to handle. Penny-pinching, unsympathetic people may not see their own characteristics, while finding them easily in others. While it is true that the world lacks compassion, seeing its absence almost everywhere in almost everyone points more to oneself than to reality. Another prime example of projections is found in religious fanatics. Their righteous indignation about a lack of values in others is not a sign of the righteous one's virtue, but a lack of thereof. Virtuous people are oblivious of their goodness and they keep busy uncovering their shortcomings, while fanatics lack such humility.

Someone once said that we see what we are. If we see the world predominately as an ugly, rotten place, we are likely to respond with our own ugliness and rottenness, which, of course, we all have. On the other hand, if all we have eyes for is our goodness, we naively believe reality to be only roses, love, and splendor. Both types of projection are potentially harmful because we have to close our eyes to the side of life that does not fit into our limited perception. In other words, projections cause us to distance ourselves from important parts of reality.

Think of the example of Empress Marie Antoinette at the time of the French Revolution. She was so disconnected from the reality of her starving people that when alerted that there was not enough bread to feed them, she is alleged to have suggested: "Let them eat cake." The moral is that projections are costly, especially so during pay-back times, when heads must roll.

To see the other as separate can be difficult, if not painful. Besides projection, we can escape the pain via identification. If we feel compelled to respond to other people's suffering with statements such as "I know exactly how you feel," chances are we cannot endure our separateness. While identification can be very helpful, overidentification is not. As opposed to bringing the other closer to us, we often end up suffocating them. We have a lot in common with others, especially with our friends and lovers, but we are not congruent with them. Acknowledging "otherness" preserves individuality and freedom.

Therefore, recognition begins with curiosity for and a healthy distance from another person. We should not assume that we know what the other thinks, feels, and needs. We should ask questions and pay attention to their verbal and nonverbal responses—even and especially when we have been friends or partners for a long time. People are not there to be conquered and assimilated but to be discovered and explored, over and over, for the rest of our and their lives.

Indeed, recognizing "otherness" causes curiosity, and curiosity builds relationships. Todd Kashdan has observed:

> As for interpersonal relationships, both trait and state curiosity predict subjective experiences and interpersonal closeness as rated by self and interaction partners, above and beyond other affect and motivational variables. . . . Highly curious individuals experience greater intimacy with novel interaction as a function of direct attention and capitalizing on positive qualities of partners and conversations and self-generating interest and fun during interaction.[34]

Both expressivity and recognition create the grounds on which we can learn from each other and grow together. Only the combined use of these skills opens us up for the dynamic experience of intimacy and change. With it we reduce—but not lose—the space between us, while expanding the space within. It is the beginning of singing one song together that echoes within each of these widening spaces.

4. Validation

The next building block of good connections—often painfully ignored by many—is validation. When we validate someone, we convey to them that we have indeed recognized them. Unless we are in possession of magical powers, there is no other way for our friends to know that we have really heard them. So, it does not suffice to talk, listen, and understand; we must also let our friends *know* that we have listened and understood.

Even when we or the other person are not aware of the need for validation, and even when we insist that we know each other inside-out, we still need it. Without validation, the best friendship or partnership will erode over time. Eventually, we might decide that the other person does not really understand us after all.

And then, of course, the other must return the favor of validation, because connections are based on reciprocity. If the other fails to do so, we ought to kindly and with a sense of urgency ask them to validate us. After letting the other know how strongly we feel about the need for validation, we could practice it together. For example, we could ask the other: "What have you heard or understood of what I have said so far?" Be sure, however, not to make the other feel as if he or she has to pass a test. Validating the other is not the easiest task to learn, especially when we ourselves were not sufficiently validated in our youth. While working on our relationships, we must be patient as well as persistent.

Most of the time, it is enough to validate the other by simply interspersing "Aha," "I understand," a nod, or a mirroring smile. However, when the issue is complex or tinged with high emotions, validation is a more demanding task. For example, it takes a lot of effort to validate someone when we are overcome with anger. Although our feeling is worth looking at, its expression is disruptive when the other needs validation. At such a time it is unwise to demand your right to self-expression. Remember, good relationships are so much more than just two people being "themselves." They are intricate, if not artistic, interplays that are as spontaneously lived as they are carefully designed. To let go of wanting instant gratification, we must relax, take deep breaths, support, and hold ourselves. This self-nourishment should enable us to switch to the other's perspective and let the other know *that*, and *what* we see from there.

5. Taking Care of Each Other

Obviously, the more intimate the connection, the more we do for the other person's happiness, and vice versa. While friendship and love cannot sufficiently be defined by doing "good" for each other, as some pragmatists tell us, there can be no doubt that good actions propel and sustain connections. The refusal to or disinterest in taking care of the other is a sign of egocentrism. If we want to expand the "point" we call ego to a field or, as Robert Stolorow would say, "intersubjective space,"[35] we must reach and look out for the other. Without sacrificing our own happiness, we have to think in terms of the other person's happiness. This entails offering help, support, and above all, availability.

In contrast to previous generations, we seem to almost condemn the notion of taking care of others. Emancipated men and woman believe in the motto: "Each individual is responsible for his or her own happiness." To some extent, this development was necessary to liberate us from an acquired, neurotic passivity, if not cowardice, as well as from the limiting, mutually exclusive roles of the sexes as "nurturers" on the one hand and "providers" on the other. People were expected to take care of each other according to their predetermined roles.

However, as so often happens, since then we have fallen from one extreme into another. While it is true that we cannot "make" anybody happy, intimate connections require an ongoing exchange of acts of love. Besides, being completely independent goes against our social nature and prevents us from active life participation. Somebody—a good friend, a family member, a partner—needs to take our hand at least sometimes, because otherwise the dance of life is not really a dance but a pitiful exhibition of individual moving flesh and neural connections.

6. Appreciation

One of the greatest dangers for long-term friendships and partnerships lies in becoming spoiled. As the novelty of any relationship wears off, we tend to become oblivious of what we have in the other, and as a result we often end up taking our best friend or life partner for granted.

Here is the remedy. When an older connection no longer engages our attention automatically, we have to give it attention consciously. In order to prevent becoming an unconscious consumer of the other, we must practice appreciation. This means we must remind ourselves regularly of our good fortune in being a recipient of our friend's voluntary—and revocable—generosity. Times may change during which we regret having succumbed to habituation, which is but a form of thoughtlessness. Indeed, all connections become brittle when we fail to count our blessings.

To illustrate the importance of this point, the little prince, the protagonist of a story written by Antoine de Saint-Exupéry, tells us about a rose. The prince had come to love a rose of stunning beauty and most delightful fragrance, which truly lit up his life. The rose's vanity and constant demands, however, required a lot of caretaking, which the little prince disapproved of and resented. It was only much later that he realized that her demands had covered up her fragility and that her actions meant so much more than her words. Much to his regret, the prince failed the relationship because he did not appreciate what the rose had meant and given to him.[36]

7. Having Fun

There are many types of omissions by which we can fail our connections. Yet there is one that often gets overlooked because it seems so mundane. Once, I asked my husband, Steven, who really does live the good and full life, what connections are all about. Without hesitation he exclaimed: "Having fun." When I raised my psycho-philosophical eyebrow, he quickly added: "Fun talking, hiking, eating, watching movies, cutting down brush together, going fishing, just doing things together." Most down-to-earth people concur with Steven, and I do too. There can hardly be anything more vital in any friendship or partnership than doing fun things together.

Fun can be a great many things. We can experience "flow"[37] together by pursuing a common goal that, as Martin Seligman points out, gives us gratification:

> The gratifications are activities we very much like doing, but they are not necessarily accompanied by any raw feelings at all. Rather, the gratifications engage us fully, we become immersed and absorbed in them, and we lose self-consciousness. Enjoying a great conversation, rock climbing, reading a good book, dancing, and making a slam dunk are all examples of activities in which time stops for us, our skills match the challenge, and we are in touch with our strengths.[38]

While gratifications last longer than pleasures, the latter are certainly part of having fun. There are simple (bodily) and higher (cognitive) pleasures that we can enhance by savoring the moment and not overdoing them. If all we do is bicker, brood over problems, gossip with our friend behind people's backs without ever doing anything constructive or fun, it may be time to simply go to the movies, hike, shop, dance, or go to a game together. Who knows how many relationships could have been saved with just a little bit of fun.

8. Bearing Pain Together

We all realize that connections are sustained not only by having good times, but also by helping each other through bad times. Life can be tough. When we feel pained by something, we might or might not feel grateful when someone distracts us. Yet when we feel completely overcome with pain, we would rather disconnect from a fair-weather friend before we let them distract us. We need fully-rounded friends with whom we can go through thick and thin, heaven and hell, sharing the joys and pains of real life.

If the person in pain can handle intimacy, he or she will naturally gravitate toward people who can bear the pain. Bearing pain together does not necessarily mean that we have wonderful and wise things to say to each other, but that we are able to witness pain without panicking. This requires us to be patient, nonjudgmental, and understanding, instead of interfering nervously, lecturing, or abandoning the other.

If we want to stay connected during hard times, we need to understand that witnessing someone's pain is not necessarily commensurate with providing solutions. Often, the one in pain just needs to talk it out or have a shoulder to cry on. Thinking things through with the other can be appropriate, as long as we do not pressure the other to accept our advice. Only when the other person indicates a readiness to take things in, may we gently help to lay out solutions. While men usually welcome solutions sooner than women, they too dislike being bombarded with them. A barrage of suggestions while in distress makes everybody feel criticized or patronized.

9. Falling in Love

The last two building blocks pertain to intimate connections. First, let me share my opinion about falling in love. Many psychologists and philosophers view falling in love with suspicion, as if it were a sin or something inherently unhealthy. Some equate the experience with a "brief psychotic episode," irreconcilable with happiness. Others believe it to be a fantasy headed for disappointment if not disaster.

While I do not believe that "falling in love" is the same as love, I see importance and beauty in this extraordinary experience. In fact, I strongly wish this experience on everybody, and here is why: When we fall in love, we find ourselves connecting on multiple levels all at once. Such a sudden, all-encompassing connection makes us feel powerful and free. We feel as if we are flying, or falling hand-in-hand with each other. It does not feel as if we are sinking or drowning. Something greater than ourselves seems to carry us while we fly or fall. Some lovers describe it as the "hand of God" or a "binding trust."

A connection like this causes us to become creative. We might feel like singing to each other, painting, writing, starting a business, building a house, or even making a baby. Falling in love is a powerful, inspiring, and thoroughly unforgettable experience. Thus it leaves traces in our mind-body that can serve us as comfort later on in the relationship, namely during times when we need it the most.

Falling in love requires us to break the boundaries that usually keep the self together. Concepts like "me" and "mine," "you" and "yours" no longer apply. We let go of much of our individual self to join with that of another, which makes this extraordinary connection so fragile and unsustainable. Even though it cannot last and must transition into something else, we ought not to hold ourselves back from it. I have yet to encounter a non-monastic, happy person who has missed out on the experience. In Ed Diener and Martin Seligman's study, the top 10 percent of the happiest people were all, but one, involved in a romantic relationship.[39]

So do not guard against the great fall. Life is too short to live it only within the boundaries of reason. As long as you take care of yourself and are kind to the other person, falling in love is healthy and surely part of happiness.

10. Saying "Yes" to Each Other

As we emerge back as two individuals, the experience of falling in love subsides. Once we have separated, we can either walk away from the connection or anchor it to a much deeper reality. Should we do the latter, we will get to know the other and how we respond to them in great detail. If we end up saying "yes" to each other, and thus affirm the knowledge that we have gained, love rises. It is as simple as that, and yet, as far as connections go, for many reasons, it is the most difficult.

To begin with, finding out about the other and our reactions to the other takes time and diligence. We need to know the other person's needs, if we are willing and able to respond to them, and how we can actively support their growth and happiness—and vice versa. Above all we must know ourselves very well, which is difficult (not just for young people). Many of us are oblivious, ashamed, or unable to verbalize our needs, a common phenomenon humorously picked up by the movie *Runaway Bride*, in which the protagonist, oblivious to her preferences and needs in life, repeatedly panics just before entering the commitment of marriage. If we love without taking care of our own or the other's needs, we will end up traumatizing ourselves or neglecting the other.

Love is different from all other experiences because our knowledge of the other person and the long times we spend together prohibit us from resorting to fantasy. Other people's flaws can be excused and overlooked, but not those of the person we love. Faced with each other's raw reality, we are triggered and challenged in endless ways. Hence love brings out both the worst and the best in us. Nothing matures us as well and as quickly as a good relationship; nothing gives us better opportunities to change and rise to the occasion; nothing can push us as often to the outer limit.

This is also why it does not suffice to say "yes" to each other on a special (wedding) day—however significant the ritual. As we continue to discover new and old parts of ourselves and the other, we have to renew our affirmation again and again. The more we embrace the other who is in constant flux, the deeper our love and stronger the connection. Just as life itself, the Other is a mysterious adventure that we must full-heartedly embrace, trusting what we know, trusting what we do not yet know. Joseph Campbell said, "The big question is whether you are going to be able to say a hearty yes to your adventure."[40] It is then that we become fully emerged and feel ourselves become alive.

We are likely to reject the other when we share a quality we prefer not to be reminded of. Who wants to look in a mirror that shows an ugly side, especially when we can look so much better in another mirror, as in the eyes of a stranger? While the solution is simple in theory, it is not easily actualized. All we need to do is become accustomed to looking directly at the ugly sides of ourselves with kind attention. Eventually we will relax about them and accept them as ours.

This is, by the way, exactly what an effective therapist does and teaches. On the grounds of acceptance, we may even be able to change some of our unfavorable sides for the better. But here the point is that we accept the other at the same rate as we accept ourselves.

It is even more difficult to say "yes" to each other in areas where we do not make a good match. Even when we have selected our loved one carefully, we will not be spared differences and thus conflict. My husband, for example, is much more security conscious than I am. While he finds me careless, I find him overly worried. Here, it is first of all quintessential to the happiness of the relationship that both partners agree on what the actual problem is. This means we have to understand the conflict from both perspectives and be able to verbalize it.

Besides understanding the conflict, loving each other in spite of differences takes humility. Ultimately we are called upon to say "yes" to the imperfections of the other by acknowledging our own. As said before, imperfection is the natural state of human beings.[41] Reconciling with this fact of life can catapult us into the realm of the spiritual, or what I call the Supreme Mode. Jiddu Krishnamurti wrote this about love: "The moment you have in your heart this extraordinary thing called love and feel the depth, the delight, the ecstasy of it, you will discover that for you the world is transformed."[42]

Let me add the last and utterly important point of fidelity. Love can rarely sustain infidelity, which is the primary reason for divorce. We talk about love and commitment in one breath for a good reason. David Buss explains that love, which is ubiquitous in all cultures, is "one of the most important cues to commitment."[43] From a biological point of view, women especially tend to select partners who seem willing and able to extend their love into the future. This ensures ongoing care for the family by both partners. For men, fidelity is especially important because it ensures paternity. While the pursuit of happiness does not always coincide with the pursuit of survival (see chapter 1), it does so here.

The consequences of avoiding or breaking our commitment are dire to happiness.[44] We need to feel safe in the relationship and be treated with tenderness and the utmost care. In other words, love is a connection that makes us feel that we have come home.

CONNECTING IN TODAY'S SOCIETY

In the distant past, when we gathered in groups to fulfill elementary needs, we naturally made space and time to connect. We are no longer tethered to basic activities such as tending to the land, producing food, constructing homes, and defending these resources. As a result, we focus on the individual as opposed to the community. The more self-focused we are, the less we realize that this self depends on community. Thinking we can do it all on our own, we leave little space and time for connections, which, ironically, depersonalizes the individual.

Our surroundings actually inhibit connections because the individual must be served at all cost. We rush in and out of cafés, and we do not care or dare to linger in restaurants. Discotheques and night clubs are so loud that it is virtually impossible to talk and connect. Overcrowded residential areas and busy shopping malls make us want to isolate ourselves and spend money, respectively. These are all normal reactions to the sensual overkill of modern spaces that serve paying and demanding individuals. While we cannot entirely evade the impact of our culture, we can implement a few small changes that will go a long way.

Return to the Home

The first change I suggest is the return to the home. We will benefit immediately by utilizing our own home more frequently for connections. There is a tendency to underutilize our homes for this purpose. Maybe we fear losing the only sanctuary we feel we have left. On the other hand, maybe we have simply lost the generosity of former generations to be a host to others and share our sanctuary. Or do we simply wish to show off what we can afford? By using a parking valet, comparing wines on the menu, and complaining about the food, we think we are bound to impress others. And by sending our children away to expensive activities, we too are bound to impress. However, when we excessively purchase kindness in anonymous places, we prevent deeper connections and lose precious bonding time.

Regardless of individual reasons and societal pressures, we need to discern that it is the home that fosters the best connections and ranks highest as a holding and learning environment. As we undoubtedly seek the best for ourselves and our children, we will have to return to our homes and bring back the happiness that can only rise in its warmth.

Let me share some tips on how to facilitate the return to the home.

1. Provide definite time frames on your invitations to friends to prevent becoming overwhelmed.
2. Make sure that for that predetermined time nothing diverts your attention from the connection. You not only give your

guests importance by putting them above all else, but also reduce the stress of multitasking.

3. Switch off all beeping devices to guard against electronic intrusions that impinge on the warm atmosphere of your home.
4. If you feel guilty for daring to take time out for your connection with others, remind yourself that true wealth is reflected by the amount of uninterrupted time you spend with your friends and family.

Beware of Time-Savers

Many of us no longer *live* our lives; we *run* our lives. And we run them as efficiently as a brokerage firm. The only winners of this Zeitgeist are businesses that sell "time-saving" products. No time-saver has the time to connect. Recently I saw an all-telling billboard that depicted the newest high-tech communication product. Next to it was this line: WHO NEEDS TO TALK? Indeed, many of us follow this implicit advice, vegetating in front of computer and television screens. We have no time to go and visit a friend because we are busy saving time.

So, because we would rather e-mail, we miss out on making physical contact with a friend. We have no opportunity to notice and feel the sadness in his eyes and cannot give him an encouraging pat on his back. No longer touched, no longer in motion, no longer invested in emotion, we gain in weight and loneliness. Time-savers are often time-takers. Beware of them and use them as little as possible.

Sanctuaries

Before we can connect with others, we need to connect with ourselves. When we have pushed ourselves too hard and feel burned out, retreating may have to come before relating with others. (Make sure, though, not to become stuck in your cocoon.) There are monasteries, retreat centers, Zen gardens, religious retreats, contemplative trips, and of course the great outdoors to help us become centered. A corner in our home could become a mini retreat center where we, and nobody else, can enjoy a book, music, a nap, or whatever else we like to do. Teachers, spiritual advisors, psychotherapists, and coaches can support us in recentering. It takes courage and resources to seek out help and sanctuaries. If, as a result, our relationships improve, it will all have been well worth it.

Connecting at the Workplace

Many of us work horrendous hours to keep up with dramatic economic changes as well as with our own personal expectations. All this toiling, even if we consider it fun, keeps us away from family and friends. This would not be quite as detrimental to our happiness if we could at least connect with our coworkers. Yet old work ethics that tell us to separate professional from private matters still prevail. I heard just recently a report on the radio about a consultant who advised firms that they could increase their efficiency in the workplace by having stricter rules in place—rules that echo a past thought long gone. The consultant said we must not look for friends and most definitely not look for a mate at work. A private phone call might just damage the bottom line. Our sole focus should be on making money.

Both employers and employees must understand that connections do not hamper, but foster productivity. If we are in constant competition with each other, we will neither work as a team, nor will we feel loyal to our company. While there is unavoidable increasing competition between companies, there should be less competition within companies themselves. It seems apparent that only close-knit, strong working environments stand a chance against exterior instability. While it takes time for the whole establishment to realize the power of connectedness at the workplace, individuals can make some changes today.

First, I suggest that we personalize our workplace. Photographs, plants, souvenirs, gifts from loved ones, drawings from kids, certificates, occasional visits from friends, members of our family, and even pets help bridge the gap between work and the rest of who we are as a person. This personalization benefits not only us, but also our coworkers. When we feel more like a full person we are more likely to become fully engaged and invested in the environment. All in all, showing ourselves leads to win-win situations for the entire system.

Second, we should reach out to others. While it was formerly common to go out for drinks after work, now most of us dart out of the workplace as soon as possible. Many skip lunches (and gain weight as a result of irregular eating habits and semistarvation). To counteract the social deterioration, we ought to make an effort to eat with others. Going out for lunch or sitting with someone in the same room even just eating a sandwich creates comfort within and between people.

It could also be helpful to make sure that we meet up with others on a more casual basis. For example, we could start conversations in corridors and community rooms, drop in on another's office/space, and find ways to briefly socialize with colleagues. If we work alone, we need to plan ahead and set up lunches and coffee breaks with others. Even just one lunch or coffee break per week makes a difference to our sense of connectedness. If physical encounters are impossible, we ought to call at least one good friend or our partner daily.

These are simple ways of staying connected at the workplace. However, in today's hectic culture, it takes effort and commitment to do even this much. In fact, it might feel painful to devote any time at all to personal connections. Yet we cannot hope for happiness if we continue to isolate ourselves for hours at a time. Living cannot begin in the remains of the day.

If our work space prohibits such small adjustments or if it consumes us altogether, we may want to consider changing course. The previously mentioned former Secretary of Labor, Robert B. Reich, resigned from his powerful position in order to be able to spend more time with his family. He enjoyed work very much, but he still resigned. Only a minority of us is this devoted to happiness.

FEELING DISCONNECTED DESPITE "KNOW-HOW"

You might agree with much of what I have proposed. You might have reset your priorities, repaired a few building blocks of connections by adding skills, and personalized your workplace. Still, you may feel disconnected. Others might trigger shame, guilt, or other self-defeating emotions in you. In this case you will most likely hold yourself responsible for the resulting disconnect. When others trigger you to become aggressive or to feel rejected or bored, you will probably hold them responsible. Regardless, you probably regret not feeling connected and know that you are missing out.

There are plenty of reasons for feeling disconnected for which professional help may be required. Yet there is a common culprit that you may be able to address immediately, which is rigidity due to a lack of compassion toward self or others. Even though we may have the skills to connect, when we lack compassion, we may not be able to use them in critical moments. All of us feel displeased and think bad thoughts on occasion. Indeed, some negativity is good and healthy. Yet, lacking compassion, we do not reduce this negativity in due time, but contribute to it.

Whenever my former client Jennifer used to feel hurt or realized that she had hurt another person, she solidified her disappointment in a matter of minutes. Soon she went from feeling a bit bad to feeling great emotional pain, which caused her to withdraw. "When I put my toe on the slide of criticalness," Jennifer described her decline, "I will go all the way down to condemnation. Only after I have completely deconstructed myself to the point of feeling utterly unlovable, I seem to be able to release the feeling." Without noticing it, Jennifer severed herself from compassion toward herself when she had wronged somebody or when somebody had wronged her.

Angela had the opposite problem. While she frequently connected with others, she pushed them away completely when she felt the slightest disappointment in them. As soon as she felt disappointment, she perceived people as completely flawed and utterly unacceptable. Angela, ordinarily a caring person, felt no compassion for others whenever she felt let down. When we lack compassion for self or others, we rigidify our negative thoughts and feelings with the effect of social isolation.

Unfortunately we are often in the dark as to these behaviors and in which direction we lack compassion. Negative responses such as blaming and shaming feel more natural to many of us, especially when promoted by our culture and family. Compassion may seem like a luxury; we know about it, but we may not dare to afford it in critical moments. Especially when we think of our world as hostile, compassion feels like reckless spending. After all, it may let us or others too easily off the hook.

As long as we do not focus on compassion and the reality of the twenty-first century, we will continue to stay disconnected from others. Compassion is more than warranted today, and no happy person can do without it. (For more on this important subject, see chapter 11.)

We may also feel in the dark about lacking compassion because we may be stuck in a paradox: sometimes in our seeking compassion, we make it impossible. Irene Pierce Stiver and Jean Baker Miller, authors of *The Healing Connection,* have observed that many people who feel disconnected have learned to hide parts of themselves. If, in the past, we were only acceptable and lovable by hiding certain parts of ourselves, we continue to hide those parts in subsequent relationships:

> As Liz builds increasingly restrictive relational images and meanings, she continues to seek connections but she can do so only by keeping more and more of her experience and her reactions to her experience out of these connections. We see this process as *the central relational paradox,* and we believe it is basic to understanding many psychological problems. . . . In keeping large parts of herself out of connection, Liz cannot relate fully to other people in the ways that lead to growth.[45]

We may be unable to connect because we crave relationships that make it impossible to show ourselves. If we were to meet someone who would be happy to engage with all of our parts, we would no longer be able to find them, like a treasure that is hidden too well. Should we have only been loved for being self-critical or aggressive, we would try to save this relationship by acting even more self-critical or more aggressive. When others complain about being "pushed away," we would feel entirely misunderstood in our effort. All we want is to help the connection. Yet we cause more disconnect.

If compassion toward self or others is the part we are hiding, we would suppress it further by bombarding the other with what we deem acceptable actions. In order to mend a relationship we impose ourselves with probing, aggressive reasoning or overbearing care-taking as opposed to exhibiting simple compassion.

A typical example is the husband who argues aggressively with his wife. While his intentions may be good, he tends to make matters worse. Unable to listen compassionately in a time of personal conflict, he continues to barrage her. Unfortunately she withdraws further and further while he feels more and more helpless. Parents of adolescents often make this mistake. Instead of preaching to and arguing incessantly with their already overwhelmed sixteen-year-old, they are often better off listening and setting clear boundaries. Too afraid to access compassion, we resort to strategies that are bound to be counterproductive.

In all of these cases, we need to become aware of the need for compassion and the reasons for not exhibiting compassion in critical moments. The immediate benefit of awareness is that we slow down the negative responses, possibly even giving ourselves a time out. By looking at our mind without judgment we stop the counterproductive responses. Slowing down our mind is in itself an act of kindness as it halts the rigid responses. As we become aware, we will eventually enable ourselves to access compassion and use it in the direction most needed. Eventually we will strike a balance between showing compassion for ourselves and for others and beginning to love our neighbor not more, not less, but *as* ourselves.[46]

Connections make us feel alive like nothing else can in the Basic Mode. They may at times cost us dearly, but happiness does not arise on its own. It needs company and it needs sharing. As we mirror and empower each other within our connections, we grow as people and actively participate in the dance of life. In a society in which social isolation is on the rise, we may not have been taught everything it takes to connect. The ten building blocks of connection can help us identify what is missing in our repertoire, which may be a simple, but crucial, skill. Happiness visits those who share their homes with others. Pets, I should mention, are welcome too.

BASIC MODE EXERCISES—CONNECTION

Something to Think About
Rate yourself on a scale from 0 (not at all) to 5 (very much so) in the ten building blocks of connection.

1. I am selective.
2. I express myself.
3. I recognize my friends/partner.
4. I validate my friends/partner.
5. I take care of my friends/partner.
6. I appreciate my friends/partner.
7. I have fun with my friends/partner.
8. I am there when my friends/partner are in distress.
9. I have fallen in love before.
10. I know my partner well and embrace her/him with all flaws.

The tally of your score is meant to make you think, instead of quantifying your experience or interpretation of it. Treat your answers as food for thought.

Imagine This
Imagine yourself in a fulfilling relationship. What makes it work? What gives you strength?

Reach Out to Others
Talk about your strengths and weaknesses in relationships. What part of yourself do you tend to hide? What part of yourself is in the forefront? Also, share what you need from another when you feel bad. If you cannot meet people, go to places where you get to do what you like to do. For example, if you like sports, join a fitness studio or gym; if you like books, join a book club. If you feel excessively isolated and lonely, consider professional psychotherapeutic help.

Explore Your Feelings
1. Switch off all diversions from telephone to television, sit down with a good friend, and let her know what you appreciate about her. Then switch sides and listen to what the other appreciates about you. It is important to be specific and thorough in this exercise.
2. Next time your friend/partner expresses his or her pain, listen attentively and do not interfere. Just be there and make this known to the other. Ask your friend/partner what she or he needs from you.

Things You Can Do

- Read *The Dance of Connection* by Harriet Lerner, *The Healing Connection* by Jean Baker Miller and Irene Pierce Stiver, *The Art of Happiness* by the Dalai Lama and Howard Cutler, *Between People* by John A. Sanford, and especially the communication chapters of *The Feeling Good Handbook* by David D. Burns.
- Watch the movies *What Dreams May Come, Life as a House, When Harry Met Sally, Cousins,* the Italian movie *Life Is Beautiful,* the Chinese movies *Happy Together* and *The Road Home,* the Australian movie *For Love Alone.*
- Seek the help of a professional if you cannot feel connected despite all efforts.
- Do fun things with your partner.
- Practice compassion toward yourself when you are too self-critical, and toward others when you are too critical of them.
- Talk to your partner attentively for ten minutes when you wake up in the morning and when you first see each other coming home.
- What could you do to make your friend/partner happy? Do it.

Spiritual Growth

We all have dark sides that get in the way of connections. What are your dark sides? What function do they have? Try not to judge yourself at this point, but sit quietly and observe your mind as you simply contemplate the matter.

Confidence

No bird soars too high, if he soars with his own wings.

Whatever we strive for and do—alone or in connection with others—we need to believe in ourselves and be assertive. Therefore I will conclude our discussion on the Basic Mode with a chapter on confidence.

AUTHENTICITY

Considering how fragile life is, we have a great need for confidence. Without confidence, it is difficult to protect what we have and love. In order to be fully functioning, responsible adults, we need to be able to stand up for ourselves. Competence without confidence will not get us anywhere. Todd Kashdan writes: "Strong abilities are not sufficient, as competency beliefs appear to be the primary mechanism for experiencing high task curiosity and persistence, increasing the likelihood of achievement success."[1]

Some people become confident by acting confident, while many others remain insecure. A successful cellist once confided to me: "Even my students would be surprised if they knew how afraid I am to make mistakes. Nobody has any idea that I control my trembling fingers with beta-blockers or how much I suffer inside." Other people, such as my former client Graham, hide their lack of confidence so well that they do not even notice it themselves. Had it not been for a sudden onset of clinical depression, Graham would have never sought out psychological help. In our first sessions, while he casually lounged across from me, he used to brag about his various successes and alleged confidence. Graham was puzzled as to why he felt struck with depression. Whenever I asked him about his present feelings, however, he started to sweat profusely, stumbled over his words, and avoided eye contact. It took him quite a while to admit to his insecurity. In spite of having never felt connected with anybody in his childhood, he had created a great story about himself, a story of success, a story of a happy child and man. This story prevented him from having any insight into his lonely, unsupported existence.

In order to survive, it is enough to just act with confidence. Yet to be happy, we must *be* confident and truly believe in ourselves. It is not even sufficient to believe in a few select parts of ourselves in which we feel competent. Believing in those is important (see chapter 5), but this cannot be the basis for happiness in the Basic Mode. That basis must be much broader and much more inclusive.

Happiness requires a belief in our authentic, total being, which is not to be mistaken for total approval or total ability. Believing in ourselves is total acceptance of everything that we are. We are not just a few select parts, but the whole of our experiences, which are dynamically interconnected and interdependent.[2] If we reject one part, such as a particular feeling, we reject the whole, because the one part connects with the rest of our being. We must not become derailed by any single experience. Being confident is realizing that every experience is part of something greater, or in other words, becoming more conscious of the whole rather than of the individual part.

EMBRACING OUR INSECURITY

Interestingly, this means that an authentically confident person does not always *feel* confident. Human nature does not permit anybody to feel authentically confident all the time, because feelings of insecurity serve a purpose. They ground us in reality, keep us on our toes, and cause us to stay connected with the group. Feelings of insecurity remind us that no individual can stand on his own in the inherently fragile world of form.

For example, when I was interviewed by a Buddhist recently, I started feeling a bit insecure but did not immediately understand why. Instead of scolding myself for the experience, I became very curious and as a consequence discovered that I had worn my usual bright-red lipstick while the Buddhist interviewer looked "the part"—that is to say, more monastic. My insecurity gave me a chance to realize my ridiculous prejudice against "Lipstick Buddhists." Thanks to my insecurity, I could let go of a rigid category that I had unknowingly formed in my mind.

While facing our insecurities may be humbling, it strengthens our ties to and kinship with others. As we stumble, we become nimble and approachable. In contrast, people who act overly confident appear mechanical, superior, and aloof.

Keep in mind that *feelings* of insecurity are different from *being* insecure. As long as we do not identify with these feelings and remain conscious of the whole of our being, we feel confidently insecure. It can even be invigorating, if not amusing, to experience occasional feelings of insecurity. By keeping a little bit of distance from the feeling by knowing that we are much more than just this one part, we become properly humbled, but not crushed. As a consequence, nothing holds us back from learning what we can and accepting what we must. Keeping in touch with the special, complex person that we are will help us handle the small stuff.

CONFIDENCE IN OUR TRUE SELF

"What," you might ask, "is so special about our True Self, the whole of our being, that we should make it the basis for confidence?"

The answer to this question is that the whole of our being is special for the simple reason that it is all we have. This, my Being, is *it*. Of course we can learn and grow. Yet right this moment, it is the only expression of life to which we have access. And as this life is the one and only, it is special. I AM. This is reality, the only reality we will ever know. If reality is not good enough to place our confidence in, nothing is.

Especially in the West, it is ingrained in us that we are what we accomplish. We measure the worth of a person by their monetary success; when we inquire about someone's wealth, we literally ask, "So how much are they worth?" Succeeding in something is wonderful, but it has nothing to do with our importance. Every drop of water in the ocean is equally important to the ocean, whether it is a drop of water from the clouds, a river, or a mud hole. A drop is a drop, and it is all it will ever be: precious to the ocean in every way and, hopefully, precious to itself.

CONFIDENCE IN THE FACE OF DESTRUCTION
You might also ask: "Aren't there authentically bad people wreaking havoc all over? How can I be confident in the face of destruction?"

We have bad behaviors, bad habits, bad thoughts, bad luck, bad moods, and so on. Yet the bad parts are not us. Nothing bad, or good for that matter, is authentically us. The bad cannot exist without the good and is interwoven into everything else. Only the whole makes sense and is authentic.

Just imagine a person who does good whenever people are looking, but does bad when they feel unobserved. Is the good side the authentic person? I think not. We all have become familiar with politicians who play up their family values or generally ethical behavior during election campaigns, but who secretly betray their family through sexual affairs and accepting illegal monies. On the other hand, think of a gang member who steals all he can but turns into a loving father when he goes home. Could we consider him authentically bad? Although he does a lot of bad, he is not bad (even though we might have to incarcerate him to protect society). There is so much more to a person than what the eye can see. There can be a lot of bad, but the whole is still filled with *Being*.

This is not to say that the parts are unimportant. Unless we are sick, each part serves an important purpose, which is to make the whole, our life, work. Although we all have reason to complain about this or that, we must have great regard for the fact that all the parts together are successful in making the whole of our Being work.

Imagine yourself as a ball. You may find the ball too small, too fat, too old, or too plain. Yet it is still a ball, and by definition round. If you take out one part of this ball, it will no longer fly in a straight line when you throw it. It will wobble. You too would wobble if you could cut out certain parts. Because you are a system in which every part connects to another, you would no longer be able to function and, if the damage cannot be compensated for by other parts, you would collapse.

Trying to rip out feelings or thoughts does not bring about positive change, but instead creates a disability. While we sometimes have to inflict injury upon ourselves—I would certainly amputate a leg to save my life—we ought to understand fully the negative consequences of such an act. Destructive acts should be our last resort.

Before I elaborate on constructive approaches to change, let me say a bit more about the link between the whole of our being and confidence. Nathaniel Branden, who has devoted much of his work to understanding self-esteem, finds that self-assertiveness is one of its "six pillars."[3] He ascertains that self-assertiveness "means the willingness to stand up for myself, to be who I am openly, to treat myself with respect in all human encounters. To practice self-assertiveness is to live authentically, to speak and act from my innermost convictions and feelings—as a way of life, as a rule."[4]

Branden proposes that authenticity is the result of knowing what we think and staying true to it. I concur, but add to Branden's purely cognitive concept of authenticity that we also need to know the rest of ourselves, which includes instincts, sensations, and feelings. Thoughts impact feelings, but feelings impact thoughts just as well. The same can be said for bodily experiences. Our instincts and sensations most certainly shape our feelings and thoughts.

Understanding only one part of ourselves is denying all the other ones that must then go underground and serve the whole in secret. This clandestine process causes anxiety and invites hypocrisy. Once we know the entire bundle of our interacting parts, our gestalt, we have found the basis for confidence. Happiness in the Basic Mode is now possible.

LOVING OUR WHOLE SELF
We are so used to taking pride only in specific parts, such as beauty, talent, or possession, for which we receive reinforcement by society. Yet what happens when a particular part loses its magic in us and others? Inevitably beauty withers, and accomplishments matter less as we grow older. Possessions can be lost. Moreover, someone more beautiful, more accomplished, or richer may come along and take our place.

Due to a psychological phenomenon called "contrast effect,"[5] any great part in which we take pride appears "less than" when compared to another even greater part. Only when we place our trust in the whole of our being can we cope well with such a loss. We will take refuge in the beauty, the accomplishment, and the abundance of the whole.

Once again, this does not mean that we should disregard individual parts of ourselves. Beauty, for instance, has biological and aesthetic value. The problem is when we identify with that one part and cling to it. If we believe that our value is determined by the degree of beauty, talent, resources, or any other single part of ourselves, we are destined to feel insecure. Believing in the strength of the whole of our being, we do not become indifferent toward, but relatively independent from, particulars.

Because we do not identify with any particular part, we also have more freedom to move and look around at the wider context. We will realize that our beauty (or any other part) is connected to and thus influenced by the rest of our being. Consequently, we will make ourselves look attractive with clothes, good nutrition, and an open, friendly demeanor. Charm can actually trump beauty in social interactions.[6] Psychologists Ann Demarais and Valerie White write how we become attractive to others by giving them attention, a smile, a light touch on the arm.[7] Thus, while still caring about beauty, we won't pin ourselves down to it.

This freedom allows us also to incorporate other people's good opinion into the whole of our being. In our quest for beauty, for example, Carlin Flora suggests we should learn to see ourselves through the eyes of others who tend to be more forgiving with alleged flaws than we are.[8] Usually the one who loves us finds us especially attractive. As Flora puts it: "You may not be able to turn off your inner hot-or-not meter. But you can spend less time fretting in the mirror and more time engaging with the world."[9]

Contrary to popular belief, focusing on our good parts is not always advantageous for our confidence. It is but another fixation on parts. Many people preach that we should believe in our good characteristics, good actions, good intentions, good nature, and so on. Scientific data supports something different. Above all we ought to believe in what psychologists call "self-efficacy."[10]

Instead of believing in how great we are, we are better off believing that we are capable. There is a significant difference between "great" and "capable." While it is pleasurable to feel "on top" and enhance our ego, happiness comes from knowing about and having access to our inner resource that is our common capability, the workings of the whole. By believing in our capability, we make it available to us. "I think I can" unlocks the strength of the whole of our being.

In a bereavement study, Jack Bauer and George Bonanno found that people recover faster from the loss of their spouse when they express belief in their ability, such as "I can do well":

> Particularly during bereavement, the sense that one is capable and strong provides a confident base for building a new life. . . . Self-efficacy works to minimize negative emotion during conjugal bereavement by establishing the sense that one can still function completely in various life domains and that one can still have meaningful relationships.[11]

Once we know the basis of confidence, namely our authentic, whole being, we must begin to focus on its workings. Eventually we will develop love for our strength and see that we can count on it. All particularities, good or bad, will look small in comparison to the workings of the whole. Loving what is great is only natural.

The more we love our authentic being and what it is capable of, the more we are able to keep things in perspective and live by the maxim "Don't sweat the small stuff."[12] The way to get to the whole cannot, by definition, be narrow and purely cognitive, but must include all types of experience. In other words, we cannot talk ourselves into confidence, just as nobody can make a decision to be happy. A relationship with the whole of our being must be built by exploring and struggling with all the various parts that make us "us." Feelings must be felt, thoughts thought, sensations sensed, good and bad sides faced and integrated. There is no way around wrestling with our various parts if we wish to be able to place confidence in the whole that they make up.

The consequence of a loving relationship with ourselves is that we no longer feel the desire to exchange a bad part for a good part, but instead we take the bad with the good. We also become more open to working constructively with the bad; that is, we learn to change without sacrificing our authenticity.

Each of us is a unique embodiment of life, and when we learn to love what is, we do not wish to be someone else. Buddha once said that we ought to be a lamp unto ourselves, and be our own confidence.[13] Naturally, as we learn to fly, we must do so with our own wings.

ON BECOMING OUR OWN BEST FRIEND

Before we can become our own best friend, we need to address a common fantasy. Many of us believe that we would feel more confident if our lives were easier or better. The imagined change—a promotion, a sudden financial windfall, an amazing scientific discovery, a prince on a white horse—would turn things around. Yet in reality, if our wishes did indeed come true, we would not love ourselves more or be more confident, which is the only change that matters. If life turned out the way we wanted in every aspect, we would realize that the good feelings that follow success are transient and do not cause happiness.

While it is natural to wish for better times, we should not make ourselves dependent upon the outcome of our wish. Once basic needs are fulfilled and we have been given opportunities to apply ourselves and grow, then confidence has little to do with circumstances. Instead it has to do with the way we relate to ourselves, which should be with unconditional, consistent positive regard. Self-love is essential to confidence. Just as a good friend is there for us when we go through hard times, we must be there for ourselves. A good friend supports us when we fail. When times are bad, self-love brings about stability and confidence when we need it the most.

Being our own best friend comes from understanding how the good and the bad are woven into one reality. (Although this thought is particularly Eastern and alludes to the Supreme Mode, I am discussing it under the Basic Mode because it effectively enhances the I-experience.) For example, if we embraced only the good for our children and did everything in our power to make their lives easy, they would not know the rewards of effort.

Nathaniel Branden points out the dangers of "antieffort," which are laziness and avoiding discomfort.[14] When we decide that our happiness is more important than transient adversity and practice living more consciously and responsibly, a positive transformation can take place:

> We notice that when we do this we like ourselves more. This inspires us to push on and attempt to go further. We become more truthful with ourselves and others. Self-esteem rises. We take on harder assignments. We feel a little tougher, a little more resourceful. It becomes easier to confront discomfiting emotions and threatening situations; we feel we have more assets with which to cope. . . . We are building the spiritual equivalent of a muscle. Experiencing ourselves as more powerful, we see difficulties in a more realistic perspective.[15]

Of course, not all difficulties turn out to be good for us. There is nothing good about the bad when it is exemplified by people who stagnate and even exacerbate their situation. Indeed, the cliché "Whatever does not kill me makes me stronger" cannot be confirmed by science.[16] Most convicts suffered abuse in their past. Helpless and resigned to the bad,[17] they are unable to turn around their fate.

Sometimes it may even be cruel having to look for the good in the bad, such as when a parent loses a child. Rabbi Harold Kushner points out that some bad things simply do not make any sense.[18] Instead of pondering the importance of death and the laws of physics, we are better off facing our new reality and mourning the old one.

With this said, the bad can still turn out to give rise to the good in the future, but only if (1) we are kind toward ourselves, and (2) we focus on good goals and good relationships (see chapter 4).

Take me, for instance. I suffered badly due to childhood abuse, and as a result I needed to give myself loving attention. Claiming my right to a brighter future, I inched myself toward my goals of becoming a psychologically healthy human being and a psychologist who enjoys loving relationships. While pursuing these goals, I realized that I had the ability to empathize with suffering people while many of my colleagues looked upon them "objectively," if not coldly. Eventually, the unhappiness of my past made me a good therapist and a believable teacher of happiness. Because my misery made me a seeker, I am now an expert in my field. Because I could make good use of the bad, I am what I am today.

If we want the bad to give rise to the good, we must be open to learning from the bad. Our pain, failures, and losses deserve our respect, because they are often the basis for future successes. Only those who can lose well will eventually win. Our problems may turn out to be opportunities if we stand by ourselves. As a result we will heal the wounds inflicted while moving steadfastly toward our goals.

BUILDING UPON OUR STRENGTHS

Living the whole of existence, our Being, happens when we are in the Supreme Mode. In the Basic Mode, however, we activate, exercise, shape, and incorporate the various parts of our Being. Unless we have no choice but to amputate parts of ourselves or punish ourselves for a behavior, the work on our Being ought to take place on positive grounds. Attempts to whip ourselves into shape are often futile.

Constructive work on our Being must begin with a profound acceptance of what at present exists. This includes our natural dispositions (for example, sexual orientation), acquired personas, our culture, and circumstances. Even if we are the only person on Earth who is willing to do so, we must embrace who we are.

Coming Out

Positive growth utilizes our current reality. Instead of tearing down undesirable behavior, it is much wiser to build up desirable behavior. As we do so, we learn to tolerate, tone down, replace, or make obsolete the undesirable. Good work on our Being begins with the recognition of who we are right now. We must "come out" to ourselves, and very possibly to others. Often, fears keep us unnecessarily isolated and constrained, so we must not let fear but reason dictate whether or not to share our reality.

"Coming out" is not only good for most gay people, but for anybody who lives in hiding as well. We tend to hide family and personal secrets (e.g., suicide, poverty, genetic diseases, alcoholism), perceived stigmata, and countless personal characteristics. The fear of being less than our ideal can be so powerful that we either constantly try to impress everybody, or hardly express ourselves at all. Then again, we may be terrified of appearing more fortunate than others. Women especially hide their light under a bushel to avoid the mortal sin of pride.[19] In all these cases, we must find appropriate ways of outing ourselves. As soon as we do, our liberation process begins. If negative feelings are all we fear, it is possible to gain confidence in the instant of coming out.

The way that I am is the way that I am. There is no need to justify reality. If people in our environment have a problem with our reality, we should note it as such, namely as *their problem*. Hopefully they will fix it, because it is futile to struggle with reality. It is our responsibility to uphold our boundaries, claim our right to be, and stand up for our reality. Upon recognizing our reality, we must support ourselves and relax, even though we may have plans for future growth.

Focusing Techniques

Although part 3 of this book is devoted to the relaxed/focused mind, here I will recommend two specific relaxation techniques for building confidence. The first one is to practice diaphragmatic breathing, which involves opening up the "lower breathing spaces of the body."[20] Shallow, upper body breathing is not enough to support our system when we begin to feel insecure. As soon as we feel ourselves wavering, we must focus only on our breathing. One breath at a time, several times in a row, we must fill our lungs with air slowly. We have to make sure that we do not hold the air in, but breathe it out slowly while pretending we can do so through our sides at the waist.

The second relaxation practice can be done either simultaneously with the first or by itself. It is simply saying or thinking intently "I am." In order to relax into these words, it is good to have repeated them slowly and deliberately many times before a crucial challenging moment. There is nothing to figure out, just to experience. Just focus intently on "I am." Before and during a challenging situation, reiterating these two words has a powerful effect.

Focusing on "I am" also helps us with our achievements. One of my clients started thinking "I am" just before hitting a tennis ball, and improved his game significantly. Connecting with a sense of our Being is accessing our greatest strength. On the other hand, it is also useful to remember "I am" in cases of failure. Even when we feel ourselves at the lowest point, we can learn to move swiftly from devastation to confidence, recognizing and allowing the reality of our dark feelings, then looking deeper within ourselves for a light in that darkness, for a voice of courage audible only when we become aware of who we *are*. To connect to "I am" is to remember who we are on a deeper level than our emotional experience, more beautifully expressed in the song "Sound the Bugle" by Gavin Greenaway.[21]

Experiencing Our Feelings to the Fullest

Besides recognizing and supporting who we are, we can also strengthen specific parts of our being. We might, for example, have little access to our feelings, which is a common problem of depressed people. Just as we would strengthen a muscle by exercising it more than we do in our usual routine, we can exercise our ability to feel.

We do this by experiencing feelings to their fullest. Instead of skipping over a faint feeling, we accentuate it with focused attention and expression. Our usual reaction might be to belittle feelings or divert our attention from uncomfortable ones. By taking the faintest feelings seriously, we cultivate what is already there and gain access to more. While our attention ought to be mostly on the feeling, it can be quite helpful to label the feeling correctly, which is described very well in the books by Buddhist teacher and psychologist Jack Kornfield.[22]

If we want to strengthen our general ability to feel, we must refrain from judging our feelings. Many of us have been instructed not to frown and not to cry, even though the full and good life requires us to feel. Contrary to a current academic trend, Bauer and Bonanno, who determined that expressing belief in ability ("self-efficacy") correlates with resilience, found that expressing negative feelings is beneficial as well.[23] When the participants of their study expressed just one bad feeling about their personality during a particular assessment period, their suffering was significantly shortened, even when they did not express self-efficacy. Expressing no negative feelings or more in this relatively short period did not show this favorable effect. The researchers found the same result in a previous study.[24] In other words, as long as we do not whine, expressing negative feelings helps us cope. According to Bauer and Bonanno: "This 'mostly good, some bad' scenario may correspond to psychological health because it allows for a generally positive view of self that also has the sense of being grounded in the typical world of occasional setbacks."[25]

Living our sensations to their fullest is necessary when we have difficulties enjoying or giving physical comfort and pleasure. If we have been touched too little, too harshly, or too rigidly for long periods of time, we often cannot relax into our body. Consequently, many people suffer from muscle tension or numbness.

Our culture also plays a role in our difficulty with feeling because it concerns itself more with the appeal of objects and bodies than with their quality and actual sensations. We like the feel and looks of "big," as in big tastes (sugar, salt, and fats), big portions (all you can eat), big sizes (super-sized beverages containing mostly water and chemicals), big packages (for small items), and big breasts (silicone). Wanting more and more, we actually sense less and less. In Germany, where big breasts, behinds, and genitalia overwhelm the media, people seem to have less interest in sexual intercourse.[26] If we want to be complete and thus confident people, we must sensitize ourselves and begin to really feel our bodies.

We can learn to do this by focusing our attention on our senses in the moment as opposed to on future satisfaction. Deliberate eating, seeing, smelling, touching and listening without distraction or thinking of the future, will help develop our senses. To enhance our feel for touch, it is beneficial to learn to give a massage. It is also good to learn to receive a massage or self-massage.[27] One easy exercise is to take hot-and-cold showers, because our bodily sensations change with the changing temperature and, preferably, changing water pressure. Exercise programs are helpful, especially when we do them consciously. Some, like yoga and tai chi, are designed for enhancing conscious awareness of the body, which is why they work very well.

If we have difficulties with sexual experience, we may want to consider what William Masters and Virginia Johnson called "sensate focus."[28] Couples who suffer from inhibited sexual desire (ISD), have difficulties maintaining a high level of arousal or reaching an orgasm can experiment with touch without attempting intercourse. One person touches the other's non-erogenous zones first, then their erogenous zones, but only for the other to enjoy, with neither one pushing forward. A climax is to be avoided in order to stay focused in the present sensation. Both partners have to find out what kind of touch the other likes and should enjoy giving as much as receiving. The practice is supposed to include more and more erogenous zones and sexual practices as days go by, from masturbation to oral sex, but the couple must still not attempt to have full intercourse. The emphasis is on giving and feeling sexual touch with loving and intense attention in the moment, as opposed to reaching a goal.

The key of reanimating a part of us is paying attention to it and utilizing it deliberately. This also holds true when it comes to thinking. While thinking dominates most of our lives, it can be ineffective and weaken our whole being. Thoughts are known to torment us because we neither notice nor direct them.

In order to think deliberately, we must first realize when we do *not* think deliberately. Cognitive psychologist Aaron Beck points out that our thoughts are often "automatic" and flawed, which tends to lower our mood.[29] Without noticing it, we think in ways that hamper our confidence. We generalize ("I am *never* as good as others"), exaggerate ("I am the worst ever"), and minimize ("Whatever I contributed means nothing now"). One bad day at work can make us doubt our entire career if we are unaware of these flawed, automatic thoughts.

To learn how to notice our thoughts, author David Burns suggests we keep a daily record of our dysfunctional thoughts and write down the corresponding deliberate, rational thoughts next to them: "It is crucial to *write down* your automatic thoughts and rational responses; do not try to do the exercise in your head. Writing them down forces you to develop much more objectivity than you could ever achieve by letting responses swirl through your mind. It also helps you locate the mental errors that depress you."[30] Thinking thoughts more appropriate to the situation—consciously and slowly, preferably writing them down on paper—helps strengthen our thinking in due time.

As we focus on and enhance a particular part of ourselves, we should not forget the whole. All parts have to be developed and become balanced in order for us to respond to reality flexibly, effectively, and thus confidently. If we trained only our thinking, eventually we would think everything to death. If we trained only our abilities to feel and to sense, eventually we would feel, hug, and savor everything to death. Going back to the analogy about the ball, it would wobble. Nothing would be missing, but something would bulge out. It cannot be emphasized strongly enough that we need to keep our eyes on the whole ball, that is, on our complete Being. As tempting as it is, we ought not to cling to any one part, because the confidence we gain from that one part will not hold up to reality over time.

As we enhance one part, we gradually and softly weaken an unwanted part of ourselves by drawing attention away from it. This is why distractions—including sophisticated, well-placed ones such as acupuncture—are effective for so many people.[31] If we decide a certain experience hampers our confidence, taking our mind off it and thinking instead about something else reduces its negative effect on us. Anger becomes weakened by practicing kindness or by focusing on something as trivial as counting numbers. A migraine headache can be successfully treated as we focus away from the head and onto other sensations. More and more people are beginning to realize that when it comes to dealing with our feelings, destructive and punitive actions aren't effective.

Discovering and Fostering Strengths

Another constructive way of working with the whole of our Being is discovering and utilizing our existing strengths. We all have strengths, but many of us do not know anything about them.

Finding our inner strengths starts with understanding what constitutes them. First of all, we have talents, which are usually only discovered when we have opportunities to make use of them. Without a guitar, it is impossible to know whether or not we have talent to play the guitar. As adults, we have to seek opportunities in order to discover, bring out, and maintain our talents. Without utilizing and fostering them, they will not be of much use to our confidence. If we want to live a full and good life, we better bring our talents to life instead of letting them slumber in the deepest corner of our mind. As columnist Erma Bombeck said: "When I stand before God at the end of my life, I would hope that I have not a single bit of talent left, and could say, 'I used everything You gave me.'"[32]

Because our educational system is oblivious to most of our strengths, so are its students. However, many of these unrecognized strengths are important assets in both our personal and professional life. They include characteristics such as emotional intelligence,[33] imagination, far-sightedness, resourcefulness, and stamina. We do not even have a good word for the strength of balance and well-roundedness. Authors Daniel Siegel and Mary Hartzell refer to this strength as "neural integration,"[34] which means that various parts of the brain work well together, enabling a person to be both logical and emotional, both concrete and abstract. Learning about our strengths gives us instant confidence; developing them gives us even more. Therefore, we are well advised to make all our strengths explicit—preferably in writing.

We can also derive distinct strengths from examining virtues, which is Martin Seligman's understanding of strengths. He found six universally appreciated virtues: wisdom, courage, humanity, justice, temperance, and spirituality, which manifested as twenty-four different strengths.[35] (The list of virtues would even be longer if we included culturally specific strengths, such as ambition and autonomy.) Let me introduce them to you:

Virtue One—Wisdom/Knowledge
Strengths: curiosity, love of learning, judgment, ingenuity, social intelligence, perspective

Virtue Two—Courage
Strengths: valor, perseverance, integrity

Virtue Three—Humanity/Love
Strengths: kindness, loving

Virtue Four—Justice
Strengths: citizenship, fairness, leadership

Virtue Five—Temperance
Strengths: self-control, prudence, humility

Virtue Six—Spirituality/Transcendence
Strengths: appreciation of beauty, gratitude, hope, spirituality, forgiveness, humor, zest

Every individual has some of these strengths, and we will benefit greatly if we find out which ones are ours. Seligman alleges that by becoming knowledgeable about our individual, so-called signature strengths, we can employ them more effectively in whatever we do. When we learn to utilize already existing inner strengths, we become "authentically happier," and I believe, more confident.

Another helpful way of grouping our strengths comes from Howard Gardner. The social scientist proposes that there are several relatively independent types of human intelligence. He recognizes eight-and-a-half intelligences: musical, bodily-kinesthetic, logical-mathematical, linguistic, spatial, interpersonal, intrapersonal, naturalist, and, to a lesser extent, existential. Gardner strongly advises us to nurture all of the varied intelligences and all of their combinations in us: "If we can mobilize the spectrum of human abilities, not only will people feel better about themselves and more competent, it is even possible that they will also feel more engaged and better able to join the rest of the world community in working for the broader good."[36]

If we fail to recognize and nurture our personal combination of intelligences, we may never feel good about ourselves and never utilize our gifts for our own and the world's benefits. Not seeing our unique combination of strengths is wasting them and robs us of the gratifying and motivational experience of confidence.

Adding On
Last but certainly not least, we can work on ourselves constructively by adding skill and competence (chapter 5) in a disciplined manner. Instead of attaching a negative and punitive attitude to

discipline, we must remain positive, encouraging, and forgiving. Positive discipline protects the rest of our Being from harm and from straying off the path of authenticity.

My tai chi instructor, Dr. Mark Cheng, is a great believer in discipline, which is inherent in Chinese culture and the martial arts. While we might not like the sound of the word "discipline" because it seems rather old-world and authoritarian, Cheng insists that it gives us freedom. In addition to what discipline can do for our lives in terms of competence, having discipline gives us access to a great resource we can rely on. Cheng comments: "Discipline gives freedom because it allows one to navigate the trials and tribulations of life with certainty. That certainty brings with it an ease of living."[37]

Adding on skills takes discipline because we are often uncomfortable about change. If, for example, we want to become more assertive, we often experience anguish over expressing an opposing position, or saying "No." This means we need to keep ourselves on track and push ourselves gently to practice the desired behavior. Positive discipline is a state of mind characterized by devotion and willingness to guide ourselves toward a goal that is hard to reach. Once we have used positive discipline for long enough, it becomes part of our mind, and our mind becomes disciplined. A disciplined mind is a steadfast tool that we can rely on in any learning situation.

Some of us have difficulties reconciling the idea of changing who we are with the Eastern idea of noninterference. Be reminded that our Being is not a static thing, but a dynamic, living whole. We are bound to change. Yet we ought not to try to turn ourselves inside out. For example, when we learn how to make a good first impression,[38] many of us grow more confident, but each of us has to determine how far we want to go with any training. Social butterflies smile a lot, appear open-minded, speak at the same speed as their conversational partner, and try to make others feel good. Since almost all of us exhibit these behaviors on occasion, it is not inherently unnatural to learn to improve. Yet if you are an introvert, you may compromise your authenticity by attempting to become a social butterfly. The right degree of change depends not on a norm or anybody's opinion, but on your personality.

LEARNING HOW TO PERSEVERE

Many of us have difficulties in persevering. It makes sense that the good and full life depends, to some degree, on perseverance. Parents, teachers, coaches, counselors, and practically everybody advises us to acquire perseverance, but hardly anybody tells us how. Helplessly, we watch ourselves halt our efforts and give up in crucial moments during important pursuits, even though we know we have the ability to persevere in other matters. Although we are otherwise able in other tasks, we may find ourselves unable to do simple things and change primitive habits.

It does not have to be this way. All of us can learn to persevere. Small changes in our perception and behavior make all the difference when it comes to perseverance. Imagine a child's struggle to learn how to walk. They are bound to become frustrated, and they will take breaks from even trying. Yet they still gather strength for the next step. Given the amount of times children fall on their bottoms, we may wonder why they do not give up. What is it that the child has that we lack when it comes to perseverance?

There are three interdependent components responsible for the child's success, which are: (1) absence of doubt, (2) acceptance of setbacks, and (3) enjoyment of the activity. We will now examine each of these components and find ways to persevere that take into account the complexities of adult brains and adult situations.

Absence of Doubt

While the immature brains of small children do not have the ability to form doubts, we certainly do. Our minds are full of thoughts. If small kids could, maybe they too would have doubts and think to themselves, "I knew that would happen! I am no good at this and I will probably never learn how to walk. I might as well give up now," and thus put a brake on their endeavors.

Be that as it may, we have to work with our minds in order to prevent doubts from arising, or at least reduce their accelerating power. There are many ways to do so, and it is our job to find out what works best for us.

It can be helpful to train ourselves to be optimistic by rebutting pessimistic thoughts systematically. We can learn to argue that there is not enough evidence for firm, negative conclusions.

Positive conclusions may be rose colored, but they are often more useful because they lift our mood and motivate us. They even help us prevail in our marriages.[39]

There are many advanced exercises for enhancing optimism. According to Martin Seligman, we can explain events more optimistically when we attribute permanent and universal causes for the good ones, and temporary and specific causes for bad ones.[40] For example, instead of making sweeping remarks about a failure, we could say: "I had a bad day [temporary] because I did not sleep well and was unprepared for this particular task [specific]." Instead of brushing successes away as luck, we could take ownership of them. Such small but conscious changes in our thinking can affect us greatly long-term.

If you are concerned about your authenticity, first make a conscious decision whether or not a particular situation warrants a positive outlook. Also, when you examine your situation and your thinking about it, you will probably find that a negative outlook is often not *you*. Pessimism is often learned via negative cultural messages that have manifested as automatic thought. By thinking about these messages and our own thinking, we often become more optimistic right away.

Another way of having few or no doubts is to prevent them from arising in the first place. Sometimes it is just a matter of mental discipline to stay focused on either the present moment or the future goal. As for the former, we can learn to hold our attention on what the task is. If we give a presentation, for example, and we have just made a blunder, our mind might let itself ponder what just happened. As our mind continues to be engaged in the present, our attention is now cut in half: one half on the past, one half on the present. We might even extrapolate into the future, which divides our attention further, until we think with a fraction of the brain power we ordinarily have at our disposal. If we were calm and focused, we would probably not overestimate the importance of a few blunders. Yet because our capacity to think is reduced, we are unable to keep our perspective. As a result, we and our presentation suffer even more.

To avoid the division of our much-needed attention, we can take less than a second to redirect our attention. Regardless of what kind of blunder we have committed, we must summon ourselves into the present by thinking "Now!" Even though we might have high aspirations, the present deserves and needs our undivided attention.

We can learn to redirect our attention by imagining a high-pressure situation where we make a blunder, and then imagine ourselves focusing on the present moment. One technique for keeping our attention on the present is to return to a key point of our work or presentation. For example, when we falter while defending our position, we must instantly return to the key argument. During a performance, we return to the most important aspect of our performance, namely a key skill, key technicality, a key word, tune, or movement. As long as we are focused fiercely in the present, we do not have the time or space to develop doubts.

Focusing on the present moment can be used as an emergency tool that enables us to stay the course. Everything we do in the Basic Mode is supposed to help us relate to a definable goal or to another being. When our relationship or goal is long-term and doubts are lurking, it is especially important to see a future (see also chapter 4). Because the imagined future competes with the immediate experience, we must be able to imagine intently what we want. Expectations are only of value when we can imagine them vividly in the now.[41] A mental representation can elicit positive feelings and keep us energized for even the longest marathon.[42]

Because life can be tough, resorting to hope and to the sweet joy of anticipation may just be what we need to keep going.[43] Imagining the future can also be a futile escape to avoid necessary action. People can live miserable lives in the name of hope. Many postpone a full and good life for decades as they keep "waiting for Godot,"[44] whether it's retirement or an afterlife.

Keep in mind, though, that imagining the future is an astounding mental tool, recently acquired in human evolution. While the tool is not always accurate and can be misused, it is still valuable as author Daniel Gilbert points out.[45] When we use the tool to motivate ourselves and to endure the aches and pains of a long-distance runner, then we use it well. Without having entertained an occasional fantasy, this book would most certainly not exist.

Depending on the situation, it is best to imagine either the ultimate purpose of our actions or an immediate, reachable goal. As for the former, Stephen Covey, pointing out how difficult it is to change habits, writes:

> It's sometimes a painful process. It's a change that has to be motivated by a higher purpose, by the willingness to subordinate what you think you want now for what you want later. But this process produces happiness, "the object and design of our existence." Happiness can be defined, in part at least, as the fruit of the desire and ability to sacrifice what we want *now* for what we want *eventually*.[46]

While I differ in regard to the "object of our existence," I agree that postponing our immediate needs for the sake of a purpose can contribute to our happiness. Hence when we want to prevent doubts from arising, we must make our greater purpose clear to ourselves, and keep our eyes glued to it.

When an ultimate goal or purpose is just too far away to provide motivation, we need to divide the path into smaller sections and pursue several subgoals. For example, in order to persevere with my book, I cannot constantly gain strength by thinking of publication. Instead I have divided my book into parts, chapters, and sections. Occasionally I keep afloat by focusing on one paragraph alone, one fact-check, or on one sentence.

We can dissect any long process into smaller, surmountable parts. Without this dissection, it is easy to become overwhelmed with doubt. If we want to lose weight, for example, and set the goal for thirty pounds, we might give up before we have lost a tenth of it. (Beware of diets that promise too much!) To set us up for success, we ought to find the amount that we are most likely to lose in a foreseeable period of time, such as a couple of pounds in a month.

Remember Joe Simpson, the mountain climber we discussed in chapter 6. He set incremental goals to save his life. Instead of giving into hopelessness at the thought of inching down a mountain with a broken leg and without water, he pictured a nearby goal. Although in great pain, this was doable. And so he did.[47] Keeping your eyes fiercely focused on one doable goal at a time keeps doubts at bay.

Acceptance of Setbacks

Still, the road to success is paved with obstacles, and often the only way to make progress is to climb in a nonlinear way. Ups and downs ought to be expected; depending on the task, there might be prolonged standstills, for instance, when we lose weight in a healthy manner of a pound or two a month. The thinking adult mind is often best served by accepting setbacks as if they were a law of nature. Just knowing that we rarely reach a goal linearly helps buffer against paralyzing frustration.

We also have to be prepared. It all begins with the right attitude, described here by columnist Ann Landers: "If I were asked to give what I consider the single most useful bit of advice for all humanity it would be this: Expect trouble as an inevitable part of life and when it comes, hold your head high, look it squarely in the eye and say, 'I will be bigger than you. You cannot defeat me.'"[48]

Anticipating setbacks prepares us by giving us a certain amount of control.[49] It is often necessary to plan what exactly we will think and what exactly we will do when we hit a setback. The better prepared we are, the easier we will move on. For example, if we are on a diet and our weight has plateaued or we have gained a few pounds, we need to say to ourselves: "I knew that this would happen at some point. Now is the time to endure this phase."

During such a phase, we have to decide whether it is best to keep doing what we were doing, or to treat the setback as an opportunity to learn and to implement changes. For example, if we are trying to lose weight, we might have to change our exercise routine before our body adjusts quickly to any particular one. If we cannot stay on a particular diet, we have to change it to one that we can be on for the rest of our lives. On the other hand, a plateau might be the time our body needs to adjust. In this latter case, we must find ways to weather the setback.

It always pays to line up various resources ahead of time to help us stay the course. The right type of encouragement at the right time by the right person often decides making or breaking it. We need to commit to a planned arrangement even when we feel sad or embarrassed. Setbacks are not the time to isolate ourselves! Sometimes we need to plan on accessing other resources, such as expert advice, a support group, or a good book. Since we know there will be setbacks, preparing for them ahead of time will spare us much anguish.

If we feel depressed despite our best efforts, chances are that our ego or I-experience has suffered injury. Ego says we should be greater than we are. Once we have tasted from the cup of success, it may have gotten to our heads just as alcohol does, and we want more to maintain the high. When we fail—and failure is inevitable—we want to slump over and sulk: "Poor me, poor me, pour me a drink." The sooner we reconcile ourselves with being human, the sooner we become real and get back on the horse.

Enjoyment of the Activity

Although not doubting and being prepared are important, it is difficult to persevere if we do not enjoy our activities. If parents persuade their child to study a subject the child detests, chances are he or she will not do well. Hence, rightfully, everybody advises us to work in a field that we enjoy and for which we are likely to develop a passion. Toddlers-to-be find it easy to learn how to walk because they love the control of pulling themselves up to a stand, the waddling, the proud eyes of cheering parents, and the funny falls—even though some really hurt. As much as we can, we ought to follow our passion in life, as opposed to following the money (see chapter 4).

On the other hand, as responsible adults, sometimes we have to deliver the goods even when it is not fun. So what are we supposed to do when we dislike an activity without which we cannot reach a certain goal? Sometimes we can redefine or reframe our goal. Other times we could find something we genuinely like in our pursuit. There is something good in just about everything. First we may have to apply our signature strengths to the task, as Martin Seligman suggests (see page 140). It is often possible to make parts of our activity more enjoyable and then concentrate on those.

If none of these techniques help, we must prevail by keeping our perspective and by tolerating the parts we dislike. Keep in mind that all beginnings are difficult. We may not like an activity at first, but then we grow to like it after a while. If push comes to shove, consider tricking yourself into the activity. Change your self-talk from: "What a drag, I still have to work out for half an hour today" to: "Maybe I won't work out the full time today. I might just start the workout and stop after five minutes." Often we will keep going once we have started.

I use this technique in my own life. When I dread the idea of paying a bill, I just put it visibly on the table. The next step is to casually put a pen on top of it, but only in order to have it ready. Then I decide to just write the date on the check, at which point I usually write and mail the whole check.

For more difficult matters, such as having to look for a job, we can also help ourselves by looking at them as tasks consisting of consecutive steps as opposed to one giant leap. The first step can be as simple as inquiring about a few good "how to" websites to become fully informed, followed by gathering support from our friends and family. Next we could look at sites for job offers, but without the pressure of having to respond, only with the intent to list them. There is no reason to call every employer on the list the same day, but we could commit to begin with just one, for practice only. One step usually leads to the next, which is why taking a few easy ones to begin with is so helpful.

It really is worth our trouble to learn how to persevere, because this ability leads to both success and happiness. Examining success in his book *Outliers*, Malcolm Gladwell identified its three components: basic ability; opportunity; and hard, hard work. Gladwell demonstrates this with an example of a student, Renee, who was given a math problem. Renee was unusual not because she could solve the problem quickly, but because she persisted and experimented much longer than other students. Gladwell concludes: "Success is a function of persistence and doggedness and the willingness to work hard for twenty-two minutes to make sense of something that most people would give up on after thirty seconds."[50]

When our success reflects who we are and helps us connect to the fragile world of form, it will also make us happy. Life is not a sprint, but a marathon. Move slowly, with a limp if you must; pause, but do not give up. Your very action will give you confidence.

After closing this chapter with the Basic Mode exercises, we will move on to part 2, which discusses the second wing of happiness, the

Supreme Mode. Hopefully I have sufficiently inspired you to take happiness by the horns and become actively engaged in areas of your life that need it. Remember though, that the reason for this engagement with life is based on the decision to live not only for survival, but for happiness. One way of experiencing happiness is to focus the mind on and pursue something and somebody outside of ourselves.

Never forget that your ambition, competence, connections, and confidence must serve your happiness. Do not become caught up in your pursuits, because they must remain subordinate to the greater goal of happiness. As the philosopher Epictetus put it:

> There is no shame in pursuing worldly success: It's normal. Your trouble lies not in the pursuit itself, but how you pursue it. You allow your frenzied, misguided desires and fears to color your judgment. So you overevaluate the intrinsic worth of your pursuits. You bank on your pursuits to give you happiness, thus confusing means with ends.[51]

Never lose yourself for somebody else or something other than your own happiness!

BASIC MODE EXERCISES—CONFIDENCE

Something to Think About
- What enables you to forgive other people's flaws?
- What role do the parts you feel most insecure about play in your equilibrium?
- Write down a plan for how you will deal with setbacks or standstills during an activity that necessitates perseverance:

_____

_____

_____

_____

Imagine This
Think of the parts of yourself that you feel most insecure about and project them onto a person you love and admire. How do you view the "flawed" parts now? How do you view the whole person?

Reach Out to Others

- Ask someone who holds you in high regard what they think of a part of you that you view as flawed.
- Ask for encouragement if you usually shy away from it.

Explore Your Feelings

What would happen if everybody could see the part of you that you usually try to keep private? What is the worst that could happen? For the sake of this exercise, explore your reasoning without debating it. Identify the feelings that underlie your thoughts. Say your feelings out loud to expose them and in order to learn whether you are merely afraid of a feeling. Remind yourself that feelings are self-generated experiences, not solid facts written in stone. By tolerating the feared feelings with this awareness, they tend to gradually lose their power.

Things You Can Do

- Watch the movies *Spirit: Stallion of the Cimarron, Gladiator, The Insider, Fried Green Tomatoes, Out of Africa, Spartacus,* the New Zealand movie *Whale Rider,* the German movie *Aimée and Jaguar,* the Italian movie *Bread and Tulips,* the Chinese movies *The King of Masks* and *Crouching Tiger, Hidden Dragon.* For perseverance, watch the true story *Touching the Void.*
- Read Russ Harris's book *The Happiness Trap* to learn about acceptance of negative experiences. In his book, Harris also introduces his acceptance and commitment therapy (ACT), which is mindfulness based.
- Practice saying "No" if it does not come easy. If you have difficulties with assertion, practice saying "I have to disagree with you. My opinion is . . ." If a person from the service industry does not treat you with respect, ask to speak to the manager. Do not speak in anger, but state your complaint with continuous respect. If a person is rude, ask: "Why would you say something like that?" Standing up for yourself does not mean that you can change someone's opinion, but that you react in spite of it.
- Take an assertiveness training class.

- If you feel insecure in social situations, learn how to make a good first impression. There are plenty of books about the subject on the market, including *First Impressions: What You Don't Know About How Others See You* by psychologists Ann Demarais and Valerie White.
- State the overall purpose of an activity. Then set a specific long-term goal and divide it into several subgoals with a corresponding timetable.
- Choose one displeasureable activity and make it more enjoyable. Either focus on a particular aspect of the activity or apply your personal strengths more to the task.
- Consider engaging in martial arts, tai chi, or yoga. Exercise increases confidence.

Spiritual Growth

Repeat "I am" frequently and breathe consciously while doing so. Pin up a note someplace visible with the two words to remind yourself of this exercise.

Part 3

The Supreme Mode

The moments of happiness we enjoy take us by surprise.
It is not that we seize them, but that they seize us.
ASHLEY MONTAGU

The Strength of Life

You will begin to touch heaven, Jonathon, in the moment
that you touch perfect speed. And that isn't flying a thousand
miles an hour, or a million, or flying at the speed of light.
Because any number is a limit, and perfection does not
have limits. Perfect speed, my son, is being there.

RICHARD BACH

We are as strong as the world we live in, which beams with creativity, spontaneity, beauty, brilliance, and balance. Still, we do not know how strong we are. We crave to be all that, while missing the fact that there is no need to crave what we already are. Without even trying, the most wonderful characteristics of the universe are part of us as we are part of them.

Certainly we can enhance our creativity, and we can let ourselves be more spontaneous and make ourselves more beautiful, just as everything can be cultivated in a garden. Yet at some level of experience, which I call the Supreme Mode, we can meet life directly, dissolve into it, or even better, we can realize that we are being continuously dissolved into it. Instead of making our life good and full, which is so crucial for our happiness in the Basic Mode, we can simply experience our existing relationship to the good and full life.

UNDERSTANDING LIFE'S STRENGTH

We can begin to get a sense of life's strength by focusing on either the macrocosm, which includes everything visible from ladybugs to celestial bodies, or the microcosm, which is too small for the eye to see. The simple fact that there are so many things to marvel at within this universe is something to marvel at in itself. We may get a sense of life's strength by looking down at the little flower growing between the cracks in the asphalt, turning toward the all-nourishing light of our sun. While being attentive, the energy of a buzzing yellow bee may suddenly appear as if to delight us. Having opened our senses, we may now hear the rustling leaves of a tree, smell its blossoms, touch its bark, and become touched by what we touch. To increase our sense of participation in this amazing life, we flock to the ocean in which we swim and become lost in it. Lakes, rivers, mountains, deserts with all their bizarre and beautiful creatures are the offspring of this wondrous, ever-productive, ever-creative universe.

Since life began on Earth, tens of millions of different species have existed, of which only a small percentage has been studied in detail.[1] Numbers are abstract. But by simply observing a creature in its ecological niche and by understanding that it is part of a habitat that is part of the greater balanced ecological system that ultimately we are part of, our mind is boggled. Such variety! Such interplay! It took a lot of time to give birth to all the species, complex animals, and biosystems. As a matter of fact, from the first life forms to *Homo sapiens*, 3.5 billion years elapsed on an earth that had already been in existence approximately one billion years.[2]

Then again, we may get a sense of life's strength by looking up into the skies. Everything that surrounds us was and is being created by the universe's forces. Our very own solar system with its orbiting planets was created about 10.3 billion years ago. Despite the enormous weight of our Earth,[3] it turns around itself, and in only one day! While the strength of Earth's gravity prevents us from "falling" into space, the sun, being one million times bigger than earth, whips us around itself with the speed of 66,700 miles per hour.

In the Middle Ages, it was believed that every star and planet orbited Earth, which gave reassurance of God's special relationship to us. When Polish astronomer Nicolaus Copernicus discovered that everything orbited the sun, Earth was dethroned and the prevalent worldview shattered.[4] To ward off feelings of insignificance, people discredited science, as if being the sole center of the universe were the only way to feel special. I think it is special that Earth takes only one year to orbit our enormous sun; that Earth turns away and toward the sun every night and every morning; that Earth brought forth life, us, in this mostly uninhabitable universe. I think it is special that we earthlings have the intelligence to discover and conclude these facts; and that it is we, Earth people, who are able to forget all these facts, experiencing only our participation in this one awesome life. When we have become receptive to the gift of life on this very special planet Earth, we feel these words of Johann Wolfgang von Goethe to be true: "Being is so kind to everyone."[5]

As I will present in the following chapters, our sense of wonder brings us closer to the experience of life participation. Unless we are exclusively preoccupied with our immediate survival, humans have always wondered about life and its origin. We now understand that the universe began fifteen billion years ago with a gigantic explosion, called the Big Bang. According to scientist Stephen Hawking, it is believed there was a point "where the whole universe, and everything in it, was scrunched up into a single point of infinite density."[6]

At such a point, there was neither space nor time, which is why known laws of physics did not apply. Yet, before even one second after the Big Bang had occurred, quarks connected to protons and neutrons. At one second, they themselves connected in order to form the atomic nucleus of light elements, such as helium and hydrogen. How amazing that this vast universe, with all its current one trillion galaxies, one of which is our own Milky Way with 300 billion stars, originates from this one single point. So much out of so little—what power lies within it all![7]

The heavier elements that we are made of, such as carbon and oxygen, came about much later but all derived from the early-born, light elements; that is, from mostly hydrogen.[8] To bring home the wonder of life's inconceivable creativity, scientific storyteller Brian Swimme summarizes: "This is the greatest discovery of the scientific enterprise: You take hydrogen gas, and you leave it alone, and it turns into rosebuds, giraffes, and humans."[9]

We have reason to marvel at this creation in which we are included. It continuously unfolds itself in us. We cannot create stars or form species, but we can intimately relate to the creative power because we are part of it. Because we are in the midst of what makes this universe tick, the creative power inherent in the universe is also inherent in us.

Some protest that there must be something outside of the universe, something distant that brought out the first elements or their components. Something could not possibly come from nothing. However, while it is impossible to picture this, something *can* and *does* come out of nothing. There is a strange sort of energy that scientists call "vacuum energy," which is everywhere, outside of and within us. It has incredible power.[10] Even if we took every visible and invisible element out of the space in front of us, this space full of no-*thing* would still "give birth" to particles!

This omnipresent vacuum energy is also referred to as "quantum fields."[11] Because this energy is not bound to anything material, it cannot be seen or measured. According to the Newtonian laws of physics, all things are determined or caused by other things. Yet in the realm of tiny particles, things work differently: they are brought into existence for no reason, out of nothing, and spontaneously.

Most of us understand that the universe and everything in it is creative, however little we may pay attention to this creativity. But how could it be that it is spontaneous? As our material, biological nature is not prepared to imagine the nonmaterial realm, we cannot imagine noncausal action. Yet, even though we cannot imagine it, when we deal with the basis of existence, which lies in things tiny enough to be tied to the vacuum energy, causal relationships do not apply. Tiny things can therefore not be measured in all their aspects with precision, because they are actually not fixed, but are instead in swinging motion, namely waves.[12]

So while the vacuum energy releases tiny particles into existence following no rules or plan, the particles themselves are also indeterminable. The reason why the base of existence creates in such a playful manner is *because it can*. It is completely free. However, this does not mean that we humans have such latitude. We aren't tiny particle waves. We aren't quanta,[13] and we aren't completely free. We are much too big, too complex. Even though many New Age books wrongly suggest so, we cannot behave as if there are no causal relationships in our lives.

Yet what we can do is become inspired by life's strength and echo it in our active life when we are in the Basic Mode. We can always grow our freedom by pursuing great goals and by liberating ourselves within the bondage of love. Beyond that—and this shall be the subject of the following chapters—we can experience the strength of life directly. If we focus on this awesome life while accessing a mental state that I call the Supreme Mode, our consciousness will allow us to realize that we too are part of the strength of life.

THE GREAT PICTURE OF LIFE
Often, we slip into the Supreme Mode when we see the beauty around and within us, in the night and day skies, landscapes, crystals, flowers, animals, art, or inspiring human behavior. Natural order comes about in symmetry and balance, but also in the accidental interplay of all things. Despite its fragility, the world is glued together in a most picturesque, deeply moving manner. When one part becomes destroyed, something new comes about.[14] While there is a tendency of things to connect, disconnection—however destructive in the short-run—often leads to expansion, namely even to greater and more complicated expressions of life.[15]

Just thinking about all this wonderful interplay may help us see parts of the great picture that life is continuously painting. Yet the full experience comes about when we stop fixating on the individual parts, the bits and pieces that we are accustomed to perceiving. In order to experience the full strength of life, we must look more deeply at the universe. Eventually we will lose our cognitive filter and see life as one whole, one body, or—as understood in Eastern thought—as one consciousness.

It may help to know that everything and everybody comes from the vacuum energy, which Brian Swimme calls the "all-nourishing abyss."[16] All is spontaneous at its base and, once big enough, abides by the laws of physics; all tends to connect, disconnect, and expand toward more complexity; and all is interdependent. While Eastern thought is diverse, it is based in the understanding that life is not a conglomeration of pieces, but one united whole.

Intellectual understanding may be helpful, but we do not need it in order to develop an intuitive sense of this whole. All we need is a mind that can focus on life and thus become aware of our relationship to it. When we feel our relatedness to life, which we can do in various degrees, we are in the Supreme Mode. No longer do we perceive distance from people or goals—a perception so necessary for happiness in the Basic Mode.

The realization of "no-distance" can go as deep as the experience of oneness with the All. As we give ourselves to the greater stream of life, boundaries lose their meaning, and ego-experiences are not being generated. As a natural result, we feel at peace and content. The more focused our mind is on life, the more we become overwhelmed with such contentment, which is akin to what Hindus call *moksha* and Buddhists nirvana.[17]

ACCESSING THE SUPREME MODE

There are many ways to access the Supreme Mode. Instead of recounting the various Eastern schools of thought, I isolate four basic components that seem most essential to them all. They are receptivity, tranquility, reliance, and lightheartedness. I regard them not so much as tools, but as intersecting, sometimes congruent, paths to happiness. A Western understanding of Eastern thought can bring the nonactive way of participation in life closer to us, which complements so perfectly the Western active way.[18]

Going back to my analogy, we can see the two modes of happiness, the Basic Mode and the Supreme Mode, as two wings of a bird, both of which are necessary to fly. We have learned about how to fly in the Basic Mode, and now we will now learn about flying in the Supreme Mode. I believe we can only be happy if we notice our flight. The Supreme Mode allows us to be in touch with the whole picture: what we are doing, what is done for us, and what is done in us. In other words, the Supreme Mode allows us to notice Being.

9

Receptivity

Indeed, I tell you the truth, any object you have on your mind, however good, will be a barrier between you and the inmost truth.

MEISTER ECKHART

Noticing the strength of life or Being in the Supreme Mode means experiencing ourselves in midst of the whole of life. It is sensing our connection in all directions to the world community.

This is, of course, easier said than done. We are used to experiencing an "I" separate from other beings and objects instead of an interconnected whole. The highly developed human cortex, especially its parietal lobe,[1] makes such a dissection possible. It does so in order for us to take better control of parts of our lives. Unfortunately we have great difficulty laying down this otherwise

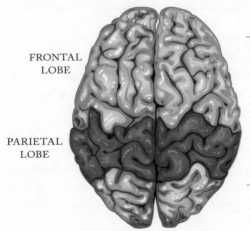

FRONTAL LOBE

PARIETAL LOBE

Parts of the human brain: the frontal lobe enables us to focus our attention; the parietal lobe enables us to differentiate between objects.

helpful tool.[2] As a result, humans have come to believe that the dissected world, in which everything appears to be separate, is in fact the real world.

For us to perceive what lies behind the scanned picture, we simultaneously have to relax the parietal lobe and activate the part of the brain with which we focus our attention, which is in the frontal lobe.[3] The goal is not to stop seeing what we are able to see now, which are bits and pieces, but to experience something greater along with it.

But where can we begin? How can we become receptive to the whole of being and its strength when we are conditioned to perceive only its parts and built-in fragility?

LOOKING AT OUR THINKING

Before I introduce ways to relax our dissecting mind while staying focused, let us prepare our minds by looking at the way we think. During meditation, we think little or not at all. The deepest meditative state is a continuous sense of complete alignment with the whole of life. It is an exceptional, boundary-less state.

But of course we do and must think in order to be fully functional human beings outside this boundary-less state. Thinking per se must not disconnect us from experiencing the strength of life. Only when our thinking is muddled or rigid does it sever our experience. Thus we need not necessarily change *what* we think in order to become more receptive. (Imposing positive thinking may or may not be beneficial.)[4] What we need to do is to examine the way we think.

By increasing our awareness of the way we think, even only slightly, we make ourselves more available to the whole of life and its strength. Just by looking briefly into the workings of our mind, we slow down and make a difference. Just by questioning obstructions to the flow of thought, thoughts flow easier. To use a Chinese metaphor, with increasing awareness of the way we think, our thinking begins to resemble the water of a healthy river, which is clear and refreshing. As we take time to look at our thinking, we notice that one thought follows another. The more we look without holding onto the old and without resisting the new, the more our thinking flows.

Looking at the way we think means to notice the speed with which we think and to notice pauses, hesitations, repetitions, ruminations, and the emotional tone, whether negative, neutral, or positive. Some thoughts seem loud, and some seem quiet. Some feel more important than others, which may trigger an immediate emotional tone and a readiness to defend or hide them. Looking at the way we think, without judgment, brings us clarity, which means we ought to refrain from judging our judgment.

WE ARE NOT WHAT WE THINK

Looking at the way we think is particularly helpful during moments when we rigidify or become confused. Most people just lash out or withdraw in such moments. Yet when we take the time and look at how we rigidify and confuse ourselves, we can quickly remove the obstructions. It is not enough to examine a particular belief and ask ourselves if we are right or not. We must go further and question ourselves more deeply. Usually what we find is that we have identified with a particular belief, or in some cases, we find that we are identified with all our beliefs. What we have come to believe seems to have become us. Being validated is therefore of the utmost importance. If a situation or a person does not fit our expectations, we cannot go with the new flow as our very existence seems in question.

Identifying with our thinking is a sign of insecurity. Instead of treating our thinking as a useful tool, we act as if we are the tool, which turns it into an automatic weapon. It is interesting that we humans have managed to make ourselves hostage to our thinking; we allow our thinking to have all the power and decide our self-worth. We do not even notice that we generate the thoughts ourselves. Thus we hang on to certain beliefs as if our life depended on them. Not only do we fear other people's inconsequential, but punitive, thoughts, but we often also fear our own. If we think we are bad, we may just be bad. Sometimes this means that we hide our true self behind particular thoughts or use our entire thinking process as a hideout.

As we question the usefulness of identifying with our thought, we de-rigidify our thinking and we become less righteous. Righteousness is based on the often unconscious assumption

that life can be grasped by thought alone. We think we have figured out how things are and should be. As a result, we no longer
consider new and seemingly incompatible thoughts. Enamored
with what we know while being closed off to what we do not
know, we have no choice but to recycle old thoughts until oblivion. This is very similar to polarized, black-and-white thinking.
We tend to disregard information that does not appear to fit into
our preferred category. Even adjuncts to our own constructs seem
suspicious, unacceptable, or too complicated.

The worst aspect of rigid thinking may be that it leads to a
lack of curiosity. Our mind is set and immovable, and thus cannot
give way to the living entity that is the whole of life.

LOOSENING OUR RIGIDITY

As soon as we look into the way we think while remaining
nonjudgmental, we loosen our rigidities. Just by looking, we dis-
identify with our thoughts and become more comfortable with
not grasping and not-knowing. Slowly we learn to approach life
the way it throws itself upon us. We realize when it's useful to try
to grasp life with thinking, and when it is not useful. We admit
when we do not know. As we are no longer completely identified
with knowing, we do not mind not-knowing.

Being comfortable about not-knowing helps us to meet life.
Not only do we ask more questions, learn, and integrate complicated thoughts, we also behave more like life itself; that is, our mind
begins to flow as life always does. Confucius, who lived and taught
morals for a new political climate in China about 2,500 years ago,
said that knowledge is knowing what we do know and what we do
not know. It is not the amount of information we have accumulated,
but the ability to distinguish between knowing and not-knowing.[5]

When we are rigid and hang on to our thinking, we lack
humility. Without humility, we cannot comfortably see the limitations of our mind. This has the effect of alienating ourselves
from much of what life is all about. We relate only to people who
think like us while rendering others dangerous, inferior, peculiar,
or pitiable. The rigid minds of fundamentalists in all religions do
exactly that. Convinced that their beliefs are the absolute truth,
they feel tightly connected with the in-group and not at all with

the out-group. Many studies show that fundamentalists, who are usually trained to think rigidly from early childhood onward, are prone to form prejudices against others more readily.[6]

But do not forget to see the rigidity within your own mind. In our quest for self-importance, self-fulfillment, and personal meaning, we too tend to cling to our thoughts. Once we think we have understood something, we begin to look at the world through the lens of that understanding. We may not notice it at first, but we really do expect that our personal belief should be everybody's belief.

Take the belief in God, for example. People kill to assert him. Others insist belligerently that God does not exist, and they cannot relate to believers. Others condemn those who deny that God has lost its principle function, that "God is dead" as German philosopher Friedrich Nietzsche put it.[7] Then there are those who proudly make thinking itself a god, while ridiculing feelings and intuition. American objectivist Ayn Rand, for example, asserts that her philosophy is: "The concept of man as a heroic being, with his own happiness as the moral purpose of his life, with productive achievement as his noblest activity, and reason as his only absolute."[8]

Dogmatic people, no matter whether they are capitalist/communist, religious/atheist, idealistic/materialistic, or Democrat/Republican suffer from their inflexible minds. Instead of enjoying variety and personal choice, they cannot relate to and feel lonely among people who do not share their beliefs. Feeling "in the right" estranges us from most people on this planet and from real life as it happens in the here and now.

In order to de-rigidify our thinking, we must understand that our preconceived notions about reality may stand in the way of experiencing reality directly. This does not mean that preconceived notions should be rejected as such, because we could not manage life without them. It does mean, however, that we should become aware of how we think and how we hold on to personal beliefs. By thinking about our thinking, we remove ourselves from our beliefs just enough to loosen their tight grip over us. Instead of being completely determined by our past and our subsequent projections into the future, awareness of our thinking makes us receptive to the stream of life as it happens.

So let us take a step back and start to observe and question the way we think. Let us ask questions like: Are we using thought for our benefit or to our detriment? Does thought help us get clarity, or does it cloud our mind? Is thought a tool, or does it run us like a robot that has discovered independence? Are we thoughtful or driven by thought? Do our beliefs serve us and our community, or do we cling to them to give ourselves more importance? How much does thought determine the value of a person?

Just sitting where we are and contemplating how we think lubricates our mind and makes it more like the watercourse that life is. With practice we begin to live the Eastern value of humility, which can open our mind and make it more receptive.

ENJOYING NOT-KNOWING

The 2,500-year-old Chinese philosophy of Taoism teaches us much about nondissected life and its direct experience. Tao can be translated into the "way" or the "essence of nature."[9] It does not stand for what nature does. Questions about why certain natural phenomena occur or what matter is made of are all covered by natural science. Instead the Tao stands for that which underlies it all, an indefinable but nevertheless real and all-connecting quality of nature.

The philosophy was founded by the legendary Lao-tzu, and its main spokesperson was Chuang Tzu.[10] Both sages were part of a culture that propagated endless rules for daily living. Living in alignment with the way of nature that is the Tao provided a much-needed sense of freedom and a more natural life.

Confucius, who lived roughly at the same time, believed that the common thread among people was to be created by binding morals.[11] A highly educated, honorable, and ambitious lower government official, Confucius realized that the increasing deterioration of his society was due to its immoral and barbaric political leaders. Hence he taught a competing philosophy, one that stressed discipline, manners, rituals, obedience to authority, frugality, sincerity, and education. His main concern was political, namely the well-being of the community. The values that he introduced prevail in much of Asia to this day and are not dissimilar to our own values.[12]

It is easy to understand that Confucius, a lifelong scholar, had an interest in Taoism. While he disagreed with its path to goodness, he respected the Taoist humility. He also used the word "Tao," even though he understood it differently. Interpreter of Chinese thought Thomas Merton distinguishes between Confucius's "Tao of man," the ethical way, and the Taoist's "Tao of Heaven," the natural way.[13]

Taoists also knew Confucius's ideas. They recognized his goodness, even though they demoted it as unnatural, like a foreign object one must acquire. Instead of abolishing Confucian ethics, Taoists went beyond them, because they believed in and identified with nature's inherent goodness.[14]

Because of the mutual respect between Confucians and Taoists, spokesperson Chuang Tzu integrated the figure of Confucius into his writings. At one point he let Confucius answer a question of his favorite student Yen Hui:

> You are familiar with the wisdom of those who know, but you have not yet learned the wisdom of those who know not. Look at this window: it is nothing but a hole in the wall, but because of it the whole room is full of light. So when the faculties are empty, the heart is full of light.[15]

It is interesting that even though education and knowing are of the utmost importance to Confucius, he leaves room for not-knowing. Acknowledging not-knowing helps us to become life-long seekers of goodness in the Confucian sense. And in the Taoist sense, it helps to surrender to the inherent goodness in nature.

Either way, if we want to become receptive to the goodness or strength of life, we too have to make room for not-knowing. We must become aware of it. For this we must learn to look inwardly, instead of only seeking for answers. Sitting and walking quietly, we gradually become curious and even excited about not-knowing. (See the section on meditation later in this chapter.)

THE VIRTUE OF SKEPTICISM

We must also learn to disagree and become skeptics of our thoughts and the thoughts of others. We need to know that we do not know, and that neither our understanding nor our perceptions are reality, but just more or less accurate representations of reality. Science, knowledge, and reason play important parts in modern societies, and we cannot afford to live without them. Yet ultimately, we must not make too much of our mental toolkit and what it can construct. There is much to learn. We will never grasp the whole of life, because our grasping mind is simply no match for the All.

Even the most advanced person is trapped within cultural boundaries, and thus is bound to draw the wrong conclusions. For example, in alignment with most abiding Jews at the time, Jesus expected the world to come to an end soon. Aristotle believed that the sun revolved around the earth. Confucius dismissed women. Buddha clandestinely left his wife right after his son's birth and later ordered his son to become a monk. Without exception and often without awareness, we are mistaken, unjust, and even cruel. Given that our minds are fallible and forever unable to grasp the whole of life, we ought to leave room for doubt.

Allowing for the possibility of being wrong takes the courage of confident adults. Skepticism is therefore not a deficiency but a sign of a mature mind that does not give in to its fears, that is above all committed to the truth, and that is willing to examine and reexamine mental constructions. Some of us fear that skepticism inevitably leads to annihilation of all values. It does not. We can be both skeptical and unequivocally rooting for our positive human potential and humanity in general.

Skeptic Michael Shermer, for example, strongly believes in the "heroic nature of humanity and in the ability of human intelligence, reason, and creativity to triumph over problems and obstacles."[16] Yet for Shermer, such a belief must go hand in hand with "the virtue of skepticism." He writes:

> Skeptics are the watchmen of reasoning errors, aiming to expose bad ideas. Perhaps the closest fit for skeptic is "a seeker after truth; an inquirer who has not yet arrived at definite convictions." Skepticism is not "seek and ye shall find"—a classic case of what is called the confirmation bias in cognitive psychology—but "seek and keep an open mind."[17]

According to studies, the happiest people in the world live in democratic countries,[18] where we can be openly skeptical and debate things freely. Because we ask more questions than when we are fed answers, rigidity melts away. Gradually we realize how little we know with certainty, and that nobody should suggest otherwise. Hence skeptics assume that no person can produce anything absolute. Only the way or quality of nature, the Tao that some refer to as God, can be considered absolute, which cannot be "thought up," defined, or grasped in any way.

However, skeptics are not necessarily receptive to the strength of life, namely experiencing happiness in the Supreme Mode. Some use skepticism to question others via ridicule. This causes others to become even more rigid and the skeptic to become even more isolated. Others use it as a tool to fight certainty only to demand it in another form. This causes more rigidity in the skeptic. French philosopher René Descartes (1596–1650), for example, used skepticism to examine his personal faulty beliefs because, so he concluded, they would negatively affect his rational thinking. Yet in his eyes, while the path to "real" knowledge begins with doubt, it arrives at certainty.[19]

Reason and rational methods were especially important during Descartes's lifetime. However, clinging to them like all powerful weapons, as religious fanatics do, does not serve happiness. While bits and pieces of life can and should be understood, the whole of life will always be over our dissecting heads.

Other skeptics are unhappy because they feel overwhelmed with the realization of uncertainty. It feels as if we have to be "in the know" in order to feel securely anchored in reality. Relaxing with the uncertainty of life does not automatically follow once we have become humble skeptics. After all, seeking control is a good strategy to secure our survival, but not necessarily our happiness.

THREE PATHS TO UNCERTAINTY

The three sections that follow can help us remain in the experience of uncertainty without creating internal havoc. With practice, we can learn to trust uncertainty and put down our analytical tools when it is time to do so.

Realizing that our cognition is not as powerful a tool as we may have assumed makes many people uncomfortable. Feelings of ineptness, powerlessness, and even anger tend to erupt. I will add further insult to such injury by quoting the interpreter of Asian thought, Alan Watts:

> For it is really impossible to appreciate what is meant by the Tao without becoming, in a rather special sense, stupid. So long as the conscious intellect is frantically trying to clutch the world in its net of abstractions, and to insist that life is bound and fitted to its rigid categories, the mood of Taoism will remain incomprehensible.[20]

Yet according to Watts, being in the "mood of Taoism" does not mean that we are reduced to a "moronic vacuity." It also does not mean that we are to discount reason or escape from it when it pleases us. Instead, it means having insight in our mind, a mind that is not only capable of dissecting reality and differentiating objects and form from one another, but a mind that also has intuitive awareness of all objects and forms, that makes up a complete picture of nature as a whole living organism that contains everything. Such awareness is likewise important for Taoists, Buddhists, and Hindus, all of whom discern that the world seen only by the dissecting eye is an illusion.

According to Eastern thought, it is not thinking but awareness that puts us in touch with the true nature of life, of which we are part. According to Shankara, the main interpreter of the sacred Hindu texts, the Vedas, we can only become aware and reveal our "innermost reality" when we are able to remove self-imposed obstacles such as our thought-generated ego.[21]

There are many different paths to awareness. I have picked the Taoist and Zen (or *Ch'an* in Chinese) Buddhist paths because they seem to fit best into secular societies and offer true alternatives to analytical thinking. Lastly I will include meditation as a means to remain constructively in the experience of uncertainty, as meditation unveils the wonder of life to us gently, naturally, and quietly.

Taoism and Wonder

As mentioned, the Tao can be translated as the "way of nature"; that is, the moving quality of nature that connects us all. As we learn to observe and feel the Tao in ourselves, we realize that we are part of something great. This realization reconciles us with the fact that our analytical mind is not as powerful as we wanted it to be.

Because we are also part of the Tao, we can redirect our attention onto the awesome whole of life. According to Lao-tzu, we can allow the experience of not-knowing because we can lean on the Tao. The way of nature knows what it is doing; there is no need to understand. We become nurtured by the Tao and strengthened by the realization of its strength. As we sense the certainty of the Tao, the need for certainty in our thinking diminishes.

The Tao is, in Lao-tzu's words, "universal like a flood" that nurtures everything and "denies nothing to anyone."[22] Without having to make any fuss at all, nature's way brings things, plants, and creatures continuously into existence. Because the Tao does not depend on mere cognition, we are free to play with the notion of not-knowing. Hence we find "the fool" a reoccurring metaphor in Asian texts, as in Lao-tzu's *Tao Te Ching*. While everybody else is concerned with appearing knowledgeable and impressing others with their sharp mind or brilliant ideas, the Taoist describes himself as the opposite:

What a fool I am!
What a muddled mind I have![23]

While others possess bright minds, Lao-tzu writes that his mind alone is "dim, dim." Not only does he admit to a lack of interest in using his cognitive tools the way others do, he seems proud of it. He stubbornly refuses to take part in business as usual, even though this sets him somewhat apart from his peers. Being different in this way has its advantages because the mind that does not know is also the mind that is open. Instead of trying to pin down reality, the open mind goes willingly with reality. Thus, the greatest advantage of the non-grasping perspective is, according to the sage, the ability to take in fully all the nourishment and offerings provided by Mother Nature.

Lao-tzu is attuned to the Tao that flows through existence. He rejoices in its quirky balancing acts and lives in a state of

perpetual wonderment. Instead of demanding more from existence, such as special favors or material goods, he notices that
existence is in itself the greatest gift we could receive. He believes
that we already live in a wonderland.

Many people ask themselves how they can arrive at such a
happy state. The little that we do know of Lao-tzu is this: he was
a sage who lived a humble, simple life that did not distract him
from realizing the greatness of existence. But do not worry. We
need not be sages to notice existence. With a little bit of insight,
we can avoid some distractions and make our lives simpler in key
areas. The smallest room suffices for reflections on life. And when
everything fails, we can employ techniques, such as using our
imagination to remove obstacles or put things "mentally" aside.

For example, when we feel overwhelmed, we can ask ourselves
what part of ourselves feels overwhelmed. It could be helpful to
ask ourselves what exactly that one part needs. If there is no time,
we could imagine a box in which we lock up the overwhelmed
part until later. In psychology, this is called compartmentalizing.
This is what Scarlett O'Hara, in *Gone with the Wind*, does when
she postpones her overwhelming problems to another day. While
her blatant greediness is not recommended by Lao-tzu, he probably would have liked how she pulled strength from focusing her
mind on her land instead of on her problems. Taking things in
stride simplifies our life. Meanwhile, we can wait or quiet our
minds with meditation, after which we can deal with our problems much more effectively.

We also know that Lao-tzu spent a lot of time in nature.
Being in an environment that has not been created by thinking
minds persuades us to stop or at least slow down our own thinking minds. Most people calm down and start praising nature
when they take a hike in the mountains. We are impressed by
the immensity of nature's manifestations; we are touched by its
beauty and awed by its power. Should we, on the other hand,
become quickly bored with nature, we benefit from going deeper
into that experience. In fact, when we let boredom overwhelm us,
we will eventually tire of generating the experience. Nobody can
resist Mother Nature when coming face to face with her. She can
fill us all with wonder.

Zen Buddhism and Wonder

How to arrive at a place of wonder from which we can receive the strength of life is taught slightly more systematically in Zen Buddhism, which evolved from Chinese Taoism. The doctrine of nonattachment and awareness in Buddhism mixed well with the understanding of the Tao, and Zen Buddhism was the result.

Although we cannot be sure of the founding of Zen with historical accuracy, according to the Zen records the Indian monk Bodhidharma (the first patriarch of Zen Buddhism) traveled to China around 520 CE to meet with the Emperor Wu of Liang. Although the Emperor did not take to Bodhidharma, the monk found a disciple, Hui-k'o who later became the second patriarch of Zen Buddhism.[24]

Hui-k'o developed the method of Zen stories that were supposed to bypass the thinking mind and push the listener, with a jolt of surprise, into awareness (meaning "awakening," or *satori*). The stories incorporated a question with a puzzling answer, which left the student filled with wonder.

For example, after Bodhidharma repeatedly refused to instruct Hui-k'o, the desperate disciple cut off his arm to get attention. Finally Bodhidharma asked what the disciple wanted:

"I have no peace of mind [*hsin*]," said Hui-k'o. "Please pacify my mind."

"Bring out your mind here before me," replied Bodhidharma, "and I will pacify it."

"But when I seek my own mind," said Hui-k'o, "I cannot find it."

"There!" snapped Bodhidharma. "I have pacified your mind."[25]

What a weird anecdote! Yet there is something Western laypeople can learn. Upon this interaction with his teacher, Hui-k'o finally managed to focus on his awareness. Although this happened suddenly, he had waited for this moment a very long time. He had known that Bodhidharma had found his own peace of mind (awareness), and he had wondered what that peaceful mind was.

The quest for this experience must have been rather unpeaceful at times. He had run out of all possible answers, and no venue he had chosen went anywhere. In other words, Hui-k'o was so filled up with his existential question, that he would have "given an arm" to find the answer. Then, at the height of his desperation, the answer came to him.

We can conclude that our own time spent wondering about our existence is not in vain. In fact, the very process of asking existential questions opens us up. It is precisely this questioning that causes us to become receptive to the strength of life.

Many older adults feel they have outgrown the existential questions that seemed to plague their minds when they were young. In reality, this is but cold comfort. Settling in the dissected world without being perplexed by the whole of life provides advantages for our survival, but not for our happiness. Survival is the basis of happiness, but being limited to the base precludes us from taking off. By recovering our existential questioning, we recover our openness to life.

The difference now is that as mature adults, our questions will no longer overwhelm us with too much emotion. They are likely less plagued with adolescent worries. Instead of wondering what life will bring us, how we see ourselves in this world, and whether or not we fit in, we may ask ourselves:

"Who am I really?"
"What lies beneath my persona?"
"Who am I without the conditioning of my culture?"
"What is life all about?"
"What makes me a part of life?"
"Am I a part of God?"
"How would I know whether or not I am a part of God?"
"What is it?"

The last question is a simple Zen question. When you choose a question you wish to ponder, be assured that the actual wording of your ultimate question is secondary to the act of asking. Also, keep in mind that the focus ought not to lie in an imaginary time, but in the here and now. Whatever you ask, do not look for the answer in the exterior world. The answer will have to do with your subjective experience, not in an object that you can point to. Whatever happened to Hui-k'o in the moment of his satori had nothing to do with cognitive understanding of his situation or a grasping of an objective truth. He had wondered before, and when he was ready, he let himself become showered with wonder while realizing: "This is it. What I am experiencing is the Tao." The answer to our prayers is in the here and now; we may wait, but we cannot expect anything in particular. Stephen Batchelor, who wrote the book *The Faith to Doubt: Glimpses of Buddhist Uncertainty*, notes:

> The deepest doubts or questions you have about existence are realized to be the key which, if turned correctly and with the right force, can open the door to their "response." This existential perplexity is the very place within us where awakening is the closest. To deny it and adopt a comforting set of beliefs is to renounce the very impulse that keeps one on track.[26]

The Lin-chi School of Zen (or Rinzai School in Japanese, founded by the Japanese monk Eisai in 1191) also uses the method of "overwhelming doubt." Here the students are confronted with a Zen problem, which is called a *koan*.[27] A koan puzzles the thinking mind to such a degree that it brings itself to the experience of absurdity. It can only be solved when the thinking mind retreats in a meditative state, and a spontaneous response can spring forward.

For example, students are asked to fill themselves up with the question of where they come from, or what they have in common with the world. Instead of analyzing the problem rationally and giving a clever response, they have to enter the experience of wonder and let a response emerge on its own. Here is a classic dialogue from Zen literature:

Question: Everybody has a place of birth. What is your place of birth?

Answer: Early this morning I ate white-rice gruel. Now I am hungry again.[28]

175

Again, Zen talk can be quite odd. Let us not analyze the response though, but turn our attention to our own sense of wonder. When art, music, or love baffles us, we ought to pay close attention to our experience. A good therapist, a child, or a curious old man in the grocery store can surprise us with a question we cannot answer.

"What are you without your pain?"
"What if the world would come to an end tomorrow?"
"When you are happy, who is happy?"
"What time is it really?"
"What makes you tick?"

Most people do not share their existential questions, but keep them private. We may want to elicit them without commenting on them, and make them our own for a while.

Most of all, we must open our eyes to the ordinary weirdness that can be observed everywhere. Every moment is serendipitous. The sound you hear right now coincides with the thought and a particular heartbeat you have only now. What a coincidence! What wonder lies in existence. Let us listen in when we wonder about existence and become aware of our wonder. Or let us imagine looking directly at existence with a calm mind. We might become strangely touched by existence, peacefully excited, quietly elated.

When we experience wonder with sustained focused attention, we do not feel like breaking the silence or talking in the same sensible way we usually do. It is often a good idea not to talk over our serendipitous moments. They are too precious. Once we are in touch with the wonder of existence, we can let this wonder grow in silence. Then, sometimes, a wondrous response erupts. We may find ourselves smiling without an apparent reason— smiling at a tree, for example, that has no eyes. In some wondrous moments, gibberish may escape our mouths. Maybe we become lost in a strange metaphor or create spontaneous art. Never dismiss such an experience.

By wondering about wonder, we invite eye-opening moments. As we refrain from defining wondrous moments and hold still, we slowly become defined by them.

Meditation and Wonder

When we trigger and immerse ourselves into wondering, we ought not to do it for the effect that it may have on us. Instead of seeking a special state in the future, such as a perfect peace of mind or satori, we are better off directing our attention onto the present experience. Another great Japanese Zen school—the Soto school, which was founded by Dogen in 1227—warns against hyped-up emotional states that we might create while waiting for something great to happen. Therefore the Soto school advocates for and teaches meditating without intent, being for the sake of *Being*, and "sitting just to sit."[29]

It becomes apparent that no matter what guideline we choose for becoming more receptive to the strength of life, our generating mind must relax while focusing on life as it is. This is what can happen in content-free prayer or meditation. De-identifying with thought, becoming skeptical and perplexed about existence, prepare us for this nonactive mental exercise. In one way or the other we need to slow down and halt what Eckhart Tolle calls our "involuntary thought process."[30] Most of us are not even aware of the constant chatter in our minds. Tolle therefore suggests something very Eastern, which is to let ourselves fall into the gaps between thoughts. The same applies for all other experiences we generate.

This effortless, highly engaged ability cannot be forced. In contrast, it is a gentle letting go. Instead of attempting to get rid of our thoughts, feelings, and sensations, we can learn to let them pass by while observing them without judgment. Some people learn this ability by paying attention to their natural breathing. Others learn it best by consciously evoking a healthy pattern of breathing. In any case, our breathing must eventually deepen and reach the last fiber inside of us. If our muscles are too tight, we can relax our mind-body via massages, hot baths, or physical exercise. Too much thought and feeling can be treated by a good psychologist; too much physical pain can be eased by a physician or therapist using acupressure, acupuncture, or biofeedback. There is not one way, but many ways of releasing the mind-body's armor.

Some people may begin meditating by paying attention to their natural experience while doing something rhythmical, ritualistic, or methodological, such as walking, attending ceremonies, gardening, or doing housework, not one of which demands much thinking. When we go through the motions without paying attention to our inner experience, we end up killing time. But when we do pay attention, we begin to feel one with the motions. Feeling one with the motions and breathing deeply, our sense of boundaries change. At first we may feel one only with the people with whom we share the activity. Then eventually, we feel one with other people, other species, plants, the soil, and the air we all breathe.

Neuroscientists Eugene D'Aquili and Andrew Newberg have found that both rituals and meditation facilitate experiences of being united with the world. Such an experience:

> often generates a decreased awareness of the boundaries between the subject and other individuals (generating a sense of community), between the subject and external inanimate objects, between the subject and any putative supernatural beings, and indeed, at the extreme, the abolition of all boundaries of discrete being leading to brief states of absolute unitary being.[31]

The Classic Meditation Posture

Besides paying attention to natural rhythmic events and movements, we can also assume a specific posture that facilitates the realization of life's strength. All major religions propose postures of reverence for the mystical experience of oneness. These postures acknowledge a reality higher than the tangible world and the self. We may look up or down to feel such reverence. Many close their eyes halfway or all the way. Kneeling and sitting seem to work best, although some people prefer to lengthen their body vertically or horizontally. Since lying down can cause sleepiness, upright postures are generally preferred, as in rhythmical dances or walking meditation.

Buddhist meditation postures attract more and more Westerners (see the exercise section for more instructions). Priest and Zen Buddhist Williges Jaeger describes the lotus position: we cross our legs, keep the back straight, the pelvis forward to let the stomach protrude, the shoulders relaxed but not slouched forward, one hand holding the other hand's thumb lightly in the lap or both hands on the knees, and the mouth closed with the tongue relaxed.[32]

Since crossing our legs in the classical lotus position (with both feet on top of the opposite legs) works only for those who have used this position since youth, I should make clear that it is perfectly acceptable to assume the half-lotus position (with only one foot on top of the opposite leg), or to sit tailor-fashion (a simple crossed-leg posture), or to sit on the legs (with or without a meditation stool or cushion), or to sit on a chair. Just do your best to sit stably with a straight back.

The classic lotus posture is one of many postures
that can be assumed for meditation.

Jack Kornfield describes the benefits of meditation as follows:

In sitting on the meditation cushion and assuming the meditation posture, we connect ourselves with the present moment in this body and on this earth. We sit in this physical body halfway between heaven and earth, and we sit erect and straight. We possess a regal strength and dignity in this act. At the same time, we must also have a sense of relaxation, an openness, a gracious receptivity to life. The body is present, the heart is soft and open, the mind is attentive. To sit in this posture is to be like the Buddha. We can sense the universal human capacity to open, to awaken.[33]

However, many people in the West prefer shifting from the Basic Mode into the Supreme Mode with a natural posture or activity. While mowing the lawn, fetching the paper, or even doing the dishes, we may suddenly become conscious receptacles of life's strength. Then our eyes move softly, almost as if they do not move at all. They see as if for the first time. They see with awe, realizing that the world is not put together like a mosaic, but that it is one piece, one picture, echoed in one experience.

All effort is gone when we take the time to notice our environment. As soon as we notice, we inadvertently stop relating to our environment as an object (an Other) outside of ourselves. We breathe deeply, see, hear, and "smell the flowers" of life. We notice that all is in a process, intimately connected to us: we are blooming, laughing, humming, bubbling, rattling, and roaring. Having slipped unintentionally from the Basic Mode into the Supreme Mode, we enjoy unexpected moments of overwhelming contentment.

Even though we cannot force the experience of being part of the whole, we must see to it that the experience *can* come to us. In other words, we should not intently await this overwhelming contentment, but remove obstacles to it. Along the same line, Jesus tells us not to *expect* the kingdom of God, but to *recognize* it "spread out upon the world."[34] If sitting meditation stills our mind, we will benefit from the posture. If sitting meditation creates intent, as in "want" or "expect," we create obstacles and will not benefit from the posture. According to the early Chinese Zen master Huai-jang, who was one of the five disciples of the sixth Zen patriarch Hui-neng,[35] intent reduces our receptivity and "kills the Buddha" that is awareness.

It is wise to experiment and observe the kind of posture that is most likely to make us feel part of the whole of life. As we relax our mind-body and focus our attention on present life unfolding, we receive. With practice, even if only for a few minutes a day, we will realize a difference in our way of being. We will likely feel more energized for the day as we become nurtured by the whole of life. Once we do not cling to controlling life, we can get a sense of our being as it lets all events, including thoughts, come through us freely. Asian philosophies refer to this as realizing that we are the boundless void or emptiness. Everything comes through us, but nothing is us. We are not fixed, but fluent as life. Because this happens all by itself, without our control or effort, we realize the peace inside of us.

Out of this peace rises a general sense of well-being, a sort of primal trust. We do not need reassurance about everything, because we notice for ourselves that the world does just fine without mental intrusions. Although before we knew that the world turns without thought, without worry, without us doing anything, now we can feel it. Although we have always known that the wind, the rain, and the ocean are without thought, now we become comforted by this knowledge. Birds find worms, fly, build nests, mate, and survive without thought, and now we smile at this. All along, we have been living much of life intuitively, but now such intuition feels *wonderful*.

BEING GRATEFUL

Most books on happiness stress the importance of gratitude, and so they should. If you want to be happy, be grateful for what you have received in the past and for what you have presently. This is not just another moral demand to be responded to with superficial gestures, so let's dig a little deeper and connect gratitude with Eastern thought.

Let's begin with some Western research about the subject. Gratitude researchers Michael McCullough and Robert Emmons have found that people who write down daily what they are grateful for—at least in the research period of two weeks—significantly increase their joy, happiness, and life satisfaction levels. In a recent study, Emmons showed that people's "set genetic point" for happiness can be increased by 25 percent if they practice gratitude regularly.[36] Martin Seligman, author of *Authentic Happiness,* incorporates gratitude exercises in his classes in Positive Psychology. According to Seligman, especially people who do not feel much gratitude should devote five minutes each night to writing down what they were grateful for that day. If they feel happier as a result, they ought to make the exercise part of their nightly routine.[37]

In order to lift our spirits it is not enough to speak the words "thank you" and display a social smile. Good manners and a sense of obligation—however important—cannot touch us deeply enough to fulfill us. What we need to do is open our eyes to "the gifts of the day," which we often and misleadingly refer to as the "little things in life." They really are not little at all.

Think about enjoying a favorite song on the radio. The fact that we can do so is wonderful. We have ears; an appreciation for music, musicians, radios; and the time to listen. The fact that we can read these lines means we have eyes, written language, books, writers, and time to read. The health we are bestowed with is phenomenally important, which we can notice even when we are not sick. Being alive is the giant among our gifts, which we can pay conscious attention to right now and repeatedly. Felt gratitude means that we no longer take "the gifts of the day" for granted, because we understand deeply how each and every one of them is interwoven with the whole of reality.

The more we open our eyes to the miracle of life in which everything is interconnected, the more we live our lives in gratitude. If we do an exercise in gratitude without a deeper understanding of the greatness of little things, the positive effect on us will cease as soon as we stop the exercise. Living our lives in gratitude is not acting gratefully, but an attitude, an ongoing celebration of life from which acting gratefully follows. Even when we have to deal with negative events and feel stressed, lived gratitude supports us. To arrive at lived gratitude, we need not make ourselves behave in artificial ways. Instead we need to foster what is naturally occurring in us.

Lao-tzu taught that nothing well-planted can be uprooted, meaning we should not worry about how we turn out as long as we ensure that we grow strong from the inside out. No exterior force is needed to steer, hold, or shape us when we tend to our interior force. "Cultivate Virtue in your own person," Lao-tzu advises us, for all that is needed is already present.[38]

Instead of making ourselves feel grateful when we are not, we may simply focus our attention on our natural experiences. We all have bad and good experiences, but often we do not notice them. Some people try to ignore the bad experiences. They pay no attention to pain and sadness, and they do everything to appear cheerful in a fabricated world of eternal sunshine. Some ignore the good. They willfully turn their heads away from potentially joyous moments, denying ever being on the receiving end. Then again, other people are not interested in any upheavals and cling to neutral experiences.

It is unlikely that anybody is successful in shutting out all bad or all good experiences. We can simply not escape entirely from the ebb and flow of life. If we want to gain access to lived gratitude, we need to lose our fixation and focus on all experiences, be they bad, be they neutral, or be they good.

My paternal grandmother used to live her life trapped in the valley of tears. She was disappointed in the course of her life, where instead of becoming a teacher, she bore and raised ten children. Nothing was ever good in her view, and nothing ever should be good. Life, according to her conclusion, was there to be endured. When she saw my mother resting in the evening, she frowned and advised her never to leave her hands idle.

Yet at the end of her bitter life, when her negative filter no longer worked, I finally saw her have a positive experience. When she felt hot and uncomfortable in her bed, my mother cooled her forehead with refreshing cologne. Suddenly my grandmother smiled and said "Wonderful. Thank you. Wonderful." It was as if she had touched heaven in that moment.

We must not wait for death to touch heaven. We must not postpone our gratitude. We must not postpone living our lives. Life leaves many good experiences for us to notice in the here and now. By acknowledging them, we are beginning to cultivate the good in ourselves. However, neutral and bad experiences must be part of the whole of life, too. Once we accept that the good experience has to pass to make room for the new, our appreciation of life will deepen. As we let all experiences pass through us and hold on to nothing, we grow less and less afraid of life.

I conclude this chapter with the words of Dorothy Thompson, which capture the spirit of Eastern thought and the Supreme Mode so well: "And only when we are no longer afraid do we begin to live in every experience, painful or joyous; to live in gratitude for every moment, to live abundantly."[39]

SUPREME MODE EXERCISES—RECEPTIVITY

Loosen Rigidities

Describe *how* you think, not *what* you think. Use terms like clear/convoluted, repetitive/innovative, slow/fast, open-minded/closed-minded, and so on.

_____

_____

_____

In the moments that you feel self-righteous, ask what purpose your rigidity serves.

_____

_____

_____

Skepticism

- Define three of your most important beliefs. Question them out loud.
- What does the statement: "Be strong; be wrong" mean to you?
- If everything were in question, what would happen to your sense of self?
- Imagine explaining to your children how they could speak with confidence while leaving open the possibility to be mistaken.

Wonder

1. Write down your existential questions. If you have difficulties formulating existential questions, imagine a wise person who has all the answers. What would you ask if you could not ask anything about the past or the future? You can also look deeply in the mirror and ask: "What am I besides my physical body? What is the real me?" Close your eyes and keep asking these types of questions. Or look at any form (such as a flower or a desk) and deeply ask yourself what nature it has.

2. Practice asking your existential questions without attempting to give answers and with a lot of loving attention. Just keep asking and develop a sense of asking the "big" questions.

Learn to Meditate
- In order to receive, your mind-body must be permeable. Try relaxing your mind-body while upholding attention. Can you keep your focus in the present moment when you relax your muscles? If not, you may benefit from counting your in-breath (1) and out-breath (2). Count all the way to ten, and then start all over. With practice, you can count each in-breath and out-breath as one. Eventually you can just pay attention to your breaths without counting.
- Experiment with different postures that relax yet help you pay attention. In order for the body to relax, it must be in a stable position: on a chair, cross-legged on a cushion (*zafu*), kneeling with your behind supported by a cushion, or on your feet (walking meditation). Focus your attention on your breath, another natural rhythm (waves, trickling water), sounds (music, birds, wind), or sensations (tingling, temperature, pressure, itching). You may also slowly scan your body and deliberately focus on anything that happens.
- To learn Tibetan meditation, read *The Joy of Living* by Yongey Mingyur Rinpoche. John Daido Loori was an esteemed Zen teacher in the United States, and his book *Finding the Still Point: A Beginner's Guide to Zen Meditation* is very helpful. You may consider engaging in a dialogue with a teacher, joining a meditation group, or taking a meditation retreat, which you can find out about on the Internet. I found my teacher via a Unitarian church that has helped me tremendously with my meditation practice.
- Instead of practicing meditation for long periods, begin by meditating for brief moments (one to three minutes) several times a day. Expand the time gradually. Do not pressure yourself, but commit to the practice. Keep in mind that there are no problems while you meditate, only opportunities. As soon as you realize any movement of your mind, you are already meditating. When you realize that your thoughts become frantic instead of slowed down, you have begun to pay attention to the chatter your mind produces.

Gratitude

- Write down what you are grateful for today. How are the "little things" big and meaningful to you? What are the "big things" that appear little in your daily life for which you are grateful? Many people benefit from keeping a daily gratitude journal.
- Is there somebody to whom you ought to express gratitude or appreciation regularly and in person? If so, make the expression of gratitude a high priority.
- Pay attention to feeling good. As the feeling ceases, express gratitude.
- Practice "letting go" by giving: listening, paying attention, reaching out, doing things for others, making donations.
- Practice "letting go" by receiving: pay attention to the many gifts from others.
- While practicing gratitude, even during awkward attempts, stay authentic.

10

Tranquility

What is this life if, full of care,
We have no time to stand and stare?
WILLIAM HENRY DAVIES

L ife is a never-ending stream of events. It will pass us by
unless we take note. If there is too much noise in our
minds, we are unable to experience our participation in
life, and we then remember little of it.

Our minds must become tranquil. In some ways, the Supreme
Mode *is* tranquility, and tranquility is therefore a recurring subject in Hinduism, Buddhism, and Taoism.

TRANQUILITY VERSUS ACTIVITY
In Eastern thought we learn about the whole of life, oneness, or
the "nondual" reality. In order to feel "one" and see beyond the
alleged duality between things and our mind, the dissecting part
of our mind must be quieted down. In other words, only the
quiet mind can reflect the oneness of reality accurately. When
Buddha's unsurpassed disciple, the layman Vimalakirti, was
asked to describe the nature of the "nondual" reality, his answer
was "thunderous silence."[1] Indeed, as the tranquil mind does not
relate to the isolated entities, the tiny dots that make up a whole,
but to the immense, all-inclusive organism they form, it has true
waking power.

In the West, tranquility is often seen as opposite to the world
of activity, which is the world that we are limited to. God has
expelled us from the tranquility of the Garden of Eden because
Adam and Eve tasted the forbidden fruit. Outside the realm of

harmony, we were all burdened with effort. Never allowed back in, God insisted: "In the sweat of thy face shalt thou eat bread, till thou return unto the ground; for out of it wast thou taken: for dust thou art, and unto dust shalt thou return."[2]

Many religious people obeyed the philosophy of effort and subscribed to a culture of work and suffering that affected even nonreligious people. The underlying assumption is that if we cannot appease God, we can at least be good enough to accept our punishment. The belief helped make sense out of the hard life most people had to endure in the past. It was mirrored and perpetuated by morals. The inevitability and moral obligation of effort felt true without anybody having to spell this out for ordinary people. Meanwhile, privileged people often kept enjoying their leisure time and regarded hard work as a sign of poverty.

While the influence of these old morals does not explain everything, it is true that people in the West are overly afraid of idleness. Suspicious of nonactivity, we have become fairly incompetent in creating meaningful spare time. Robert Kubey and Mihaly Csikszentmihalyi have done studies that suggest that people feel best when engaged in externally structured activity.[3] I doubt this is the case for practicing Buddhists, who create positive feelings during meditation and the meditative life.

Stefan Klein, who compiled research about how to generate positive feelings, also comes to the conclusion that it is easier to find happiness in activity than in nonactivity.[4] Indeed, several researchers confirm that people rate their leisure time lower than their work time on a satisfaction scale. Joseph Veroff, for example, found that 49 percent of a group of working men claimed that work was more satisfying than leisure, while only 19 percent claimed the opposite.[5]

Apparently we have difficulties in finding fulfillment when we do not aspire to external goals. In my opinion, this is because we are disconnected from each other (see chapter 6). In addition, we are both biased toward activity and uneducated about nonactivity.

LOSING OUR FEAR OF INACTIVITY

To tackle the bias toward activity, we must lose our fear of inactivity. It is not defying God; it is not a sin or an obstacle. Let's begin by learning how to distinguish between nonactivity and inactivity, as the latter really is often bad for us.

In much of Eastern thought, nonactivity is considered creative nondoing that inspires and fulfills. We may also understand it as a realization of creation. If we want to use the word "passivity" at all, it is "active passivity." By no means does it mean slouching in front of a television or computer screen for hours at a time, which only tires us. To the contrary, nonactivity energizes us and helps ideas spring forward as no mental commotion holds them back. It heals, strengthens, and enriches.

To rid ourselves of our fear of nonactivity, we must address the need for balance. It is commonly agreed that everything in excess stands in the way of happiness. Nonactivity is good because we experience a nurturing connection with life. But if we overdo nonactivity, we may not feel like fighting for worthy goals or value any sort of passion. As a result, we may harbor contempt for people's ambitions or belittle their wants and needs.[6] However, some inactivity is part of a good balance as evidenced by when we relax nearly all of our effort in sleep or when we are moderately lazy. But even in the Supreme Mode we somewhat exert ourselves because it takes effort to focus on life. Consciousness is a costly event in our body. Yet too much sleep or slouching causes depression, dimness, overall mind-body weakness, weight gain, loss of sexual appeal, and loss of libido.

In other words, of course activity is good—unless we overdo it. Besides stressing our body, overdoing creates unhealthy life patterns. If we exaggerate our pursuit of connections, we could end up developing compulsions, such as the compulsion to help others. Codependency is, despite recent controversy, still a common problem, especially among women.[7] Becoming compulsive in the pursuit of goals can drive us away from friends, family, and lesser goals, such as personal hygiene, exercise, and proper nutrition. Even the strongest proponent of goal-oriented activity, Mihaly Csikszentmihalyi, concedes that we can become addicted to the enjoyable flow-experience it may generate. According to Csikszentmihalyi, surgeons, for example, describe operations as being addictive, like "taking heroin."[8]

In addition, there are plenty of not-so-good activities that we engage in. Bad goals or mere greed make tranquility impossible.

Some overly busy people sadly shake their head when someone suggests they take time out. They simply cannot sit still, read a book, or go for a walk. Even well-off people feel they must over-work. A normal work load causes them to feel guilty or inferior to their contemporaries. Indeed, many are not just excessively busy, but take pride in being so. Being busy is in vogue today as idleness used to be for the rich in former times. Our Western work ethic and various compulsions—such as having to check messages, having to respond to all messages immediately, having to take "this call," having to talk about business, having to say "I am busy," having to put business before friendship and one's per-sonal advantage before the team's and even the family's—have created a different type of poverty: "we have no time to stand and stare."[9]

It takes real courage to go against the mainstream and to seek tranquility. But although tranquility is enriching, we may be the only person in our circle who values its wealth. Let me entice you to go against Western bias with the words of Lin Yutang (1895–1976) who believed in "the capacity for true enjoyment of idleness":

> It must come from an inner richness of a soul in a man who loves the simple ways of life and is somewhat impatient with the business of making money. There is always plenty of life to enjoy for a man who is determined to enjoy it. If men fail to enjoy this earthly existence we have, it is because they do not love life sufficiently.[10]

Women and men have to learn to love life sufficiently. It is tranquility that takes us there.

CREATING EXTERNAL TRANQUILITY

Opening our eyes to the whole of life is easier when our surround-ings are tranquil. Earthly goods, positive earthly goals, intimate relationships, and children enrich our lives, but noise and turmoil are part of that package. Nuns and monks, who abdicate so much of that earthly life, are blessed with much more external tranquil-ity than most laypeople. I have spent a few weeks in a convent and can give testimony to the heavenly silence that resounds there.

All surrounding events can be taken in clearly and consciously. They are not just some bothersome noise or superfluous action. Everything has meaning as it becomes noticed. Everything flows in and out of one's mind with less resistance. It is safe to assume that a quiet place lends itself to Supreme Mode experiences.

Yet how much tranquility lies in most jobsites? How about driving our cars through rush hour traffic, squeezing into over-crowded buses, sitting in squeaking subways? Do parents ever have a chance at quiet? There are so many parties and confer-ences to attend, so much paperwork to be handled, so many needs to be balanced. Many places are frantic and loud. Making a phone call can be stressful because we have to speak to auto-mated voices that keep us on hold. Every device beeps, and everybody expects, if not demands, that we make use of them. Efficiency was supposed to give us time, yet in reality, it con-sumes time. Even if we had a sanctuary in our very own house, we probably would not have the time to use it. What is there to do in the face of all this commotion?

Although modern living cannot be as quiet and simple as the monastic lifestyle, we can still tone it down. It is tricky to give advice on the subject, because our individual life circumstances and priorities vary so much. What is good for the goose is *not* necessarily good for the gander. But do not discount the idea of toning down point blank. Even if you cannot incorporate all the following suggestions, you may be able to make small adjust-ments that will go a long way. The more you value tranquility as a necessary path to the Supreme Mode, the more you will avoid inner and outer turmoil. So let me make some broad suggestions that you can tailor to your needs and add onto freely.

"Not Now, Please"

The first suggestion concerns our personal electronic connections. Almost all of us are wired up to our armpits and continually avail-able for the benefit of others.

While it is true that not being available is often disadvanta-geous, most of us go too far in pleasing others. Just as we can use a "Do not disturb!" sign in a hotel, we have the freedom to deter-mine when someone can communicate with us. When we get back to the other person within a considerate time frame, they are unlikely to take offense. This also holds true for family members. It is not unloving to miss a call. Taking a call at an inopportune moment actually prevents us from paying close attention. The loving thing to do is to assure that we give ourselves entirely, and do so abundantly.

On the other hand, we might feel alone or uncomfortable when we disconnect our electrical devices. Due to the pervasiveness of modern technology, we may have become accustomed to consulting with others before deciding anything at all. Because we *can* consult, we may feel we *should* consult. Buying a particular kind of cheese can make us anxious if we believe our partner should have a say in the matter. Walking out of a store without giving our partner an opportunity to tell us what they need may suggest we are inconsiderate. As a result, we may infantilize our family circle and unconsciously create anxieties that we should no longer have as adults. Breaking such habits will reestablish confidence in our family, as well as create more external tranquility.

We may also feel uncomfortable turning communication devices off even briefly because we crave the feeling of being wanted. It feels good and looks cool to be in demand. Holding a cigarette and waving it in front of our face is out, whereas talking on a cellular phone is most definitely in. Such behavior may be acceptable in young people, yet as adults we ought to be able to stand on our own and overcome such insecurities.

Whatever the reason for wanting to be accessible at all times, we ought to have better rules of engagement. Some of us could determine that we will not be disturbed during meal, nap, or vacation times. When we are already engaged in a conversation, we most certainly should not divide our attention. Others may find peace in designating a specific time frame during which relative tranquility can be enjoyed. The important thing is to consistently tone down our electronic accessibility. A quick switch to the "off" mode may be all it takes to create an ambience of greater peace and tranquility.

Lower the Volume

Toning down can be as easy as lowering the volume on our electronic devices. If there is a regulator, feel free to use it.

Unfortunately, parents do not have that choice with their children. Screaming "Be quiet!" only makes matters worse. Being quiet ourselves, on the other hand, sets the tone for the family. Especially with younger children, it is more effective to whisper intently "Please be quiet" than to raise our voice. Occasionally we can have a whisper contest to find out who can whisper the longest.

Clear rules also help during times of conflict. We must negotiate with older children, of course. Good rules are: (1) never yell from one room to another; (2) never call each other names; and (3) never slam doors. Eventually—and yes, this will take time—the family tone will be more agreeable. In the meantime, closing the door may be the only thing we can do.

Creating a Sanctuary

While we may not be able to retreat into a sanctuary often or for a long period of time, a short period of almost perfect external tranquility may make a great difference in our lives. We could make one small room or corner of a room our own. (I converted my closet to a tiny meditation room.) A cushion or chair to sit on, and a simple candle, flower arrangement, room fountain, or a religious symbol will suffice. We may listen to natural sounds; play quiet, meditative music; smell the flowers; or burn incense. If we like Asian traditions, we can put up a Buddha statue, altar, or other symbols that set the atmosphere for us. (If you are fond of Tibetan Buddhism, see Robert Thurman's book *Infinite Life* for more detailed instructions.)[11]

Most important, however, is that our sanctuary be simple, uncluttered, and undisturbed. When I was a student, I could only fit a bed, a desk, and a chair in my room. So I sat upright in my bed every morning, with a warm cup of tea in my hands, doing nothing, focusing inwardly. Whatever your sanctuary, just sit there quietly praying, meditating (see chapter 9), contemplating, breathing, wondering "Who am I?" "What is it?" "Am I curious?" being only in the moment, consciously away from all turmoil for a designated five to fifteen minutes every day. The voice of silence may touch you and stay with you throughout your day.

Losing Clutter

The idea of the sanctuary can extend to the house or apartment we live in. Regardless of personal taste, we can all tone down our environment by losing the clutter in our surroundings. In rich countries, letting go of things is often the key. Decide whether to trash it (if it is unlikely that anybody will use it), donate it (think what it could mean to poor children and homeless adults), or sell it (but refrain from replacing it). We can also install more storage place to hide the clutter from our eyes, unless this inadvertently creates a new clutter area. Keep in mind that less stuff translates into more external tranquility.

Because of our survival instinct, we may experience discomfort when we are about to let go of clutter. To horde things may make us feel secure, while giving them up may trigger anxiety and regret. Yet if we want to give happiness a chance, we will learn to tolerate such transient feelings, if necessary with the help of a psychologist. Whether you are a moderate pack rat or a full-blown obsessive-compulsive, committing yourself to a saner external life will eventually reward you with a saner internal life. The good and full life makes all your effort worth it.

With the help of the Chinese system of *feng shui*, we can transform our homes into more open and livable places. Karen Kingston wrote a practical book on how to lose the clutter of ordinary life in the spirit of feng shui.[12] If you need help arranging your living space to become more balanced and tranquil, this book is for you.

More Activities in the Home

Our home is no longer our castle, because we abandon it for most of the day. Almost all social activities are organized and placed outside the house. Kids suffer because they are being schlepped all over the place after school, and adults are exhausted from taking them there. Instead of inviting our friends and family for coffee in our home, we meet at cafés. Instead of cooking for people, we meet them at restaurants.

So the suggestion is: rediscover your home for social activities. Socialize often, but try to do so more frequently in private homes. As far as outside activities go, instead of starting new activities every few months, limit yourself to two particular activities for at least a year or two. It takes commitment, but it is ultimately more enjoyable when we focus on specific activities and become more competent. Inadvertently, you will be rewarded with more external tranquility.

UNDERSTANDING OUR BUDDHA-NATURE

External tranquility has value because it helps us access the Supreme Mode, but it is not the access itself. The access lies in the mind alone. Only when we have become independent from the world insofar as we feel right and contented in it, will we enjoy inner peace and calm. The tranquil mind *is* tranquility. It is both our path and our destination.

In Buddhism the tranquil mind is often called "Buddha-nature." The word "nature" in this context does not refer to our biological nature. Instead it refers to what is essential to our Being—that is to say, our awareness. We may consider awareness to be the most important, and in some ways the most real quality of our mind. Sustained awareness enables us to see the world in its natural state, "as is," without being dissected by our mind. It is in all our potential to see the natural world with our natural mind.

It is important to note that the word "Buddha" in "Buddha-nature" does not point to a person. "Buddha" is not a name, but a principle or state that we can all attain. It simply means "awakened," "blossomed," "enlightened."[13] The famous person who carried this title was born around the fifth century BCE. His given name was Siddhartha Gautama. He trained his mind to transcend any particular Other, any particular experience, form or mental formation or mental construct (which I also refer to as particularizations), and he advised others how to go about such training.

Siddhartha Gautama was not a god, and he never claimed to be one. It is said that a man who passed Gautama on a road, impressed by his extraordinary radiance and peaceful presence, asked him:

"My friend, what are you? Are you a celestial being or a god?"
"No," said the Buddha.
"Well, then, are you some kind of magician or wizard?"

195

Again the Buddha answered, "No."
"Are you a man?"
"No."
"Well, my friend, then what are you?"
The Buddha replied, "I am awake."[14]

The reason for pointing this out is that we should not put a barrier between us and the tranquil mind that some call Buddha-nature. The tranquil mind is not reserved for superhuman, mystical beings, or for superhuman, mystical circumstances. It is for all of us, and it applies to ordinary life, be it in the East or in the West.

Gautama grew up as the son of a king in Kapilavastu, which lies at what is now the Indian-Nepalese border. He married, but he left his wife and newborn son to seek liberation from the suffering that he perceived in the world. After years of calming his mind as an ascetic, he decided to change his approach. He began to eat in moderation, and he relaxed his effort. Eventually and with enormous determination, he became aware of his awareness and began to reside in it. Gautama had discovered his Buddha-nature.

THE FOUR NOBLE TRUTHS

Retracing the steps of his own process, the Buddha taught Four Noble Truths. They are designed to help us become aware of our own awareness, namely the tranquil mind that is the Buddha-nature. I will elaborate on them in a way that is intended to make sense to the Western mind.[15]

The First Noble Truth: The Truth of Suffering

There is no use denying that life is fragile, that it entails death, disease, frailty, losses, and failures. Abuse and deprivation can hit us hard, especially during the vulnerable years of childhood. People may pretend that there is no pain in life. We may willingly forget, or we may willingly look the other way.

Yet pain is real. It has been there in our past, is here right now, and will be there in our future. Maybe we are convinced that pain is an avoidable choice, as some New Age people suggest with phrases such as "It is all in your mind" or "Mind over matter." The truth is that we cannot control life to such a degree that it becomes pain free. Pain, discomfort, and displeasure are inherent in all sentient beings, regardless how conscious, devout, educated, good, or strong we may be.

Psychological pain is also real and unavoidable. It hurts when we do not get what we need over a prolonged period of time, such as attention, affection, or love. A friend may unexpectedly decide to end the friendship. Someone we love may become sick or die. When we become old, our extended family may decide to abandon us. Reasons for psychological pain are numerous, and it is no less devastating than physical pain.

If we desire to experience full-life participation, we must, according to Gautama, first of all accept the existence of all pain as part of the human condition. Only when we are willing to look at this reality can we make peace with life. Such peace can then be the platform from which we either instigate or manage change.

Therefore Gautama laid down his premise about suffering first. It is of utmost importance in Buddhism to recognize our own and other people's pain as the first step toward a better and more fulfilling life. By recognizing our own pain as part of reality that we wish to embrace, we have an opportunity to develop empathy. With this empathy, we can actively help ourselves and others, as well as reinforce a sense of connectedness with the world. Holding hands with all sentient beings and understanding deeply the existence of all our pain increases inner tranquility. Instead of fighting life, we begin to accept it.

Should we also accept unnecessary pain and suffering? So many times we just give in to anger, fear, and greediness; indulge in our frustrations; and hurt others. Along these lines, Alan Watts interprets the Buddha's First Noble Truth to mean that "life as we usually live it is suffering."[16] It is a good point to make, especially when we look at the Third Noble Truth (see page 199). Yet Buddha thought it wise to first ground ourselves in reality. A radical acceptance of the existence of all pain prevents us from lofty ideas and the various forms of escapism such as esotericism or fantasy.

Hence the Buddha, who started his own journey with the observation of real people suffering, set a sobering tone for his teachings: birth is suffering; decay is suffering; death is suffering; sorrow, lamentation, pain, grief, and despair are suffering; not to get what one desires is suffering; in short, the five groups of existence are suffering.

Once again, there is no use denying that life is fragile. We can look at the world with the eyes of acceptance, but pain will remain part of this world. Only after facing this fact do we benefit from further refinement of the mind, which brings us to the second part of Gautama's guidelines.

The Second Noble Truth: The Truth of the Origin of Suffering

There is a difference between the existence of pain and the experience of pain. When we relate to reality as something outside of ourselves, which our brain—especially the parietal lobe—suggests, our perceived distinct self relates to distinct categories. Instead of simply not liking the "bad," we reject it. Instead of simply enjoying the "good," we cling to it.

Buddha believed that the reason why we human beings suffer so much is because of our clinging. Every time we cling to something, our ego-experience becomes activated or reborn. As we tend to identify with our ego-experience, we set ourselves apart from the rest of the world and become trapped in suffering. Gautama realized that anything that can give us pleasure—such as sensations, thoughts, fantasies, and feelings—has the potential to set off craving.

So, while pain is pain, we add suffering to this pain and fail to comfort ourselves because of our desires. When we particularly want something, we lose our perspective on everything else. Metaphorically speaking, we pin ourselves to the ground and prevent the wind from sweeping us back up into the sky where we could fly. The good things from the past have long died, but we keep holding on to these corpses. The good in the present has to be guarded with suspicion. The good in the future has to be worried about. We are swayed by good and bad events and take no refuge in ourselves. Blind to the fact that the good and the bad are connected, that life takes unexpected turns, we only look to the direction of what we deem "good."

However, we all know that there are also benefits to clinging. For example, tenacity helps us reach our goals. Hope can succor when it seems futile. It is only human to mourn our losses. Letting go at the same speed as life is for robots. If we have a heart at all, we will need time to work things out and to cherish memories.

The Buddha would likely agree. His guidelines are not to instruct us to live mechanically and detached from others. Pain exists because it plays an important role in life, a role that we can help define. Yet pain is not all that we are. We ought not to identify with it. Utilizing pain and consciously deciding to cling to some experience may be a tool. Clinging blindly to pain is self-defeating, and the cause of unnecessary suffering.

The Third Noble Truth: The Truth of the Extinction of Suffering

We cannot erase pain from reality, but we can end unnecessary pain when we no longer cling to what we perceive is good. We can learn to look at the world of ups and downs as a whole. Our awareness of the whole gives us the freedom to refrain from automatic reactions, such as automatically clinging to the good. Our awareness or Buddha-nature is the only steady, unshakable thing in an otherwise dynamic world. The Buddha said: "Just as a rock of one solid mass remains unshaken by the wind, even so neither forms, nor sounds, nor odors, nor tastes, nor contacts of any kind, neither the desired nor the undesired can cause such a one to waver; one is steadfast in mind, gained is deliverance."[17]

Everything that we perceive as separate from our awareness, created by the ego-experience, can entice us to cling. Greed and hate are especially enticing because they tend to be intense and long lasting. Awareness keeps us from identifying with our ego-experience. As long as we are predominately aware of the whole, ego-experiences have lost absolute power. Our all-encompassing look at life protects us from becoming stuck in particularities, and thus from becoming overwhelmed.

The idea of becoming liberated from feelings, such as hate and sorrow, seems especially difficult to integrate into contemporary Western thought. Many of us have come to understand feelings and do not wish to be liberated from them. Feelings connect us to our body and our environment. Indeed, expressing them is often liberating, invigorating, and, if done correctly, interconnecting.

Buddha's words are subject to various interpretations. Being overcome with anxiety or depression, you might, for example, benefit from the conclusions of Tibetan Buddhists. They attempt to nip negative feelings in the bud by avoiding negative thoughts. When thought is distorted, such an approach is in alignment with cognitive therapy.[18] Indeed, we all need to control our thoughts when and preferably before they cause harm. As the human condition of imperfection causes us to "lose" our mind occasionally, we could wreak havoc in no time. In other words, we should all cultivate the ability to "hold our horses" and to direct them.

In general, however, Westerners move toward the integration of feelings. Other interpretations of Buddha's words seem more fitting for that direction. The emotional extremism of methodologies in the sixties and seventies that elevated feelings to the level of gods has long been tempered. In part thanks to that extremism, the topic of emotional intelligence has seeped into the most conservative circles.[19] Appropriate emotional expression has become part of the entire spectrum of social interaction from personal to public relationships. Nobody suggests we ought to act blindly on feelings. Instead of deeming negative feelings as "bad," we have begun to accept their existence and possibly even learn from them.

The interpretation I find most promising in regard to Western integration has less to do with control and more with retreating into and trusting our awareness. Just looking intently at our turmoil in stillness dissipates negative feelings. This is the thinking in Zen Buddhism. The Vietnamese Zen Buddhist Thich Nhat Hanh, for example, teaches how to sit with and accept pain and discomfort.[20] We should not just be conscious of our pain in the Freudian sense. In Thich Nhat Hanh's teachings, it becomes clear that we are not asking our ego-experience to push itself into the forefront and direct our every action. Instead we should operate from our still mind that focuses on whatever moves, including emotion. From here we can let go.

When we relate well to the whole of life, we remain aware of all phenomena in the moment. We say "Yes." We may dislike an experience and may want to counteract it; such a response is natural and often necessary. Still, we should not antagonize the reality of the moment. Deeply aware that everything has passing existential value, instead of an immediate personal advantage, we can bear the pain without becoming lost in it.

The path to such an attitude takes effort, but the attitude in itself is effortless. It is commensurate with deeply experienced patience that, once we have found our way to it, makes us realize that we have arrived. It is being there.

Similar to this interpretation of Buddha's words is the stance of Taoism, which is one of the parents of Zen Buddhism. Lao-tzu wrote:

> Because when a man is in turmoil how shall he find peace
> Save by staying patient till the stream clears?[21]

And muddy water does indeed become clear when we let it stand still. Stillness while living is thus the Buddha-nature.

The Fourth Noble Truth: The Truth of the Path That Leads to the Extinction of Suffering
Learning to live from awareness is not an easy path. First, Gautama advises against excessive measures. As you may recall, he himself realized his Buddha-nature only after ending his life as a spoiled prince and then as an ascetic. What Gautama calls the Middle Path lies somewhere between self-indulgence and self-mortification. More often than not, we benefit from avoiding extremes and finding a middle ground. Otherwise we cling to our method. The Middle Path helps us also avoid unhealthy consequences of both indulgence and deprivation.

THE EIGHTFOLD PATH
Gautama suggests following the so-called Eightfold Path that addresses various aspects of our life:

1. Right Understanding
2. Right Thought
3. Right Speech
4. Right Action
5. Right Livelihood
6. Right Effort

7. Right Mindfulness
8. Right Concentration

These general guidelines tell us two things: where to look for the many hindrances to awareness, and all the hindrances that have to be removed just "right" to live from the vantage point of awareness. What exactly we need to do depends on who we are. According to Gautama's own tradition, which was what we now call the Hindu tradition, we cannot be told by any teacher what to do. Instead we have to find out by ourselves through introspection and engagement in a dialogue with a teacher. This goes back to the understanding that our Buddha-nature cannot be acquired or given to us. We have to discover it.

However, few Westerners relate to a guru or wish to have a personal consultation with a master teacher. In my opinion, there is no good reason to copy a method from a different culture if this method does not fit in with our own. We can learn from the written word, diverse worldviews, classes, psychotherapy, sermons, nature, events, and experience. Serious, honest, and concentrated discussions help our process tremendously, but they can also happen between any two emancipated human beings, and not necessarily just with a guru. Thus we ought to seek such dialogues with friends and family members and reciprocate the attention they give us. The key is not to please each other, but to grow within a connection (see chapter 6), because together we may stumble from obstacles to an awareness that we would not find otherwise. And when it comes to our own mind, isn't it true that we often do not see the trees before seeing the forest?

As to the eight areas of our life, they address the need for wisdom (1–2), ethical conduct (3–5), and mental discipline (6–8).

Wisdom
Although we are all different, we are alike in that we are drawn to take the easiest route, which, of course, is not always the "right" one. For example, in the name of living fully in the present, some of us live as if there were no tomorrow. This, so we tell ourselves, gives us freedom (such as to make money however we please) and preserves our spontaneity (such as to have sex when and with

whomever we feel like). Such an adolescent view of the world fosters materialism and other addictions, which we can hardly call indicative of freedom. Hence, a "right understanding" of how things work in the real world includes the fact that all of our actions have consequences, just as the Eastern concept of *karma* suggests. Regardless of which terminology we choose, understanding cause and its multiple, personal, and global effects ought to be made part of our own wisdom.

Ethical Conduct

In regard to ethical conduct, I like to list the five precepts that give guidance in Buddhism. They are not unlike our own Western guidelines as to what constitutes negative behavior and how it impedes the good and full life. They are:

1. Do not kill.
2. Do not steal.
3. Do not indulge in sexual misconduct.
4. Do not make false speech.
5. Do not take intoxicants.

Despite their similarity to our Western guidelines, the precepts are not commandments. They are given from a human to humans. We are supposed to integrate them sensibly and responsibly in our life. Former Buddhist nun and author Martine Batchelor emphasizes: "Ethics in Buddhism does not mean blind rules and regulations. They do not exist to force you to do something, but to make you reflect on your motivations and actions."[22]

Some people may take this liberty to mean that they can behave unethically if such behavior gives instant peace of mind. Alan Watts, for example, the otherwise excellent scholar who informed thousands of Westerners with great insight and wit about Eastern thought, fell into that trap. Against medical advice, he abused alcohol to such a degree that it might well have contributed to his early death at the age of fifty-nine. While we all have shortcomings, he did not think of his as such. After all, he only did what felt right to him at the moment. Alcohol, so he said, made him feel "sexy" and probably more spontaneous.[23]

In regard to the Basic Mode, our shortcomings are likely to hamper our pursuit of goals. They are sure to aggravate our intimate relationships. If we do not resist our negative behavior, we might do more harm to ourselves and others. Just trying to behave ethically makes others feel more cared for and less neglected. Conquering our shortcomings is a great gift to those who need and love us.

With respect to the Supreme Mode, by giving in to destructive impulses and habits, we rob ourselves of opportunities to experience Being. Thus unethical behavior decelerates growth and hinders full life participation. Tolerating the emptiness that we may experience when we refrain from drugs, for example, may help us discover a different side to ourselves. In other words, by trying to be a "good" person, we might meet the "real" person.

While the real person may be less desirable and a bit too vulnerable at first, we may find a gateway to humanity in this real person. Humbled and stripped of fake identities, we may realize how we fit right into life's strength and fragility, light and darkness, and ups and downs. Who knows where the naked truth of our plain self will take us? A little less grandeur may free our consciousness from restraints that we can hardly anticipate.

Mental Discipline

As to the mental discipline that Gautama's Eightfold Path suggests, there are many ways to help us become focused human beings, one of which is meditation (see chapter 9). With meditation, we practice attentiveness without fabricating mental products or forms. Attentiveness can be achieved by focusing on our breath, a specific object, or on all phenomena. The Zen practice is called *zazen*, which can be interpreted as either "one-pointed" concentration, the aforementioned koan introspection (content-free wondering), or "just sitting" (*shikantaza*). The latter is a high state of concentration on what is. It is great general attentiveness via the means of zazen that makes us see our interconnectedness with the whole of life.

While the average Westerner will not sit quietly for hours at a time, we have to understand that paying attention to Being will not just happen to us. True, we are all somewhat aware of our surroundings and our inner experience, because otherwise we would constantly trip and fall, gag and falter. But we are aware of very little. We leave out anything that does not seem important to immediate survival. We leave out anything that seems to muddle our ego-experience. We leave out "the other side" that does not fit in with our scheme.

Total awareness needs practice. Slowing down, looking around, looking inward, looking deeply, and listening carefully are essential to this practice. To see and acknowledge, we must learn to honor the mundane, live from a place of humility, and willingly assume the other perspective. Seeing all is embracing all. Embracing all is relating to all. Relating to all is wondering. Wondering is giving our ego-experience less importance. Giving our ego-experience less importance is seeing all. It takes lifelong devotion to develop our awareness of the whole. Our Buddha-nature is within us right now, but it hides underneath many obstacles. It is our job to leave no stone unturned and to remove as many as we can.

Yet, with all these allusions to making an effort, such as removing obstacles and practicing concentration, let us not forget that the tranquil mind itself is effortless. The poet Rainer Maria Rilke once described the tranquil mind as a house deep inside of us that cannot be disturbed by outside noise.[24] Although we have to find our way to this house, we do not have to build it. Retreating into this home, we see the whole, sense our participation in it without holding on to it or being exasperated by anything in particular. We notice the fleeting existence of it all. In other words, by not identifying with the stream of life as it passes through existence, we experience relative freedom and clarity. While dreams may come true, or tragedy may come upon us, we never entirely lose our sense for the whole of life.

In the end, it does not matter how we name this sense. Some call it Supreme Identity (Muslims),[25] some Unity Consciousness (neuroscientists like Eugene D'Aquili and Andrew Newberg),[26] some Buddha-nature, and others something else altogether. What counts is that we all have the ability to notice that we are more than our individual bodies. Because we can be aware of everything, everything is represented in us and in full operation.

Let me close this section with a simple but beautiful definition of the Buddha-nature given by Stephen Batchelor, who spent ten years as a Buddhist monk in both the Tibetan and Zen traditions: "Consider the Buddha-nature as a kind of awareness. To say that we all possess Buddha-nature could mean that we are all aware (perhaps very dimly) of a dimension of depth and mystery at the root of our lives."[27]

SURRENDERING TO THE FLOW OF THINGS

The reality of things and events may not be as we first see it when we are in the active mode—that is, the Basic Mode. In the Basic Mode, we see and pursue goals and separate entities. We quickly react to what appears to go wrong on the surface. When we look deeply, as we can in the Supreme Mode, we not only see our pursuit, but that which underlies it as well.

In the Supreme Mode, we could, as we do in science, extricate distinct variables and examine reality systematically. But we could also be simply aware of life's interconnecting principles. This way, our mind remains open, clear, and relatively independent from what happens on the surface. All things and all events pass through our mind without rushing to clinging thought or goal-oriented, aggressive action. For this reason, we have the ability to surrender and to not interfere in the Supreme Mode.

Noninterference is essential to the parent of Zen Buddhism, Taoism. Seeing through turmoil, the mind stays calm and steadfast. Patiently and with utmost confidence in the natural flow of things, it observes and resists not. The river flows quietly when it is unobstructed and given its way freely and affirmatively. Lao-tzu remarks that "those who flow as life flows" are not dependent on outside conditions. In modern terms me might say that if we make peace with life's fluidity, we are in no need of tranquilizers, alcohol, television, excessive material stuff, or other crutches. As we give ourselves to the flow of life we become naturally calm, steadfast, and more resilient.[28]

Sometimes surrender reveals itself when we literally lay down our weapons and tools, accept a hopeless situation, and give up with dignity. There are plenty of situations in which such surrender is warranted. For example, while we ought to fight for our

206

lives and develop new and better medications, we ought not to fight when death is pending. Death is part of life and—however much we could have avoided it in a particular situation—when it is here, it is here. When a cup of milk is spilling, it is milk spilled. It is too late to regret any action once the action is inevitably in process. When there is nothing to do for the time being, doing is clinging and causes suffering. A mind able to access the Supreme Mode will not rush to pursue a goal that can no longer be attained, but realize the moment and let it go.

Then again, we also surrender when we do not struggle against the reality of a moment during which we are doing what can and must be done. Such doing does not interfere with events that need, should, or will have to happen in that moment of time and space. It is sensible action, aligned with the natural flow of things. For example, it does not make sense to shout angrily at the milk or try to shove it back into the cup. Rather, we could immediately pick up the glass and prevent the milk from dripping on the floor using a towel. Having let go of the milk, our mind is cleared and free to act in accordance with a new set of circumstances. Such action can also be called nonaction, as it is refrains from interfering with the imminent action.

Weathering the Perfect Storm

To illustrate surrender as well as difficulties to surrender, let me tell you the story of my perfect storm. During the holidays, my entire family came down with the flu. An infant, two toddlers, and two adults ran fevers and hurt all over. Heavily medicated, my husband, Steven, felt compelled to go to work and take care of an emergency at his office. In the midst of this already bad situation, I twisted my ankle and fell down the stairs while carrying my feverish two-year-old son. There was no way to buffer my fall, because I had to protect him from possibly greater harm. Thankfully, our nanny, Barbra, arrived at the front door just as I hit the floor. This gave me a chance to take myself to the hospital, where I received a splint for my broken left foot. While I was hurting physically, I felt more anger than anything else. Instead of comforting myself, I resented my fate, which only added to my misery.

The next day, I struggled to take care of myself and my three children. My infant was lying next to me on the sofa; diapers, water, and food were all in reach. The other two kids had only mild fevers and were rather content watching television. Suddenly the telephone rang. Refusing to accept my limitations, I quickly hopped up two steps to the other room without my crutches. Having beaten the answering machine (Ha!), I picked up the phone and learned that Barbra had caught the flu and was unable to come. Feeling guilty and exasperated, I hopped down the two steps as quickly as I had hopped up them, and fell again. Despite the splint I broke my big toe. Just as I was rolling with pain, my boy held his dirty diaper over my head saying, "Look, mama, poopoo!"

I assure you the scene would have seemed too exaggerated even for slapstick comedy. I felt the pain, my helplessness, and utter exhaustion, and as one child started crying and the telephone began ringing once again, I started laughing despite it all. "If I die today," I thought, "people will laugh during my eulogy." Life was playing with me, and while the joke was on me, I could laugh at it or, better, I could laugh *with* it.

I was certainly not happy in the usual sense of the word, but I finally arrived at a point of total clarity. I was in pain and burdened with responsibility I could no longer handle. I realized that. The extreme situation had forced me into the present. There was no escape into the future, no goal, no worry. There was no escape into the past, no regret, no anger. I got up in pain, wiped everything clean, and provided for my children until my husband arrived home a few hours later. After the second fall, something made me rise to the occasion. From then on, my focus was fierce, and my actions were sensible. I did not observe myself as if standing right next to myself, as some people describe themselves when in a shock. I was observing myself while completely being there. I had finally surrendered.

Experiences like mine can trigger dramatic attentiveness and learning. It has long been known that too much stress is harmful to the mind-body. Yet new research has shown that we can also change and grow from it.[29] Besides examining positive responses after the fact, we can also look at our ability to be completely mindful during stressful events. As opposed to operating from our ego-experience, stress may urge us to pay attention to each unfolding event. From here we can extrapolate that mindfulness and surrendering to the natural stream of things is also possible during ordinary circumstances. We will find that if we do not resist the moment, be it good, neutral, or bad, we are as full (of changing experiences) as we are empty (of anything fixed).

UNDERSTANDING DETACHMENT

One of the biggest misunderstandings about Buddhism is that surrendering to the moment is commensurate with emotional detachment. Buddhist detachment means to live from awareness, which does not preclude us from feelings, but rather from identifying with feelings.

The Japanese poet Kobayashi Issa (1763–1827), for example, expresses great sadness in his haiku. Among other hardships, he had endured poverty, the loss of his mother in early childhood, and the death of his three young children. Yet while he saw the mud on a nightingale's feet, he did not lose sight of the spring blossoms.[30] After his one-year-old daughter, Sato-jo, died of smallpox, he wrote a one-breath poem about the world being of dew, beautiful dew, but dew that reflects not only that which is joyful, but that which is sad, indicated by Issa's words: "And yet, and yet . . . "[31]

Issa is aware of the transience of life forms and accepts it. He has come to love the world as it is. At the same time, he is aware of his sadness. Instead of describing his feeling as a fixed state of mind though, he sees movement in it. The flowing of the words "And yet, and yet . . . " bring lightness and joy to the haiku. Even in Issa's darkest feelings lies love for this life. It is the very dewdrop he lost, his daughter Sato-jo, that reminds him of the beautiful flow of life.

So no, we do not stop caring when we surrender. Instead we only stop second-guessing reality, and thus we no longer "wobble" between actions and thoughts.[32] In no way do we engage in a futile struggle (as opposed to a real cause). In tune with reality, we are realistic. We travel with the stream of life.

DEEPENING OUR AWARENESS

During times when reality seems too harsh, we can deepen our awareness of the whole of life. By sitting or walking quietly, with our mind focused and wide open, we should receive strength. Issa, who felt one with the smallest creature, used to do just that. The Zen poet had experienced painful losses in his life, such as child loss, and drew great comfort from nature, describing dignified, sad frogs contemplating the mountains.[33]

When reality presents itself favorably, surrendering to it can give us the sweetest pleasures and deepest joy. So often we let a good moment pass unfelt, uncelebrated, unnoticed. We turn our minds away as we struggle with reality, which we may consider not good enough or too good to be true. Greediness or self-doubt may plague us. Our mind may also be too busy for the present moment. Preoccupied with the past or the future, we may never just be there.

As stated earlier, surrendering not only helps us experience the fragility of life, but also the strength and beauty of life. If we do let ourselves be moved by the good, we may feel as described in *Memoirs of a Geisha:* "I hadn't felt such bliss in as long as I could remember. Like a ball tossed in the air that seems to hang motionless before it falls, I felt myself suspended in a state of quiet timelessness."[34]

The tranquil mind is the ball that does not move, while everything else moves around it. Our mind stays centered while our actions flow along.

TRANCE AND TRANQUILITY

Trance is a state of mind that we access spontaneously and frequently during the course of a day. Although trance is as natural as breathing, we usually do not notice it. As unobtrusive as a trance state is, it gives our over-utilized thinking mind a well-needed break. Our thinking relaxes as our unconscious comes more to the forefront.

We access a trance state in many ways, such as when we daydream, use our imagination, focus on a rhythm, or try to retrieve old information. Try to remember your favorite vacation, for example. Do it right now. You probably rolled your eyes up a little or stared briefly, and then waited for the information to come to you. The moment before the retrieval is nothing but a light trance.

If you wished to deepen this state, you could imagine your vacation in more detail or change the memory creatively. If you have gained access to the trance state by paying attention to a rhythm, such as by dancing, chanting, reiterating words, or observing waves, you would also deepen a trance state, possibly with closed eyes and fewer distractions. Afterward, you will probably find that you are more in touch with yourself and have gained perspective. As a result of this experience, you might, almost magically, feel more apt in regard to your pursuits and more content with your being.

Many of us think that the thinking mind is an all-powerful tool and deem the unconscious mind as unimportant or nonexistent. Others want nothing to do with the unconscious because they associate it with the Freudian animalistic id that is bad or embarrassing. According to psychoanalysts Sigmund Freud and Carl Gustav Jung, the unconscious is the seat of our personal and/or interpersonal conflicts.[35] Most people are not keen on conflict, let alone their own. While a trance in Tibetan Buddhism and Hinduism is widely embraced, it is often shunned in the West because it would cloud our mind and reduce attentiveness. In any of these cases, we fail to understand the unconscious mind and its extraordinarily beneficial power.

First of all, we need to understand that the unconscious mind is very important to our survival. If we had to learn and process all information with our thinking mind, we would be at a terrible disadvantage in our biological environment. There is simply too much data around to filter it all through thinking. Timothy D. Wilson writes in his book *Strangers to Ourselves: Discovering the Adaptive Unconscious:*

> We take in 11,000,000 pieces of information per second, but can process only 40 of them consciously. What happens to the other 10,999,960? It would be terribly wasteful to design a system with such incredible sensory acuity but very little capacity to use the incoming information. Fortunately, we do make use of the great deal of this information outside of conscious awareness.[36]

This is why German psychologist Gerd Gigerenzer and his fellow researchers call the adaptive tools of the unconscious, namely simple heuristics, "fast and frugal."[37] They work well, as they are specific to the situation, but not too specific. Our unconscious also filters out noises and other distractions. This is an ability that enables us to concentrate on important matters or on matters that we are in the habit of dealing with consciously.

Without thinking much about it, we take a lot from our surroundings into account. We realize the Zeitgeist. We do not even notice how our own thinking and choices are influenced by it. Even people who claim not to have a fashion sense will tend to dress as the current times suggest. While we may believe that we have thought of something truly original, it was most certainly thought of previously by many other thinkers. And for those of us who consider ourselves independent, morally superior beings, it is quite humbling to notice that we too have merely assimilated cultural values. Our unconscious filter is therefore not only of utmost importance to us as individuals, but also for the cohesiveness and harmony of our group.

Nobody could seriously wish to be without the unconscious. Only the unconscious keeps working when we sleep. It saves many lives many times during the day as we move through traffic without thinking. It adjusts our heart rate and blood pressure. It protects us from overheating and suffocating by sweating and breathing correctly. Living our lives without these unconscious tools is impossible. However flawed, the unconscious mind will always be an invaluable resource to us all.

We should also better our psychological understanding of the unconscious to reap its full benefits. It makes sense that bits and pieces of our conflicts reveal themselves when we bypass conscious judgment, as in dreams. Such revelations may reduce some people's unhappiness. However, focusing on conflicts, as many followers of Freud do, is not good advice for well-functioning people. A scholar of mythology, Joseph Campbell saw something far more positive in the unconscious mind. He called it the "deep, dark ground that is the support of our conscious lives."[38] Milton Erickson, the most important clinical hypnotherapist who ever lived, tapped into and utilized directly that support. With it he helped countless patients with a wide variety of symptoms, and he also alleviated his own polio symptoms.[39]

THE RELATIONSHIP BETWEEN TRANCE AND AWARENESS

Before I elaborate on ways we can tap into our supportive unconscious without formal hypnotherapy, I will answer Zen Buddhists' concerns about trances. They often believe that trances lead us further away from awareness. At face value, the concern is valid, because we really do dim our awareness somewhat when we are in a trance.

However, the first point I would like to make is that during a trance state we are still in control of our actions, as Milton Erickson pointed out numerous times.[40] The circus acts in which people are made to act like a chicken are magic shows with willing performers. In real life and during an intentional trance, we give ourselves permission to relax the conscious controller of perceptions. We let ourselves trust our unconscious processes for exactly as long as we want to. Nobody can make us do anything in a trance that we do not want or of which we disapprove.

Second and most importantly, while we do dim our awareness of conscious processes during a trance state, we increase our awareness of unconscious ones. Gradually, the focus on the unconscious builds stronger bridges between the conscious and the unconscious mind. We learn to open our eyes to what usually remains unseen, and thus we widen the scope of our perceptions. In other words, a temporary reduction in conscious awareness ultimately increases overall awareness.

For example, a person who is more or less oblivious of his feelings or cannot use his creativity, will discover paths to these inner resources. After getting in touch with them, his awareness will include psychological and creative awareness. He will ground himself in reality and thus become fit for relationships and problem solving. Psychological health is always an asset and may, if we so desire, help us access the ultimate experiences in the Supreme Mode. If we are well-rounded and functioning, we are more prepared to face the emptiness of particularities that we encounter when we become keenly aware of our oneness with the world.

To understand the unconscious, we should also know the following: our mind is just as interconnected as the whole of life.
There are no absolute distinct areas. The conscious mind is not
over here and the unconscious mind over there. (This intercon-
nection is also true for the Basic Mode and the Supreme Mode,
which we will discuss later on.) When we focus our mind, we
merely activate and deactivate vaguely defined areas. Unless we
are in a coma, no such area is ever completely shut off or completely in control. When we relate to the world as distinct from
us, as we do when we focus fiercely on a goal in the Basic Mode,
we experience ourselves as effective and completely engrossed
partakers. When we relate to the world as nondistinct from us—
as in the awareness of being in the Supreme Mode—we realize
our existing participation. Yet in between these extreme experiences lie many variants, one of which is trance.

Eugene D'Aquili and Andrew Newberg have given much
attention to the most extreme experience in the Supreme Mode.[41]
They use the term "absolute unitary experience," which is commensurate with the Buddhist nirvana and Hindu moksha. Instead
of looking at the extreme as a distinctively different experience,
they see it as part of a continuum. Aesthetics, love, and spiritual
experiences of reality (via dreams, visions, or mandalas) as well as
a profound sense of deep unity would all be increasingly intense
experiences on that continuum. Before the absolute unitary experience, D'Aquili and Newberg place "various progressively intense
trance states" on this continuum. Just as in the experience of the
whole of life, we blur boundaries of individual things when we
are in a trance.[42]

Finally, the authors arrive at the end of the continuum, namely
at the "state of blissful unity with the world."[43] They hypothesize
that it is the most balanced state due to equal and consistent acti-
vation of our quiescent and arousing systems. (Both systems make
up our autonomous nervous system.)[44] In this state, we manage to
blur all boundaries while staying completely alert.

I think it is apparent that while trance does not equal that
state, it too is tranquility. The continuum tells me this: existence
brings forward a wide potential to experience the world. We can
experience it via (1) boundaries, (2) blurred boundaries while

relaxing conscious awareness, and (3) blurred boundaries while maintaining conscious awareness. All these experiences help us relate to the world, and all contribute to happiness that is full life participation.

HOW TO ACCESS TRANCE STATES

Let me now discuss some ways to access and deepen natural trance states.[45] It is helpful to think of our unconscious as the seat for many resources that support our well-being. To name but a few, there is the unconscious resource of comfort (which, for example, tells you how to place your fingers while holding this book), trust (which tells you to relax at least somewhat at this moment), curiosity (which tells you to remain open and seek new information), and creativity (which tells you to play with ideas and imagine new experiences). When we focus our attention not on the content, but on the actual resource, we are more likely to sink into a trance. Observing our unconscious resource will make this part more accessible and simultaneously relax our mind-body.

Comfort

Take a moment to realize how your fingers are positioned in order to hold this book. Most likely you have not concocted a plan as to how each of your fingers must go about doing this. While you did not need thought to place your fingers, you did need the wisdom of your body. Instead of thinking of your anatomy and intricate brain connections, pay direct attention to the comfort that has led you do this. Close your eyes or lower your eyelids. Focus on the natural rhythm of your breath. While honing in on the sensation of your fingers, your hands, arms, the tilt of your head, and your general posture, examine your relationship to such comfort. You may just think "comfort," or breathe into the realization of comfort. Feel free to experiment until you find your way to comfort.

Trust

Now take a moment to realize that you are paying attention to these written lines. You might not be 100 percent concentrated, but you have managed to concentrate and relax enough to read this. You have screened and actually continue to screen your external environment for potential danger, and you have come to the unconscious conclusion that "It is safe enough to read at this time." Apparently you also trust your reading and comprehension skills, at least sufficiently so, to continue reading. We walk down stairs without measuring each step. We stretch out our hand to shake another hand at the exact right time. Earth turns and gravity keeps us grounded, and we do not doubt that. Yet many of us examine only our mistrust; few pay attention to existing trust. We may wish for more trust. By simply observing trust in the same way as we observe our comfort, our wish will be granted.

Curiosity

So much of the time we think we should know something. To be "in the know" makes us feel confident. Yet the pressure we put on ourselves is quick to undermine our confidence. Releasing that pressure and enjoying the sense of "not knowing" is observing curiosity, which is as humbling as it is invigorating. So, pay attention, enhance your sense of curiosity, and begin to "love your questions," as the poet Rainer Maria Rilke put it.[46] Having found answers elevates us; the process of getting there touches us deeply and changes us at our core.

To enhance our curiosity, we could ask ourselves: "Is it acceptable not to know?" If we like to shake our head at that question, we may continue to ask: "Am I curious to find out how it feels to accept not knowing?" We can also ask ourselves: "Am I curious now?" Placing our attention inward, we may then proceed to wonder about that curiosity and wonder about our wonder. While we wonder about our curiosity, mental pressure dissolves. Time stands still, and we can begin to relax into our curiosity. Wondering about wondering is a wonderful way of becoming less full of ourselves and more "simply human."

This section on curiosity will probably remind you of the meditative doubt provoked by the aforementioned Zen questions, the koans. Trance is just another way of practicing "existential perplexity." To remind us, let us read these lines by Stephen Batchelor on "great doubt," which next to "great faith" and "great

216

courage" are so important in Zen Buddhism: "It means to keep alive the perplexity at the heart of our life, to acknowledge that fundamentally we do not know what is going on, to question whatever arises within us."[47]

The practice of observing curiosity in a trance is different from Zen practices, but in the end it serves a similar purpose. We become humble, less self-focused, and—as our inner eye relaxes—we open up to the world that we cannot grasp. We recognize that we frequently don't even grasp our own actions; our unconscious mind is much too involved in processing the triggering data. With the practice of meditation, we become more attentive overall. Regardless, we will remain—at least partially—ignorant of many inner processes. This too is something to be aware of. This too is truth.

Once again, the fact that we are also guided by our unconscious mind is not a bad thing. There are certainly times during which we are much better off slowing down in order to think things through. This makes instinctive reactions, such as panic or blind rage, less probable. And as the author of *Blink*, Malcolm Gladwell, points out, we have to continuously cultivate our unconscious mind.[48] He notes, for example, that we must consciously feed it associations such as women/competent and blacks/intelligent. Unchecked unconscious associations can cause biases that lead to very poor judgment.

Still we should be willing to utilize our unconscious readily and with appreciation. Gladwell cites studies that demonstrate that conscious processes, such as verbalization, actually hinder unconscious processes, such as generating spontaneous insight.[49] In other words, thought can separate us from our instinct. I have found that the recognition of not-knowing connects us with our instinct and that the deeper we relax into this recognition, the better our mind works for us. All we need to do is track the experience of not-knowing. Then, naturally, curiosity may rise. If we let it, it can then lead us to new information, places, and vistas.

At this point, you may still wonder what I mean by tracking an experience and how to access a trance state. If so, take the state of not-knowing as a starting point. Try not to figure out what to do. You cannot think yourself into a trance. Ask yourself how it feels "not to know" (instead of what feeling it may trigger). Stay with that simple experience, breathe naturally, and focus on what is happening. "What," you could ask, "is that part in me that wonders about not-knowing and wanting-to-know?" Close your eyes and let your mind go on an unconscious search. Tracking your search means to observe it as it happens.

Creativity

Even if you believe you are not creative, your dreams prove that you are. When you relax your thinking mind as you fall asleep, you relax your judgments. Your mind composes unreasonable, unconventional, frightening, and fantastic stories. No inner judge demands that they have to make sense. Hence your mind is free to take unusual perspectives from which intricate problems can be solved. Pharmacologist Otto Loewi dreamed up his experiment about the chemical transmission of nerve impulses that won him the Nobel Prize.[50] Along these lines, psychologist Deirdre Barrett demonstrated that subjects who concentrate on a particular problem before sleep are likely to dream up solutions.[51] Not all dreams are that valuable, but all dreams are in essence creative.

You will have a much easier time accessing the resource of creativity when you are comfortable and trust your curiosity. What this tells you is that all trance states are connected. By accessing one resource, you facilitate access to another. Just picture a painter. He needs a blank canvas and a somewhat blank mind. If our mind is fixated and rigid, there will be no natural flow in our creation or no creation at all. Even if the painter has a clear picture or plan in mind, there has to be a point of letting go and becoming surprised by his own actions. Therefore every creation begins with a certain amount of comfort with the creative act and trust in our creative abilities. Via the experience of not-knowing, you (or a part of you) have to let yourself be driven to the creation.

Just by reducing the pressure of having to know and eliminating the attached fear, you become more creative. You unblock your creative energies. This is so because it is necessity, not fear, that is the mother of invention. Sometimes all we have to do when we encounter a necessity is to start doing: our unconscious resource of creativity often kicks in automatically. If it does not, you may consider relaxing your mind via soft music or dim lights. Some need to remember the supporting words of a good friend. You can also try to bypass your thinking mind with fast and free associations as we do in brainstorming, alone or with others.

If relaxation techniques make you sleepy, you have relaxed too much of your mind. (Alcohol or television have that effect too, and are the enemies of creativity.) It is important to pick and use your relaxation technique wisely. You may want to counterbalance your relaxation with an energizing activity. You can utilize the energy of doing sports or listening to music, for example, and kick-start your creativity.

You can also imagine a great feeling, an inspiring event, an incredible achievement or person. Start by breathing with awareness and paying attention to your natural rhythm. When you are centered, focus your attention on a good experience you would like to absorb or utilize. Contrary to popular belief, good feelings, not bad, are best for creativity, as shown in Alice Isen's research.[52] Negative feelings give us reasons to be creative, but positive ones are usually more energizing.

So imagine something positive in detail, and place yourself in the midst of it. At the height of your experience, start working on your project. You may have to refine or correct your creation as the unconscious ignores many rules. Still, the creative flow has begun.

Let's assume you have writer's block. Imagine yourself at a moment in your life when you performed very well, felt impassioned or exuberant. Notice how you were pleased. Explore, in your imagination, how you were breathing, what you thought, and what you felt. Take your time to paint a complete picture of how well you felt, including the environment you were in. Maybe you will benefit from picking a symbol that will remind you later of this wonderful feeling. Then pick up the pen and start writing. If you wish, you can intermittently recall the symbol that might continuously trigger your good experience.

Sometimes it is easier to imagine someone or something else. For example, you could imagine a master writing a very successful, fulfilling book. Imagine the significant steps the master takes to reach his goal and how good it feels to be on the right track.

Then picture the master's happiness on receiving a note that his book will be published. You could even imagine awarding him a prize for his outstanding creative work.

Now, take his place and become him. Breathe his air, feel his feelings, see with his eyes, think his thoughts, give an acceptance speech. Then, abruptly, take this positive experience to your own creative work. If this causes inadvertent pressure, change the image. For example, picture a bubble of creative energy hovering over your head or the energy of doing the first step. All you need is a kick-start in order to come into your own.

Psychologists have long used creativity and imagination to relax deeply, overcome fears, and enhance performances. Besides becoming energized, we can learn from the pictures created in our imagination just as we do from perceptions. Indeed, according to neuroscientists, imagination causes brain cells to grow.[53] While some Eastern schools of thought have reservations about trance states, many do utilize them for spiritual purposes.

For example, Tibetan Buddhism uses meditative imagination in its dominant religious practice of the Tantric vehicle of Vajrayana. During ritual symbolic visualizations, practitioners gradually absorb what they focus on. In deity yoga, for example, this would be the divine personality of a Buddha form. Author Rebecca McClen Novick explains: "Deity yoga requires an active imagination, but is not simply make-believe; it is a system of deep psychological training. A sense of divine identity must be cultivated whereby one regards oneself as an embodiment of the very deity one is visualizing."[54]

By relaxing our thinking mind and imaging a powerful, positive force, we become part of that force or at least familiarize ourselves with it. The Dalai Lama describes deity yoga as a "rehearsal for Buddhahood."[55] The logic is simple and persuasive: if we can imagine enlightenment, we are closer to the experience.

Our unconscious can support just about all learning processes. As trance is tranquility too, we learn quietly in it, which in itself can reinforce and enhance tranquility. In other words, tranquility brings forth more tranquility. Thus, if we include the tranquility of trance states and embrace the unconscious mind as part of reality, we can only gain. Our mind transforms itself as we become more aware of and kinder toward the whole of life. While trance is not the empty mind—we do hold images and follow desires—trance helps us relate to ourselves with loving-kindness. Less perfect a state than the tranquility of emptiness or nirvana, it reminds us of the less-than-perfect being that we are. And when we begin to live with who we are in peace, the best of us, the mensch in us, can show its face.

THE PRACTICE OF HUMILITY

It is easier to describe what tranquility is not than what tranquility is. We all agree that it is not tranquility when we succumb to competition in the struggle for survival. To embrace and work with our biology is one thing; to be driven by it, yet another. When we are driven, we feel we must control, must achieve, and must preserve our advantages.

One sign of this compulsion in our culture is that we want to feel special all the time. It is not enough that we frantically and often unconsciously seek advantages. We also seek a proper rationale for why we deserve them. Being content with anything average or below average goes against this rationale and can feel morally wrong. As we are special, we owe it to ourselves and others not to settle for less.

To accomplish our goals, we are willing to wage wars. Our religious group is special to us, which means we feel entitled to take from others who are not so special. Our nation feels special to us, which is why we feel justified to take others' resources. Our children feel special to us, so we allow them to cheat to get better grades and "work" the system. Our individual needs feel special to us, so we feel justified in exploiting our environment. We torture our minds with envy, fear, and greed. Self-assured and self-seeking, we suffer and cause suffering. No gains in power, security, and love could ever be enough, because the competition does not rest. So we actively struggle and fight or passively struggle and resent. Whatever war we wage, it feels justified.

When we are that driven, compassion falls by the wayside. Wanting to ride high consumes us. It seems like a weakness to care for the fallen ones. There is work to do and we do not want

221

anyone to stand in our way. Feeling connected in general becomes rare. Others ought to think of us as above them or as above average. They must join us in our hope of or belief in being special. Not only does this give us assurance, but others may also cater to us and grant us even more advantages. Eager to make us their allies, they may hope to advance themselves in some way. To level with an other is a risk, because the other may take advantage of us. Many of us can only connect with blood relatives; victims of abuse and neglect cannot even do that.

Let me reiterate what I said in the beginning of this book: we are all biologically-driven animals. There is no need to feel guilty about this, because there is no way to escape this reality. We can even celebrate this reality and have fun with it. We are special in that life finds a unique way to express itself in us. Each of us counts and has a right to be.

Yet we also need to realize that we are much more and much less than individuals. We are part of the whole of life and thus have a lot more in common with others than we are different from them. Gradually, we need to see more eye to eye with the world than to look up or down. Tranquility is feeling special while operating from an ordinary, common place.

By now we have come closer to defining what tranquility is as opposed to what it is not. Now, imagine someone who thinks very highly of him or herself. After a while of paying him or her homage or pretending to do so, we probably feel like saying: "Come down already! Be a mensch. Be one of us!" Thinking we are different from others alienates others. Nobody feels intimate with a gorilla pounding his chest. Unfortunately, while we have little patience for other people's feelings of superiority, we have difficulties recognizing our own. This is so even though almost all of us share a deep longing to relax and to belong. Who among us does not wish to come together as a simple, grounded, and compassionate human family?

Tranquility is not just the acceptance of our animal nature; it goes much further. It is also the acceptance of a higher consciousness. It is the consciousness of being a part of the greater Being that makes us "simply human." Being rooted in this consciousness is what makes us the human animal, as opposed to just the animal.

Let us take the example of the Buddha. Like all of us, he was driven by his biological nature as he ate, drank, and had friends and favorites. His son Rahula, who became his novice at the age of six, received special attention and became an important disciple. The Buddha had high aspirations and wished to overhaul the prevailing religious thinking of his time. Yet he discovered that he was much more than a seeking and struggling being. He is known for his still posture, settled into the awareness of Being. This settled or awakened state did not advance him in measurable ways, which is why the Buddha called it "unexcelled" in the Diamond Sutra.[56] Yet it did bring out his humanity, beautifully captured in one of his sayings in the Dhammapada. After pointing out that all beings fear death and love life, the Buddha continues that we ought to see ourselves in others to avoid inflicting harm. If we were to hurt others, the Buddha doubted we could ever be happy, reminding us that we are all alike.[57]

Being aware of everything that is outside and everything that is inside, we can bond with others as well as with ourselves. Beyond that, however, we can become a witness of our biology. Living from the consciousness of the whole of life means not just to tolerate our experiences, but also to observe them as they extinguish themselves passing through the mind. In the words of Stephen Batchelor:

> Letting go of craving is not rejecting it but allowing it to be itself: a contingent state of mind that once arisen will pass away. Instead of forcibly freeing ourselves from it, notice how its very nature is to free itself. To let it go is like releasing a snake that you have been clutching in your hand.[58]

What we see when we observe our life is that all things are impermanent, including our drives. As we observe that which comes in and out of our mind, we see that nothing is fixed. All form, including thoughts and feelings, are but guests. If we like the guests, we may like to engage and focus on them, but ultimately each guest must leave. We can invite a good guest and discourage a bad one. Whatever we do—and lots can be done with thought—in the Supreme Mode, we hold onto nothing.

Even our dearest political, psychological, or spiritual approaches must be dropped for us to be "simply human." If we clutch to them as objects, they will become cold techniques and obstacles to the quiet feeling of connectedness within the universe.

NOTHING SPECIAL

As we observe ourselves, we become tranquil, and our mind becomes as clear as a blue sky. Clouds pass by. Thoughts happen, feelings happen, events happen. Yet we do not have to disconnect from the fact that each thought, feeling, and event is but a cloud, followed by another, and still another. For example, when we give a talk and say something wrong, we can let it go. New and better thoughts will come and flow out of our mind. Being "simply human" means accepting the dark clouds, mistakes, and misfortunes as we know of the perfection of the sky. In other words, life is not perfect, but the grounds on which it happens—God, the Way, Tao, or essence of life and its experience in conscious awareness—is perfect.

When we are in the Supreme Mode, we do not eradicate bad thoughts and feelings here, and praise good thoughts and feelings there. We move beyond distinction. We do not use the sword to divide. We feel at peace with the process of life as it unfolds. The natural consequence of the experience of peace and tranquility brings out our humanity. As Zen Buddhists put it, we become natural, spontaneous, and "simply human." Trusting the perfection of the Way gives us the courage to let go of the idea of being special. We can lean into life's flow and enjoy our leaning. Humility can rise when we are no longer afraid of not being special.

For Zen monks and nuns, the notion of "nothing special" (Chinese: *wu-shih;* Japanese: *buji*) is very important.[59] Even the most accomplished Buddhist realizes that they themselves as a person or their enlightenment is "nothing special." For example, after Fa-yung had a talk with the Fourth Patriarch in China (579–651 CE), he is said to no longer have received special attention from the birds.[60] He no longer stood out. At a certain point in our maturation process we do not need to stand out anymore, and we find great strength in adjusting to the flow or the natural order of things.

WISDOM FROM LAYMAN P'ANG

Let me conclude this chapter with two stories about a Chinese layman named P'ang (740–808 CE). He had studied for several months with Zen master Shih-t'ou and had come to understand the tranquil mind well. When he was asked what his daily activities had become, he answered that they were not unusual, that he felt himself "naturally in harmony" with them. He experienced no conflict, neither grasping nor discarding anything.[61]

Later, the layman traveled with his daughter Ling-chao, who worked hard selling bamboo baskets. He is recorded to have said that the mind reflects circumstances when it can be just "as is." Not distinguishing between what should be and what is, between existence and nonexistence, he felt like "an ordinary man who has settled his affairs."[62]

Not unlike hardworking bees and climbing plants, we do our work and strive. Yet in the end we are just a part of the greater oneness. Recognizing our humble existence in this marvelous life is the greatest tranquility and thus the greatest access of all to the Supreme Mode.

SUPREME MODE EXERCISES—TRANQUILITY

The Value of Tranquility
Contrast the value of activity with the value of nonactivity in your life:

For example: Getting to "X" place in life	Noticing I am already here (peace)

External Tranquility
- Making small but permanent changes brings permanent results, as opposed to short-lived, big changes. Commit yourself to a few of these changes in order to create more

serene surroundings, such as turning off electronic devices,
not watching television on certain days, or listening to
quiet music.
• Disciplined attempts to create external tranquility are of value
too, because they help you realize what really matters. Perform
tasks you tend to avoid (such as cleaning and organizing) or
apply a difficult rule (such as "I will not use my cell phone
during meal times"). Explore the impact of these changes.

Buddha-Nature
• After reading about Buddha-nature, meditate on the
question: "What is my Buddha-nature?"
• To experience calm insight, one must radically accept the
existence of pain, discomfort, and death. What stands in the
way of your acceptance? Become quiet as you contemplate
this question.

Surrendering
• In the middle of a pursuit, stop yourself and tell yourself to
let go of what you wanted to accomplish. Think or say "Yes"
while you focus on the moment. Take deep breaths until you
feel at peace with just Being.
• Sit quietly and pay attention to the transient form of noise.
Trace the noise to its origin. Follow the noise into oblivion.
• Watch the Korean movie *Why Has Bodhi-Dharma Left for
the East?*
• Read Byron Katie's book *A Thousand Names for Joy* to
address the issue of surrendering.

Trance Is Tranquility Too
What relaxes your mind-body? Imagine it with your eyes closed.
Let yourself occasionally daydream. What idea, motto, or message would you like to absorb? Write it down and stare at it
while you relax.

Practice Humility
• Question how you feel in relation to others. In what ways
do you feel inferior to others, and in what ways do you feel

superior? Pay attention to how you distance yourself from others every time you lower yourself, or look down on others.

- While we are not all the same, we are all One. How do you connect within the One?

11

Reliance

Who knows for certain? Who shall here declare it?
Whence was it born, and whence came this creation?
The Gods were born after this world's creation:
Then who can know from whence it has arisen?

None knoweth whence creation has arisen;
And whether he has or has not produced it:
He who surveys it in the highest heaven,
He only knows, or haply he may know not.
CREATION HYMN OF THE RIG-VEDA

L eaning on something that is bigger than our individual self is essential to happiness because life is too complex to control it in all of its aspects. When we try anyway, we lose the serenity needed to enjoy life. There are plenty of times during which we must rely on ourselves and take control. Even those times, though, have to be approached with the understanding that our personal power is limited. Somehow we must maintain the right perspective that allows us to surrender to the moment. As long as we remember who we are, namely part of the body of existence, we do right by assuming control. But we must also know how to rest our head on this body of existence in the Supreme Mode. Awareness of the whole body of life gives us reason and permission to relax our effort.

EMBRACING UNCERTAINTY
Reliance is part of being human, but it has different faces as we mature. As children we rely on parents and family in general. As we grow up, we must become self-reliant and relatively independent. Reliance in the Supreme Mode does not mean to give up that self-reliance, but to go beyond it. It makes us rely on God,

the Way, or the whole of life with the understanding that it will not treat us like children. Parents suggest that their children are safe and secure as long as they listen to them. As we mature, we realize that there is no such security in life. Life does not provide absolute certainty. Too many variables are involved. Adults have to accept the uncertainty of life in order to learn mature ways of reliance in the Supreme Mode.

There is a tendency in religious people to relate to the Way or God as children do toward parents. Often this leads to disappointment. No parent-like figure, no God with eyes and hands, no *deus ex machina* will reach down from heaven and take care of our every need.[1] We are, as adults, no longer the rightful recipients of parental care. Not that there is anything wrong with calling God lovingly and humbly "our father," or the Way "our mother." But let us not forget that what we relate to is not a person and does not behave like one either. Consequently there is no way of controlling it with our will or prayer. We can only change our own receptivity (chapter 9) to the Way or God. As far as life goes, it does what it always does, namely creates and sustains itself with the highest care and intelligence.

Accepting the uncertainty of life is one step toward reliance in the Supreme Mode. The next step is to realize that this uncertain life is still dependable. If we do not take this step, we will find it necessary to assume too much control. We will continue to treat existence as lacking natural, ordering principles, as barren of intelligence, as some lifeless, hollow thing that we must bend to our will. It is our actions of course that lack intelligence as we exploit and damage our very own environment and work ourselves voluntarily to the ground. If we felt one with the strength of life, we would reciprocate its generous care of us, cherish and protect it, and with it ourselves. Life as we know it on Earth will vanish if we go on treating it as a separate, unintelligible thing. While existence renews itself continuously and reliably, its actual manifestations are vulnerable to destruction. If we assume too much control and practice self-reliance as a religion, we end up destroying faster than life can repair.

Since the manifestations of life are perishable and there is not much security in the Way or God, we could ask ourselves what there is left to depend on. It is true that reliance in the Supreme Mode does not give the same comfort as believing in a parental God. Yet once our eyes are open to the miracle of life and we deeply understand that we owe every breath we take to the Way or God, we can find unique and enormous strength in it. While we will not be spared tears, we will thus cry fewer of them.

Above all, as we mature, we can find comfort in knowing that life never ceases to be dynamic. We can be certain that nothing is for certain. The constancy in life's flow gives reassurance of its awesome and eternal power. As we partake in this life, we partake in this power.

Driven Westerners especially need to come to terms with the limits of control and the necessity of reliance in the Supreme Mode. Let me concede again that controlling that which we can control can be very good for our confidence.[2] The belief that we can control everything feels even better but is dangerous. It is a Western ideal to enhance this exaggerated sense of control. Happiness in Eastern thought comes from realizing Being in which there are no separate objects (others) to control. Reliance on God or the Way of life is a sign of such realization. Life is like water that runs through our fingers when we try to catch it. When we hold still we notice that we are bathing in it, and that it holds and supports us constantly.

WHAT NOT TO RELY ON

Throughout history countless leaders have used their persuasive powers to make people rely on them and their philosophies. We were and are being told that we benefit from relying on kings, dictators, governmental, financial, and religious institutions with their respective rules. Many leaders have claimed divine connections to increase credibility to their claims. Without making too much trouble for the leaders, we have maintained their order, filled their pockets, and lifted their status while neglecting our own interests. Deriving comfort from the assertion of power and the promise of certainty, it is easy to become compliant. We like the idea of certainty in the midst of the many eruptions in an ever-changing world.

Our willingness to rely on certainty is also apparent in the fact that our brain can be tricked easily. We are susceptible to optical illusions and cognitive biases because they paint a much rosier, self-serving picture of the world of form than it is. Gerd Gigerenzer points out: "Certainty has become a consumer product.... The illusion of certainty can be created and exploited as a tool for political and economic goals. ...The illusion of certainty is already manifest in our most elementary perceptual experiences of size and shape."[3]

Hence our minds tend to see things as we like to see them. According to our unconscious expectations, whatever we see ought to fit into our existing, safe schemata. Our mind completes incomplete pictures and chooses perspectives according to our existing understanding of the world. A half-circle becomes a full circle; a black shape behind a white shape becomes a shadow; a gold-plated ring becomes a solid gold ring; beautiful and rich people become bright and righteous. As Gerd Gigerenzer puts it: "The eye does not have sufficient information to know for certain what is out there. But our brains are not paralyzed by uncertainty."[4]

The illusion of certainty works fine and is actually an essential survival tool. We could not accomplish much if we perceived uncertainty everywhere. Yet the illusion of certainty can also be counterproductive. Such is the case when we become overpowered by events. Sudden deaths, illness and accidents, old age, puffed-up dreams, and ailing hearts remind us: the world of form is a world of foam, unstable and utterly unreliable. The disillusionment may cause bitterness, or worse, indifference toward the world of form. Or we may simply concede our own foolishness in having believed false promises and having harbored hopes for a distant future. If we have no-*thing* to fall back on at such a point, we risk becoming depressed. On the other hand, hanging desperately onto some-*thing* and our measure of it makes us anxious.

Relying solely on what we see and on what we have come to expect can also lead to serious practical and theoretical mistakes. Because we expect things to be a certain way, we act a certain way, regardless of reality. For example, if there is no step where we expected one, we may fall and break a bone. If there is a step where we expected none, we still may fall and break a bone. Our actions reflect our beliefs about reality. When our beliefs are too rigid, we frequently miss the mark of reality.

As brilliant as Albert Einstein was, he too was a victim of his expectations. He discovered by his calculations that the universe was expanding. Yet his finding defied everything he had believed about the universe. This led the scientist to add a "cosmological constant" to his equation that turned the universe back into a set space. Einstein only realized his "greatest blunder" when Edwin Hubble held reality right up to his face with a telescope.[5]

Einstein also refused to accept that tiny particles behave unpredictably. According to quantum mechanics, we cannot claim certainty on an elementary level. Einstein was deeply troubled by this and claimed: "God does not play dice." As it turns out, "God" does. Tiny particles do not have a definite position and speed and behave without rhyme or reason.[6]

Buddha, much in accordance with the Hindu tradition, knew not to rely solely on form and our expectations of it. He pointed out that every-*thing*, in any form, be it tangible or in our minds, is transient:

All formations are transient; all formations are subject to suffering; all things are without a self. Therefore, whatever there be of form, of feeling, perception, mental formations, or consciousness, whether past, present, or future, one's own or external, gross or subtle, lofty or low, far or near, one should understand according to reality and true wisdom: "This does not belong to me; this am I not; this is not my Self."[7]

The message is clear: Do not turn yourself over to something that, by its very nature, cannot last. Transient things are only relatively dependable. We ought not to make them the ultimate power with which we identify. While we need things, thoughts, and images, they cannot be our gods. We must reserve an accessible space in our minds that is free of certainty as it relates to form. Accordingly we should not make other people our ultimate power. Instead we may rely on something that is really no-*thing* and everlasting. This could be a principle, a common threat or ultimate cause of reality, a spirit, or, as we find in Eastern literature, a supreme consciousness or awareness. Such a no-thing is empty of form, empty of Self, and thus eternally reliable.

If we do not reserve such a space in our minds, we will give our hearts and minds to tangible objects (money or possessions) and intangible objects (thoughts or beliefs). In our all-too-human search for certainty, we will anchor ourselves to form and go under with it when its time has come to dissolve. In contrast, if we reserve such a space, we will let go of form with less suffering as we find continuous support in our ultimate reality.

Of course, there will still be pain when we lose something and someone we love. There will still be a sense of insecurity when our expectations are not met. Yet if we have practice being in the Supreme Mode, we will still have eyes for and be aware of the rest of reality. Used to experiencing our ultimate reality, our God or the Way that serves as our inner light, we continue to see when there is no-*thing* to see. It will not cease to shine, even though it may not always look bright. Our own self may form thoughts of a promising future, but the light already shines in the present. Here it awaits us when we are once more ready to experience it in its full brilliance.

RELYING ON SOMETHING GREATER THAN OURSELVES

That no-*thing* that we can rely on in good and in bad times has been described in many different ways using very different languages in all cultures of the world. Before I use Eastern terms, let me point out our own Western ones.

The Western, father-like God figure that punishes badness and rewards goodness is quite removed from the actual experience of an ultimate reality. This is not to say that people who adhere to this patriarchal understanding cannot have such a spiritual experience. It can happen spontaneously or be brought forward with many actions, for example with praying, singing, dancing, or sharing a meal. However, certain modern or mystical concepts point more directly to the experience of an ultimate reality.

What all concepts have in common is that they refer to the ultimate reality as something greater than the individual self. Twelve-step programs call it a "higher power" and for the same reason adhere to the group rule "principles before personalities." This is so because humility is essential to the ability to receive from and rely on an absolute reality. Looking up in reverence is therefore part of many places of worship. We are meant to feel small in relation to a Gothic cathedral's window, a raised relic or book, an oversized painting. Male Jews put on a skull cap called the *kippah* to remember respectfully that God is above everything. The Islamic understanding of God being "great" and "high" reflects much of the same: we are small in relation to the absolute reality we wish to experience.

Also, the absolute reality is often described as somewhat independent from us. Although it is woven into the web of existence, there is no two-way causal relationship between us and it. In other words, the absolute does not need us to be or act a certain way in order to exist. It is a constant and is nonreactive to our human, changing experiences. On the other hand, we can relate better to it, see it, and *be* it more clearly when we are attuned with it.

For example, the philosopher Epictetus, a former slave of the Roman Empire, saw goodness as a major force and principle: "Goodness exists independently of our conception of it. The good is out there and it always has been out there, even before we began to exist."[8]

There has been a long philosophical debate over what constitutes goodness and whether or not it truly is independent from our culture with its changing needs. Yet once we understand the goodness in question, it makes sense to see that it operates separately from our doing or experience. The key is to notice that a principle or spirit behaves unlike the ever-changing world of form. It may manifest more or less, and be known to few or many. Regardless, it does exist and once we have detected it, we can have access to it.

Although the absolute reality is greater than we are, detecting it is not so easy. It is like a constant sound that we have learned to block out and can no longer hear. According to mystics, we must become open and fully content in the present moment in order to perceive it. Instead of seeking an Other, we must become tranquil and settle within our subjective experience. We could call such action object-free prayer, which was well-known to the Christian monk Meister Eckhart (1260–1327). Although unpopular with his medieval contemporaries, his teachings resonate with many spiritual people today. Much in alignment with Zen Buddhist thinking, the mystic advises us not to seek anything in our prayer (action) but the presence of God:

> The just man loves God for nothing, neither for this nor for that, and if God gave him wisdom or anything else he had to give, except himself, the just man would not look for it, nor would it be to his taste; for he wants nothing, seeks nothing, and has no reason for doing anything. As God, having no motives, acts without them, so the just man acts without motives. As life lives on for its own sake, needing no reason for being, so the just man has no reason for doing what he does.[9]

All Western religions have a branch of mysticism, such as Jewish Kabbalah or Islamic Sufism, that stresses the importance of direct experience of the absolute power. To a mystic, mere adherence to a religion is insufficient, which would explain that why on average, religion increases happiness only moderately.[10] Paying lip-service does not get us far when we are accessing the Supreme Mode. What is needed is a touch of God, a conscious sharing of the absolute reality or Way. Only when we experience our connection religion does what it promises to do, namely "link together" socially and spiritually.[11] For us to experience God's or the Way's touch, we must turn inward. Once again Meister Eckhart:

> The most powerful prayer, one well nigh omnipotent, and the worthiest work of all is the outcome of a quiet mind. The quieter the mind, the more powerful, the worthier, the deeper, the more telling and more perfect the prayer is. . . . A quiet mind is one which nothing weighs on, nothing worries, which, free from ties and from all self-seeking, is wholly merged into the will of God and dead to its own.[12]

So, we might say that even for us Westerners the most important way to rely on our absolute reality is with tranquil mind. In quiet we become aware of what is greater than ourselves. In quiet we become consciously touched by its power and in turn feel empowered ourselves. Focusing, praying, and being consciously with the presence of our absolute reality helps us to rely on something that really is no-*thing* during good and bad times. Even when we are not in the very process of praying, we can feel our absolute reality backing us. When we are sufficiently acquainted with our higher power and have made tranquility our home, we can venture out and almost forget about it. Returning to it frequently will make us feel most secure in this insecure world.

RELYING ON EFFORT

Judaism, Christianity, and Islam all stress the importance of doing and being good as a means to feel close to God, our absolute reality. These religions tell us to study, follow traditions, do good deeds, sacrifice, pray, and do self-inventories all in their distinct ways with a distinct understanding. Because it can be hard to do the right thing, the prescribed paths are all full of effort. In the eyes of Western religions, it is necessary to pray and live "by the book" in order to make ourselves worthy of God. Supposedly, we are made in God's image, free to strive for goodness, but we *are not* good. Our nature has potential, but is limited, if not soiled by original sin, as many Christians are raised to believe.

Emphasis on effort is also present in the East, especially in Hinduism and the Theravada tradition of Buddhism. Highlighting the differences between their traditions and our own helps us rely on effort in a less guilt-ridden and more constructive way. Let's take a look at how effort is understood in Hinduism and in Theravada Buddhism.

Effort and Hinduism

The greatest difference between the traditions is probably how human nature is understood. Throughout the East, we are considered "good" in our deepest nature, even when we commit bad acts. We are seen as part of the gods, the whole of life, or simply the natural balance of things. In Hinduism, for example, we are seen, along with the rest of the world of form, as an expression of the divine. Accordingly, a worldly life does not oppose a spiritual life.[13] We are already close to the absolute reality because we are it already right now, albeit, in the Hindi eye, only in part.

The reason for prescribing sustained effort is that until we look beyond that part, we become entangled with it. It is our task then to learn, quite arduously, how to open our eyes to our complete nature that is called *Atman*.

In Hinduism, to see only the material part of the divine is considered a fixation or bondage. It causes the continuous cycle of reincarnation that is called *samsara*. The cycle of being reborn over and over symbolizes our inability to break away from bad habits. Reincarnation is therefore seen as a problem, because it testifies to our ignorance of the absolute reality, or Brahman. Besides, it is samsara that causes suffering. Therefore every Hindu hopes to free her- or himself from this cycle; the Hindi term for this freeing is *moksha*.

Let us now examine more closely what sort of action takes effort in Hinduism, and what effect it has on the individual. Author Mark William Muesse explains that traditionally there are three ways to escape the world of samsara.[14] The first one is the way of action, followed by the way of wisdom, and then the way of devotion. All three ways are described by the word "yoga," which is a process of many practices (and much more than the physical postures as we think of in the West).

Most Hindus pursue the way of action in one form or the other, which requires sustained effort. The four main worthy goals of action are: duty (*dharma*), the acquisition of wealth (*artha*), pleasure (*kāma*), and lastly moksha. If Hindus wish to realize moksha, which is the highest of the four goals, they have to leave the first three goals behind. Yet first comes first in Hinduism. The actions that bind us to the world of form are necessary until one's station in life permits one to disregard them. These actions all produce karma, which can be either good or bad; it is action and its consequence. Muesse defines karma as follows: "In the Hindu view, karma is the principle of justice, ensuring that the effects of one's actions return to the agent. Karma is what binds the soul to the cycle of endless existence and determines its station in future existences."[15]

Only a few people from the Brahmin caste (priests and intellectuals) are in the position to disregard actions that produce karma and realize moksha.[16] Because for most people, producing no karma seems unattainable in this lifetime, and producing good karma is the most important religious discipline in Hinduism. Doing one's duty (dharma) as prescribed for one's gender and caste is one way of accomplishing that. Other actions are:

- rituals (uttering the name of a deity, ritual bathing while uttering mantras, prayers, burning incense during worship, and so on)
- participating in rites of passage that strengthen the community
- festivals (there are as many festivals in India as days of the year, which mirrors the countless deities)
- pilgrimages (as in Christianity and Islam, pilgrimages are very important; the land "India" itself is holy to Hindus and an expression of many deities; visiting various holy places marks many Hindus' lives)[17]

The actual actions are not that dissimilar from Western ones. What is different is the understanding of what constitutes good actions. Instead of being private events that take place between the individual here and God there, they are highly communal. Good acts connect us in a positive way to the community; bad acts in a negative way. Whatever we do, we affect the whole system around us. In other words, our effort of doing "good" has good consequences for ourselves, and also for the whole. And while it would be much better for us to remove ourselves from the world of form and experience only the great oneness, doing the right thing is still very valuable, and for the time being it is good enough.

There is no need for us Westerners to start believing in reincarnation, deities, or karma. We benefit from understanding the Hindu way and from integrating its essence into our own approach to life and happiness. For example, we can alleviate the pressure of having to live a narrowly defined "good life" as prescribed by the executive branches of religion and others. No form of goodness is redundant. We shall neither dismiss other people's goodness nor become arrogant about our own.

- There is goodness in practicing social norms and adhering to the law. No instincts guide us when it comes to specific rules because they differ from group to group and from time to time.

- There is goodness in caring for ourselves and our families.
  As long as this is practiced consciously, it does not need
  to be selfish (as in looking out for the survival of only
  our genetic material), or something that distracts us from
  more profound, spiritual endeavors (as suggested by some
  Buddhists). It is also not more of a burden than any other
  form of goodness. Indeed, taking good care of one's own
  family reduces suffering in a fundamental way. Thus for
  many people, it is the most heroic, loving, peace-bringing,
  and fulfilling contribution they can make to the world.
- There is goodness in caring for our nonblood-related
  family of all sentient beings and our physical environment.
  Whether we are motivated by love or political activism, this
  form of goodness saves real lives.

Doing "good" in any way we can is what matters because it
brings out the mensch in us or at least in the ones we affect.[18]
All forms of goodness liberate us spiritually because they make
us relatively independent from outer conditions and help us see
more than the eye can see. This is so because we become guided
by a vision, a principle, an understanding that supersedes the
material and, to an extent, our survival. Thus goodness helps us
unleash our full potential and, as Hindus would say, bring out
Atman—our transcending, true nature.

This is not to deny that goodness has its price. Besides losing
out on the advantages that materialistic or selfish behavior offers,
goodness takes effort. Unlike in the Basic Mode, however, effort
in Hinduism must not be aimed at a specific goal or person, but
at an indefinable process that may lead to an indefinable experience. By doing the good, we may come to feel the good. Instead
of aspiring to reach a specific outcome, we can become the outcome and embody goodness. We can make it alive in us as it sits
there like a seed in soil awaiting fertilization. And as we walk on
the path of goodness, we may stumble on something far greater
than the original good deed we performed. We may feel Brahman,
the touch of God, the essence or the Way of nature, or the absolute reality.

If we just do good deeds because authority tells us to, we miss
out on spiritual liberation. In Christianity, for example, our good

shepherd may threaten us with hell and exclusion from heaven. Subsequently we learn to do the right thing out of fear of the shepherd and God. Each deed then becomes a concrete effort to avoid punishment and a means to make it into heaven, which we relate to as an object, a godly but specific goal. Of course in Hinduism there are plenty of people who are driven by punishment and reward just as we see in Western religions. Yet Hindu thought encourages a completely different, less linear approach toward goodness. Karma—part of Hindu and Buddhist thought— is supposed to raise our awareness of the whole world system, our communal circle, our ever-expanding family.

Good deeds in Hinduism are therefore not intended to help the individual reach a distant goal, but to connect the individual to others in the physical world right now. As good begets good, and bad begets bad in unforeseeable ways, karma strings us all together. Being strung together, our lives make sense.[19] Goodness need not be a technique that we use to relate to an external goal. Instead it can evoke a feeling of family from deep inside of us. It must not be forced but allowed into our lives, just as we allow our brother to be our brother and our sister to be our sister. Thus deeply felt goodness must not be dictated to us, but it can be triggered as a spontaneous response we have toward our family.

Still, karma is not only there for its own sake, but is also a means to an end, a path to an objective. Our positive deeds are supposed to catapult us into a better life after death, a better station after we become reborn. Thus karma keeps binding us to the material world in which we perceive ourselves as a subject and others as somewhat separated from us. My brother and my sister may be close to me, but they are not me. Living by the social law of cause and effect brings us closer to the world, but in itself does not make us feel "one" with it. As long as we experience an "I" doing something to or for a "you," we maintain some distance to the world.

It is possible, however, to get to the experience of oneness by generating good karma, just as it is possible for two people to feel united as one. (It is never fixed where one experience ends and another one begins in our consciousness, as I will show later.) Sometimes when we do "good" spontaneously and without any expectation of a return, our distance from the world may shrink to nothing. Instead of making our participation in the world happen with effort in the Basic Mode, we may slip into the realization of our already existing participation in the Supreme Mode. This is precisely why we find reliance of effort to various degrees in all religions.

Effort and Theravada Buddhism

As pointed out earlier, the Theravada tradition of Buddhism, the "doctrine of the elders," emphasizes effort as Hinduism does.[20] The Theravada tradition, also called Hinayana, is based on the Pali Canon (the oldest Buddhist collection of scriptures to survive in its entirety) and flourishes in the countries of Southeast Asia except in Vietnam. Just as few Hindus can reach liberation and realize their oneness with Brahman, few Buddhists of this tradition can reach nirvana, which is the deliverance from samsara (the endless cycle of rebirth). In fact, no members of laity can ever make it to the experience of "simply being," namely being in the here and now without grasping the physical world. Nirvana or enlightenment is only for Theravada monks who have become holy beings (*arahants* in Pali) via their own efforts.

The way to this deliverance is arduous and requires practice in various disciplines. First and foremost, Theravada Buddhists are supposed to follow the teachings of Buddha, such as the Four Noble Truths that include the Eightfold Path (see chapter 10). The Theravada Buddhist is supposed to develop insight/wisdom (*prajna* in Sanskrit) by abstaining from evil thoughts and actions and by purifying the mind with ethical conduct and meditation. The demand to turn ourselves into good people, to mold and control our minds, resembles the demand of Western religions.

Although this way of thinking pushes enlightenment far away to a distant goal, the implications for the daily life in the here and now are powerful. In addition, Theravada Buddhism adheres to the concept of the "righteous king," that is, a king who protects and spreads Buddhist teachings, the Dharma. (King Asoka, c. 268–239 BCE, became the prototype after converting to Buddhism.) For better or worse, religion and politics are therefore intertwined in Theravada Buddhism.[21] The fundamental

Buddhist values of courage, patience, tolerance, and nonviolence are to be practiced by everyone.

It is self-apparent that leaning onto these Buddhist values betters life for the community. Also, these values reduce hatred, greed, and fear—experiences that cause considerable turmoil in our minds. This is especially so when we like to enjoy having a good conscience. Theravada Buddhism helps the individual to get to a place of inner tranquility, which prepares the mind for not clinging and freedom. Being a good person is thus of incredible importance to both the individual and to society.

Yet it feels as if the struggle to be good can also stand in the way of one's inner peace and the experience of nirvana. Clinging to goodness may be necessary to the experiences in the Supreme Mode, but it does not appear to be sufficient. The least we can say is that reliance on our individual effort can be a good beginning, but somehow we have to go beyond it.

RELYING ON COMPASSION

Relying on individual effort and becoming a disciplined, good person prepares our mind for the Supreme Mode or may help us access it. Compassion, part of all major religions, leads us even deeper into the realization of being part of life. It has incredible connecting power. Instead of being a mere moral or rational choice, compassion is more visceral, a movement of the whole mind-body union. We are naturally inclined to experience compassion for close family members, and this inclination can be utilized for the ever-widening circle of our world family.

A compassionate person acknowledges that she or he does not sit alone in his or her lifeboat, but that others are always present. Any effort we muster to advance ourselves will therefore affect another. There has never been a king who did not help bring up at least a small circle of friends around him. If we decide to aspire to more than power and aim also for happiness, we will try to help bring up many more people around us. Happiness cannot be achieved by empowering only ourselves, even though such is an essential goal for the disempowered among us. Happiness comes from the feeling of holding hands with each other, from knowing that the other could be us and—in a spiritual sense—is us. It comes from giving, forgiving, and desiring other people's happiness.

According to Western religions, salvation comes largely when we love our neighbor as ourselves. In Judaism, Christianity, and Islam the creation is interlocked with the creator, and if we love one, we are expected to love the other. We may believe in a particular law, prophet, or savior, but the experience of life's essence or God must trump this particularization. The God of the Bible had come to care more about compassion and faith in God than about religion: "He hath showed thee, O man, what is good; and what doth the Lord require of thee, but to do justly, and to love mercy, and to work humbly with thy God?"[22]

I will not suggest that Buddhism emphasizes compassion more than Western religions. Growing up, I was generously instructed in believing in the power of love, in acting on behalf of the disadvantaged and sick, and in forgiving wrong-doers. And I know others within their own religion or moral upbringing were, too. Indeed, the Dalai Lama's pitch for compassion is nothing new to the West.[23] What I will say is that there are noteworthy differences in approaching the subject, differences we can learn from.

First, I like to point out that in Buddhism it is stated clearly that compassion is not limited to the person next to us. It is also our own person. We are to be compassionate with ourselves. While this may be implicit in the statement: "Love your neighbor as yourself," it is explicit in many Buddhist texts. Strong, negative sentiments stand in the way of inner tranquility because they linger too long in our minds, cause clutter, and thus obstruct our experience of the present moment.

In addition, compassion is to go beyond "persons," that is, beyond our own species. Buddhist texts state that all sentient beings deserve lovingkindness (*metta* in Pali) and compassion (*karuna*). No being is outside the circle. There is no in-group and no out-group. None can be killed in the name of religion. Even animal sacrifice is forbidden. To define the object of our compassion so widely, opens our eyes more widely. It encourages us to embrace larger parts of the world and gets us away from dissecting the world into little pieces. While we still see separate beings, we see them within a huge group. The more lives we include in the group, the more we feel ourselves as partakers of life as such.

Compassion and Mahayana Buddhism

Compassion is an important virtue in all of Buddhism. Yet in Mahayana Buddhism, a tradition that originated about 200 years after the Theravada tradition, it plays an extra, intriguing role.[24] Mahayana Buddhists view compassion not merely as a helpful tool that turns the individual into a better person. Instead compassion is supposed to shift the individual's focus away from his or her own self and onto the community of all sentient beings. According to Mahayana Buddhism, focusing on one's own salvation creates desire, and because desire is clinging to form it is considered an obstacle to nirvana. In other words, the desire not to desire, the clinging to nirvana, keeps us in a vicious circle. Compassion would free us from ego-centered desires.

The agenda not to become trapped in ego while seeking nirvana is evident in the Mahayana ideal of the bodhisattva. In the words of scholar Malcolm D. Eckel, a bodhisattva is a "future Buddha or 'Buddha-to-be' who postpones nirvana in order to help others achieve nirvana."[25] A bodhisattva and everybody who desires to be one train their minds to be motivated by wisdom and compassion. Such a mind, called *bodhicitta,* is considered our innate potential. The Dalai Lama, who is considered a manifestation of the great bodhisattva of compassion Avalokiteshvara, defines bodhicitta as "kindness combined with the highest intelligence."[26]

The training of our mind begins with expressing our aspiration to become clear and present-minded (Buddhahood) for the sake of all other beings. Furthermore we are to live a virtuous life (in this tradition follow the six *paramitas:* charity, morality, humility, zestfully doing "good," meditation, and wisdom).[27] We can learn from Mahayana Buddhism that first our individual happiness is tied to the community. There is no happiness in making it to heaven alone! Second, our happiness is tied to how we treat ourselves. We need to exhibit compassion to ourselves because we are just as much a part of the whole of life as everybody and everything else. The renowned Zen Buddhist D. T. Suzuki is alleged to have said that we become perfect when we love ourselves in the all to which we belong. Compassion must be spread joyfully, in all directions.

We need a lot of psychic energy while committing good deeds in Mahayana Buddhism. Ethics in Buddhism does not mean to follow rules and regulations blindly. Only deeply felt compassion connects us to the whole of existence. Mahayana Buddhist and writer Martine Batchelor explains that we bring such authenticity about when we reflect on our motivations and actions.[28] In other words, we need to look inside continuously while we are giving to others. When we find resistance or a feeling of resentment we need to acknowledge it with curiosity and compassionate understanding. As we give our true inner experiences attention and guidance, they eventually fall into alignment with our deeper Buddha-nature (see chapter 10).

Also, authentic or "great compassion"—a Mahayana term—is more of a gut reaction or a holistic response that comes about without hesitation. The longer we practice giving from the heart, the more effortless our effort will feel. The same is true for meditation: the more we meditate, the easier it becomes. "Effortless effort" is therefore an important concept in Mahayana Buddhism. Martine Batchelor advises us to practice meditation and compassion this way:

> Try with dedication but without expectation; do not judge or blackmail yourself. Be intent and attentive without grasping at any result. This is cultivating effortless effort—trying not too much and not too little but just enough . . . try gently without forcing yourself. Effortless effort is characterized by a light but steady intention that is energized with inspiration.[29]

Let me point out two more of the many differences between Mahayana Buddhism and Western religions in regard to compassion. First, in Mahayana Buddhism we should not feel as if we are handing down gifts of compassion with a sense of superiority. Instead, we should feel related within a system of unfathomable reciprocity. According to Buddha, we ought to be simultaneously the givers and recipients of compassion.[30] There is only one diamond with many facets reflecting each other, only one "flower ornament" (which is the name of the famous Avatamsaka Sutra).[31] When we give to others, we give to ourselves. When we take from others and cause suffering, we take from ourselves and cause suffering in ourselves. Happiness becomes therefore something like a moral obligation in Mahayana Buddhism.

Second, in Mahayana Buddhism reliance on personal effort as described in Hinduism and Theravada Buddhism becomes less important. This is beautifully exemplified in the concept of celestial beings. They are highly advanced bodhisattvas and Buddhas who reside in the heavens.[32] There is, for example, the bodhisattva Avalokiteshvara who—according to the Lotus Sutra—takes any form to save a devotee in need. Simply chanting the mantra OM MANI PADME HUM ("Ah, the jewel in the lotus") can invoke Avalokiteshvara's compassion.[33]

Amitabha (Amida in Japanese) is yet another important celestial Buddha who resides in the Pure Land heaven, a prevalent tradition in China and Japan. The Pure Land reformer Honen (1133–1212) goes so far as to abandon all self-reliance and asks of the devotees to have radical faith alone. They are merely to repeat Amida's name in order to get access to the Land of Perfect Bliss:

> Those who believe this, though they clearly understand all the teachings Shaka [Shakyamuni the Buddha] taught throughout his life, should behave themselves like simpleminded folk, who know not a single letter, or like ignorant monks or nuns whose faith is implicitly simple. Thus without pedantic airs, they should fervently practice the repetition of the name of Amida, and that alone.[34]

This turning away from the reliance on effort was great news to many Buddhists. No longer are only a few selected holy monks eligible to develop the clear-mindedness of a Buddha. A great many people, laypeople included, could save themselves by giving or receiving compassion. This is the reason for Mahayana Buddhists calling their own tradition the "great vehicle" and the Theravada tradition the "lesser vehicle."[35]

What follows is a brief description of a form of reliance even less centered on the individual. By looking at these various forms of reliance as complementary, you can integrate them best into Western thought.

RELYING ON VIRTUES

Chaos without a positive counterforce brings death and suffering. Everything that is brought into existence by chance must instantly meet order to avoid obliteration. This is true for the microcosm and the macrocosm, the organic and inorganic world, for plants and animals. When tiny particles are released from the vacuum energy, they must meet "friendly" and as of yet unknown conditions, or return to no-*thing*.[36] Eventually life depends on the laws and rules of nature.

To the extent that we do not create finer and more humane organizing principles, we remain completely in the hands of nature. Its rough order dictates that on average the most fortunate succeed while the less fortunate fail. Neither group could ever relax. To bring out our full human potential, we must invent more refined ordering principles and alter them as needed.

If our ordering principles are to be successful, they cannot be too imposing. When we force harmony onto people, we end up with an army of disciplined but joyless, if not brutal, underlings as seen in Nazi Germany. The goal of harmony has to be reconciled with the goal of freedom.

Frequently the desire to be free tends to supersede the desire to live harmoniously. While the flame that burns for freedom in the human heart can become a small, barely flickering point of light, it is virtually inextinguishable. Accordingly, African-American slaves were never comfortable with the imposed order of their captors. In spite of great risks, many continuously concocted ways to escape. Former slave Frederick Douglass recounts this story after having defended himself against a white overseer:

> This battle with Mr. Covey was the turning-point in my career as a slave. It rekindled the few expiring embers of freedom and revived within me a sense of my manhood. It recalled the departed self-confidence and inspired me again with a determination to be free. The gratification afforded by the triumph was a full compensation for whatever else might follow, even death itself.[37]

As soon as we see a chance to live freely, we reject imposing conventions and bondage. This is also true for women who have been "kept" like children by their fathers and husbands for much of history right here in the West. To maintain the old order in families and in society, girls were not to go to school, not to learn a profession, not to speak up aggressively, and not to vote (until 1918 in Germany and 1920 in the United States). Women are still pushing through the glass ceiling and, as a whole are literally unstoppable in their desire for equal rights and opportunities. It is apparent that harmony is needed to live in a humane society. Yet while harmony allows us to breathe with ease, we shall not forget that freedom allows us to breathe in the first place.

Confucius and Virtue

The Chinese sage Confucius was painfully aware of the tension between harmony and order. As he saw his civilization fall into violence and barbarity, instigating political change was of the utmost importance to him.[38] Harmony, so Confucius believed, could only be brought upon by virtue. The primary source of his thoughts, the *Analects of Confucius,* reveals his distrust of laws that punish people after the fact. Instead Confucius believed that people have to desire righteousness and order themselves harmoniously with roles and rituals. Contrasting exterior with internal forces, he said: "Lead them with political maneuvers, restrain them with punishments: the people will become cunning and shameless. Lead them by virtue, restrain them with ritual: they will develop a sense of shame and a sense of participation."[39]

Confucius laid out countless rules about how to relate to other people and insisted that a leader had to set an example and become a "polestar."[40] Accordingly, the sage lived by his own rules while leaving ample room for passion, love, and self-expression.[41] Naturally, it does not make sense to emulate all Confucius's rules from 2,600 years ago. Nevertheless Confucius can help us become happier people in the here and now. It is still true that a "sense of participation" comes about when we live virtuous lives, even though we have to find modern ways that address the concerns of the twenty-first century.

Before I suggest some of these ways and concerns, let me point out the following facts. There is no higher percentage of people imprisoned in any country than currently in the United States of America where one in a hundred adults is behind bars.[42] Apparently we strongly believe in punishment, especially for minorities, who tend to be punished more harshly than whites for the same crimes. Overall we like to use fear to control people. Fear persuades bad people to suppress their aggression and good people to raise their aggression against bad people. Fear makes us want to sacrifice our sons and daughters to commit aggressive warfare and accept torture as a means to an end.

But we also have many virtues at work here in the West. Just as Confucius suggested, we believe in respect, discipline, and education as a means to govern ourselves. While some values are deteriorating (just think of how pervasively the elderly are disrespected) and our leaders are often involved in scandals, we may argue that overall the majority strives to be good. In the United States especially, we march with optimism and enjoy giving. Still, despite our values, we seem to be headed for disaster: the polar ice cap is melting, forests are dying, and species are becoming extinct every day. Neither wealth nor opportunity is distributed fairly. We overeat, overwork, and are overextended. Wars are being waged and too many prisons built. While we talk about "finding balance," we live to optimize, maximize, and excel.

Before we can rely on values, we need to understand what we want to accomplish with them. Confucius understood the concerns of his time, and he had a clear vision of what the future should bring. China was in the process of falling apart. While China had been united by the Duke of Zhou five hundred years before Confucius, Confucius was witnessing its collapse. Simon Leys explains: "Confucius believed Heaven had chosen him to become the spiritual heir to the Duke of Zhou and that he should revive his grand design, restore the world order on a new ethical basis, and salvage the entire civilization."[43]

Confucius's world was China, namely a highly hierarchical and patriarchal China with appointed leaders and feudal lords. Our world is much more egalitarian and reaches far beyond national boundaries. Confucius believed that his countrymen needed to relate to their community and know their role in life well. I doubt that we in the modern West even know who our community is, let alone how to relate to it. Most of us are lost in our individualism and lack of a conscious, uniting vision for the global community.

If anything, we are marching together through the malls enticed by television ads of which we are barely conscious. While feeling very much in control of Mother Nature, we are really her slave as we constantly wish to gain advantages over others. We are obsessed with having more money, more power, more beauty, and more comfort than our neighbor and even our brother and sister. As a result of obsessing over "having," we incessantly take from nature as opposed to feeling part of nature. We are, as Daniel Quinn points out in his novel *Ishmael*, the Takers, presiding pompously over the world and grabbing what we can: "As long as the people of your culture are convinced that the world belongs to them and that their divinely-appointed destiny is to conquer and rule it, then they are of course going to go on acting the way they've been acting for the past ten thousand years."[44]

In full alignment with Confucius, Quinn goes on to suggest that we cannot change ourselves with laws, but that we need to change our minds.

It is time to pause and think about our priorities. First, as we discussed in chapter 1, we must acknowledge that we are driven by our biology and struggle for survival. Second, we have to ask ourselves if we wish to limit ourselves to this struggle or if instead we want to expand. The path provided by our biological nature helps us to survive. We may encounter happiness on this path, but only as long as it serves the ultimate goal of gaining an advantage over others. However grand we feel when we reach this goal, we will remain small-minded and—even when we don't know it— operate below capacity.

If doing well in life fails to fulfill our human potential, we must transcend this feeling that I call our I-experience. We can only participate fully in life if we understand who and what else belongs to this life. It is not just "I," our own family, race, and class. It is not just our own nation. It is not just all people and it is not even just all sentient beings. It is the community of all things and beings. Our virtues will only create harmony if they help us relate to the whole of life.

So when we exercise the virtue of compassion, we ought to have the members of the other church or religion in mind. The virtue of charity should go beyond our own kid's school. The girl whose parents cannot afford the uniform that would entitle her to attend school is our daughter, too. If we want to exhibit the virtue of respect, we must bow to the people who are different from us. All old men are our fathers and grandfathers; all old women are our mothers and grandmothers. The air that becomes polluted in one part of the world will contribute to the global warming that affects us all. We shouldn't only be concerned with our own backyard, but with our entire planet.

Just as it helped Confucius to envision China as one whole, so we must envision all things and beings as one harmonious whole. We need leaders who propose overarching ideas, unifying strategies, and exemplify all encompassing virtues. These leaders will be brought on by people who have grown tired of politicians' egos and wish to see their global community come together and prosper as a whole. Each person committed to happiness—as in "full life participation"—will push forward a new political reality. And as long as we know where we are going on the path of virtue, each of us contributes to making this reality come true.

RELYING ON INDEFINABLE BEING

Virtues can be objectified and pursued as goals in the Basic Mode. The more we feel virtues to be part of our psyche, the less effort we need to live by them. Thus Confucius's idea of cultivating our virtues from within as opposed to imposing them from the outside steers us toward the Supreme Mode. Changing our minds gently, but with all our might, is commensurate with the concept of effortless effort in Mahayana Buddhism. Both Confucianism and Theravada Buddhism prefer and rely on the trained over the untrained mind. In the West we refer to the trained mind as our better or second nature.

There is yet another form of reliance, namely one that does not distinguish between the trained and untrained mind. It is reliance on something whole and indefinable. We may look at it as some quality or virtue woven into the nature of all things and beings. It is what Western religions would call God's omnipresence, and our reliance on it, faith. The great Eastern religions speak of it in many different ways because they are based in the notion that we are essentially good.

Taoism and Indefinable Being

The philosophy of Taoism makes the essence of our nature, namely the Way or Tao, its single most important hallmark. Instead of slicing and dicing nature, Taoism looks to its movements. And as movement escapes words, whose purpose is to fixate, Taoism necessitates direct experience.

In order to talk about the indefinable and our experience of it, Lao-tzu reluctantly referred to it as the Tao. In order to stay true to the fact that the indefinable cannot be defined, Lao-tzu's words are sometimes more mystifying than clarifying. Instead of reading these words with our analytical mind, we have to hone in with our whole and open mind.

In one poem, Lao-tzu says we should be like empty bowls. Because the flow of life streams out of us as soon as it streams into us, nothing becomes stuck. We can neither become deprived of nor filled up with too much life. The flowing characteristic of life is the opposite of our desire to make things static, to single out parts of life, to isolate and interpret, to define and distill things as we do when we favor or disregard certain thoughts and feelings. The never-ending stream of life is a constant and abundant harmonizer of all things.

Thus, the Tao makes all things equal. It connects all things, smoothes out all differences, and balances everything. An "inside job" is done quietly without drawing attention to itself, yet all is done thoroughly and well. The Tao makes us wonder like children and ask questions for which we may not receive answers. In Lao-tzu's words, "It seems to be the common ancestor of all."[45]

In order to get to the experience of the indefinable, we are to become a receptacle for life or the Way. Being empty means to be open to the changing events of life, without preconceived notions or automatic sorting mechanisms. Lao-tzu speaks of "unity" and "harmony," and he compares the Tao to a parent. Pointing to our kinship with nature, Lao-tzu hopes to evoke a feeling of basic trust in us. Thus, instead of describing a "good" or a "bad" thing that nature does, he alludes to the relentless and soft strength with which it does everything. Accordingly, Taoism is not about trusting everything that comes out of nature, which is definable, but the fact *that* everything comes out of nature. Instead of judging nature piece by piece, we can judge it by its ability to create balance among all pieces.

We may pick up on the indefinable by looking at nature's overt movements. Outdoors we can feel the wind moving through our hair, birds flapping their wings silhouetted on billowing clouds, dogs chasing squirrels, children skipping. And then there is water, a symbol for the indefinable. Most of us like to be around it. As water is coming down a mountain, crashing, trickling, flowing, or rising up and ebbing down, embracing us wholly, carrying us without effort, we are being appeased and invigorated. It feels good to be in nature. There is little that distinguishes us from water or from others when we are in its presence. We all like to take off our shoes and walk or play along the shoreline. Nobody gives importance to formalities, manners, or how our hair looks when we throw a ball. Neither position nor possession matter when we try to catch a wave on the surfboard.

At least once in a while, it is good to be less concerned with convention and enjoy our own simple nature. The hidden movement in nature, the eternal dynamic that brings out the overt movement, can be experienced wherever we are. Everything is brought forward by the Tao. And it is hidden within us all. When we rely on the indefinable, flowing nature of nature itself the way Taoism suggests, we feel good in our skin wherever we are. There is so much pressure to question ourselves, to change, adjust, repent, and redeem. But while we ought to live a virtuous life, we must stop short of identifying with it. There is a natural goodness in us that goes deeper than our acquired goodness. Keeping in touch with this goodness, the indefinable, gives us relief and a profound acceptance of who we are in essence.

Reliance on the indefinable strength that moves nature may seem difficult at first, especially in the Taoist tradition. While God is also indefinable in Western traditions, we usually make

God an entity that cares and plans ahead. When he does not seem to care or when bad things happen to good people, we fault ourselves for not understanding. In Taoism, no entity and no consciousness is attached to nature's Way. Lao-tzu writes about the Tao, saying that it does all the work without claiming anything. It also takes care of every person's needs without having to feel in power. "Thus it [the Tao] may be called 'The Little,'" he writes.[46]

While all things begin and end with the Tao, and while there seems to be direction and order, there is no lord in Taoism who watches over the indefinable strength inherent in nature.

Why should we entrust ourselves to nature's way when it cannot even do what any human can do, that is care and plan? Feeling little ourselves, it seems counterintuitive to rely on what can be deemed "the Little."

To make this leap of trust, we must take a step back, away from our personal little feelings, away from nature's perceived mistakes as manifested in bits and pieces and tangible misfortunes. With some distance we can see the whole picture much more clearly. We need to be in the right position to realize that it is within nature to find its way even though it is blind. It does not need eyes. It does not need to plan and care with consciousness. Blindly it puts together a well-balanced whole, and it does so in good and in bad times, in sickness and in health, in life and in death.

The Tao does not deem a particular fortune to be either good or bad. If we compare its workings with a puzzle, it is not identified with any single piece. Any form of latching on would halt the creative process. The pieces come about without hesitation, "of itself, so" (*tzu-jan*), which is the Chinese meaning for nature. And they come together as they fit. Every piece completes the whole. Within each piece lies the answer or key for another, as symbolized by the famous Chinese yin-yang symbol.

Accordingly, every bad fortune lays the groundwork for good fortune, and vice versa. As we take a step back from particularities, we learn to see "opportunity" in a "crisis" (both words can be translated as *weiji* in Chinese).[47] Even when we cannot find anything good in a personal crisis, understanding nature's way helps us accept crisis as a necessary complement to opportunity, and therefore as part of life.

The Chinese yin-yang symbol stands for how seemingly
contrary forces are interconnected in the natural world.

Zen Buddhism and Indefinable Being

Taking a step back, we can see how everything fits together. Zen
Buddhism provides the know-how of taking a step back and
gaining perspective. Just as in Taoism, Zen Buddhism relies first
and foremost on direct experience as opposed to scripture and
proper action. Zen Buddhists find the Mahayana sutras and five
precepts (do not kill, steal, indulge in sexual misconduct, make
false speech, and take intoxicants)[48] important, but these people
know that they are not equivalent to the actual experience of a
Buddha. Zen master Huang Po (d. 850 CE), for example, who
lived by the six paramitas[49]—charity, morality, humility, zestfully
doing "good," meditation, and wisdom—stated: "When there
is occasion for them, perform them; and, when the occasion is
passed, remain quiescent."[50]

Huang Po stood by his virtues, but in honor of the natural flow
in the whole of life, he did not practice them rigidly. When it is
time to think good thoughts and do good deeds, we must do so. At
other times we need to think no thoughts and just do a good job
whether it is gardening, cleaning, doctoring, walking, or sitting.
If a job requires thinking, Zen followers tend to think relevant
thoughts in support of the job instead of drifting off or engaging
in useless worrying. Zen is a simple and honest experience of the
now. In other words, Zen is not about "doing the right thing in
the pursuit of a distant ideal," but rather about authentic being.

Accordingly, Zen masters do not ask us to get rid of our desires or bad thoughts. For instance, Zen master Suzuki Roshi, who left Japan in 1959 to teach Western students in San Francisco, tells us to practice Zen by observing "things-as-it-is." Discipline is important to Zen because it keeps us from acting out bad thoughts and gets us to practice meditation, but we cannot rely on discipline alone. What we need is a lot of courage to take the "bad" into account.[51] In this way Zen Buddhism is unlike Tibetan Buddhism: the Dalai Lama instructs us to maintain a positive state of mind at all times. We ought to "face and oppose the disturbing emotions that endanger our peace of mind" with so-called antidotes for every kind of negativity. If we, for example, intend to speak badly of someone, the Dalai Lama says that we ought to imagine excrement in our mouths.[52]

Our individual expression of life, our personal being, depends on everything that happens in a given moment that makes it indistinguishable from life we share, that is the All or Being in general. We cannot help but relate. Our mind and the puzzle pieces we call life are therefore both indefinable and "one" in Zen. Mind is just another puzzle piece of Being. While we have many real interchanges with others, there are no definite distinctions between us and our surroundings. We cannot escape our mind, we cannot escape the puzzle, and we cannot escape the reliance on the indefinable. Yet only when we are conscious of our reliance on the indefinable do we become creatively engaged with life. Awareness allows us to see, reflect, and invoke the ultimate creation of indefinable being called life.

To shed further light on these crucial teachings of Zen, American Zen master Ta Hui (Donald Gilbert) wrote a wonderful, humorous book called *The Upside Down Circle*.[53] He explains that awareness is not the ability to narrow our attention, build new habits, and follow directions. Instead, it is like being on top of a mountain that allows us to look in all directions. A mind that has the ability to rotate 360 degrees is flexible and stays young through the ages. It does not wobble or become rusty. It notices the many definable particularities (convictions, beliefs, and other preconceived notions), but it does not become stuck in them. It is as fluid as water and as smooth as a mirror reflecting the creative approach of life.

When we live with awareness of the indefinable, we experience life more deeply. Soon we forget whether we are intentionally or unintentionally good. Soon we forget whether we are good at all. When we understand Being and are skilled in focusing on it, the mind knows by itself what life wants it to do. Our behavior will reflect life because our mind has accepted that we are this life. Therefore, Zen does not first and foremost rely on effort, training, and education that bring out a second nature. Instead Zen relies on an inborn virtue of our mind; that is, our intuitive knowing. While it needs to be uncovered, it is present in us all. We all have the potential to work in the same way as nature does. As Zen master D. T. Suzuki puts it: "To such a person his life reflects every image he creates out of his inexhaustive source of the unconscious. To such, his every deed expresses originality, creativity, his living personality. There is in it no conventionality, no conformity, no inhibitory motivation."[54]

The practice of awareness or mindfulness helps us rely on our indefinable being. In Zen it is often done by a particular kind of meditation, namely the sitting meditation zazen (see chapter 10). While zazen is the formal practice, we do best when we always practice mindfulness. When we walk or eat, we should just walk or eat. So many times we let ourselves be distracted from living. It is up to us to bring ourselves back to the moment and notice the thoughts, feelings, and sensations passing through us. Instead of worrying about the future, we can realize the now. Instead of gulping down our food, we are better off paying attention to the texture, the tastes unfolding, the mood it triggers, the people who surround us. We will learn that all particular things are essentially related, as if mirrored by each other. Gradually or suddenly we will learn to discover the all in the one.

This is captured beautifully in the Avatamsaka Sutra, the Mahayana text that literally means "flower ornament."[55] The simplest way of explaining the essence of this sutra is that by looking at one flower deeply, we can see the essence of all flowers and—as everything is in essence alike—the whole world. In the words of Vietnamese Zen master Thich Nhat Hanh, one flower contains all non-flower elements.[56] These non-elements are the sun that shines on the flower, the minerals that nourish it, the wind that carries its pollen, its gardener, and the gardener's bread maker. Noticing the small things in life is a popular piece of advice for a very good reason.

Living with awareness makes us see the inherent virtue in the most mundane thing. Seeing the ordinary "suchness" of each thing is seeing Being everywhere. Let me offer you a few lines of "The Sandokai" written by Sekito Kisen (Chinese: Shitou Xiqian, 700–790 CE):

> Darkness and brightness stand with each other
> like one foot forward and the other behind in walking.
> Everything—all beings—have their own virtue.
> You should know how to apply this truth. . . .
> If you don't practice in your everyday life as you walk,
>   how can you know the way?
> The goal is neither far nor near.
> If you stick to the idea of good or bad, you will be separated
> from the way by high mountains or big rivers.[57]

Let us not remain "separated from the Way," and begin instead to look at Being as an interconnected whole in which the least of us has purpose. Reliance on the indefinable is looking deeply into our constantly changing Being that comes about "of itself, so" (tzu-jan).

Thus we realize that we do not have to be in control of everything at all times. Many answers will come to us. It is OK to relax. Awareness is also about looking at life widely, because then we realize that the impetus of action is inherent in all of existence and that many things work themselves out with time. Looking widely, we realize that everything and everyone is a mixed bag: the good comes with the bad, and the bad comes with the good. It is OK to feel good while there is bad in us and on our beloved Earth, as long as we take the indefinable into account. Accepting ourselves, our neighbor, and Earth "as is" brings about peace, compassion, and contentment.

Let me close this challenging section with this summary: reliance on the indefinable is unlike other forms of reliance because there is no Other to rely on. It is more of a faith in Being, a basic trust in what is right now, an awareness of our True Self that relates to everything and makes no distinctions. As Professor Shin'ichi Hisamatsu puts it best: "In Zen, true authority is that Self which is itself authority and does not rely on anything. . . . True authority is where there is no distinction between that which relies and that which is relied upon."[58]

All forms of reliance are important if we wish to live a happy life. Without the forces of individual effort and unifying virtues such as compassion, we become unanchored in the world. Martine Batchelor explained to me on one occasion that Buddhism should never divorce itself from virtuous action, because otherwise it could be used for continuous self-centeredness.[59] I wholeheartedly agree. Yet, we cannot rely on effort and the practice of virtue alone. The realization of participating in life can only come about when we are fully aware of this life and live from this vantage point.

Our deep and wide attention to the nourishing virtues inherent in every thing and every one provides a positive platform for change. Our sense of oneness will cause us to do something about the abundant, needless suffering within and around us. Thus, reliance on the indefinable helps us in our efforts to do "good." No one form of reliance is dispensable; no one form is enough. Just like interlocking principles or pieces of a puzzle, the forms of reliance must all be lived in order to facilitate happiness in the Supreme Mode.

SUPREME MODE EXERCISES—RELIANCE

Effort
What are your most treasured beliefs or convictions? How can they help you to become more disciplined about your efforts? What could help you develop new or better habits?

Question Your Values
List your most important moral values.

_____

_____

_____

_____

Ask yourself: Who are the deserving recipients of your values? Can you widen the circle?

Question Your Personal Categories

1. Begin by underlining one word of each of the following pairs that you feel best describes you:

woman/man	single/married	mother/father
funny/serious	rich/poor	fair/dark
above average intelligence/ below average intelligence	ugly/pretty	good/bad

2. Now, describe yourself in categories. Write down only experiences that are relevant to the now (for example, "I am warm," "I am reading").
3. Also, write down what you are *not* right now (for example, if you are *not* in a smart or parenting mode at this very moment, write: "I am not being smart at the moment" or "I am not parenting right now").
4. After you are done writing, quiet your mind.

This exercise facilitates the awareness of life itself, because most identifications fall away at any given moment.

Compassion

Commit more acts of kindness than you ordinarily would, and register how this connects you to others. If you have difficulties being kind to strangers, imagine them to be family. If you feel judgmental about someone, find the same flaw within yourself. Can you forgive yourself? Can you forgive the other? What stands in the way of forgiveness?

Mindfulness

- Sit down and become still. Focus on one thing deeply and fiercely as if your life depended on it. Sharpen your senses as best you can and label what you experience, such as "blue" when you stare into a flame or "nervous" when you look into your own body.

- Spend time outdoors and look deeply and widely at the overt movements in nature.
- When you drive the car, switch off the radio and your cell phone. Pay attention to your hands on the steering wheel, the things and people you pass, the sounds that occur as part of driving. Add more and more mundane practices such as ironing and grocery shopping to practice mindfulness.

12

Lightheartedness

To be the fountain of the World is
To live the abundant life of Virtue,
And to return again to Primal Simplicity.

LAO-TZU

Evidently we cannot be happy when the world weighs heavily on us. Lightheartedness is as crucial an ingredient to happiness in the Supreme Mode as connection is in the Basic Mode. Only the light heart can hear what Hermann Hesse called the "eternal music of the spheres."[1] Surely we are all part of this composition, but only the light heart realizes this participation.

Hesse considered the realization of our participation a rare occasion, mostly occurring in childhood. I believe that it should not be that rare. We can learn to uncover our ears and hone in on the song of creation frequently and to some degree consistently. There are ways that take us back to the lightheartedness we once possessed as children even though now it takes insight to find them. Part of this insight can be taught, while other parts must be experienced directly.

THE NATURE OF LIGHTHEARTEDNESS
In order to clarify what lightheartedness is, we can look more closely at those who have it in abundance: children (albeit not those who at a young age have been forced to become little adults or those who while away their hours in front of the television). It would be those bouncing balls of energy, relatively free from cultural bondage, uncensored, unspoiled, unreasonable, if not impossible. Yes, from them we can learn and derive insight about what it takes. It is the little ones who can teach us a lesson.

Let us begin with their light feet. We tend to associate mobility with lightheartedness for a good reason. Lighthearted children are physically and mentally active as their muscles, bones, and neural connections grow. Their little worlds change to bigger worlds and their individual changes and motions echo the changes and motions of life in general. We can conclude that lightheartedness correlates with an energetically moving and changing mind-body.

When we picture lighthearted children, we do not see them planning for the future, but rather living for the moment. Because of their present-mindedness, they detect the littlest bug and tiniest airplane moving through the sky. While not listening well, they do seem to hear everything. They are attentive and hence thoroughly impressed by the world. Every day is an adventure during which the miracle of life is discovered.

Another side of lighthearted children is that they move swiftly from question to question. They do not have all the answers we think we have; they just enjoy asking questions. In comparison to adults, lighthearted children appear humble and simpleminded. Instead of using knowledge, they go by their gut and follow their intuition. Accordingly, their activities are more visceral. Using their hands and feet, playing with mud and clay, dancing, singing, playing soccer, and having gutsy adventures are perfect activities for our little balls of energy. As their whole mind-body engages without intrusive thoughts about the future, they become easily lost in their games and "vibrate in perfect accord with nature."[2] In other words, they are aligned with nature.

When we look back at our childhood, we are often inclined to give a romanticized version of what really happened. We think that we were mostly happy and that most everything was a blast. Not even the lighthearted children that I am thinking about have these ongoing, happy-go-lucky experiences. Life is not a romanticized advertisement for baby food, but is tough from the beginning. Lighthearted children cry, whine, and get angry just as all children do. Yet when the time of "feeling bad" has passed, they move on to higher and better places. In other words, they do not hang on (for long) to ideas of a more perfect world, but accept the world wholeheartedly, let go, and adjust. As they are more or less empty of particular expectations and identities, they come out of bad situations whole where adults tend to come out crushed. And while we ponder, they make light of their misery and inconsistencies with nonsense and laughter, which is lightheartedness in a nutshell.

Here is the list of the eight apparent qualities that characterize lighthearted children:

1. Moving and changing energetically
2. Living for the moment
3. Being awed by the miracle of life
4. Simplemindedness
5. Intuition
6. Aligning with nature
7. Wholeheartedness
8. Smiles, nonsense, and laughter

Before we find ways to reawaken these qualities in ourselves, we must ask why we lost them in the first place.

ON BECOMING AN ADULT

The older we become, the more disappointments we accumulate. Children fall and bruise themselves a lot; they get their feelings hurt, and their hopes of "super-greatness" crushed. By the time we are adults we have endured a lot more falls and bruises, heart breaks, and disillusionments. This alone could account for the dwindling lightheartedness many of us register.

In addition to mounting negative experiences, we understand more about their causes and how to avoid them. We use cognitive reasoning for risk assessments and predictions that protect us and our families that have become our new priority. Unfortunately, reaching into our cognitive tool box we often hamper our lightheartedness. Also in adulthood, encounters with what is novel become rare events. It seems as if losing some of our lightheartedness is the price we have to pay for becoming responsible adults.

It is clear that we cannot and should not go back to the childlike ways of our past. While it is useful to examine the nature of lightheartedness by looking at those who embody it, it is immature and even dangerous to hang on to our childhood. There are those who take pride in not committing to anything but their personal pleasures. Some of them take drugs and others get high on their feelings of superiority over those who do commit. If we hang on to our childhoods, we are more likely to become indifferent than lighthearted.

The paths I will discuss in the following section are designed by adults for adults. They will show us how to live for the present while also living for a future; how to enjoy the process while also setting goals; how to live from the gut while also thinking things through; how to accept the world wholeheartedly and play around while also taking charge and taking things seriously.

The skills we use in the Basic Mode are important for our survival and our happiness, which is why we must practice them to reach and maintain a degree of excellence. Also, we ought not to forget that we need to invite and cultivate receptivity, tranquility, and reliance in the Supreme Mode before we can become lastingly more lighthearted.

At times, the practices in the Supreme Mode will contradict each other, which is necessary in order to develop our consciousness. For example, instilling doubt as a practice of receptivity (chapter 9) is necessary before we can come to the lighthearted state of no doubt and intuitive knowledge. Exercising tranquility prevents our mind-body activities from being chaotic and ineffective. And living a virtuous life based on the complexities of life facilitates an adult version of simplemindedness. Contradictions work the whole of our mind and stretch it to its limit. With more flexibility we can become as "mindfully mindless" and "sensibly goofy" as we wish.

REDISCOVERING THE NATURE OF LIGHTHEARTEDNESS

Now we'll explore eight qualities that will help us to rediscover the nature of our lightheartedness.

Moving and Changing Energetically

It is a well-known fact that exercise uplifts our spirit. We feel good for about two hours after taking only a ten-minute brisk walk. More rigorous aerobic exercises have antidepressant-like effects and improve cognitive functions such as memory and learning.[3]

According to Harvard professor John J. Ratey, there are three levels of change that occur when we activate our muscles and help our blood circulate.[4] The first one is systemic, because activity in the frontal lobe increases, which helps us focus. The second one is cellular. Via exercise we increase levels of neurotransmitters that carry signals between cells as well as a special family of proteins such as the brain-derived neurotrophic factor (BDNF) that builds the very infrastructure of the cells. Ratey calls BDNF our brain fertilizer as it builds and maintains cell circuitry. The third level of change is altogether new cell growth. As neuroscientist Astrid Bjørnebekk has shown, with exercise's help we can grow completely new brain cells in the hippocampal area of the brain which is heavily involved in memory.[5]

As laid out in John Ratey's book *Spark,* this new science of exercise and the brain tells us that by moving our body we inoculate ourselves against stress, improve our thinking, and also feel better.[6] Exercise is therefore essential to lightheartedness, especially as we age and our levels of hormones and neurotransmitters drop.

Besides physical exercise, mental exercise has a great impact on our overall well-being. Also well researched is the fact that getting out of our comfort zone by interjecting exciting events into our lives and learning new skills keeps our brain fresh and agile.[7] Breaking routines can be as easy as trying out new foods, brushing our teeth with the opposite hand, or reading a type of book we ordinarily would not. Not only is it possible to become mentally fitter in terms of gathering and applying knowledge (crystallized intelligence), but also in terms of sorting through and solving new problems (fluid intelligence). As Susanne M. Jaeggi and a team of researchers have demonstrated, the more we train and challenge our mind, the more we can improve it.[8]

Most of us know that we feel better when we exercise our mind and body regularly. We also realize that doughnuts make us feel sluggish while fresh fruits and vegetables make us feel light and energetic. (A well-balanced diet is as essential to lightheartedness as exercise.) Yet for so many of us, getting our mind-body moving is hard. Starting with the best intentions, we usually do not follow the advice given by countless well-meaning individuals and organizations.

There are reasons why we do not do what is best for us, and these need to be addressed. The main reasons for settling into a state of immobility are our aging bodies, limited time and resources, and the fact that a life of habit has its advantages.

There is no doubt: the older we become, the harder it becomes to move. Clearly we need more motivation to get to the gym than when we were younger. And when we do make it to the gym, we must endure looking at young people who are fitter for one reason alone: they are younger. If you have any sense of competitiveness as I do, this is not exactly encouraging. Yet even when we have risen above such admittedly ridiculous competitiveness, we still feel stiffer, overall achier, and more tired than only a few years ago. When I was in my early forties, I already had to stretch for fifteen minutes before it was safe to move.

Also, as far as mental exercise goes, we have less reason to train our minds because the world has already become more accessible. We are no longer judged by our report cards and are long past our first job interview. Furthermore, we have figured out that our alliances, communication, and political skills carry as much weight as our agile minds. All these facts are real; no book on "age is only in our mind" can rationalize them away.

As we grow older, we also have changing priorities. Unlike when we were young, we carry a lot of responsibilities on our shoulders. Who has the time to jump around in the gym? Besides, the routine that we have settled into saves us much-needed energy, while exercise causes a certain amount of discomfort and uncertainty. Eating the same meals with the same ingredients at the same places is relaxing. Without time-saving, predictable routines we would never be able to get through the demanding days we have as responsible adults.

Before each of us can get our mind-body moving, we need to acknowledge these reasons for why it is hard to do so. Furthermore we have to counter these reasons, not point by point, but with a new paradigm that is based on both Western and Eastern thought. Our entire attitude toward age has to change.

We all feel the consequences of age. While modern techniques make them less severe, no amount of denial and rejuvenation gimmicks can make them disappear. However, we can learn to work with the reality of age by realizing its value and understanding its challenges. With the help of Eastern concepts we may come to respond to our changing mind-body with better decisions. Changing our paradigm is the basis for all change to come.

The value of age should be apparent to us, but in the youth-obsessed West, we are blind to it. Age makes youth possible because only as a whole—as yin and yang—life can go on. Older people are less self-absorbed, more experienced, and ready and willing to pass on that experience. And once we are over our greediest phase, which seems to peek at middle age, we actually become happier people. Contrary to popular belief, research has shown that old age brings us back the lightheartedness we once enjoyed. Professor of psychology Linda Carstensen speculates that this may be due to more appreciation of life as death approaches.[9] With age comes wisdom, and the world can simply not do without that wisdom.

We can only hope that we have successfully transmitted our invaluable experience before death. Finally, seeing value in our personal finality as an integral part of reality may be the ultimate gift for new generations. There may be nothing as important to our planet as respect for life and death. Yet, if we do not see value in aging and death, we cannot expect younger people to see it either.

Lighthearted people do not go around rejecting reality, but most of us certainly do. In love not with life but with youth, we judge everything from the perspective of youth. Young people tend to look at older people not as works in progress, but as finished products. If we do not outgrow that perspective, we may not find it necessary to keep learning. Without thinking it through, we simply expect that we will be sitting on our laurels and that life will become easier. On the other hand, if we keep a sense of lightheartedness that enables us to hop swiftly from one experience to the next, we can accept that life is a continuum. Life is an endless adventure with changing conditions and challenges and never-ending opportunities.

When we see life as a whole in which all parts have equal value, as Eastern thought suggests, we see it as one organic process. Instead of hacking life up into goals and phases with the highest one being "early retirement"—which is code for "laziness when still young"—we live life like a tree from the inside out. Until its death, a tree never ceases to grow, year after year, ring after ring.

Apart from yoga and martial arts, Eastern thought is not famous for its exercise programs. However, its love for whole-ness lends itself to a positive understanding of age. Zen master Baizhang Huaihai (720–814 CE), who may have set up the first monastic rules of Zen Buddhism, is known to have said: "A day without work is a day without food."[10] Staying mentally engaged and active is a very important notion in Buddhism, and in Zen this notion clearly includes the body.

As with many Zen practitioners, the San Francisco Zen teacher Suzuki Roshi continued to work throughout his life. Although in the end he was very ill, he taught Zen and worked in the garden in the typical, deliberate Zen style. Once, when he moved stones in the garden, his worried wife scolded him for cutting his life short. Roshi replied: "If I don't cut my life short, my students will not grow."[11] Active engagement keeps us tied to life as well as to young people who benefit most from a vivacious, wise mind. Zen master Donald Gilbert explains that this world is a "world of change," and that it is best not to resist it: "If one seeks happiness or security in the world of change, only change will be found."[12]

We are better off accepting change and ourselves as "works in progress." Subscribing to a paradigm that values the whole of life, that understands it as a continuous flow, and that does not wait for better, perfect times, we are bound to make better decisions. Yes, it does become harder to keep our mind-body moving as we age, just as other aspects of life become easier. It may be as difficult for us to learn something new and exercise as it is for children to sit down and learn multiplication tables. If we expect our children to meet their challenges, we should not pass up our own.

So adults, let us roll up our sleeves, go to work on ourselves, move our bodies, and move our minds—for our own and for other people's benefit! The question is not who can afford to work their minds and bodies, but who can afford not to do so? If we do not live life up, it will feel short to us even though in reality—thanks to medical advances—it has become long. Habits are good, but some need to be broken, replaced, or done away with. Putting movement back in our lives will help us enjoy this long life and increase our awareness of our participation in it.

Living for the Moment

Being devoted to the moment and really living it may be the aspect of lightheartedness that provides the greatest challenge for adults. I know many people who are familiar with Eastern concepts, practice meditation, and understand the importance of "now." Still, their reoccurring question is: "How can we fully experience being in the now when we have important goals to pursue?" It seems as if we cannot afford to take our eyes off the ball, especially when time is a factor. The "now" and the future seem irreconcilable.

We need to understand that immersion in the present does not preclude us from thinking about the future. As long as we surrender to the reality of the moment, which requires focused attention and trust, thoughts about the next moment are natural and not harmful. It is harmful, however, when our thoughts prevent us from focusing on the present moment or when we begin to resist the moment. It is not thinking but mindlessness that is the biggest thief that robs us of our lightheartedness.

Mindfulness gives us peace of mind because, while we recognize the bad that may lie ahead, we also recognize that we are woven into the strongest conceivable fabric called existence. Of course our heart cannot feel light when disaster strikes. As a Western psychologist, I would think it maladjusted to skip over all so-called negative feelings. Everything has its rightful place in an authentic life. Still, we must not become stuck in that place. Instead we must recognize how we are being helped by millions of real, simultaneous relationships. We keep living these working relationships and thus refrain from isolation. As we see ourselves in others, we are also more likely to reach out for help. Living in the awareness of being part of a wider, supportive system, we are more capable of dealing with the moment and moving on with natural optimism and confidence.

Just as thoughts about the future do not necessarily take away from the moment, neither do thoughts about the past. There is nothing wrong with having a functional memory and no Buddhist wishes us to lose this function. However many of us spend too much time living as if we are still in the past. When we try to make everything fit into our story, we gradually lose sight of the present moment. Children spoil the moment by regretting the immediate past ("If only I could have gotten that toy"); adults spoil it by wishing that long stretches of our past were different ("If only I could have had better parents; if only I could go back and make better decisions"). The longer we have dealt with the past, the more evanescent the present moment tends to feel. While time never rushes, we rush to conclusions and let the past speak with unquestioned authority.

It is actually quite easy to let the past overwhelm us and dictate what we should experience in the present. According to Nobel Prize winner Daniel Kahneman, we have a built-in bias that favors memory over immediate experience.[13] This is so even when our memory is faulty, for example when we attributed the wrong cause to a negative event. Our survival instincts steer us to safety to prevent our being sorry about our decisions. In alignment with Buddhists, Kahneman questions the value that we place on what is passed when it comes to happiness.

While most psychologists determine happiness by rating it in retrospect, Kahneman is curious about our "online" happiness, that is our present experience. He has found that it and our memories operate on different tracks; for example, we can be a lot happier right now than our so-perceived unhappy past. It does not come as a surprise then when Kahneman advises us to be attentive, or in Buddhist terms, to practice mindfulness.[14]

Zen Buddhist master Thich Nhat Hanh has been teaching mindfulness to Westerners for many years. When he speaks, he speaks quietly and slowly. Between his very consciously spoken words is plenty of space. These spaces have meaning because they allow for continuous connection with our Being and with Being in general. As we pay fierce attention to "now" the past stops haunting us and the present stops worrying us. We become peaceful, nourished, and light at heart. Thich Nhat Hanh gives this example:

> I did sitting meditation alone, and I was in touch with the moon, the sky, and the mountains. It was very nourishing, just sitting here with a cup of tea. After that I invited the brothers and sisters

to do walking meditation. The moon was still there in the sky, and I knew that going walking like that and getting in touch with the early morning, the sky, the moon, the mountains, the trees, and the animals that are alive in the mountains was good for me also.[15]

Meditation or content-free prayer is a fierce practice of mindfulness. We can also set aside time to practice mindfulness on a particular day, which is what observant Jews do on the Sabbath. They refrain from work and, if orthodox, from *anything* that involves work for the whole day.

Another way of practicing mindfulness is watching what we eat. My Orthodox Jewish friend revealed to me that eating kosher was his way of eating with awareness. Fasting and vegetarianism do the same for millions of people. Also, slow, conscious eating of unprocessed, simple foods is a good practice. Realizing the effects food has on our body—how it smells, tastes, and alters our mood as well as its connection to the sun, soil, and water—is a great way to increase our attentiveness to the moment.

There is a very effective Buddhist practice of mindfulness that, at first, does not at all sound like a practice that leads to lightheartedness. It is the practice of contemplating our own death. It is not helpful to imagine how painful death can be. Instead of focusing on the pain and loss, we must focus on the inevitability and unpredictability of death.

Try this exercise: Quiet your mind. Breathe in, thinking "life." Breathe out, thinking "death." Upon reaching an even breath, become aware of the fact that you will die. Realize the uncertainty of not knowing when you will die. Breathe into this uncertainty.

As you become conscious of the oneness of life and death and, simultaneously, of the contrast between life and death, you become thrust into life, which is the current moment where you belong.

Contemplating death causes us to gain perspective and deep appreciation. We cannot change death. But our perception of death intensifies the experience of life, which suddenly seems more special and its moments more worthy of savoring. In other words, understanding death is understanding life. We should all concur with comedian Joan Rivers, who replied to the question of what makes her happy: "At my age, breathing."[16]

Being Awed by the Miracle of Life

Children's mindfulness leads them to be impressed by the world and to discover the miracle of life. Discovering the miracle of life is a part of lightheartedness because it fills us with energy and wonder.

It is easy for children to become excited about their encounters with life when most of these encounters are novel. For adults, on the other hand, novelties are rare and routines take their place. Things become "old" easily. To counterbalance this ubiquitous progression into routine, some of us become compulsive novelty-seekers, chasing all kinds of adventure. But such seeking and chasing is incompatible with tranquility, a doorway to the Supreme Mode that is much more accessible and saner than any other. Thankfully, there is another, saner way to become alert and to instill awe.

Looking intently, and taking time to do so, is one of these ways. When we look at things or organisms as if we could look through them, we begin to see their *suchness*. Not only do their forms and colors become more striking, their very existence begins to speak to us and touch us deeply. We feel a strange kind of kinship with the Other. The more we focus and realize our kinship, the more we melt together with what we revere, until we no longer experience an inside and an outside. Gradually we live the wonder of oneness and feel it without naming or conceptualizing it.

For this way of looking to work and to make us lighthearted, we must make room for the experience. For most adults, the I-experience (ego) fills up most of the conscious mind. Generating thoughts and feelings for the sake of helping our genes survive produces this I-experience. The I-experience highlights not our commonalities but our differences, which helps us see and respond to our distinct interests and our distinct survival. As a result, the I-experience usually makes us forget who we are in essence, namely not at all distinct, but an interconnected part of the whole of life.

Unable to relate to the whole of life, we become defined by distinct facts and events that we often repeat unnecessarily in the form of routines. Of those distinct facts and events, we only pay attention to the seemingly useful ones. In Hinduism the world of facts and events is called *maya*, which basically means "to measure, form, build, or lay out a plan."[17] Maya isn't reality itself, but a way to make reality more "user friendly." Unfortunately, the I-experience relates only to the small world of useful pieces and—to the extent that we are identified with the I-experience—takes up all our mental space.

Before proceeding, let us concede once again that the fragile side of life necessitates that we relate to it as maya in the Basic Mode. I do not think we can sustain any growth if we dismiss or ignore our biological nature. We are not "inherently dysfunctional" for perceiving differences and for having I-experiences, as some suggest.[18] Instead we are bestowed with extremely valuable biological instincts and biases. They are imperfect, but essential. If we look at them as part of the whole of life as opposed to dysfunctions that we wish to eliminate, we refrain from creating the duality of "body" (that strives for survival) and "consciousness" (that just is, even without a body). In the Supreme Mode there are no such distinctions, as everything is interconnected and mirrored by the other.

In the words of Lao-tzu, there is no inherent difference between the body and the mind, between the inner and outer life, between external and internal reality. They are dependent on each other, bringing each other out. What matters is not even how strongly we feel about our reference points as long as we remain open-minded and "see." Even opposing things are related and inconceivable on their own. "The core and the surface are essentially the same" writes Lao-tzu.[19]

If we wish to describe the essence of who we are and flourish as human beings, we ought not to separate the surface from the core—the body from consciousness—but fill our mind with wonder, as Lao-tzu says in the poem. Out of an unwavering love for life as a whole, we become aware and make room for the miracle of life. Now we are in the best position to grow in a way that promotes happiness as well as survival, a way that curbs our instincts, works on our biases, fosters reason, unleashes our great compassion, and allows us to be present and still. Now when we look deeply, we are not just using a technique, but we open up to existence.

More and more people have the desire to open up and experience the miracle of life. Unlike earlier times, the miracle of life is not just reserved for a few artists, poets, and idealists as the

French philosopher Henri Bergson suggested. Thanks to the new accessibility of Eastern thought and the growing desire to feel one with God, we now have the tools to develop our human potential. We realize that through the process of attrition and the disempowerment of the I-experience, we begin to see the whole of life as opposed to only its pieces. Henri Bergson wrote:

> Deep in our souls we should hear the strains of our inner life's unbroken melody—a music that is ofttimes gay, but more frequently plaintive and always original. All this around and within us, and yet no whit of it do we distinctively perceive. Between nature and ourselves, nay, between ourselves and our own consciousness a veil is interposed.[20]

We can all learn to take off this veil, see the miracle, be awed by it, and listen and dance to its music. There is no reason why we—the working people, students, mothers, and fathers—should not also be able to realize that there is this music that invites us to swing along.

Simplemindedness

As adults, it is our job to look for answers to problems and offer solutions for future generations. Yet while this job is enormously important for our survival, knowing that we do not know what actually matters is just as important for our happiness. Doctor Faust, the protagonist of Johann Wolfgang von Goethe's famous tragedy, was plagued by "not knowing." He felt completely lost in the world. The tragedy shows what happens to us when we feel we must know everything before we can love life.

All his life Faust yearned to see the absolute reality, which he called the "secret force." He looked for it in scripture, but did not find it. He looked for it in the moral life, but did not find it there either. This was so dissatisfying to the poor professor, that he started looking for it in the immoral life. Let us hear from him:

> No dog would want to live longer this way!
> Hence I have yielded to magic to see
> Whether the spirit's mouth and might
> Would bring some mysteries to light,

That I need not with work and woe
Go on to say what I don't know;
That I might see what secret force
Hides in the world and rules its course.[21]

The tragedy describes Faust's downfall as he makes a pact with the devil and causes tremendous suffering: Faust makes false promises to a woman who trusts him completely, then he impregnates and abandons her, which indirectly causes the death of the woman and their unborn child. Obviously Faust never found the secret force by living immorally. Angels had to save him, but they did so only after Faust's miserable death. With all that Faust had done to innocent people, we may be surprised to learn that he was given access to heaven merely because of his striving. The angels, carrying his soul, exclaimed:

Who ever strives with all his power,
We are allowed to save.[22]

Apparently there was nothing wrong with Faust's ambition to gain insight. Quite the contrary; the angels were advised not to see heresy in his intent, but a key to heaven. This sort of striving is not the same as wanting to *have* more, but to *be* more; that is, to be more like God. Faust had the desire to recognize God, but he did so by looking for an identifiable object, an "it" with which he could identify. He tried to relate to God as an object, as opposed to the omnipresent process of Being.

As you may recall from chapter 9, intense striving also has a place in Eastern thought, namely in Zen Buddhism, where it is utilized as a propelling force to solve riddles (koans) that cannot be answered rationally. Having no "it" in his mind, but striving only to be with God, would have eventually disempowered the ego behind Faust's striving and led him to awareness. Awareness is seeing life as it is and recognizing that it is a miracle deserving of our love. The tragedy ends therefore with words of love. Faust's mistake was only that he had forgotten his own godly essence, his innermost, indivisible being that is his soul.[23] Such sin can be forgiven with unconditional love, symbolized in *Faust* by Jesus's mother Maria.[24]

If Faust had been more open to the simple experience of being that is already in communion with God, he would not have tried so hard to identify some thing outside of himself. There is no need to identify with any "it." To the extent that we do, we decrease our awareness and our ability to simply and directly experience life. If we, for example, are entirely identified with our beliefs, we close our minds to experiences that contradict these beliefs. My belief in being right in an argument can make me feel confident, but righteousness can also prevent me from hearing the other side. If we make any belief, possession, or another person our God, we block the path to unconditioned, simple experience.

As we learn again and again from Eastern thought, we must take a path that goes through our own experience and then beyond in order to become independent from whatever we cling to. Many of us make our religion's founders and teachers our God. While their examples, teachings, or in Eastern terms, dharma, may be shining lights, no one can enlighten us. We have to simplify our own minds and stop identifying with any thing it produces.

Ninth-century Chinese Zen master Lin-Chi (Rinzai) used these words to steer us away from identification with form:

> Whether you're facing inward or facing outward, whatever you meet up with, just kill it! If you meet a buddha, kill the buddha. If you meet a patriarch, kill the patriarch. . . . If you meet your parents, kill your parents. If you meet your kinfolk, kill your kinfolk. Then for the first time you will gain emancipation, will not be entangled with things, will pass freely anywhere you wish to go.[25]

It is apparent that Lin-Chi intends to shock us by using Buddha the person or Buddha the image as a metaphor for all form. It must have been his hope that we would become energized, maybe even defiant, and gather the courage we need to let go of fixed ideas and the sense of control they provide.

Indeed, it does take courage to retreat or leap into awareness, the simplest state of mind. We may fear that not identifying with anything will make us feel stupid or defenseless in the struggle for survival. Yet, as Eckhart Tolle says, we will be rewarded for letting go and leaping into what he calls the "light of consciousness" through which all experiences pass: "That is Being, that is the deeper, true I. When I know myself as that, whatever happens in my life is no longer of absolute but only of relative importance. I honor it, but it loses its absolute seriousness, its heaviness."[26]

We could also say that by diminishing our Faustian mind—the part in us that has to know "it" in order to feel good—we will increase our simple sense of Being. We must not wait for our death to experience our communion with Being, as Faust did. We can acknowledge our fears of not knowing and hang loose in the simplicity of Being. We can go through those fears and end up feeling freer and lighter than ever before. We can rest assured that in reality nothing has to die for us to see the secret force—except maybe the notion of this secret force. Giving way to the realization of the secret force is all that is required. Once given, we take things more lightly while remaining fully connected to reality until maybe, someday, we feel as if we have grown wings. When D. T. Suzuki was asked how it feels to have attained satori, he is said to have answered: "Just like ordinary, everyday experience, except about two inches off the ground."[27]

Simplemindedness means knowing the same kinds of aches and pains as everybody else, and using the same kind of cognitive tools as everybody else. Indeed, our intellect can be as complicated as we wish it to be. It is only that our ordinary experiences are lived from a different perspective, namely one of tranquility, receptivity, and reliance. From here we see beauty in this life. Whether there is hardship or not, we cannot help but love life for its beauty—humbly, simply, and devoutly.

Intuition

When we are free from the compulsion to dissect everything into nameable pieces, free to see the whole, we notice how things unfold and happen without willful interference. Not always to our liking, but surely without much effort and hesitation, nature lets things spring up and change. This is true also for our internal life. Most everything that happens within us happens spontaneously, almost magically, or *tzu-jan* ("of itself, so"), which is, as you may recall, the Chinese understanding of nature. In fact, even willfully produced thoughts are in part spontaneous since they spring up from consciousness.

As we grow older, most of us become less intuitive and make less use of our intuition. We gradually close ourselves off to gut reactions because we increasingly rely on form—on what we know and on the notion that we should know. While knowledge does not automatically hamper intuition—just think of Albert Einstein!—clinging to knowledge and the knowable most certainly does.

In contrast, age-appropriate ignorance in children almost guarantees greater access to intuition. Because children jump from one creative idea to another, we perceive them as more lighthearted than the creatures of habit that we often become. Children are spontaneous natural events, like hurricanes leaving nothing in place, like clouds painting the skies, and, luckily, more often than not, like rainbows enchanting us with fleeting appearances.

Nobody wills a rainbow into existence. Nobody paints the rainbow. There is no doer and there is hardly any effort involved when we are intuitive. This is why in Zen Buddhism, awareness, intuition, and effortlessness are closely related subjects. We cannot will ourselves to be intuitive, but we can allow it to happen, or better yet, invite it to happen and then wait. Intuition thrives when we relate to the world openly; that is, with few or no preconceived notions. I-experiences must not interfere too much. For example, when I want to write creatively, I find it's best if I start off with mostly vague ideas, which then develop freely as the ink flows over the paper.

Also, my ink flows easier when I see myself as a simple delivery person, a kind of servant, not at all preoccupied with my skill, worth, effort, or ambition. What needs to be in the forefront is basic trust of the simple good in me and in all that exists. I must understand deeply that the good that we may call God, Tao, or the Way of nature is our all-nurturing stream that runs through all cells and inhabits every space in between.

As the Trappist monk and great inter-religious scholar Thomas Merton explains:

> Instead of self-conscious cultivation of this good (which vanishes when we look at it and becomes intangible when we try to grasp it), we grow quietly in the humility of a simple, ordinary

life, and this way is analogous (at least psychologically) to the Christian "life of Faith." It is more a matter of believing the good than of seeing it as the fruit of one's effort.[28]

Instead of holding myself in high esteem, I hold writing, the written word, and above all the reader in high esteem.

If we wish to invite a greater intuitive sense, we must cultivate our talents with devotion and discipline. Letting ourselves become inspired by others is part of this cultivation. Yet in crucial moments, we need to relax our effort and let things happen to us. The provocative Chinese Zen master Lin-Chi warned us against too much effort, because it is effort that gets us in trouble in the first place. It takes effort to produce the I-experience that creates the illusion of separation from the whole. According to Lin-Chi, the trouble is that we refuse to accept that we ourselves generate the I-experience. Not doing anything would prevent us from generating anything, which he considered a good beginning:

> All the ten thousand kinds of contrived happenings operate in a place that is in fact no place. Therefore the more you search the farther away you get, the harder you hunt the wider astray you go. . . . As long as you seek something it can only lead to suffering. Better to do nothing.[29]

Paying attention to the moment, dressing, walking, sitting, unveils the "secret force," and with it our intuition.

Another piece of advice by Lin-Chi is to go against our fears and doubts. While acknowledgement of uncertainty in the world of form causes us to be receptive and aware, doubting our very awareness, which is free of form, hampers intuition. In Lin-Chi's words:

> Whatever confronts you, don't let yourself be imposed on. If you entertain even a moment of doubt, the devil will enter your mind. . . . Learn to put a stop to thoughts and never look for something outside yourselves. When an object appears, shine your light on it. Just have faith in this thing that is operating in you right now. Outside of it, nothing else exists.[30]

Letting go of fears and doubts is easier said than done. Many of our fear-based experiences are triggered instantaneously and do not, in my opinion, even need to be thought about. Years of early training have created habits in us, and breaking our habits can be enormously challenging, as Zen master Donald Gilbert said:

> Awakening is sudden, after which deliverance is gradual. Even after awakening, the accumulated karma (the old habit patterns) has a tendency to respond to circumstances in the old familiar ways. . . . Thus, it is after satori that the way to true practice is open.[31]

The good news is that we can untangle the mind and undo almost all damage, if this is what we set out to do. Some of us have to combat especially robust fears and doubts with therapeutic techniques, maybe even with psycho-pharmaceuticals. Others have to learn formal meditation techniques or deep, content-free prayer in order to train the mind to become tranquil. Many have to do all of the above and more, at different moments in life. Yet I am convinced that millions of us benefit already from:

- understanding that self-doubt (doubt of awareness) is counterproductive
- engaging in simple awareness exercises
- focusing on the spontaneously unfolding miracle of life

The more we become acquainted with simply being, the more we realize the greatness of life that unfolds within us, every minute we live, with every breath we take. When doubts emerge, we can notice them, bow to them in honor of their existence, and direct our attention to Being. Without fretting and pondering, we gradually and naturally learn how to respond to life creatively, "out of the box," with good common sense, from the gut, without trying hard, but lightly and right on target.

Aligning with Nature

When we experience ourselves as being totally in control of our lives, we overburden ourselves with responsibility. Yet this is exactly what our modern times suggest: our good thoughts, good intentions, good decisions are said to determine our fate, attract money, love, health, and happiness. But should we really be in the position to reign over our lives like that? If we indeed pulled all the strings, would we have time to notice anything else but these strings or what they are attached to? Aiming to control, we would lose the humility needed to accept imperfection as normal and lovable. Afraid of causing all personal misfortune ourselves, we would grow afraid of the slightest negative thought or negative intention—of our own shadow, to borrow a Jungian term—or we would be afraid of simply omitting positive thoughts.

Thankfully, nobody has ever been in total control, and things do just happen. It is good to take charge of what we can and change what we can. Yet we must not pretend that we are "on top of the world" when in reality we are just a part of it. Acknowledging that we are a part of a wide system invites us to relax our I-experience. We do not become inactive, but act without losing sight of the system. Instead of acting as if we were alone on this planet, we continuously notice our exchange with it, become clued in, informed, prompted, inspired, and guided by it.

If we come from awareness, we take on as much responsibility as is fitting. We keep our team in mind under all circumstances. Thus we would act much more effectively or, again in the words of philosopher Henri Bergson, we would "vibrate in perfect accord with nature."[32] Such action is less burdensome and conducive to lightheartedness. The Taoist and Zen term for such action is *wu-wei*,[33] which means "nonaction," or as the Soto school calls it, "motiveless action."[34] Acting in accord with nature is not inaction, but harmonic action. As Thomas Merton explains: "His [the sage's] action is not a violent manipulation of exterior reality, an 'attack' on the outside world, bending it to his conquering will: on the contrary, he respects external reality by yielding to it."[35]

Yielding to nature or reality can mean many things, from giving up utterly to working hard. Yet our action connected to the whole of reality will not be determined by rigid ideas originating from I-experiences of what that reality *should* be, but by the reality itself in which we are so deeply entrenched. Without holding reality in high regard, we will hardly be in the position to notice relevant changes, details, inconsistencies, or aspects and people we dislike. Open-minded, simpleminded, aware we must be, not naive, but wise like adults who love the world more than their image of it.

Only then can we be ready to act swiftly, appropriately, and constructively for the common good that is also our good.

Underlining the importance of promptness and readiness in nonaction (wu-wei), the Chinese Zen monk P'u-hua (or Fuke in Japanese d. 860 CE) who roamed through the streets ringing a handbell, said that he responds the way reality presents itself, whether it is negative or positive. We might conclude that one ought not to deny or ignore the bad, but to act in accordance with it. Therefore, one ought not to be swayed or seduced by the good, but act in accordance with it too. No matter from what direction life would hit us, we ought to strike back in alignment with it. P'u-hua continues:

> What comes from four corners or eight directions,
> I strike like a whirlwind.[36]

The notion of being in sync with reality, of "striking back as reality hits," to pick up P'u-hua's strong analogy, is well-known in martial arts. Fighters who give up active control while utilizing the existing energy of their opponents become far better fighters. For this to work, they must take in every move of the other person in one single perception, just like a mirror reflecting the many aspects of one image from moment to moment. Fighters who can do this look almost superhuman; hence the depictions in movies of Chinese martial-art fighters. They are light as feathers, uplifted not by their separate self, but by nature herself—our reality.[37]

To fully take in reality, we must be able to look beyond ourselves—beyond our wants, fears, expectations, personal preferences, and even beyond our dreams. We must, in a way, forget about ourselves, not like people who commit self-neglect or martyrdom, but like people who understand deeply that they are inseparable from the rest of the world. This sort of self-forgetting is really a self-finding—finding of a self that cannot be defined, a self that is related to the whole of life—that is, the True Self; that is, this life.

Mystics of all religions talk about self-forgetting, as did the famous Islamic philosopher and poet Jalal al-Din Rumi, who wants us to be just like melting snow, to wash ourselves of ourselves.[38] His poem has striking similarity to a Zen Buddhist poem by Basho who wrote:

The snow whisk,
sweeping sweeping,
forgets the snow.[39]

Forgetting about ourselves creates the necessary space or, as Buddhists say, "emptiness" in us to take in reality. As we take in this reality, we will not feel empty though, but fulfilled with that reality.

As soon as we awaken to being part of reality, we stop resisting what it brings to us. We no longer try to run away from the truths we encounter continually but feel propelled to act in accordance with them. No more lying to ourselves and willfully misunderstanding others! Once we open our eyes to being part of the oneness, we want to act our part. The ones who had preferred to strive against our civilization, begin to feel that oneness "accords with, and is the source and base of civilization."[40] When we realize how wonderfully stuck we are in the game of life, we will have a much better time playing it. After all, it is a lot more enjoyable when we play the game with open eyes. Instead of charging at the goal like a mad person, trying to call all the shots, or feeling left out, we will actually catch and throw the ball.

Wholeheartedness
Accepting the world wholeheartedly comes easily to children because they do not yet know how unfair and painful life can be. Embracing life while having the ability to understand complex matters and bring about change is *our* challenge.

When someone who was dear to my family died, my son remained relatively lighthearted. "Don't worry Mama, tomorrow he will be back," he assured me. For children, ignorance *is* bliss. I, on the other hand, was devastated and overwhelmed with grief. In the midst of my grief I asked myself if I had sadness *in* me, or if I *was* sadness. Despite maintaining this watchful eye on my reactions, I was sadness. And that is just how it is when we have to let go of someone we truly, deeply love.

When we love—not spiritually, but passionately—we are bound to feel strongly on occasion. There is nothing wrong with earthly love. It is not pure, but it can be a deeply fulfilling part of life. In general, when we care deeply about something or somebody in particular, we can temporarily be overcome by particular experiences, such as disappointment and anger. However, as long as our feelings pass through a fully developed consciousness that can focus and maintain awareness of Being, strong feelings only add to the good and full life.

For example, although I occasionally get angry with my husband, I keep an eye on all my feelings and on what the relationship needs. I may be experiencing strong feelings, but I do not have to forget about the bigger picture of our love and our common interest. I can observe the particular experience of anger but not lose touch with the rest of myself.

A fully developed consciousness can shift its focus swiftly from the defined to the undefined realm, from the Basic Mode to the Supreme Mode. We rely on such a consciousness even when we are not aware of it. Until we die, none of us becomes suddenly severed from our consciousness. Our consciousness is always there for us. What distinguishes people with a fully developed consciousness from people without one is not whether they have certain experiences, but what they do with them. If we resist, hang on to, or become lost and confused in them, our consciousness is not fully developed. If we experience deeply, but we stay clear, tranquil, and remain ready to move on, our consciousness is fully developed.

A fully developed consciousness depends on our love for the whole of life and on the habit of realizing our participation in it. It usually means that our experiences are not overwhelming and are more often than not positive. On the other hand, during times of unusually powerful emotions, we can still accept experiences that are overwhelming or negative. Alan Watts wrote that realizing our participation in life, which is what Easterners call having nondual awareness, helps us in all our affairs:

> In this state man is supremely happy because even though he
> may be involved in a conflict with pain and evil, even though he

may feel the very human emotions of fear, anger, and love, he lives his life with a whole-heartedness and abandon born of the understanding that all things are fundamentally acceptable.[41]

We cannot always be in the Supreme Mode, but good access to it determines whether or not we suffer unnecessarily, bounce back swiftly, and feel light while living. Accepting every part of life wholeheartedly is seeing essential goodness, God, or the Tao in everything. Deep spiritual joy and gratitude arise when we see how good existence is even when we feel or deem something "good" or "bad." Not distinguishing on the deepest level of the human experience reconnects us to the lightheartedness and thus the wholeheartedness of children. "Like an innocent child," as Jack Kornfield puts it, "we can rejoice in life itself, in being alive."[42]

Smiles, Nonsense, and Laughter

Siddhartha Gautama, the Buddha, was concerned with suffering and how to end it. He was a remarkable person, practicing meditation, living as a monk, delivering serious sermons. Why then is Buddha so often depicted as less than serious; that is, smiling and laughing? Apparently, he was setting an example. We are to smile and laugh with him. But why?

To answer this question, it is beneficial to clarify why human beings smile and laugh in the first place. Understanding the biological origins of positive nonverbal displays is helpful in revealing the Buddha.

Human beings are interdependent, social animals who rely on bonding with others. Displaying amiable, nonthreatening expressions such as a smile is thus essential to our survival. Nonverbal expressions are means of communication that we tend to give more credence to than the more voluntary verbal means. Raising the corners of our mouths is distinctly different from other nonverbal expressions such as anger, disgust, or indifference. Therefore the smile says quickly and effectively: "All is good and well." Not only do we communicate this message to others, but also to ourselves. When we smile, we actually reinforce our internal experience in a feedback loop. And when we put on a happy face—the kind that gives us wrinkles around our eyes—this internal communication has the power to improve how we feel.[43]

The so-called social smile helps us deal with the complexities of our daily split-second interactions, which enhances our happiness indirectly. The so-called felt smile, the "Duchenne smile," directly enhances our happiness.[44] Both the social and the felt smile intend to say that "All is good and well," and cause us to lighten up others and ourselves.

Laughter has yet another biological origin. Researchers have asked themselves in what way the physical arousal with repetitive vocalizations ("Ha-Ha-Ha") is sensible behavior. At first, laughter seems like a rather superfluous indulgence of human beings, but not to neurobiologist Robert R. Provine. He points out that laughter evolved from tickling and playing. According to Provine, laughter developed from a ritualized panting sound of rowdy play triggered by tickle: "In the great apes, laughter was emancipated from its original context in the labored breathing of play, the heavy panting now signaling playful intent or anticipation, even when the ongoing level of activity does not demand labored breathing."[45] From this we can conclude that laughter evolved from the ape's panting to the "sophisticated" human "Ha-Ha-Ha."

To appreciate the significance of this conclusion, we must understand that play is essential to all higher developed animals. It provides the many opportunities we need to practice complex living. The lion cub has to play at hunting with its mother before it goes out into the wild. We have to play house before we start a family, and we have to play competitive games before we start a career. Both tickling and laughter arouse our body. Thus, so Provine says, playing is fun, which is an important motivational factor in nature.

Finally we have to clarify why we laugh when there is nobody to tickle and play with us. Play for humans is not limited to the physical realm. The idea of playing is enough to make us giggle. From idea of play to verbal play and humor is but a small evolutionary step. And this is where it all begins to make sense. To a Buddha, life is *lila*, which is Sanskrit for play and sport.[46] Because Siddhartha Gautama's faith was based in what we now call Hinduism, he considered all of the world's hustle and bustle as a wonderful, sometimes painful, but always divine play.

In this reality, which is the outcome of creative play by the Absolute Reality (Brahman), the Hindu Gods seem to play hide-and-seek. For example, the goddess Bhudevi hides as Earth, and Ganga as the river Ganges.[47] We people are left to realize that deeper reality. Scholar of Hinduism Klaus Klostermeier explains that life is considered a game in Hinduism because there was no need for God to create the universe. The creation is more of a divine pastime. The game that life is begins with the God Brahma and ends with Shiva.[48] Krsna, who is a manifestation of Vishnu, sustains the game and plays it well. His divine playfulness (lila) is indicated by his relationship with the *gopis*, especially with the most devoted one named Radha, who became his consort.

In this Hindu story line, we all make good and bad moves in this play depending on our awareness of the Absolute Reality. In Western terms, we could say that we live our lives well when we stay connected with what matters on the deepest level. As we move, life moves. Nothing is planned out in advance in the game of life, because everything depends on our moves and on life's moves. Life itself does not have a definable goal.

The idea of life having no other point but itself is shared by mystics such as the medieval priest Meister Eckhart:

> For if Life were questioned a thousand years and asked: "Why live?" and if there were an answer, it could be no more than this: "I live only to live!" And that is because Life is its own reason for being, springs from its own Source, and goes on and on, without ever asking why—just because it is life. Thus, if you ask a genuine person, that is, one who acts [uncalculatingly] from his heart: "Why are you doing that?"—he will reply in the only possible way: "I do it because I do it!"[49]

We may give our individual life a purpose, a sense, but at the same time we need to understand that life by itself has no sense. It is the "no sense," or nonsense that we must respond to with love and devotion. Lightheartedness comes about by letting life or God unveil itself while playing the game. When we become good players *in* life, as opposed to being passive or clutching to egotistical ideas *about* life, we become content. The moment we hang onto our "creaturely ideas," so Meister Eckhart says, God fades away.[50] After having discovered the art of no longer clutching to form, but of living from awareness, Buddha lived life in the affirmative. This means that ultimately what brings out his smiles and laughter is awareness.

Therefore awareness is, once again, key to happiness. Awareness makes us realize that the game of life is "all good and well" despite its essential senselessness. On the other hand, our actions should make sense, unless it is time to be silly. We tend to make sense as long as we understand the dynamic nature of the game of life. If we become rigid, our game is somewhat off because we are directly juxtaposing this nature.

When we become aware of rigidity, we expose and hopefully correct it after shaking and waking ourselves up with laughter. To a certain extent, our very survival depends on our realignment with the flow of life. The philosopher Henri Bergson points out that we laugh at rigidity because we need "the wide-awake adaptability and the living pliableness of a human being."[51] Bergson gives the example of a man who stumbles and falls as he fails to adjust his gait to the road's conditions. He explains: "Through lack of elasticity, through absentmindedness and a kind of physical obstinacy, as a result, in fact, of rigidity or of momentum, the muscles continued to perform the same movement when the circumstances of the case called for something else."[52]

Laughter can therefore be used intentionally to point to rigidities and to bring about insight. This is done particularly well and often in Zen Buddhism. Zen master Donald Gilbert, who teaches by means of cartoons, points out that:

> Humor is a key to knowing because it depends on intuitive flashes that reveal the Truth and the incongruities in the subject at hand. Humor is a romp: it is open and fun-filled. It is in this attitude of openness that one can participate and have flashes of insight.[53]

The "incongruities" are the interruptions in the flow of life. Once we become aware of them, we can laugh and loosen the rigidities. Thus we go from laughter to insight, from "Ha-Ha" to "Ah-Ha."[54] Writer and minister Conrad Hyers calls the humor in

Zen "comic midwifery."[55] As you will see in the following examples, Zen anecdotes are full of laughter.

Zen masters are often referred to as fools, even if they do not take the name of one, as Japanese master Ryokan actually did.[56] Yūan-wu, who started using the anecdotes for the puzzling koan method,[57] spoke of the legendary Indian monk Bodhidharma as "this fellow who talks nonsense."[58] Surely Bodhidharma would not have minded! When he arrived in China, the Emperor Wu asked Bodhidharma about the primary truth of the holy teachings. All he replied was: "Vastly empty and nothing holy."[59] We are invited to laugh along, because we probably would have tried to gain the emperor's respect had we been in the Bodhidharma's shoes. Eventually—and this is the hope of many Zen teachings—we learn to poke fun at ourselves and stop taking ourselves too seriously. With our laughter, we demote the I-experience to "nothing." And right at that instant, we may realize that "nothing" was disrespected after all.

Often Zen men and women induce laughter in doing or saying something silly. One of my favorite anecdotes is when master Ho-shan (Kwasan) was asked by a monk what "truly transcending" is. Instead of explaining himself, Ho-shan pretended to play a drum, saying: "Dong, dong, doko-dong, doko-dong!" He replied the same way when asked to explain the "truth itself" as well as the "one who is neither mind nor Buddha." Suzuki interprets this nonsense:

> It is in fact not Kwasan himself that plays the drum and laughs, it is the "truth itself," it is the "one who is neither mind nor Buddha," it is "that which has truly transcended," that plays the drum and laughs. Is it not really good to see that each, though differently designated, goes through this wonderful performance?[60]

When the I-experience is not in the way of life, life is original and surprises even us. Ho-shan was probably amused by his own performances. He did not overthink any question, but let the answer jump out of his gut like a jack-in-the-box. When we go with the flow of life, as opposed to standing in its way, our mind is quick to respond.

Sometimes the quick response is noticing the (only) good in the bad. There is a very famous Zen story in which a man is chased by a tiger. To save himself, the man grabs a root and swings to the other side of a cliff. There, another tiger awaits him. To make matters worse, two little mice begin gnawing at the root he is hanging on to. The man is terrified. Suddenly he detects a strawberry growing close by, which he picks and eats with delight, thinking to himself, "Ah, how delicious it is."

Zen practitioners realize that life is full of surprises, and because life is not dull we must not be dull either. The old masters used to throw things at each other, poke each other, yell, bark, and respond to riddles with riddles. Zen master Sengai underlined his extraordinarily happy calligraphies with little poems. One of these calligraphies depicts a *go* game. Like in chess, players of go find themselves cornered ("in the midst of death") and can only free themselves via a complex solution. Sengai writes: "There are things even the wise fail to do, while the fool hits the point. Unexpectedly, discovering the way to life in the midst of death, he bursts out into hearty laughter."[61]

Why the laughter? It is funny to recognize that solutions are found in the most unlikely places. We cannot think them up, but they come to us, springing up like jacks-in-the-box, as long as we keep our eyes wide open to all parts of all places. Embracing the interplay of everything, we become better players, and we also become thoroughly entertained.

Sometimes our awareness of the flow in life makes us keen, fierce, and strong doers. Other times we totally surrender and let ourselves go. It is then that we abandon ourselves to experience, and let the moment do to us whatever it wants.[62]

Here are some final anecdotes, both about the great scholar of Eastern thought Alan Watts. Toward the end of his life, when he was just about to impress with his intellect, he expressed himself in a slightly different fashion to his friend Al Chungliang Huang: "Yah . . . Ha . . . Ho . . . Ha! Ho . . . La Cha Om Ha . . . Deg deg te re . . . Ta De De Ta Te Ta . . . Ha Te Te Ha Hom . . . Te Te Te . . . " and went dancing off with his friend.[63] Alan Watts's daughter Jano described him as "Never dull. He was a man full of fun and surprises." The night before his death, he played with balloons that reminded him of his spirit leaving his body.[64]

So what can you learn from this inquiry into smiles, nonsense, and laughter? Obviously awareness is the key to lightheartedness and thus to the Supreme Mode, but it can hardly be prescribed. You, like everybody else, will have to find your own way to lighten your heart and learn to be seriously silly at the right times. To foster your humor, it helps to understand that life is a game. It requires you to tend to important business with great skill, but without thinking of yourself as too important. And do not forget to laugh at your own rigidities. It is easy to find someone else funny. Yet the best lessons are learned from exposing and laughing about your own absentmindedness. You will find that your I-experiences will decrease in frequency and intensity at the same rate as your awareness increases. Such laughter is exceptionally freeing, catapulting you right into the Supreme Mode and away from the ground.

SUPREME MODE EXERCISES— LIGHTHEARTEDNESS

Move Your Mind-Body
- What would you tell your children if they told you that it is too hard to go to school and learn new things?
- Write into your schedule when you will exercise and when you will learn something new for yourself. Next to the entries, write why you should follow through even if you find it hard.
- Read *Spark* by John J. Ratey, MD, et al. to become educated in the science of exercise and the brain, and visit the resource page on andreapolard.com for more information on exercise and nutrition.

Practice Mindfulness
Only if you can forget about your goals and love the moment for what it is right now can you be lighthearted. Take time out during your busy day and pay attention to every detail of the present moment: your breath, any passing sounds, the way you hold your fingers, what exactly you see, taste, and smell.

Unwavering Love for the Whole of Life

Life cannot always be "happy-go-lucky." We must mourn our dead, protest, bear pain, seek solutions under pressure, get our kids to eat vegetables. Nevertheless, we must fundamentally be in love with life. What would help you to embrace the whole of life despite its pains and fragility? What would you advise your adult children if they came to you for advice on unwavering love for the whole of life? How can you see the miracle in all life?

_____

_____

_____

_____

Foster Your Humor

We are not all stand-up comedians, thank God, but we can all foster our humor. Some of us need to simply give ourselves permission to laugh. Some have to dig deeper to find out why we look at the world, including ourselves, too seriously. All of us need to come down from our high horse! Are you, for example, too smart or too important to laugh? Do you feel responsible for the world's problems, or are you simply too sad to laugh? Do you feel you were wronged and must punish your environment? Whatever it is, commit yourself to the practice of poking fun at yourself.

Learn to Be Silly

- Watch silly movies like *Young Frankenstein, The Producers, Zoolander, Bowfinger, Heartbreakers, Borat, The Blues Brothers, There's Something About Mary, A Fish Called Wanda,* or *Airplane;* or make one yourself.
- Have a singing/karaoke contest.
- Make faces in the mirror.
- Play on the floor with the kids or the dogs.
- Go to an amusement park; ride a roller-coaster.
- Put on a Halloween costume. Let your kids dress you up on Sunday afternoons.
- Produce a show for children or ask them to produce one for you.

Conclusion

A Synthesis of Western and Eastern Thought: The Theory of Elastic Consciousness

Make everything as simple as possible, but not simpler.
ALBERT EINSTEIN

And if the dialogue proceeds well, the final synthesis
will be greater than, and different from, what any
of the participants initially brought to the table.
HOWARD E. GARDNER

My inspiration for writing this book came from observing that most people's knowledge about happiness is by and large rudimentary, and that the so-called experts do not help by oversimplifying the subject. My premise is that we need to honor the complexities of life and reflect them in a comprehensive understanding of happiness.

To provide such an understanding, I found that the common denominator in a wide variety of accounts of happiness was the experience of participation in life. Being happy in this sense means rising above the experience of self and tapping willingly into the stream of life that takes us along for a ride. Happiness goes beyond "feeling good" and allows for negative states of mind, which do—and to some extent, must—occur in the authentically lived life.

To do justice to the complexities of life, I further examined the diverse and strangely paradoxical accounts of happiness. It became apparent that they could be divided into two groups, pointing to two mental modes in which we experience our participation. They are the Two Wings of Happiness.

The first one is active and based on life's fragility. It is the Basic Mode where we focus on and strive toward the seemingly distinct, definable realm of life, such as an external goal or another person. Experiences in this mode require effort. The other mode is nonactive and based on life's strength. It is a Supreme Mode where we focus on the whole of Being in which we all partake, a focus that has no clear distinctions but is consciousness itself. Once learned, this focus takes little or no effort in the usual sense and gives us strength and nourishment.

It is tempting but ultimately unhelpful to explain happiness from only one mode. For example, proponents of the active approach to happiness claim that awareness is really an objective and that the path to happiness is packed with effort and action. Even though there is truth in this belief—for example, many Eastern religious practices require discipline—such claims are flawed. Enlightened states of mind are neither definable nor can we get there with willful desire. Taking action is supposed to become effortless (as in Tibetan Buddhism)—wu-wei that is non-action or motiveless action (as in Zen Buddhism and Taoism). To explain awareness with the goal-oriented approach of Westerners therefore misses the point.

On the other hand, proponents of Eastern approaches to happiness often insist that all we need is awareness, after which everything else falls into place. Skill building is mostly an afterthought, if mentioned at all. The monks and nuns for whom most of Eastern religious literature was written were to lay aside their ambitions, which are essential for success in careers, sports, and games. And if we wish for enduring and enriching relationships, we must have passion and communication skills for which a peaceful heart may be a basis, but is no substitute.

BALANCING THE TWO MODES

Neither Western nor Eastern thought alone can teach us to respond well to life as it really happens, and neither one alone lends itself to full life participation. To illustrate the importance of practicing both, the active Basic Mode and the nonactive Supreme Mode, let me share a story told by Paulo Coelho in his book *The Alchemist*.

There once was a young man who wished to learn the secret

of happiness from a wise man. Much to the young man's surprise, he found the wise man busily engaged with merchants. After a long wait, the young man asked for advice, whereupon the wise man told him to look at the wise man's magnificent palace and to return in two hours, all the while holding a spoon with two drops of oil without spilling them.

Upon the young man's return, he had nothing to report about the splendor of the palace because his sole focus had been on the drops of oil. The wise man sent him out again with the same assignment. This time the young man marveled at the beauty of the palace while forgetting all about the drops of oil.

The wise man gave him this advice: "The secret of happiness is to see all the marvels of the world and never to forget the drops of oil in the spoon."[1]

Using my terminology, the secret of happiness is to focus on the miracle of life in the Supreme Mode without neglecting our primary pursuits in the Basic Mode. If we are committed to making happiness a priority, time and experience will help us access the two modes in a balanced way. We will improve our relationship to the All by learning to relate to the many, and vice versa. Eventually we will balance our ambition with tranquility; our self-confidence with reliance on something larger; our competence with the receptive state of not knowing; and our serious transactions with Buddha's lighthearted laughter. Eventually we will develop a consciousness capable of narrowing and broadening its attention flexibly and as needed for full life participation.

THE UNION OF THE TWO MODES

For the purpose of clarification and training, I have introduced the Basic Mode and the Supreme Mode separately. However, the more we learn to access the two modes, the more we realize that they are by no means mutually exclusive or even two distinct states. In reality, the two seemingly opposed Basic and Supreme Modes overlap, interplay, and complement each other. We only have one consciousness. There are no completely distinct areas of the brain, only different patterns of neural activity.

Let me therefore conclude with a simple (but not too simple) theory of happiness that incorporates both mental modes. It is the Theory of Elastic Consciousness, which helps integrate the information we've discussed about the various types of engaging experiences in the Basic and the Supreme Mode.

Instead of looking at the Basic Mode and the Supreme Mode as mutually exclusive mental modes, it is more accurate to say that between focusing on a so-perceived distinct Other and focusing on nondual Being, there are countless possibilities. For example, we can focus on a goal or person with varying intensity. This happens as we focus and withdraw our attention from different focal points slowly or continuously, as opposed to abruptly or disjointedly.

Our consciousness can reach outside of itself with varying degrees of intensity and varied focus. The following diagram indicates the varying degrees of focus while in the Basic Mode.

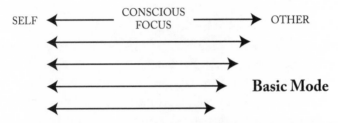

In the Basic Mode we focus on the Other
(other beings or external goals) with varying degrees of intensity.

Although fierce attention to a focal point is the more optimal state of mind, it would tire us out too much if we performed at this level all day long. As always, perfection is for the gods, and imperfection the human condition. Also, if it wasn't for the full range of focused attention, we couldn't tell the difference between feeling in or outside the stream of life. Finally, variety is part of our biology and something without which Mother Nature could not do.

However, the more our consciousness withdraws its attention from a particular Other, the lower the level of active participation. If we become inactive for too long, we will eventually reach a critical point where we deaden our minds. In other words, if we continually interact only loosely with the external or seemingly discrete world while remaining unaware of Being, the rubber band becomes limp. Instead of recuperating we become sluggish and our minds too muddled to experience our participation in life. Unfortunately this is the fate of too many people who resort to surfing television channels and computer sites or other mind-less acts of consumption. When we no longer feel like exerting ourselves, there comes a point at which we must refocus on Being.

Just as in the Basic Mode, our consciousness in the Supreme Mode can be more or less focused on itself; that is, on Being. The experience of feeling one with life without interfering cannot always be optimal. We simply do not always feel the same degree of being one with life. It is possible to feel continuously awake and enlightened, but the extent to which we experience this must vary. Even the most aware person must sleep and rest. Most of us enjoy occasional distractions. One moment we could enjoy the sight of a bird passing by; in another moment we could pay closer attention to the bird in its environment, feel a glimpse of nature's balance, or feel one with the bird in its balance. All degrees of focus on Being will make us feel somewhat part of life.

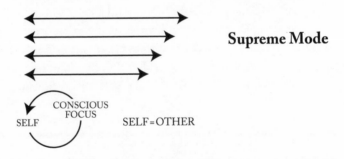

Supreme Mode

In the Supreme Mode, we focus our consciousness onto itself and experience nondual awareness with varying degrees of intensity.

We experience ourselves overwhelmingly as participants in life when our consciousness is fully elastic, which means it can enjoy all degrees of attention on either an Other (another being or external goal) or on itself (Being). Preferably we have numerous peak experiences in either mode, but mostly there will be varying degrees as well as blends of experiences.

Let me give you an example of blended experiences that you've probably had yourself in a particularly good relationship. When we connect skillfully with each other in the Basic Mode, we can also slip into an experience of oneness in the Supreme Mode. Moments like these are more likely to happen when we are not under time-pressure[2] and feel mutually empowered.[3] Greek philosopher Epicurus wrote more than two thousand years ago that friendships can "help us obtain that quietness of mind and body which is the supreme pleasure."[4] The quietness of mind comes from reaching out to the other first, followed by mutual understanding and reciprocity on many levels.[5]

Special nerves in our brain, so-called mirror neurons, are in part responsible for the experience of mutuality or oneness. When we are focused on someone else, these neurons fire in concert with the other person's mirror neurons.[6] Instead of relating to the other as an object, we make him or her part of us and engage in what philosopher Martin Buber referred to as an "I-thou relationship."[7] Also, our boundaries with one another can be blurred in the intense feeling of romantic love that is "bigger than both of us" according to Eugene D'Aquili and Andrew Newberg.[8]

Let us now look at what I call the elastic consciousness. This is the whole spectrum of a consciousness, a consciousness capable of both actively relating to the world and understanding its existing relationship with it not just optimally, but in various degrees of intensity.

THE ELASTIC CONSCIOUSNESS

An elastic consciousness allows us not only to alternate between and within the modes, but also to focus on a worthy, external goal or another person while maintaining some awareness of Being. In other words, it is possible to bring the Supreme Mode into our Basic Mode; it is possible to feel our connection with Being while we are exerting ourselves. When we feel continuously supported by a strong sense of Being in the Supreme Mode and use ample skills in the Basic Mode, we can take on the hardest task and solve the hardest crisis. Having developed an elastic consciousness, we never feel as if we were standing apart from our own lives. We continue to fly whether we need to fly high or low. We can live happy lives, no matter what.

A balance between the Basic Mode and the Supreme Mode comes about naturally and gradually after (1) committing ourselves to happiness as opposed to merely surviving well, (2) giving extra energy to our body with good nutrition and exercise to afford the luxury that happiness is, (3) understanding both modes, and (4) practicing both modes.

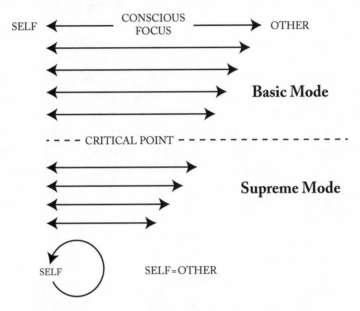

The elastic consciousness is capable of keeping its focus with changing intensity, shifting from external to internal focal points, from experiencing various degrees of tension between "self" and Other in the Basic Mode, as well as various degrees of nonduality in the Supreme Mode.

We may also have to continuously remind ourselves that the pursuit of happiness is a good moral choice. Unlike perpetual pleasure seeking in the survival mode, happiness is not only good for us individually, but for our wider communities as well. When we feel ourselves as part of life, we wish to create, love, and give. There is nothing wrong with spreading our wings and flying all we want. As Barbra Streisand puts it in one of her songs: we don't have to settle for only "a piece of sky."[9]

Yet we must never forget how tempting it is to drift off into the egocentric, consumerist approach that is currently spreading throughout the world. Our "wanting more" must not be reduced to wanting more objects, more recognition, more security, more possessions, all of which are really settling for only "a piece of sky." It is the flight we should aspire to, both toward something or someone that is worthy in the Basic Mode, and for its very own sake in the Supreme Mode.

To avoid drifting off into survival mode and to promote elasticity in consciousness, we need to watch over ourselves and maintain a relatively high level of awareness. While we cannot always sink into our awareness like we do in the Supreme Mode, we can always check whether or not our actions and nonactions are in accord with happiness. Happiness will always be based in a choice. We depend on our awareness to stay on the right track and to live all degrees in both the Basic Mode and the Supreme Mode of our consciousness.

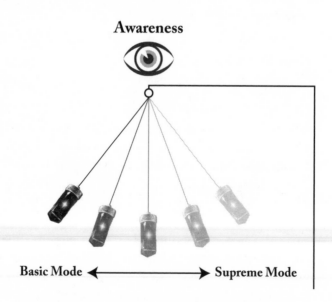

Awareness

Basic Mode ◀——————▶ Supreme Mode

Awareness of our Basic Mode and Supreme Mode
helps our consciousness stay elastic.

I trust that by learning about the two modes of consciousness and by practicing them, you too will be visited frequently by the guest of happiness. Just do not try to use force, and try to refrain from grasping. Instead, give kind attention to your life so that you do not destroy the "winged life,"—as William Blake advises in his poem "Eternity"—but remain open to the experience of joy always.

Notes

INTRODUCTION

1. The two modes are complementary, just as the yin-yang polarity. The symbol
   ☯ is rooted in Chinese philosophy. Alan Watts explains that the Chinese do
   not view light and darkness, life and death, good and evil, positive and negative in conflict. They "are all different aspects of one and the same system, and
   that the disappearance of either one of them would be the disappearance of
   the system." Alan Watts and Al Chung-Liang Huang, *Tao: The Watercourse
   Way* (New York: Pantheon Books, 1975), 20. Later in the same book, he says,
   "The yin-yang principle is not . . . what we would ordinarily call a dualism, but
   rather an explicit duality expressing an implicit unity" (26). The two mental
   modes, the Basic Mode and the Supreme Mode, are such a unity.

2. Happiness and unhappiness are not mutually exclusive categories. Diane
   Swanbrow, "The Paradox of Happiness," *Psychology Today* 23, (1989):
   37–39.

3. This is in reference to the song *A Piece of Sky*, which is sung by Barbra
   Streisand in the movie *Yentl*, directed by Barbra Streisand (1983).

Part 1

HAPPINESS AND THE TWO MODES OF CONSCIOUSNESS

CHAPTER 1—THE TWO WINGS OF HAPPINESS

1. Barbara Frederickson, "What Good are Positive Emotions?" *Review
   of General Psychology* 2 (1998): 300–319. Also, Barbara Frederickson
   and Thomas Joiner, "Positive Emotions Trigger Upward Spirals toward
   Emotional Well-being," *Psychological Science* 13 (2002): 172–75.

2. Deborah Danner, David A. Snowdon, and Wallace V. Friesen, "Positive
   Emotions in Early Life and Longevity: Findings from the Nun Study,"
   Journal of Personality and Social Psychology 80 (2001): 804–13.

3. Economist Richard Layard points out, "Happiness is that ultimate goal
   because, unlike other goals, it is self-evidently good. If we are asked why
   happiness matters, we can give no further, external reason. It just obviously does matter. As the American Declaration of Independence says,
   it is a 'self-evident' objective." Richard Layard, *Happiness: Lessons from a
   New Science* (New York: Penguin, 2005), 113.

4. Michael R. Cunningham, "Measuring the Physical in Physical Attractiveness: Quasi-experiments on the Sociobiology of Female Facial Beauty," *Journal of Personal & Social Psychology* 50 (1986): 925–35.

5. Aristotle (384–322 BC), the famous philosopher of ancient Greece, son of Nichomachus, student of Plato, and teacher of Alexander the Great, believed that happiness was the ultimate goal in a human life. All other goals would serve happiness. Many people nowadays reject happiness as a selfish endeavor. Aristotle saw no ethical conflict though. For him the community came first, and the individual second. However, happiness would always start with the individual. Happiness is virtuous activity that fulfills our proper function in life. Aristotle wrote that "we may almost say that the great majority of mankind are agreed about this; for both the multitude and persons of refinement speak of it as happiness, and conceive 'the good life' or 'doing well' to be the same thing as 'being happy.'" Aristotle, *The Nicomachean Ethics*, trans. H. Rackham (London: Harvard University Press, 1934), Book I, iii. 8-iv. Furthermore "the Good of man is the active exercise of his soul's faculties in conformity with excellence or virtue, or if there be several human excellences or virtues, in conformity with the best and most perfect among them." (Book I, vii. 15) But in order to be happy one would need a whole list of things: sufficient goods, health, opportunity to practice one's excellence and virtue, friends, and good luck (Book I, x. 14–xi). Definition of happiness, (Book I, vii. 13–16).

6. Martin Seligman and Mihaly Csikszentmihalyi, two of the founders of positive psychology (which postulates that focusing on psychological disorders and suffering does not lead to happiness), write about the importance of positive institutions in Martin Seligman and Mihaly Csikszentmihalyi, "Positive Psychology. An Introduction," *American Psychologist* 55, No.1 (2000): 5–14.

7. Taking the road less traveled pertains to many situations, particularly those of immigrants. Immigrants who leave their safe harbor frequently encounter unexpected hardship. The majority of people usually prefer to stay in the homeland. As my research revealed, voluntary immigrants are more interested in freedom and opportunity than in security. Andrea Floren Polard, "Leaving the Circle: The Phenomenon of Emigration," a dissertation research project submitted in partial satisfaction of the requirements for the degree of Doctor of Psychology in Clinical Psychology at Ryokan College, Los Angeles, California (1998).

8. For more about comparing notions in regard to happiness see Ed Diener, Marissa Diener, and Carol Diener, "Factors Predicting the Subjective Well-being of Nations," *Journal of Personality and Social Psychology* 69 (1995): 851–62.

9. For more information about societal change, see Layard, *Happiness*.

10. Gregg Easterbrook wonders why people do not feel happier even though they live longer, healthier, and richer lives. See Gregg Easterbrook, *The Progress Paradox: How Life Gets Better While People Feel Worse* (New York: Random House, 2004). In this context it is also interesting that according

to a study, lottery winners are no happier than before their win after a period of adjustment. P. Brickman, D. Coates, and R. Janoff-Bulman, "Lottery Winners and Accident Victims: Is Happiness Relative?" *Journal of Personality and Social Psychology* 36 (1978): 917–27. Also a good article about prosperity and happiness is Shlomo Maital, "The Pursuit of Happiness: If We're So Rich, Why Aren't More of Us Satisfied?" *Barron's* (May 1, 2000): 70.

11. Although happiness has become an important subject, I think that our highest priority ought to be the reduction of suffering in poor, devastated, and discriminated-against communities and countries. Happiness will evade us if we remain indifferent to the suffering of others.

12. Anaïs Nin as quoted in Dan Millman, *Living on Purpose: Straight Answers to Universal Questions* (Novato: New World Library, 2000), 4.

13. Darrin M. McMahon, *Happiness: A History* (New York: Grove Press, 2006).

14. Paul Watzlawick, *The Situation Is Hopeless But Not Serious: The Pursuit of Unhappiness* (New York: W.W. Norton, 1993).

15. To learn more about the science of exercise and the brain, read John J. Ratey and Eric Hagerman, *Spark: The Revolutionary New Science of Exercise and the Brain* (New York: Little, Brown and Company, 2008). For further references on exercise and nutrition go to the resources section following these notes, or visit andreapolard.com.

16. Nancy Cantor and Catherine A. Sanderson, "Life Task Participation and Well-Being: The Importance of Taking Part in Daily Life," *Well-Being: The Foundation of Hedonic Psychology*, eds. Daniel Kahneman, Ed Diener, and Norbert Schwarz (Russel Sage Foundation: New York, 2003), 230–43.

17. Aristotle wrote: "Without friends no one would choose to live, though he had all other goods." He also emphasized that the social good is more important than the individual good, and thus that political science is the highest practical concern in life. Aristotle, *The Nicomachean Ethics*, Book VIII, 1155a5.

18. Csikszentmihalyi is a strong proponent of happiness being linked to goal-oriented activity, an idea that goes back to Aristotle. His in-depth analysis of how activity can lead to a sense of flow and happiness is rich and highly valuable to anybody interested in committing his or her life to happiness. Mihaly Csikszentmihalyi, *Flow: The Psychology of Optimal Experience* (New York: HarperCollins, 1990).

19. Csikszentmihalyi, *Flow*, 4. Csikszentmihalyi also believes that reflection (the contemplative life, in Aristotle's terms) should ideally complement or support activity (the active life). One can only reflect upon one's action when in touch with one's experience (ibid., 226). Aristotle however viewed contemplation as the highest form of virtuous activity. Therefore reflection, as in thinking things through, is not part of the Supreme Mode, but the Basic Mode as defined in the Two Wings of Happiness. Reflection in Eastern understanding does not equal thinking. It is a quiet state of mind that lets thoughts pass while observing them along with all other experiences.

NOTES

20. Genesis 1:22–28 (Authorized Version)

21. Matthew 6:28–30 (AV).

22. First translation of Lao-tzu's poem by Witter Bynner, *The Way of Life According to Lao-tzu* (New York: Perigee, 1994), no. 37.

23. Second translation of Lao-tzu's poem by John C. H. Wu, *Lao-tzu: Tao Teh Ching* (New York: St. John's University Press, 1961), no. 37. Watts interprets the Tao as "the flowing course of nature and the universe" in Watts and Huang, *Tao: The Watercourse Way*, 49.

24. The excerpt by Hermann Hesse is my own translation and paraphrasing of the *Betrachtungen über das Glück* (1949).

25. For my research on Eastern philosophies and religions I used Junjiro Takakusu, *The Essentials of Buddhist Philosophy* (Hawaii: University of Hawaii, 1947). Also, for a scientific explanation of experiencing oneness, please read Eugene D'Aquili and Andrew Newberg, *The Mystical Mind: Probing the Biology of Religious Experience* (Minneapolis: Fortress Press, 1999).

26. This excerpt by Hermann Hesse (1949) is my own word-by-word translation, also from the *Betrachtungen über das Glück* (1949).

27. Source for early translation of *A Harem in Bismarck's Reich: The Delightful Diary of Shah Nasreddin* (1873) no longer in print. Current translation, Idries Shah, *The Pleasantries of the Incredible Mulla Nasrudin* (New York: Penguin, 1993), 110.

28. Alan Watts, *The Wisdom of Insecurity: A Message for an Age of Anxiety* (New York: Vintage, 1951), 62.

Part 2

THE BASIC MODE

CHAPTER 3—THE FRAGILITY OF LIFE

1. From Rilke's poem "Autumn." Rainer Maria Rilke, *Selected Poems of Rainer Maria Rilke* (New York: Harper & Row, 1981), 89.

2. From Frost's poem "Nothing Gold Can Stay." Robert Frost, *The Poetry of Robert Frost: The Collected Poems Complete and Unabridged*, ed. Edward Connery Lathem (New York: Henry Holt, 1969), 222–23.

3. "We have to come to grips with the fact that every boy has an inner life, that their hearts are full. Every boy is sensitive, and every boy suffers. This is a scary idea for many adults, who, consciously or unconsciously, don't want to acknowledge a boy's emotional vulnerability. But when we do acknowledge it, and we use this understanding to advance our own emotional education as parents and teachers of boys, we can help them meet the shadows in their lives with a more meaningful light." Dan Kindlon and Michael Thompson, *Raising Cain: Protecting the Emotional Life of Boys* (New York: Ballantine Books, 2000), 20.

4. This quote refers to the "Serenity Prayer": "God grant us the serenity to accept the things we cannot change, courage to change the things we

can, and wisdom to know the difference" written by German philosopher Reinhold Niebuhr.

5. "For our purpose, we will define a habit as the intersection of *knowledge, skill,* and *desire.* . . . But knowing I need to listen and knowing how to listen is not enough. Unless I *want* to listen, unless I have the desire, it won't be a habit in my life. Creating a habit requires work in all three dimensions." Stephen R. Covey, *The Seven Habits of Highly Effective People: Powerful Lessons in Personal Change* (New York: Simon & Schuster, 1989), 47.

CHAPTER 4—AMBITION

1. This does not mean that we should stay in relationships that once had love but are now reduced to abuse and neglect.

2. Dan Buettner, "The Secrets of Long Life," *National Geographic* (Nov. 2005): 2–26.

3. This quote from Franz Liszt is my own translation. The original says: *Glücklich, wer mit den Verhaeltnissen zu brechen versteht, ehe sie ihn gebrochen haben.*

4. Reference to Ed Diener is based on an interview in which he explains the ingredients to happiness, among which he lists the following: "Having long-term goals that are congruent with another, and that are pleasant to work for. If you want to be a lawyer but you hate conflict, you are going to be messed up." John H. Richardson, "Dr. Happy," *Reader's Digest* 161, No. 967 (2002): 94–99.

5. Seligman describes how we all have "signature strengths," which I have listed in chapter 7. Martin Seligman, *Authentic Happiness: Using the New Positive Psychology to Realize Your Potential for Lasting Fulfillment* (New York: The Free Press, 2002).

6. Gail Evans, *Play Like a Man, Win Like a Woman: What Men Know About Success That Women Need to Learn* (New York: Broadway Books, 2000), 178.

7. Csikszentmihalyi has coined the term "flow" for Western science and made it popular in his book *Flow.*

8. Ibid., 50.

9. Robbins promotes taking control over one's mind. However, even with this extremely Western position, he concedes that there are limits to this approach. Anthony Robbins, *Awaken the Giant Within: How to Take Immediate Control of Your Mental, Emotional & Financial Destiny* (New York: Fireside, 1991), 372.

10. Csikszentmihalyi writes extensively throughout his book *Flow* about the importance of clarity and feedback, as well as the difficulties we have when we lack them.

11. The reason for calling this knowledge "popular" is that it is preached widely in Western schools and can now be called a part of our culture. Quote from Jeffrey Kluger, "Ambition: Why Some People Are Most Likely to Succeed," *Time* 14 (Nov.14, 2005): 48–59.

12. Dean Simonton, PhD, is a professor of the psychology department at the University of California, Davis. His expertise is in genius, creativity, leadership, talent, and aesthetics. Kluger, "Ambition," 48–59.

13. Campbell frequently advises us in his interviews, "Follow your bliss," because this is what makes us feel alive. He believes that "if you do follow your bliss you put yourself on a kind of track that has been there all the while, waiting for you, and the life that you ought to be living is the one you are living," Joseph Campbell, *The Power of Myth with Bill Moyers* (New York: Anchor Books, 1988), 150.

14. Joseph Campbell, *An Open Life: Joseph Campbell in Conversation with Michael Toms* (New York: Harper & Row, 1990), 24.

15. The German poet Johann Wolfgang von Goethe traveled through Italy during the years 1786 to 1788. Johann Wolfgang von Goethe, *Italienische Reise* (Stiebner: München, 2008).

16. Having to leave father and mother as part of one's salvation is a reoccurring theme in the New Testament, for instance, Matthew 4:18–22 (AV).

17. Dr. Cloninger is Wallace Renard Professor of Psychiatry, Professor of Psychology and Genetics. He wrote the highly recommendable book *Feeling Good: The Science of Well-Being* (New York: Oxford University Press, 2004). His approach is interdisciplinary and includes Eastern ideas, since his focus is on reaching higher levels of awareness. The reference is from Kluger, "Ambition," 48–59.

18. This statement is inspired by Kevin Leman who answers the question about whether one can be ambitious without losing one's values, "Yes, as long as you maintain integrity, never cutting corners to 'win at any price.'" Kevin Leman, *Winning the Rat Race Without Becoming the Rat: The Psychology of Winning in Business* (Nashville, TN: Thomas Nelson, 1996), 233.

19. Seventy-seven percent of driven students in a suburban high school in the United States admit to having cheated according to an anonymous school survey administered by the Student Forum during the 1998–99 academic year. This information was found in Peter Demerath and Jill Lynch, *The Social Construction of Advantage in a Suburban U.S. High School: Techniques of the Authoritative Self.* Paper presented at the annual meeting of the American Anthropological Association (2002). In Peter Demerath, *WHS Student Culture Study.* Report. Social and Cultural Foundations Section. School of Educational Policy and Leadership. From the Ohio State University study, (2005) we learn that 70 percent of the high achieving students were stressed out "frequently" or "all the time." Female students were more vulnerable to stress. They also achieved on average higher grades than the male students and seemed more immersed in competitive learning.

20. Demerath, *WHS Student Culture Study,* 5.

21. Peter Demerath, "The Social Cost of Acting 'Extra': Students' Moral Judgments of Self, Social Relations, and Academic Success in Papua New Guinea," *American Journal of Education* 108:3 (2001), and Peter Demerath, "Negotiating Individualist and Collectivist Futures: Emerging

Subjectivities and Social Forms in Papua New Guinean High Schools," *Anthropology & Education Quarterly* 34(2) (2003): 136–57.

22. Having applied the game theory of John von Neumann and Oskar Morgenstern to the evolutionary process, Wright is hesitantly optimistic about the direction of human development. Non-zero-sum-games do not always have to result in win-win situations. We must play the game correctly in order to achieve only positives. Robert Wright, *Nonzero: The Logic of Human Destiny* (New York: Pantheon Books, 2000), 6–7.

23. Covey, *Seven Habits*, 48.

24. Ibid., 151. "The Time Management Matrix" has the following quadrants: (1) Urgent/Important; (2) Not urgent/Important; (3) Urgent/Not Important; and (4) Not Urgent/Not Important. Often our dreams are in the second quadrant: they feel important to us, but not necessarily urgent. If we want to make things happen for ourselves, we need to shift them into the first quadrant.

CHAPTER 5—COMPETENCE

1. When we learn anything, the nerve cells in our brain (neurons) grow extensions (dendrites) to connect with other neurons. F. Engert and T. Bonhoeffer, "Dendritic Spine Changes Associated with Hippocampal Long-term Synaptic Plasticity," *Nature* 399 (1999): 66–70.

2. Hermann Hesse wrote the poem "Stufen" ("Stages") as part of his book *Das Glasperlenspiel.* English translation: Hermann Hesse, *The Glass Bead Game: (Magister Ludi),* trans. Richard and Clara Winston (New York: Picador, 1990), 444.

3. R. M. Ryan and E. L. Deci, "Self-Determination Theory and the Facilitation of Intrinsic Motivation, Social Development, and Well-Being," *American Psychologist* 55 (2000): 66–78.

4. Seligman and Csikszentmihalyi say, "When these needs are satisfied, Ryan and Deci claim that personal well-being and social development are optimized. Persons in this condition are intrinsically motivated, able to fulfill their potentialities, and able to seek out progressively greater challenges . . . Ryan and Deci's contribution shows that promises of the humanistic psychology of the 1960s can generate a vital program of empirical research." Martin Seligman and Mihaly Csikszentmihalyi, "Positive Psychology: An Introduction," *American Psychologist* 55 No.1 (2000): 5–14. Also Abraham H. Maslow, *Toward a Psychology of Being* (New York: Van Nostrand, 1968) and Abraham H. Maslow, *Religions, Values, and Peak-Experiences* (New York: Penguin, 1994).

5. Gisela Ulmann, PhD, teaches at the Psychological Institute of the Free University in Berlin and promotes a non-theoretical approach in our dealings with children. She suggests looking at each child and her unique circumstances to find out what stops her from developing well. The fundamental assumption in her book *Über den Umgang mit Kinder (How to Treat Children* [my translation]) is that all children develop as long as they

are given the tools, opportunities, and reasons to do so. Gisela Ulmann, *Über den Umgang mit Kindern. Orientierungshilfen für den Erziehungsalltag* (Hamburg/Berlin: Argument Verlag, 1987).

6. Erik Erikson, leaning on Sigmund Freud's developmental theory, looked upon development as a succession of stages through which we all have to move, one of which is the latency stage between the ages of five or six to twelve. Erikson believed that we learn much about curiosity, imagination, and skills during this stage. When we master this stage successfully we will develop a sense of competence. I propose that teenagers begin to react more strongly to societal conditions toward the end of this stage, probably because of their cognitive development. It is a tumultuous time, because at this stage of life we are all beginning to find out who we are and want to be in relation to our current culture. Erik H. Erikson, *Identity and the Life Cycle* (New York: International Universities Press, 1959).

7. There really is no need to be "excellent" in mundane activities such as opening a door or using shower gel. It is therefore fine—and prudent—to be mediocre in most of our life's affairs. Yet, if we seek an advantage or happiness, we should be willing to allocate more energy to designated areas.

8. Ryan and Deci distinguish between "intrinsic" and "extrinsic" motivation, stating that the former is supposed to correlate with happiness. This distinction does not take into account that other living beings can make us feel a part of something. Just looking at someone else scoring a goal can make us feel happy. If wanted, our children—a wondrous work in progress—can bring tremendous joy into our lives. Any gardener or hiker can give testimony to their positive experience. This is why I usually prefer the distinction between being motivated by the "animated" and the "non-animated." We just love to see or feel the living, grow, and excel. Ryan and Deci, "Self-Determination Theory," 66–78.

9. In *Raising Cain*, the authors write, "Harsh discipline—by which we mean both physical punishment in the form of hitting or spanking, and verbal intimidation, which includes belittling, denigrating, scapegoating, and threatening—is not the answer for any child. Not ever. And yet boys are like lightning rods for harsh discipline, much more so than girls. Many parents acknowledge that they use a more disciplinary style with their sons than with their daughters." Kindlon and Thompson, *Raising Cain*, 53.

10. Todd Kashdan, et al., "Curiosity" in *Character Strengths and Virtues: A Handbook and Classification*, eds. C. Peterson and M. E. P. Seligman (Washington, DC: American Psychological Association and Oxford University Press, 2004), 125–41.

11. Robert B. Reich is University Professor at Brandeis University and Maurice B. Hexter Professor of Social and Economic Policy at Brandeis's Heller Graduate School. He was the secretary of labor under President Bill Clinton. Reich does not believe that most individuals can stand up against the modern, frantic Zeitgeist. Even though my book is written for individuals who can develop the determination to live a balanced life today, I share Reich's opinion that external conditions have to be improved for

the general population to offer more people the chance to become happy. The quote can be found in Reich's book *The Future of Success* (New York: Knopf, 2001), 222.

12. Todd Kashdan and F. D. Fincham, "Facilitating Curiosity: A Social and Self-Perspective for Scientifically Based Interventions," *Positive Psychology in Practice*, ed. Linley and S. Joseph (Hoboken, NJ: Wiley), 482–503.

13. Ibid., 490. Many of Kashdan's concrete suggestions are discussed further in Peterson and Seligman's handbook *Character Strengths and Virtues*, which I highly recommend. Kashdan gives examples such as "Create tasks that capitalize on novelty, complexity, ambiguity, variety, and surprise"; "Provide encouragement and supportive feedback for efforts"; "Emphasize the meaningfulness of activity and efforts." See note 10 above for information on *Character Strengths and Virtues: A Handbook and Classification*.

14. Edward Hirt, PhD, a social psychologist at Indiana University Bloomington, found in his research that there are gender differences in evaluating the lame excuses (self-handicapping) people take for a lack of performance. Women do not believe other people's excuses and are quick to identify missing motivation. Women tend to apply themselves more in the work place, while men believe more in competence. Edward Hirt, "I Know You Self-Handicapped Last Exam: Gender Differences in Reactions to Self-Handicapping," *Journal of Personality and Social Psychology* (Jan. 2003): 177–93.

15. Evans, *Play Like a Man*.

16. Barbara Ehrenreich, *Nickel and Dimed: On (Not) Getting By in America* (New York: Owl Books, 2001), 195.

CHAPTER 6—CONNECTION

1. The story of Simon Yates and Joe Simpson can be seen in the movie *Touching the Void*, directed by Kevin Macdonald (2003).

2. J. Sutton-Hibbert and Y. Simon, *Amazing Stories of Survival: Tales of Hope, Heroism & Astounding Luck*, (People 2006): 80–81.

3. In this article by Nicholas Christakis and Paul Allison, we learn that elderly people have a higher mortality rate when their spouse dies, and also when their spouse is hospitalized. Nicholas A. Christakis and Paul D. Allison, "Mortality after the Hospitalization of a Spouse," *The New England Journal of Medicine* 7 (2006): 719–30.

4. Robert Coombs, who wrote a literature review about marital status and personal well-being, found that 70 percent of chronic problem drinkers were either divorced or separated, and only 15 percent were married. Single men are more than three times as likely to die of cirrhosis of the liver. Robert H. Coombs, "Marital Status and Personal Well-being: A Literature Review," *Family Relations* 40 (1991): 97–102.

5. "Studies indicate that depressive episodes occur twice as frequently in women than in men," American Psychiatric Association, *Diagnostic and Statistical Manual of Mental Disorders*, 4th ed. (1994), 325. These studies

pertain to major depressive episodes. While children of both sexes suffer equally from the less intense form of depression (dysthymic disorder), women suffer two to three times more often from it than men. American Psychiatric Association, *Diagnostic and Statistical Manual,* 347.

6. References for this finding are L. Verbrugge and D. Balaban, "Patterns of Change, Disability and Well-Being," *Medical Care* 27 (1989): 128–47; I. M. Joung, et al., "Differences in Self-reported Morbidity by Marital status and by Living Arrangement," *International Journal of Epidemiology* 23 (1994): 91–97; Coombs, "Marital Status and Personal Well-Being: A Literature Review," 97–102.

7. Most of us already know this to be true from experience, but many philosophers and scientists struggle to integrate this phenomenon in their theories. Aristotle and his followers, for example, point out how important friendships are but cannot weave this observation into their theories.

8. From an evolutionary point of view, other people are important because they help us with our individual goals as well as the goals we have for the family and group. David Buss writes that women want a mate who is able and willing to invest resources in their children, willing and able to physically protect the family, will show good parenting skills, and will be compatible enough in goals and values to enable strategic alignment without inflicting too many costs on the family. David M. Buss, "Human Mating Strategies," Samfundsøkonomen, 4 (2002): 50. Csikszentmihalyi writes that couples can only be happy when they have common goals as well as interest in each other's goals in order to facilitate flow. Csikszentmihalyi, *Flow,* 81.

9. When one measures purely the quantity of positive feelings in groups of parents that are not identified by backgrounds, research has shown that parenthood does not correlate with happiness. D. G. Myers, *The Pursuit of Happiness* (New York: Morrow, 1992). Children, however enriching they are to couples who wish to have them, reduce the level of contentment between the parents, especially during pre-toddler times and puberty. Contrary to popular belief, children do not mend relationships, but challenge them. Yet good working relationships should weather the storms well. Also, couples do report that children bring great meaning to their lives. While they might not help the couple feel better with each other, they make the individual happy. Stefan Klein, *Die Glücksformel oder Wie die guten Gefühle entstehen* (Hamburg: Rowohlt Taschenbuch Verlag, 2003), 168. I hope to see more research done on the subject, particularly research that takes into account variables such as the age of parents, their education, and their expressed wish for parenthood.

10. Even though Aristotle felt that the active life and the contemplative life were the highest form of happiness, he considered friends an invaluable asset and wrote: "Without friends no one would choose to live, though he had all other goods." (Aristotle, *The Nicomachean Ethics,* Book VIII, 1155a5). He believed that true friendship includes mutual advantage and pleasure, but above all, love for the same values. Thus, using the terms of his time, he emphasized the growth of the individual within friendship and community.

11. Diener and Seligman found that the twenty-two students who had rated themselves as "very happy" were significantly more socially active than the study's control group. The fact that feeling connected was even more important than religion or amount of sleep might be explained by the group's youth. Young people might not emphasize the need for relaxation. Ed Diener and Martin E. Seligman, "Very Happy People," *Psychological Science* 13 (2001): 81–84.

12. Happiness correlates highly with extroversion, even when people just act extroverted. W. Fleesen, A. B. Malanos, and N. M. Achille, "An Intraindividual Process Approach to the Relationship between Extraversion and Positive Affect: Is Acting Extroverted as 'Good' as being Extroverted?" *Journal of Personality and Social Psychology* 83, 6 (Dec. 2002): 1409–22.

13. Jean Baker Miller and Irene Pierce Stiver, *The Healing Connection: How Women Form Relationships in Therapy and in Life* (Boston: Beacon Press, 1997), 30.

14. Factors predicting the subjective well-being of nations in, Ed Diener, Marissa Diener, and Carol Diener, "Factors Predicting the Subjective Well-Being of Nations," *Journal of Personality and Social Psychology* 69 (1995): 851–62.

15. John Barlow experienced something similar in Africa and rejects the Western way of pursuing happiness, citing Chuang-tzu who believed that happiness is the absence of striving for it. John Perry Barlow, "The Pursuit of Emptiness: Why Americans Have Never Been a Happy Bunch," *Forbes*, December, 2001, forbes.com/asap/2001/1203/096.html

16. Daniel Kahneman explains in an interview with Carlin Flora that when people are asked in the very moment of their experience with a friend or family, they report feeling happier with friends because of their full engagement. As we do not pay the same amount of attention to family as we do with friends, family would recede into the background. Carlin Flora, "Happy Hour," *Psychology Today* (Jan./Feb. 2005): 42.

17. Harriet Lerner gives advice on how to make good conversation in her book: Harriet Lerner, *The Dance of Connection: How to Talk to Someone When You're Mad, Hurt, Scared, Frustrated, Insulted, Betrayed, or Desperate* (New York: Harper Collins, 2001), 239.

18. John A. Sanford is a highly experienced Jungian analyst and has written many valuable books on relationships, one of which I make reference to: John A. Sanford, *Between People: Communicating One-to-One* (Mahwah, NJ: Paulist Press, 1982), 91. This book is particularly good for learning about the "power of creative listening," "guilt and communication," and "indirect communication." It gives practical advice on how to improve one's communication skills.

19. Dalai Lama and Howard C. Cutler, *The Art of Happiness: A Handbook for Living* (New York: Riverhead Books, 1998).

20. David M. Buss, *The Evolution of Desire: Strategies of Human Mating* (New York: Basic Books, 2003).

21. Ibid., 59. Buss states:

> The importance that men assign to a woman's attractiveness has reasons other than her reproductive value. The consequences for a man's social status are critical. Everyday folklore tells us that our mate is a reflection of ourselves. Men are particularly concerned about status, reputation, and hierarchies because elevated rank has always been an important means of acquiring the resources that make men attractive to women. It is reasonable, therefore, to expect that a man will be concerned about the effect that his mate has on his social status—an effect that has consequences for gaining additional resources and mating opportunities.

> It is important to understand the biological tendencies. We should not forget, however, that we do have the choice to alter our behavior in a way that promotes both sexes' happiness. The biological view offers no excuse to behave like animals. I believe that we do have the freedom to either act or not act on these dispositions.

22. Ibid., 34.

23. Ibid. Buss points out countless studies that give evidence about the pervasiveness of these dispositions in all cultures: men have a strong tendency to look for beauty; women for resourcefulness. This is true even when women have resources themselves (45). Aging and less attractive men tend to choose very young women when they are in the position to do so. See Donald Trump, etc. (64). Apparently, it is not easy to overcome one's biology, and many people are not even interested in trying.

24. The term "aggressively asexual" was coined by professor Dr. Gottfried Lischke, who used to teach at my German alma mater (Freie Universität Berlin). Of all my teachers, he influenced me the most. Not only did he inspire me to write, he also urged me to take biology into account. He taught that we can all rise above our biology with the human powers of humility, awareness, and civility.

25. Sigmund Freud, *The Complete Psychological Works of Sigmund Freud*, ed. J. Strachey (London: Hogarth and the Institute of Psychoanalysis, 1955).

26. Buss, *The Evolution of Desire*, 36.

27. C. T. Hill, Z. Rubin, and L. A. Peplau, "Breakups Before Marriage: The End of 103 Affairs," *Journal of Social Issues* 32 (1976): 147–68. Also, "Successful long-term mating requires a sustained cooperative alliance with another person for mutually beneficial goals. Relationships riddled with conflict impede the attainment of those goals. Compatibility between mates entails a complex mesh between two different kinds of characteristics. One kind involves complementary traits. . . . The other kinds of traits crucial to compatibility with a mate, however, are those that are most likely to mesh cooperatively with one's own particular personal characteristics and thus are most similar to one's own." (Buss, *Evolution of Desire*, 35.)

28. Buss, *Evolution of Desire*, 263.

29. Ibid., 264.

30. From a biological point of view, it makes sense for men, who can sire countless children, to have affairs and resist commitment. I think we also have to take into account that modern women depend less on men's financial contributions and are also exposed to a diverse group of men in working environments. All these factors make affairs and divorce more likely. Yet, raising children together must have been the preferred strategy in our evolutionary history, as human offspring need intense caretaking for a long period of time. Ibid., 35, 41, 61.

31. Concerning gender differences, see W. Wood, N. Rhodes, and M. Whelan, "Sex Differences in Positive Well-Being: A Consideration of Emotional Style and Marital Status," *Psychological Bulletin* 106 (1989): 249–64. Also, S. Nolen-Hoeksema and C. L. Rusting, "Gender Differences in Well-Being," *Well-Being: The Foundation of Hedonic Psychology* eds. D. Kahneman, E. Diener, and N. Schwarz (New York: Russell Sage Foundation, 2000). It is still unclear why women report that they experience more emotions. Sex differences are often caused by biology, but also by socialization, and, most importantly, by an interaction of these highly variable factors. It makes sense to assume that the cognitive act of expressing emotions increases both the intensity of emotions as well as our awareness of them.

32. Many books on happiness emphasize how futile it is to express negative emotions. Yet millions of people know that crying and even some well-placed anger can help as long as one is cognizant of one's feelings.

33. See note 5, chapter 1.

34. Kashdan, "Curiosity," *Character Strengths and Virtues*, 135. To enhance one's curiosity, the reader should also read chapter 5 in T. B. Kashdan and F. D. Fincham, "Facilitating Curiosity: A Social and Self-Perspective for Scientifically Based Interventions," *Positive Psychology in Practice*, eds. P. Linley and S. Joseph, (Hoboken, NJ: Wiley, 2004).

35. R. D. Stolorow, B. Brandchaft, and G. E. Atwood, *Psychoanalytic Treatment: An Intersubjective Approach* (Hillsdale, NJ: The Analytic Press, 2000).

36. Antoine de Saint-Exupéry wrote his story *The Little Prince* in order to teach what is important in life, for example how to love someone. He stresses the significance of really knowing someone: "In those days, I didn't understand anything. I should have judged her according to her actions, not her words. She perfumed my planet and lit up my life. I should have never have run away. I ought to have realized the tenderness underlying her silly pretensions. Flowers are so contradictory. But I was too young to know how to love her." Antoine de Saint-Exupéry, *The Little Prince* (New York: Harcourt, 2000), 24ff.

37. Csikszentmihalyi, *Flow*, and also Mihaly Csikszentmihalyi, *Finding Flow: The Psychology of Engagement with Everyday Life* (New York: Basic Books, 1997).

38. Seligman, *Authentic Happiness*, 108.

39. Diener and Seligman, "Very Happy People," 81–84.

40. Joseph Campbell, *The Power of Myth* (New York: Anchor Books, 1991), 206.

41. The imperfections we should be willing to accept are not, however, abuse (including deceitfulness) or severe and chronic neglect. These should all be considered "deal breakers" in the interest of our happiness.

42. Jiddu Krishnamurti (1895–1986) was raised to be a spiritual leader but, remarkably, rejected this predetermined role. Instead, he became an independent writer and encouraged people to think for themselves.

43. Buss, *The Evolution of Desire*, 42.

44. Sometimes, however, breaking our commitment will increase our happiness. Also see note 41.

45. Miller and Stiver, *The Healing Connection*, 81.

46. In *The Art of Loving*, Erich Fromm says: "The idea expressed in the Biblical 'Love thy neighbor as thyself' implies that respect for one's own integrity and uniqueness, love for and understanding of one's own self, cannot be separated from respect and love and understanding for another individual. The love for my own self is inseparably connected with the love for any other being." Erich Fromm, *The Art of Loving* (New York: Perennial Classics, 1956), 54.

CHAPTER 7—CONFIDENCE

1. Kashdan, et al., "Curiosity" *Character Strengths and Virtues*, 485.

2. Our experiences include our context, which means that we are connected with the entire surrounding world as well. To realize that we are part of something so big as total reality gives us the deepest form of confidence. This will be further discussed in part 3.

3. Nathaniel Branden lists the following as the Six Pillars of Self-Esteem: the practice of living consciously, self-acceptance, self-responsibility, self-assertiveness, living purposefully, and personal integrity. Nathaniel Branden, *The Six Pillars of Self-Esteem* (New York: Bantam Books, 1994), 118–19.

4. Ibid., 119.

5. Due to the "contrast effect," we quickly change our perception of just about everything. For example, when a man rates his wife immediately after having looked at a pin-up girl, he rates his wife as less attractive than he would ordinarily do. D. T. Kenrick, S. E. Gutierres, and L. Goldberg "Influence of Erotica on Ratings of Strangers and Mates," *Journal of Experimental Social Psychology* 25 (1989): 159–67. Also, D. T. Kenrick, S. L. Neuberg, K. L. Kierk, and J. M. Krones, "Evolution and Social Cognition: Contrast Effects as a Function of Sex, Dominance, and Physical Attractiveness," *Personality and Social Psychology Bulletin* 202 (1994): 210–17.

6. See "charming" study by H. S. Friedman, R. E. Riggio, and D. F. Casella, "Nonverbal Skill, Personal Charisma, and Initial Attraction," *Personality and Social Psychology Bulletin* 14, No. 1 (1988): 284–90.

7. A. Demarais and V. White, *First Impressions: What You Don't Know About How Others See You* (New York: Bantam Books, 2004).

8. Concerning forgiving ourselves for alleged flaws, see study by T. Gilowich, V. H. Medvec, and K. Savitsky in which participants were asked to wear an embarrassing T-shirt and meet a room full of strangers. They consistently overestimated the amount of people who remembered the image. T. Gilowich, V. H. Medvec, and K. Savitsky, "The Spotlight Effect in Social Judgment: An Egocentric Bias in Estimates of the Salience of One's Own Actions and Appearance," *Journal of Personality and Social Psychology* 78, No. 2 (2000): 211–22.

9. Carlin Flora, "The Beguiling Truth About Beauty," *Psychology Today* (May/June 2006): 62.

10. The term "self-efficacy" is used in social psychology. More about this concept in Albert Bandura, "Self-Efficacy: Toward a Unifying Theory of Behavioral Change," *Psychological Review* 84 (1977): 191–215. Also see Albert Bandura, *Self-Efficacy: The Exercise of Control* (New York: Freeman, 1997).

11. J. J. Bauer and G. A. Bonanno, "I Can, I Do, I Am: The Narrative Differentiation of Self-Efficacy and Other Self-Evaluations While Adapting to Bereavement," *Journal of Research in Personality* 35 (2001): 424–48.

12. Richard Carlson, *Don't Sweat the Small Stuff—and It's All Small Stuff.* (New York: Hyperion, 1997).

13. Buddha is known to have said:

> Therefore, Ananda, be ye lamps unto yourselves, be ye a refuge to yourselves. Betake yourselves to no external refuge. Hold fast to the Truth as refuge. Look not for a refuge in anyone beside yourselves. And those, Ananda, who either now or after I am dead shall be a lamp unto themselves, shall betake themselves to no external refuge, but holding fast to the Truth as their lamp, and holding fast to the Truth as their refuge, shall not look for refuge to anyone besides themselves—it is they who shall reach to the very topmost Height. But they must be anxious to learn.

Jack Kornfield, *Teachings of the Buddha* (Boston: Shambhala, 1996), 125.

14. Branden, *Six Pillars,* 307.

15. Ibid., 308.

16. Friedrich Nietzsche, *Nietzsche: The Anti-Christ, Ecce Homo, Twilight of the Idols and Other Writings* (Cambridge: Cambridge University Press, 2005), 154.

17. The concept of "learned helplessness," passivity, and depression is discussed in the following literature: C. Peterson, S. Maier, and M. E. P. Seligman, *Learned Helplessness* (New York: Oxford University Press, 1993); M. E. P. Seligman, *Learned Optimism* (New York: Knopf, 1991).

18. Harold Kushner made an important contribution in how to relate to God when one suffers tragedy. Instead of feeling punished by God, he stresses that some bad things happen in spite of God, not because of God. In Eastern traditions, God, or the One, is often seen as both "the good" and "the bad"; not as an entity that rewards or punishes, but as the All that

entails everything. Harold S. Kushner, *When Bad Things Happen to Good People* (New York: Anchor Books, 2004).

19. Jesus is known to have preached about the right kind of living. Talking about God, boasting, and showing off one's righteousness may lead away from God. Instead, doing the right thing without profiting *directly* from it leads to God. This, however, does not mean that one ought to hide one's (moral) strength either. One can inspire other people, including oneself, if one is cognizant of one's strength, and lets it shine through. Subsequently inspiration can lead to the celebration of goodness as it runs through our blood, or, as Jesus understood it, as it is embodied in our Father God. Jesus said: "Ye are the light of the world. A city that is set on a hill cannot be hid. Neither do men light a candle and put it under a bushel, but on a candlestick; and it giveth light unto *all* that are in the house. *Let your light so shine* before men, that they may see your good works, and *glorify* your Father which is in heaven." Matthew 5:14–16 (AV). (Italics added by this author.)

20. Dennis Lewis, *Free Your Breath, Free Your Life: How Conscious Breathing Can Relieve Stress, Increase Vitality, and Help Your Life More Fully* (Boston: Shambhala, 2004).

21. The song "Sound the Bugle" by Gavin Greenaway, Trevor Horn, 2002. Sung in the movie *Spirit.*

22. Jack Kornfield, *A Path with Heart: A Guide Through the Perils and Promises of Spiritual Life* (Bantam Books: New York, 1993). Also, Jack Kornfield, *Meditation for Beginners: A Complete Video Instruction to the Inner Art of Meditation.* Sounds True, 1996.

23. Bauer and Bonanno, "I Can, I Do, I Am," 424–48.

24. J. J. Bauer and G. A. Bonanno, "Doing and Being Well (For The Most Part): Adaptive Patterns of Narrative Self-Evaluation During Bereavement," *Journal of Personality* 69 (2001): 451–82.

25. Bauer and Bonanno, "I Can, I Do, I Am," 442.

26. While Germans are much more subjected to nudity, pornography, and prostitution, their sexual activities may be declining. One explanation may be that the German population is aging, just as in the United States. A. Mazur, U. Mueller, W. Krause, and A. Booth, "Causes of Sexual Decline in Aging Married Men: Germany and America," *International Journal of Impotence Research* 14 (2002): 101–106. On the other hand, even younger Germans may become increasingly reluctant to engage in sexual intercourse with their long-term partners. According to the psychologists of the Georg-August-Universität, Germany, Peter Breuer and Ragnar Beer, 17 percent of all couples (13,483 young and older men and women) have sex less than once a month, 57 percent have sex once a week. While Ragnar Beer informed me personally that the poll the researchers took was about decreasing sexual pleasure over time in long-term relationships, there might be truth to the public perception that Germans suffer from more and more "unlust." Peter Breuer and Ragnar Beer. "Unlust," *Rheinische Post,* November 28, 2005, Germany.

27. Concerning Western self-massage see Kristine Kaoverii Weber, *Healing Self-Massage: Over 100 Simple Techniques for Reenergizing Body and Mind* (New York: Collins & Brown, 2005). Concerning Eastern, Taoist self-massage see Mantak Chia, *Chi Self-Massage: The Taoist Way of Rejuvenation* (New York: Destiny Books, 2006).

28. William H. Masters and Virginia E. Johnson, *Human Sexual Response* (Philadelphia: Lippincott Williams & Wilkins, 1966).

29. A. T. Beck, A. J. Rush, B. F. Shaw, and G. Emery, *Cognitive Therapy of Depression* (New York: Guildford Press, 1979).

30. Burns uses parts of Aaron Beck's cognitive theory. David Burns, *Feeling Good: The New Mood Therapy Revised and Updated* (New York: Harper, 1999), 71.

31. According to Klaus Linde, et al.'s study on 302 people who suffered from migraine headaches and who were treated with acupuncture, sham acupuncture, or waited as a control group: "Acupuncture was no more effective than sham acupuncture in reducing migraine headaches although both interventions were more effective than a waiting list control." As Klaus Linde explained in a personal e-mail, this result may be due to the focused attention by: (1) a caring other; (2) unspecific physiological effects of needling; and (3) high positive expectations. K. Linde, et al., "Acupuncture for Patients with Migraine," *The Journal of the American Medical Association* 293, no.17. (2005): 2118–25.

32. Erma Bombeck (1927–96) worked as a journalist before her first child was born. Eleven years later, she began a humor column that was syndicated in two hundred newspapers by 1968, and in more than eight hundred by the late 1970s.

33. Daniel Goleman, *Emotional Intelligence: Why It Can Matter More Than IQ* (New York: Bantam, 2005).

34. Daniel Siegel, MD, and Mary Hartzell, MEd, have described successful interactions with children that lead to neural integration. "Integration is the linking together of separate components of a larger system. Neural integration is how neurons connect the activity of one region of the brain and body to other regions. . . . We feel that our minds exist in that of the other person. This can be seen as the integration of the activity of two brains: neural integration, interpersonal style." Daniel J. Siegel and Mary Hartzell, *Parenting from the Inside Out: How a Deeper Self-Understanding Can Help You Raise Children Who Thrive* (New York: Penguin, 2003), 77–78. In my example, I refer to the integration of the left and right hemisphere of the brain.

35. Compare Seligman, *Authentic Happiness,* 134–61. You may want to take Martin Seligman's questionnaire to identify your signature strength: authentichappiness.com.

36. Howard Gardner proposes that the various intelligences can be treated like discrete categories even though it may turn out that they are interrelated. The Harvard University professor thinks that if we recognize that

there are different types of intelligences "we will have at least a better chance of dealing appropriately with the many problems that we face in the world." Howard Gardner, *Multiple Intelligences: New Horizons in Theory and Practice* (New York: Basic Books, 2006), 24.

37. Dr. Mark Cheng granted me an interview and wrote this as part of an e-mail to me. He explains that the sort of discipline that allows for certainty requires awareness of one's moral/ethical standards and of the challenges that one may encounter. He further explains that one can only arrive at such discipline with instruction, meditation, experience, and "stress-proven systems of thought." Dr. Cheng is the director of the Chung-Hua Institute in Santa Monica, California.

38. About sex-appeal and making a first impression, see S. Paulsell and M. Goldman, "The Effect of Touching Different Body Areas on Prosocial Behavior," *Journal of Social Study* 122 (1984): 269–73. For the effect of touching different body areas on prosocial behavior see J. D. Fisher, M. Rytting, and R. Heslin, "Hands Touching Hands: Affective and Evaluative Effects of Interpersonal Touch," *Sociometry* 39 (1975): 416–21.

39. In regard to optimism and marriages see Seligman, *Authentic Happiness,* 201ff. Also F. Fincham and T. Bradbury, "The Impact of Attributions in Marriage: A Longitudinal Analysis" *Journal of Personality and Social Psychology* 53, (1987): 510–17. Optimism is actually a pervasive bias when most people make predictions. David A. Armor and Shelley E. Taylor explain that optimism works even though it may not lead to accurate predictions because we are (1) not indiscriminately optimistic, (2) motivated to live up to positive predictions, and (3) because we can escape disappointment by optimistically reinterpreting the situation. D. A. Armor and S. E. Taylor, "When Predictions Fail: The Dilemma of Unrealistic Optimism," *Heuristics and Biases: The Psychology of Intuitive Judgment,* eds. Thomas Gilovich, Dale Griffin, & Daniel Kahneman (Cambridge: Cambridge University Press, 2002), 334–47.

40. One can find such exercises in Martin Seligman, *Learned Optimism* (New York: Alfred A. Knopf, 1991), chapter 12.

41. A. Twersky and D. Kahneman have found in their research that when we can imagine something, we are likely to overestimate the likelihood of its occurrence. While we ought to understand that this may lead to unfounded optimism, we can employ this distortion to our benefit by deriving motivation from our mental image during times that we need it the most. A. Twersky and D. and Kahneman, "Availability: A Heuristic for Judgment Frequency and Probability," *Cognitive Psychology* 5 (1973): 207–32.

42. Mental imagery activates corresponding brain regions. See K. O'Craven and M. Kanwisher, "Mental Imagery of Faces and Places Activates Stimulus-Specific Brain Regions," *Journal of Cognitive Neuroscience* 12 (2000): 1013–23. In fact the brain does not distinguish between what it sees in reality and what is imagined.

43. The joy of anticipation can even be found without complicated mental images in primates, as brain researchers Wolfram Schultz et al. realized

when their monkeys' dopamine neurons fired in expectation of getting fed. Humans have the same underlying basic neural feedback system when they expect a reward, even though we are the only animal that has the ability to project into the future what has yet to be experienced the first time. W. Schultz, P. Apicella and T. Ljungberg, "Responses of Monkey Dopamine Neurons During Learning of Behavioral Reactions," *Journal of Neurophysiology* 67 (1992): 145–63. Also: W. Schultz, P. Apicella and T. Ljungberg, "Responses of Monkey Dopamine Neurons to Reward and Conditioned Stimuli During Steps of Learning a Delayed Response Task," *Journal of Neurophysiology* 13, no. 3 (1993): 900–913.

44. *Waiting for Godot* is an absurdist play by the Irish writer Samuel Beckett (1906–89), in which two tramps are waiting for the arrival of Godot, who never comes. Without their hope of meeting Godot (which may stand for God or anything we place our hopes on), they are stripped of purpose and energy. Yet with their hope intact, the two are inactive and reminiscent.

45. Daniel Gilbert points out in his excellent book the fact that projecting into the future in great detail without yet having had the actual experience is a relatively newly acquired tool in evolutionary history and specific to *Homo sapiens*. We have the ability to plan (and be anxious about) the future due to our frontal lobe. "We think about the future in a way that no other animal can, does, or ever has, and this simple, ubiquitous, ordinary act is a defining feature of our humanity." Daniel Gilbert, *Stumbling on Happiness: Think You Know What Makes You Happy?* (New York: Knopf, 2006), 4.

46. Covey, *Seven Habits*, 47.

47. See the movie *Touching the Void*.

48. Esther "Eppie" Pauline Friedman Lederer, better known as Ann Landers (1918–2002), is best known for writing an advice column for forty-five years.

49. A. Arntz, M. Van Eck, and P. J. de Jong have found that the group of volunteers that received twenty foreseeable high-intensity electric shocks coped better than the group that received only three, but unforeseeable jolts. The group left in the dark reported more fear, sweated more profusely, and had higher heart rates. The more we know about our future setbacks, that is their likely occurrence, the more control we experience. A. Arntz, M. Van Eck, and P. J. de Jong, "Unpredictable Sudden Increases in Intensity of Pain and Acquired Fear," *Journal of Psychophysiology* 6 (1992): 54–64.

50. Malcolm Gladwell, *Outliers: The Story of Success* (New York: Little, Brown, 2008), 246.

51. Epictetus was born approximately two thousand years ago. He was a slave in the Roman Empire, but then became a famous philosopher. Surely he understood the value of ambition and the rest of the tools discussed in this book. However, he never lost sight of his priorities. His manual on virtue, happiness, and effectiveness, *The Art of Living*, which is still in print, pays tribute to that. Sharon Lebell, *Epictetus, The Art of Living: The Classic Manual on Virtue, Happiness, and Effectiveness* (New York: Harper Collins, 1994).

Part 3

THE SUPREME MODE

CHAPTER 8—THE STRENGTH OF LIFE

1. The United Nations Environment Programme's *Global Biodiversity Assessment* estimates that only 1.75 million species have been described so far, of which over half are insects, including 300,000 beetles. *Global Biodiversity Assessment,* ed. V. H. Heywood (Cambridge: Cambridge University Press, 1995). See also enviroliteracy.org.

2. These estimated statistics about the universe can be found in Stephen Hawking, *The Universe in a Nutshell* (New York: Bantam Books, 2001), 168.

3. The Earth weighs about 6,585,600,000,000,000,000,000,000 tons.

4. Nicolaus Copernicus (1473–1543), who must have anticipated the upsetting consequences of his findings, released them only at the very end of his life. David Bergamini, *The Universe (Life Nature Library)* (Morristown, NJ: Silver Burdett Press, 1987), 14ff.

5. Walter Kaufmann, *Goethe's Faust* (New York: Anchor Books, 1962), 491.

6. Stephen Hawking explains that the Big Bang is a "singularity," which is "a point in spacetime at which the spacetime curvature becomes infinite." Everything was scrunched up into a single point of infinite density. At such a point—according to the singularity theorem—"general relativity breaks down." There was no "time," and our known laws of physics did not apply. One million years after the Big Bang, matter connected to form the first stars. Billions of years later, stars burned up, and helium and heavier elements—which we are made of, such as carbon and oxygen—came about. Stephen Hawking, *The Universe in a Nutshell* (New York: Bantam, 2001), 78ff. Even though nothing is *known* about this time, I ought to mention theoretical possibilities described by Hawking later in the same book. In the beginning, the universe was very small, which means that there were only a small number of rolls of the dice. "Because the universe keeps on rolling the dice to see what happens next, it does not have just a single history, as one might have thought. Instead, the universe must have every possible history, each with its own probability." We would have to find out how the histories started to predict how the universe developed. The histories of the universe (in imaginary time, which is an abstract mathematical construction) "can be thought of as curved surfaces, like a ball, a plane, or a saddle shape, but with four dimensions instead of two . . . If the histories of the universe in imaginary time are indeed closed surfaces, as Hartle and I proposed, it would have fundamental implications for philosophy and our picture of where we came from. The universe would be entirely self-contained; it wouldn't need anything outside . . . the vast universe can be understood in terms of its history in imaginary time, which is a tiny, slightly flattened sphere." (ibid, 80–81).

7. Mathematical cosmologist Brian Swimme has recognized the importance of continuing the old tradition of telling stories about the universe, stories that we can relate to. While supported by science, he hopes to evoke

real experiences about and with the universe, so that we understand better what role we play in its vast ever-expansiveness. See Brian Swimme, *The Hidden Heart of the Cosmos: Humanity and the New Story* (New York: Orbis Books, 1996) and also Brian Swimme and Thomas Berry, *The Universe Story from the Primordial Flaring Forth to the Ecozoic Era: A Celebration of the Unfolding of the Universe* (New York: Harper Collins, 1994).

8. Hoimer von Ditfurth wrote a wonderful book called *In the Beginning There Was Hydrogen* (my translation). Hydrogen is the gas from which everything else developed. Hoimer von Difurth *Im Anfang war der Wasserstoff* (Muechen: Deutscher Taschenbuch Verlag, 1997).

9. Brian Swimme's website, accessed September 26, 2011, brianswimme.org/media/excerpts.

10. Hawking gives this definition of vacuum energy: "Energy that is present even in apparently empty space. It has the curious property that unlike the presence of mass, the presence of vacuum energy would cause the expansion of the universe to speed up." Hawking, *The Universe in a Nutshell*, 208.

11. Swimme, *Hidden Heart*, 97.

12. See Heisenberg's uncertainty paper, 1927. I found the information on plato.stanford.edu/entries/qt-uncertainty/. According to physicist Werner Heisenberg's uncertainty principle, the more precisely the position is determined, the less precisely the momentum is known in this instant, and vice versa. For example, electrons around the atomic nucleus have a position but are also standing waves that fit in the atom. When we measure the position, we cannot predict the wave and vice versa.

13. Stephen Hawking writes that Max Planck suggested in 1900 that light always comes in little packets called "quanta." When we observe a particle/wave by shooting low- or high-energy photons (that is low- or high-frequency wavelengths) at it, we get either uncertain information about its velocity or its position (Hawking, *Universe in a Nutshell*, 42). Later in the same book, he defines the quantum, "Quantum (plural quanta): The indivisible unit in which waves may be absorbed or emitted," (ibid., 206).

14. However, nature's ability to bounce back has its limits. When we disturb the natural balance too much, the ecosystem may not recover. In these cases, there can hardly be any comfort in the eventual results of the destruction. If we humans continue to destroy the natural balance, we also continue destroying many species, of which, one day, we may be one. Also, I worry along with the Chinese Taoist Chuang Tzu, "I know about letting the world alone, not interfering. I do not know about running things. Letting things alone: so that men will not blow their nature out of shape! Not interfering, so that men will not be changed into something they are not! When men do not get twisted and maimed beyond recognition, when they are allowed to live—the purpose of government is achieved." Thomas Merton, *The Way of Chuang Tzu Chuang*, 70.

15. Ditfurth writes the following about the development of the universe: "Intelligence does not exist because nature was capable of creating brains

that produced the phenomenon of intelligence in the end of a long developmental chain . . . Nature has not merely created life, but also brains and our consciousness because it already had sense, imagination, and direction from the first moment of existence. The main point is that *principles were at work* that already reign in the inorganic world." Difurth, *Im Anfang war der Wasserstoff,* 11–12. Later in the same book, Ditfurth characterizes the entire evolution of the universe as the outcome of the two principles: "The first was the principle of connection . . . to ever more complex, higher levels. The second was the principle of expansion, which led to more independence from the environment the element disconnected from." (ibid., 341) (my translation from German).

16. Swimme, *Hidden Heart,* 97.

17. Stephen Cross writes: "For most schools of Hinduism . . . *moksha* is release from the individual condition itself: the release of consciousness from the limiting forms in which it is enclosed, as the relative nature of these is experienced. Thus moksha is not a deprivation but an expansion of consciousness beyond the bounds of individuality. It is essentially positive—not, as the Buddhist nirvana is often and perhaps incorrectly represented as being, simply the ending of sorrow." Stephen Cross, *Way of Hinduism* (London: HarperCollins, 1994), 127.

18. To remind the reader, "nonactive" is not synonymous with "inactive." While being active, we can be focused in the moment, not on a future goal, and we can be aware of how activity is happening, as opposed to our individual effort.

CHAPTER 9—RECEPTIVITY

1. The parietal lobe is part the cerebral cortex of our brain that contains the orientation association area, which receives, among other things, input from the visual receiving areas. It is crucial for integrating visual, auditory, and somaesthetic information, which, according to many researchers including Rhawn Joseph, enables us to differentiate between objects within and beyond our grasp: "It seems likely that the 'self-other' or the 'self-world' distinction that philosophers and theologians have discussed throughout the ages may be a function of the left orientation association that evolved from its more primitive ability to divide objects in space into the graspable and the nongraspable." (D'Aquili and Newberg, *Mystical Mind,* 34).

2. Many authors who write about Eastern thought judge the analytical human experience negatively. I believe that if we desired to integrate Eastern into Western thought, we ought to maintain our respect for the analytical perception that is praised so much in Western thought. The fact that we can scan the world and make it more manageable is a wonderful, natural accomplishment.

3. The frontal lobe of our brain contains the attention association area, which is connected with our limbic system (which modulates emotions) in the mid-brain. The frontal lobe is involved in impulse control, judgment, language, memory, motor function, problem solving, sexual

behavior, socialization, and spontaneity, and it assists in planning, coordinating, controlling, and executing behavior (see also en.wikipedia.org/wiki/Frontal_lobe). Without it, as Gilbert points out, we could not look into the future, which would rob us of an exclusively human attribute. See Gilbert, *Stumbling on Happiness,* 12. Yet when we activate the attention association area, we can also focus on the present moment and enhance our experience of the life that takes place. The orientation association area is heavily interconnected with the attention association area, which is the reason that paying attention has an effect on our space and time experience. Both the orientation and the attention association areas are involved in what D'Aquili and Newberg call "a sense of 'egocentric spatial organization' or how things are spatially oriented to ourselves." D'Aquili and Newberg, *Mystical Mind,* 35.

4. Positive thinking has become a buzzword in popular culture, self-help books, and in cognitive psychology. The frenzy is based on the verifiable experience that focusing on positive thoughts with great discipline—as exemplified by Tibetan Buddhists—can generate positive emotions. This is due to the strong neural connections between the various parts of the brain, i.e., the attention association area and the limbic system (see note 3). Yet negative thinking can be very important to our overall being as well, as Paul Pearsall points out in his self-help book *The Last Self-Help Book You'll Ever Need: Repress Your Anger, Think Negatively, Be a Good Blamer and Throttle Your Inner Child* (New York: Basic Books, 2005). For example, hopelessness may be adequate to our situation, while self-imposed optimism may put unnecessary pressure on people. Instead of being optimistic, Pearsall suggests, we are better off surrendering, and acceptance may be best for us (ibid., 43). Negative experiences may also help us face situations, be honest with ourselves, and be heard and helped by others (ibid., 44). According to Pearsall, blaming others occasionally and effectively may also end bad situations (ibid., 55).

5. Russell Freedman, *Confucius: The Golden Rule* (New York: Arthur A. Levine Books, 2002), Author's Note.

6. Bob Altemeyer, "Why Do Religious Fundamentalists Tend to Be Prejudiced?" *International Journal for the Psychology of Religion* 13, no. 1 (2003): 17–28. B. Hunsberger, and L. M. Jackson, "Religion, Meaning, and Prejudice," *Journal of Social Issues* 61:4 (2005): 807. B. Duriez, "A Research Note on The Relation Between Religiosity and Racism: The Importance of the Way in Which Religious Contents Are Being Processed," *International Journal for the Psychology of Religion* 14, no. 3 (2004): 177–91.

7. Friedrich Wilhelm Nietzsche (1844–1900) was a German philosopher who freed himself from the thinking of his time of which he had felt himself a captive. In retrospect, he described the three stages he underwent: (1) belief in cultural innovation, (2) annihilation of tradition and Christian values ("God is dead" even though humans are in need of believing in God), and (3) acceptance of the world in which all strive to power, and hope that the ones who do adhere to values and show compassion. Nietzsche was one of

the most tragic figures of German culture. In an attempt to free himself, he was brutally honest with himself and others. While he was a very fragile person with overflowing compassion, his thoughts offended everyone: Jews, Christians, women, fellow philosophers, friends, and potential mates. While he suffered many emotional problems, his cognitive rigidity and inability to receive comfort from the world (as opposed to his own thinking) are most striking to me. While I admire his commitment to what he deemed the truth, I pity him for thinking that he had found it. In the end, it was his certainty that invited the Third Reich to use and abuse his philosophy. A greater punishment for his rigidity is hardly conceivable. Nietzsche's auto-biographical statements are summarized in Friedrich Nietzsche, *Ecce Homo: How One Becomes What One Is* (New York: Oxford University Press, 1887). Some paragraphs start with headlines such as these: "Why I am so intelligent," "Why I am so wise," "Why I write such good books." The aphorisms throughout his writing are all written with forceful conviction. In the story of Zarathustra, a prophet-like young man meets an old holy man in the forest. The latter invites the younger to join his holy path. The younger one declines, and bewildered, thinks to himself that the old man had not yet received the news of God's death. "God is dead" has become the saying for which Nietzsche is famous. He rejected the values we attach to God because they led to childish hypocrisy. The values Nietzsche (Zarathustra) proposed were based on insight into human nature and an attempt to replace the God-given values that can no longer work for modern men and women. Friedrich Nietzsche, *Thus Spake Zarathustra: A Book for All and None* (Calgary: Theophania Publishing, 2011).

8. This quote is found at the end of the highly entertaining book *Atlas Shrugged* by Ayn Rand, founder of the objectivist philosophy. Ayn Rand, *Atlas Shrugged* (New York: Penguin, 1985), About the Author.

9. Watts interprets the Tao as "the flowing course of nature and the universe." Watts and Huang, *Tao: The Watercourse Way*, 49.

10. Merton reminds us that we cannot be certain about the existence of Lao-tzu, who allegedly wrote the Tao Te Ching, yet we can be certain about the historical existence of the "greatest of the Taoist writers." Merton, *The Way of Chuang Tzu Chuang*, 15.

11. Merton writes: "The Tao of Ju philosophy is, in the words of Confucius, 'threading together into one the desires of the self and the desires of the other.'" (Ibid., 21)

12. T. R. Reid spent some years living in the East and discovered many similarities between our systems of values: "What the Asians have learned from Confucius and other great teachers of the Eastern traditions is essentially the same as what Americans and Europeans have learned from Socrates and the Judeo-Christian teachers of Western traditions. The basic precepts are the same." T. R. Reid, *What Living in the East Teaches Us About Living in the West* (New York: Vintage, 1999), 241.

13. Merton distinguishes between two kinds of understanding of the Tao. The first is more conventional and was freely used by Confucius. It is an

"ethical Tao" or the "Tao of man," the manifestation in act of a principle of love and justice." Merton, *The Way of Chuang Tzu,* 21. Later in the same book, Merton writes that while the way the legendary founder of the Chinese philosophy of Taoism, Lao-tzu, as well as its greatest spokesman, Chuang Tzu, understood the Tao is not bound to human convention. It is the "Tao of Heaven," (ibid., 21) the indefinable way or essence of nature that we cannot be separated from as we could from an object or objective, but that we can realize when our minds are receptive to the experience.

14. Alan W. Watts, *The Way of Zen* (New York: Vintage, 1985).

15. From Merton we learn that Confucius's favorite student, Yen Hui, wants to leave his master to go to Wei in order to convert the Prince of Wei to more ethical governing. Confucius discourages him from leaving because Yen Hui was not able to be one of them, but would have come as a superior stranger trying to "break in the door." Having inner unity and peace is a necessary prerequisite for connecting with people and stands thus before knowledge. Merton, *The Way of Chuang Tzu,* 50–53.

16. See Michael Shermer, *The Science of Good & Evil: Why People Cheat, Gossip, Care, Share, and Follow the Golden Rule* (New York: Times Books, 2004), 260–62.

17. Ibid., 260–62.

18. World Database of Happiness, accessed October 18, 2011, worlddatabaseofhappiness.eur.nl.

19. Daniel Garberl, *Descartes' Metaphysical Physics* (Science and Its Conceptual Foundations series) (Chicago: University of Chicago Press, 1992).

20. This quote continues: "and the intellect will wear itself out. . . . The idea is not to reduce the human mind to a moronic vacuity, but to bring into play its innate and spontaneous intelligence by using it without forcing it." Watts, *The Way of Zen,* 19–21).

21. Cross writes, "Shankara is concerned with removing the ignorance of our own nature which keeps us bound to the phenomenal world; with clearing away the self-imposed obstacles which stand between us and an immediate apprehension of our own innermost reality. . . . For this school of thought [Vedanta], it is not so much more faith in gods which is required, but more skepticism about the reality of the world and of the individual self which experiences it." Cross, *Way of Hinduism,* 60. Vedanta "can mean both the Upanisads and systems of Upanisadic philosophy and theology. The Upanisads were the last portion of the Veda (in the wider sense) and, according to Vedantins, constitute the core purpose of the Veda, because they teach final emancipation from the cycle of birth and death." Klaus K. Klostermaier, *A Concise Encyclopedia of Hinduism* (Oxford: Oneworld Publication, 1998), 200.

22. "The Great Tao is universal like a flood. How can it be turned to the right or to the left? All creatures depend on it, and it denies nothing to anyone. It does its work, but it does no claims for itself. It clothes and feeds all, but it does not lord it over them: Thus it may be called 'The Little.' All things

return to it as their home, but it does not lord it over them: Thus it may be called the 'Great.' It is just that it does not wish to be great that its greatness is fully realized." Wu, *Tao Teh Ching*, no. 34.

23. Ibid., no. 20.

24. Watts, *The Way of Zen*, 84ff.

25. Ibid., 87.

26. Stephen Batchelor, *The Faith to Doubt: Glimpses of Buddhist Uncertainty* (Berkeley: Parallax Press, 1990), 16.

27. Watts, *The Way of Zen*, 107. In the same book, Watts writes that the word "koan" comes from the word *kung-an*, which means "public document" or "case." "The student is expected to show that he has experienced the meaning of the koan by a specific and usually nonverbal demonstration which he has to discover intuitively." Examples of koans are "Everybody has a place of birth. Where is your place of birth?" "How is my hand the Buddha's hand?" "How is my foot like a donkey's foot?" (ibid., 105).

28. Ibid., 106.

29. Ibid., 107.

30. Eckhart Tolle made Eastern ways accessible to Westerners. He writes, "The fact is that, in a very similar way, virtually everyone hears a voice, or several voices, in their head all the time: the involuntary thought process that you don't realize you have the power to stop. Continuous monologues or dialogues. . . . Sometimes this soundtrack is accompanied by visual images or 'mental movies.'" Eckhart Tolle, *The Power of Now: A Guide to Spiritual Enlightenment* (New York: New World Library, 1999), 14.

31. D'Aquili and Newberg, *Mystical Mind*, 95.

32. Williges Jaeger is both a Christian priest as well as a Zen master; he originated a meditation center in Würzburg, Germany. He describes the Western traditions of turning inward, becoming peaceful and fulfilled. Williges Jaeger, *Kontemplation: Gott Begegnen—Heute* (Freiburg in Breisgau: Herder, 2002), 18.

33. Kornfield, *A Path with Heart*, 35.

34. This quote is from the Gospel of Thomas (known as "doubting Thomas"), which is a list of 114 sayings attributed to Jesus and discovered only in 1945 in Egypt: "When will the kingdom of God come?" "It will not come by watching for it. It will not be said, 'Look, here!' or 'Look, there!' Rather, the Father's kingdom is spread out upon the earth, and people don't see it." Stephen J. Patterson, Hans-Gebhard Bethge, and James M. Robinson, *Fifth Gospel: The Gospel of Thomas Comes of Age* (Valley Forge: Trinity Press International, 1998), 32.

35. Huai-jang (d. 775 CE) was the immediate disciple of the sixth and last Chinese Zen patriarch, Hui-neng (637–713 CE). He emphasized that enlightenment cannot be attained, but must come to us: "To train yourself in sitting meditation (*za-zen*) is to train yourself to be a sitting Buddha. If

you train yourself in za-zen, (you should know that) Zen is neither sitting nor lying. If you train yourself to be a sitting Buddha, (you should know that) the Buddha is not a fixed form. Since the Dharma has no (fixed) abode, it is not a matter of making choices. If you (make yourself) a sitting Buddha this is precisely *killing the Buddha*. If you adhere to the sitting position, you will not attain the principle (of Zen)." Watts, *The Way of Zen*, 110.

36. Gratitude researchers have found—in their two-week research study— that if a group of people writes down what they are grateful for on a daily basis, they significantly increase their joy, happiness, and life satisfaction levels. M. E. McCullough, S. Kilpatrick, R. A. Emmons, and D. Larson, "Gratitude as Moral Affect," *Psychological Bulletin* 127 (2001): 249–66. Also, Robert A. Emmons, *Thanks! How the New Science of Gratitude Can Make You Happier* (Boston: Houghton Mifflin, 2007).

37. Seligman, *Authentic Happiness*, 75.

38. Wu, *Tao Teh Ching*, no. 54.

39. Dorothy Thompson (1894–1961).

CHAPTER 10—TRANQUILITY

1. Here, I am alluding to a story from the Vimalakirti Sutra, a text that had significant influence on Zen Buddhism in China. In this text, we learn from a layman named Vimalakirti, who surpassed all other disciples of Buddha. When asked about the nature of the nondual reality, his reply was: "thunderingly silence." Watts, *The Way of Zen*, 81. According to Takakusu, just as the Indian monk Bodhidharma who came to China demonstrated with his gazing at a wall, the saintly layman of Vaisali, Vimalakirti, showed that one can attain perfect enlightenment without appealing to words or order. Via silence one can gain instant access to one's natural insight in the "nondual" reality. Junjiro Takakusu, *The Essentials of Buddhist Philosophy* (Columbia, MO: South Asia Books, 1998), 120ff. Also, Charles Luc, *Ordinary Enlightenment: A Translation of the Vimalakirti Nirdesa Sutra* (Boston: Shambhala, 2002).

2. Genesis 3:19 (AV). The Western worldview is greatly influenced by the understanding that human nature is bad or imperfect as exemplified by the Bible's story about Adam and Eve's original sin. (Muslims and Jews do not believe in original sin, but both world religions point to ways to make humans perfect or more worthy.) Despite God's command not to eat from the tree of knowledge of good and evil, so the story goes, Adam and Eve could not resist temptation. Not knowing the distinction between "good" and "bad" was a peaceful paradise, and knowing the distinction ended Adam and Eve's carefree existence once and for all. As a consequence, suffering was put upon the couple and all human beings. While Buddhists believe that we can enter a non-distinctive state of mind, our Buddha-nature, much of the Western world tends to believe in God's eternal punishment. A return to innocence is not possible according to pervasive Western beliefs. "So he drove out the man: and he placed at the east of the Garden of Eden cherubim, and a flaming sword which turned every way, to keep the way of the tree of life." Gen 3:24 (AV).

3. R. Kubey and M. Csikszentmihalyi, *Television and the Quality of Life* (Hillsdale, NJ: Lawrence Erlbaum, 1990).

4. Stefan Klein, *Die Glücksformel oder Wie die guten Gefuehle entstehen* (Hamburg: Rowohlt Taschenbuch Verlag, 2003).

5. J. Veroff, E. Douvan, and R. A. Kulka, *The Inner American* (New York: Basic Books, 1981). Also, John P. Robinson, *How Americans Use Time* (New York: Praeger, 1977).

6. Dr. Lin Yutang was a Chinese-American writer, translator, and editor. He lived predominately in the United States, where he was educated at Harvard University. Lin Yutang, *The Importance of Living* (Baltimore: Patterson Press, 2008), 155.

7. Melody Beattie is the author of several popular self-help books on co-dependency. The cluster of symptoms described by the author has never made it into the DSM, which is the main manual used to classify psychological disorders. Nevertheless, thousands of people can identify with codependency, as one can conclude from the overwhelming responses and the many self-help groups that originated based on the ideas expressed in Beattie's books. Beattie has been harshly criticized for preaching self-care, because caring for others would be healthy, fulfilling, and the "moral" thing to do. Codependency, however, describes a compulsion, not the healthy behavior of giving. No compulsion can be seen as good, because it robs us of a healthy choice and a balanced life. It may be interesting to examine whether the criticism rests on either the fear of discouraging giving under any circumstances as we have too little in this world, or the fear of losing the predominate female group who gives without asking anything back in turn. Melody Beattie, *Codependent No More: How to Stop Controlling Others and Start Caring for Yourself* (New York: HarperCollins, 1987).

8. Csikszentmihalyi was aware of the possibility of becoming addicted to flow. He writes,

> Almost any enjoyable activity can become addictive. Instead of being a conscious choice, it can become a necessity that interferes with other activities. Surgeons, for instance, describe operations as being addictive, like 'taking heroin.' Thus enjoyable activities that produce flow have a potentially negative aspect: while they are capable of improving the quality of existence by creating order in the mind, they can become addictive, at which point the self becomes captive of a certain kind of order, and is then unwilling to cope with the ambiguities of life.

Csikszentmihalyi, *Flow*, 62.

9. The last line of the poem "Leisure of William Henry Davies" goes as follows: "A poor life this if, full of care, / We have no time to stand and stare." Helen Ferris Tibbets, *Favorite Poems Old and New: Selected for Boys and Girls* (New York: Doubleday, 1957), 78.

10. Yutang, *The Importance of Living*, 154.

11. See chapter 2, "Physical Preparation," "Mental Preparation." in Robert Thurman, *Infinite Life: Seven Virtues for Living Well* (New York: Riverhead Books, 2004).

12. Karen Kingston, *Clear Your Clutter with Feng Shui* (New York: Broadway, 1999).

13. Thurman, *Infinite Life*, 87.

14. Kornfield, *Teachings of the Buddha*, xxxi.

15. Ibid., 28ff. All following quotes regarding the Four Noble Truth are from Jack Kornfield, *Teachings of the Buddha*.

16. Watts points out that the way we usually live life is in suffering because we tend to frustrate ourselves by fighting the present as a passing moment and by suppressing our spontaneity. See Watts, *The Way of Zen*, 46.

17. See note 15.

18. Burns, a cognitive therapist, explains that anxiety and depression are caused by cognitive distortions, as opposed to realistic thoughts. Burns also warns against positive distortions, because they cause us to make wrong decisions in our life. David D. Burns, *The Feeling Good Handbook* (New York: Plume, 1999), 27. Later in the same book, Burns points out that appropriate negative feelings are very important and natural: "Sometimes it's best just to accept bad feelings and pamper yourself and ride things out until the clouds pass and you feel better again." Ibid., 30.

19. Daniel Goleman's best-selling, widely accepted, and debated book *Emotional Intelligence* is really a cultural phenomenon.

20. Thich Nhat Hanh is a Vietnamese Zen Buddhist monk who has helped to heal the wounds of the Vietnam War, for which he was nominated for a Nobel Peace Prize. He exemplifies humble humanity and peace. He wrote numerous introductory books on Buddhist meditation and mindfulness.

21. Bynner, *The Way of Life*, no. 15.

22. Martine Batchelor, *Meditation for Life* (Boston: Wisdom Publication, 2001), 52.

23. Monica Furlong writes that Watts was suffering from an enlarged liver due to drinking. His doctor warned him to stop drinking, which—much to the relief of family and friends—he temporarily did. When he was noticed to resume drinking during a party, he explained: "If I don't drink, I don't feel sexy." Especially in small groups he seemed to have felt shy and inhibited. Monica Furlong, *Zen Effects: The Life of Alan Watts* (Boston: Houghton Mifflin, 1986), 189.

24. Rainer Maria Rilke, *Letters to a Young Poet* (Frankfurt: Insel Verlag, 1958), 21.

25. It is the highest goal in Islam to be close to God (the Muslim name being Allah). Usually, this is accomplished through the five pillars of Islam: (1) faith in the Oneness of God and the finality of the prophet-hood of Mohammad, (2) establishment of five daily prayers, (3) concern for and almsgiving to the needy, (4) self-purification through fasting (Ramadan), and (5) pilgrimage to Mecca for those who are able. The

Sufis go further in their attempt to become united with God, including additional devotional prayers, night vigils, and fasts. A divine utterance (*hadith qudsi*), which are words directly from God, says that the devotee might eventually become so loved by God that God would become his eyes, ears, hands, and feet. Mohammed M. Ayoub, *Islam: Faith and History* (Oxford: Oneworld, 2004), 155. In another book about Islam, we learn that the Sufi's understanding of true reality is recognizing God. Such a metaphysical knowledge or "spiritual realization," is the removal of the veils that separate man from God and from the full reality of his own true nature. It is the means of actualizing the full potentialities of the human state. J. L. Michon, J. L. and R. Gaetani, *Sufism: Love & Wisdom* (Bloomington: World Wisdom, 2006), 22.

26. D'Aquili and Newberg, *Mystical Mind.*

27. Batchelor, *The Faith to Doubt*, 78.

28. Bynner, *The Way of Life*, no. 15.

29. Carol D. Ryff and Burton Singer, "Flourishing Under Fire: Resilience as a Prototype of Challenged Thriving," *Flourishing: Positive Psychology and the Life Well-Lived*, eds. Corey L. M. Keyes and Jonathan Haidt (Washington, DC: American Psychological Association, 2003), 15ff; Elaine Wethington, "Turning Points as Opportunities for Psychological Growth," *Flourishing*, 37ff; Christopher Peterson and Edward Chang "Optimism and Flourishing," *Flourishing*, 55ff. All of these authors write about rising to life's challenges.

30. The poem by Kobayashi Issa that I am referring to is: "world over Hell viewing spring blossoms." David G. Lanoue, *Issa: Cup of Tea Poems* (Berkeley: Asian Humanities Press, 2001), 19.

31. Issa wrote this haiku (short, Japanese poems of seventeen syllables) upon the death of his child; it transmits the sorrow over the transience of the world. It can be found in R. H. Blyth's translation of Kobayashi Issa, *A Fly and I: Haiku* (New York: Random House, 1969).

32. As recommended by the Chinese Zen master Yün-men Wen-yen (d. 949 CE): "In walking, just walk. In sitting, just sit. Above all, don't wobble." Watts, *The Way of Zen*, 135.

33. Lewis Mackenzie, *Autumn Wind Haiku: Selected Poems by Kobayashi Issa* (Tokyo: Kodensha, 1999), 5.

34. Arthur Golden, *Memoirs of a Geisha* (New York: Vintage, 1997), 206.

35. Sigmund Freud (1856–1939) brought the concept of the unconscious to life, which is why he is the most influential personality in psychology. Yet his understanding was very different from a modern understanding. He believed that the unconscious mind keeps us away from unbearable psycho-sexual conflicts caused by our biological drives clashing with reality. Freud believed that we are determined by our biological drives. He did not accept Carl Gustav Jung's (1887–1961) theory that human beings are more accurately characterized by their desire for self-fulfillment than by their biological drives. Freud also did not accept Jung's notion of a

collective unconscious. This would be the part of the unconscious that all humans have in common, because we all go through the same basic conflicts and resolutions. Even though Jung's understanding of the unconscious was more positive than Freud's, neither one focused primarily on the unconscious as the seat for resources, as Milton Erickson did. Today, there is a great revival of the use of inner resources and the healing mind-body connection. Even Harvard Medical School advertises for relaxation and hypnosis to strengthen our body and mind. See "Take a Break from Stress," *Newsweek*, Sept. 27, 2004.

36. Timothy Wilson, *Strangers to Ourselves: Discovering the Adaptive Unconscious* (Cambridge, MA: Harvard University Press, 2002), 24.

37. G. Gigerenzer, P. M. Todd, and The ABC Research Group, *Simple Heuristics That Make Us Smart* (New York: Oxford University Press, 1999).

38. The complete quote by Joseph Campbell after being asked by Bill Moyers why a myth is different from a dream, is as follows: "Oh, because a dream is a personal experience of that deep, dark ground that is the support of our conscious lives; a myth is the society's dream. The myth is the public dream and the dream is the private myth. If your private myth, your dream, happens to coincide with that of the society, you are in good accord with your group. If it isn't, you've got an adventure in the dark forest ahead of you." Campbell, *The Power of Myth*, 48.

39. Erickson suffered from polio and "stumbled over" trance on his own when he was very young. He treated himself and others for pain, psychological disorders and issues, and he utilized the unconscious mind for countless learning experiences. Many consider him the best hypnotherapist of all times. Milton H. Erickson, *The Seminars, Workshops, and Lectures of Milton H. Erikson: Creative Choice in Hypnosis*, vol. 4, ed. E. L. Rossi and M. O. Ryan (New York: Irvington, 1992); Milton H. Erickson, *The Collected Papers of Milton H. Erickson on Hypnosis: Hypnotic Alteration of Sensory, Perceptual and Psychophysiological Processes* (vol. 2) and *Hypnotic Investigation of Psychodynamic Process*, vol. 3, ed. E. L. Rossi, (New York: Irvington, 1992).

40. Once, a student of Erickson gave no sign of wanting to come out of the peaceful state of trance. Finally, Erickson became frustrated with the subject and said: "For God's sake, snap out of it. After all, you are just in a stupid trance." The student instantly came back to his senses and started laughing. This story was recounted to a class I attended with hypnotherapist Terry Anges, PhD, who used to be a student of Erickson's.

41. D'Aquili and Newberg, *The Mystical Mind*.

42. Ibid., 98.

43. Ibid., 98.

44. Ibid., 97.

45. Not everyone is hypnotizable. Obviously, it is dangerous to access a trance when conscious thought is necessary, such as when driving in traffic. Some psychological disorders should not be treated with hypnosis.

46. Rilke, *Letters to a Young Poet*, 21.

47. Batchelor, *The Faith to Doubt*, 16–17.

48. "Our unconscious thinking is, in one critical respect, no different from our conscious thinking: in both, we are able to develop our rapid decision making with training and experience." Malcolm Gladwell, *Blink: The Power of Thinking Without Thinking* (New York, Boston: Little, Brown, 2005), 237.

49. Ibid., 120: "If you wrote a paragraph on Marilyn Monroe's face, without telling me whom you were writing about, could I guess who it was? We all have an instinctive memory for faces. But by forcing you to verbalize that memory—to explain yourself—I separate you from those instincts." Also: "In short, when you write down your thoughts, your chances of having the flash of insight you need in order to come up with a solution are significantly impaired." Ibid., 121.

50. William Dement, "Problem Solving," *Some Must Watch While Some Must Sleep* (San Francisco: W. H. Freeman, 1974), 98–102.

51. Deirdre Barrett had seventy-six subjects "incubate" dreams addressing problems chosen by the dreamer nightly for one week. Approximately half of this group believed to have dreamed about the problem. Most of this half thought they dreamed up solutions. Personal problems were more conducive for resolve than non-personal ones. Deirdre Barrett, "Comment on Baylor: A Note About Dreams of Scientific Problem Solving," *Dreaming* 11:2 (2001): 93–95.

52. As one of the first researchers on good feelings, Alice M. Isen and her team showed the beneficial effect of positive emotions. She showed, for example, that medical doctors who experience positive emotions are more likely to make accurate diagnosis than medical doctors without positive emotions. See A. M. Isen, A. S. Rosenzweig, and M. J. Young, "The Influence of Positive Affect on Clinical Problem Solving," *Medical Decision Making* 11 (1991): 221–27; A. M. Isen, "Positive Affect and Decision Making," *Handbook of Emotions*, ed. M. Lewis and J. M. Haviland-Jones (New York: Guilford Press, 2000), 417–35.

53. When we learn anything, the nerve cells in our brains (neurons) grow extensions (dendrites) to other neurons. (By the way, the Canadian psychologist Donald Hebb assumed as early as 1949 that learning had to be linked to individual nerve cells.) This occurs after learning something for only half an hour. Our brain literally forms itself throughout our life span if we make it work, as with new learning materials. See F. Engert and T. Bonhoeffer, "Dendritic Spine Changes Associated with Hippocampal Long-Term Synaptic Plasticity," *Nature* 399 (1999): 66–70. That mental imagery can grow the brain in almost the same way as hands-on experiences do, is shown in neuro-psychological studies. See K. O'Craven and M. Kanwisher, "Mental Imagery of Faces and Places Activates Stimulus-Specific Brain Regions," *Journal of Cognitive Neuroscience* 12 (2000): 1013–23.

54. Rebecca McClen Novick, *Fundamentals of Tibetan Buddhism* (Freedom, CA: The Crossing Press Freedom, 1999), 149.

55. Ibid., 149.

56. The word "unexcelled" awakening is used in the Diamond Sutra, also called Vajracchedika. Red Pine, *Tripitaka, The Diamond Sutra: The Perfection of Wisdom* (Washington, DC: Counterpoint, 2001).

57. Thomas Byrom, *Dhammapada: The Sayings of the Buddha* (New York: Shambhala Pocket, 1976), 36.

58. Stephen Batchelor, *Buddhism without Beliefs: A Contemporary Guide to Awakening* (New York: Riverhead Books, 1998), 9.

59. Watts, *The Way of Zen*, 126.

60. Ibid., 152.

61. Nelson Foster and Jack Shoemaker, *The Roaring Stream: A New Zen Reader* (Hopewell, NJ: The Ecco Press, 1996), 65.

62. Ibid., 66.

CHAPTER 11—RELIANCE

1. *"Deus ex machina* ('god out of the machine') describes an unexpected, artificial, or improbable character, device, or event introduced suddenly in a work of fiction or drama to resolve a situation or untangle a plot. . . . The Latin phrase *deus ex machina* has its origins in the conventions of Greek tragedy, with ancient Roman dramatists continuing the use of the device." (en.wikipedia.org/wiki/Deus_ex_machina). "In modern terms the deus ex machina has also come to describe a being, object, or event that suddenly appears and solves a seemingly insoluble difficulty, where the author has 'painted the characters into a corner' that they can't easily be extricated from." (lanedemoll.com/Gallerypages/ContentPages/Flashbacks/machina.htm)

2. Peterson writes in his article "Personal Control and Well-Being" that a sense of control is often beneficial to people's experience, unless they really have no influence on the outcome. If we do not feel that we have control, we could develop learned helplessness (see Peterson, Maier, and Seligman, *Learned Helplessness*). However, Peterson also points out that one can assume too much personal control, which manifests in risk-taking behavior, hostility, perfectionism, anxiety, and paranoia. He concludes: "Attempts to enhance the well-being of people need to consider personal control, among other factors, but at the same time to avoid assuming that more is necessarily better." Christopher Peterson, "Personal Control and Well-Being," *Well-Being: The Foundations of Hedonic Psychology*, eds. Daniel Kahneman, Ed Diener, and Norbert Schwarz (New York: Russell Sage Foundation, 1999), 299.

3. Gerd Gigerenzer, *Calculated Risks: How to Know When Numbers Deceive You* (New York: Simon and Schuster, 2002), 11.

4. Gerd Gigerenzer, *Gut Feelings: The Intelligence of the Unconscious* (New York: Viking, 2007), 43.

5. Swimme, *Hidden Heart of the Cosmos*, 71.

6. Hawking writes about German physicist Werner Heisenberg's famous uncertainty principle. Based on Planck's hypothesis that light always comes in little packets he called quanta, Heisenberg stated that the more accurately one tries to measure the position of a particle, the less accurately one can measure its speed, and vice versa. This means that whether or not we perceive a wave or particle depends on the way we measure, because the high-frequency wavelength disturbs the velocity of the particle, and the low-frequency wavelength disturbs the position more. (Hawking, *The Universe in a Nutshell*, 41.) Hawking goes on to say in the same book that Einstein continued to work on the quantum idea but was deeply disturbed by the work of Werner Heisenberg and others who developed quantum mechanics. "Einstein was horrified by this random, unpredictable element in the basic laws and never fully accepted quantum mechanics. His feelings were expressed in his famous dictum 'God does not play dice.'" Ibid., 24.

7. Kornfield, *Teachings of the Buddha*, 38.

8. Lebell, *Epictetus*, 91.

9. David O'Neil, *Meister Eckhart, from Whom God Hid Nothing: Sermons, Writings & Sayings* (Boston: Shambhala, 1996), 7.

10. Research has shown that religion reduces *un*happiness. Apparently we cope better with life's fragility when we believe in something sturdy. On average, however, religion increases happiness only moderately (Seligman, *Authentic Happiness*, 61). Religion encourages and teaches us how to focus on the indefinable realm. Any such practice would have to facilitate our access to the Supreme Mode. Also, religion is helpful to the extent that it fosters a sense of connectedness, which is essential to happiness (see chapter 6). Religion does not automatically give purpose to everyone.

11. The Latin word base *religio* means "to bind or link together."

12. O'Neil, *Meister Eckhart*, 15.

13. Cross, *Way of Hinduism*, 128.

14. Mark W. Muesse, *The Great World Religions: Hinduism*, Course Guidebook, (Chantilly, VA: The Teaching Company, 2003), 24.

15. Ibid., 50.

16. Castes divide society in India into four main groups, which are determined by birth and manifested in one's vocation and purity. The highest caste is the one of the Brāhmins (priests and intellectuals), followed by Kśatriyas (warriors and administrators), the Vaiśyas (farmers, business people, cattle herders, artisans), and Sùdras (peasants and servants). See Muesse, *Great World Religions: Hinduism*.

17. Ibid., 25.

18. Goodness is defined as a way of being that benefits not only the individual, but also the group.

19. Wilhelm Schmid writes in his short philosophical work on happiness (in my own translation): "So we may say: sense is interconnectedness, and senselessness is the lack of interconnectedness. This is true for the simple sentence: if we see an order or connectedness in the words, if we see the formulation of a statement, the sentence makes sense. Otherwise we would refer to it as nonsense." Wilhelm Schmid, *Glück: Alles, Was Sie Darueber Wissen Muessen Und Warum Es Nicht Das Wichtigste Im Leben Ist* (Frankfurt am Main: Insel Verlag, 2007), 46.

20. When the Buddhist king Asoka (c. 268–239 BCE) reigned in India, the first missionaries left for Sri Lanka where the "tradition of the Elders," the Theravada tradition, grew. As Eckel explains, the tradition raised the concept of the "righteous king." The concept is still evident in Thailand and with the democratic activist Aung San Suu Kyi of Myanmar (Burma). She received the Nobel Peace Prize in 1991 for her nonviolent resistance to Burma's military regime. David M. Eckel, *The Great World Religions: Buddhism*, Course Guidebook (Chantilly, VA: The Teaching Company, 2002), 35.

21. While there are good examples of mixing politics with religion as noted in note 20, Theravada Buddhists in Sri Lanka have used their religion to wage a bloody war with the Sri Lanka Hindus. Eckel, *Great World Religions: Buddhism*, 39.

22. This Bible quote, Micah 6:8 (AV), was found in Gregg Easterbrook's book *Beside Still Waters*. Easterbrook writes:

> But surely in that contest our Maker would consider compassion and morality infinitely more significant than religion. Plain words are what matter most about scripture, and among the plainest words in the Bible are those that appear at the chapter head, quoted from Micah, one of the final Old Testament books: 'What does the Lord require of you but to do justice, and to love kindness and to walk humbly with your God?' Here we find an unambiguous directive that women and men seek the spiritual; we find no requirement for any particular religion. God wants our feet on the path, but hardly cares what brand of shoes we wear.

Gregg Easterbrook, *The Progress Paradox: How Life Gets Better While People Feel Worse* (New York: Random House, 2004), 284.

23. The Dalai Lama proposes that happiness is mostly the result of living a life of compassion. Dalai Lama, *The Path to Tranquility* (New York: Penguin, 1998).

24. Mahayana Buddhism began around the Common Era. While the texts (sutras, such as the Avatamsaka Sutra) were likely written after the Theravada texts (Pali Canon), Mahayana Buddhists claim they were passed down directly from Buddha. Takakusu writes that it is said that because no ordinary person understood a word of these sutras, the Buddha preached them to a selected few, namely bodhisattvas, while continuing to preach the Āgamas to the others. Generally, both the Pali Canon and the Āgamas on the Theravada side and the sutras on the Mahayana side are considered *Buddhavacana* (the word of the Buddha). The Mahayana

doctrines represent a departure in Buddha's philosophy (Buddha not as a God, but merely "the awakened one") and a turn to a religion. Mahayana Buddhism speaks of gradations of Buddhahood, with Buddhahood on top, preceded by a series of lives as bodhisattvas. The Buddha as we know him is supposed to have had countless lives before his final one. Takakusu, *Essentials of Buddhist Philosophy*, 112ff.

25. Eckel explains that advanced practitioners of the bodhisattva path (in the ninth or tenth stages) achieve extraordinary, superhuman powers that make it possible for them to reside in the heavens. Such bodhisattvas are called celestial Buddhas and bodhisattvas (Eckel, *Great World Religions: Buddhism*, 27). Avalokiteshvara ("Lord who looks down with compassion") or Kuan-yin (in Chinese) is one of the most important celestial bodhisattvas. In Tibet, Avalokiteshvara is manifested in the form of the Dalai Lama. Amitabha is the compassionate "Buddha of Infinite Light" in the Pure Land tradition, which is practiced mostly in China and Japan (ibid.).

26. Novick, *Fundamentals of Tibetan Buddhism*, 113.

27. I leaned on D. T. Suzuki's (1960) translation of the paramitas, 72–73.

28. Martine Batchelor writes: "Ethics in Buddhism does not mean blind rules and regulations. They do not exist to force you to do something, but to make you reflect on your motivations and actions." Batchelor, *Meditation for Life*, 52.

29. Ibid., 78.

30. Ibid., 85. "He (Buddha) said that there are four types of people: those who give only to others, those who only give to themselves, those who give to neither, and those who give to both themselves and others. He encouraged people to cultivate the fourth option."

31. The Avatamsaka Sutra is a voluminous, relatively recent work of Mahayana Buddhism. It greatly influenced Zen Buddhism, which—in connection with Taoism—rose in China in the first millennium. The image of the Avatamsaka Sutra is a network of gems that reflect each other. We can also notice the connecting, spontaneous nature in all our mind/experiences, be they related to convention or no-convention. See Thich Nhat Hanh, *The Ultimate Dimension: An Advanced Dharma Retreat on the Avatamsaka and Lotus Sutras* (Boulder: Sounds True, 2004), and Watts, *The Way of Zen*, 70.

32. See note 25.

33. Eckel explains that the OM in the mantra OM MANI PADME HUM is the sacred syllable of the Vedas (basic sacred texts in Hinduism) and that the sound HUM conveys power. However, a mantra's power does not lie in the meaning of words, but in the phrase itself. Eckel, *Great World Religions: Buddhism*, 27.

34. Ibid., 54.

35. Ibid., 24.

36. The so-called vacuum energy releases particles at random. Why some return to this energy while others keep in existence is not yet known. (See also note 10, chapter 8.)

37. Frederick Douglass, *Narrative of the Life of Frederick Douglass: An American Slave, Written by Himself* (New York: Pocket Books, 2004), 98–99.

38. Simon Leys, *The Analects of Confucius* (New York: W. W. Norton, 1997), xxiii.

39. Ibid., *Analects* II:3.

40. "The Master said: 'He who rules by virtue is like the polestar, which remains unmoving in its mansion while all the other stars revolve respectfully around it.'" (Ibid., II:1).

41. Confucius described himself as a passionate person, believing in love and ecstasy. Leys gives the following example: "When his beloved disciple Yan Hui died prematurely, Confucius was devastated; his grief was wild, he cried with a violence that stunned people around him; they objected that such as excessive reaction did not befit a sage—a criticism which Confucius rejected indignantly." (Ibid., xxi–xxii).

42. Adam Liptak, "1 in 100 U.S. Adults Behind Bars, New Study Says" *New York Times,* Feb. 28, 2008.

43. Leys, *Analects of Confucius,* xxiii.

44. Daniel Quinn, *Ishmael: An Adventure of the Mind and Spirit* (New York: Bantam/Turner Book, 1992), 249.

45. Wu, *Tao Teh Ching,* no. 4.

46. Wu, *Tao Teh Ching,* no. 34. This poem concludes with: "It is just because it does not wish to be great that its greatness is fully realized."

47. According to Wikipedia, the word *weiji* could be split off in *wei,* which means danger and *ji,* which has a variety of meanings, one of which is opportunity (wikipedia.org/wiki/Chinese_word_for_%22crisis%22).

48. Kornfield, *Path with Heart,* 109.

49. See note 27.

50. John Blofeld, *The Zen Teaching of Huang Po: On the Transmission of Mind* (New York: Grove Press, 1958), 30.

51. Mel Weitsman, *Branching Streams Flow in the Darkness: Zen Talks on the Sandokai* (London: University of California Press, 1999), 28.

52. Quote from the Dalai Lama, *Path to Tranquility,* ix. The main theme in the Dalai Lama's book *The Art of Happiness* is that compassion alone leads to happiness. The Dalai Lama promotes a vigorous training of the mind to accomplish a constant positive state of mind. Understanding the indefinable/emptiness has a place in his philosophy, but it is not made explicit in his book on happiness. The great authority of the Dalai Lama and his emphasis on effort and the definable realm (virtues, rules, and so on) may have led to an approach that is more in alignment with the West. Accordingly there is no cultivation of "great doubt" in Tibetan Buddhism. Stephen Batchelor, who used to be an ordained Tibetan monk, reports that doubt is missing in this school. When he heard about the Buddhist practice of mindfulness—a practice not included in Tibetan Buddhism—he

was tolerated, and not encouraged. Doubt was not part of his school's curriculum; students were expected to take a leap of faith. Batchelor writes: "Just as Tibet was a country sealed off both by its geography and its political intentions, so is Tibetan Buddhism a sealed, hermetic system of thought and practice that makes excellent sense if studied in its own terms but gets problematic if looked at from outside its own parameters. . . . Once inside the system, there is no room for doubt. The teacher is enlightened, the path complete and perfect." Batchelor, *The Faith to Doubt*, 9.

53. Zen master (Ta Hui) Donald Gilbert was a monk in the Cho Ke Order of Korea. He was born in Oakland, California, in 1909. He was recognized a Zen master by his teacher, the venerable Dr. Seo Kyung-bo of Korea. He was also a cartoonist and wrote a delightful book using this craft. His cartoons are full of insight and are highly recommended to all interested in Zen. For example, Gilbert writes, "Climbing the mountain, one finds the view unobstructed at the top. This is intuitional knowing. All directions are now 'one direction.' The 'one direction' springs forth from pure consciousness or Mind." In my words, once we have the freedom to turn around all ways, the answer of the moment can come to us. Donald Gilbert, *The Upside Down Circle: Zen Laughter* (Nevada City, CA: Blue Dolphin, 1988), 77.

54. D. T. Suzuki, Erich Fromm, and Richard De Martino, *Zen Buddhism and Psychoanalysis* (New York: Grove Press, 1960), 15–16. When the book was written, psychoanalysis was still in vogue. Zen Buddhists did not find connecting with psychoanalysts far-fetched. Reaching into the unconscious via free association is vaguely akin to reaching into one's deep, spontaneous nature via thought-discouraging methods, such as koans. Nowadays, cognitive therapy is in vogue. Tibetan Buddhism connects with today's psychology. Positive, more effective thinking is accomplished by cognitive restructuring, and this seems similar to the compassionate mind undergoing rigorous mental training. Interestingly, current popular Zen Buddhists point more to the cognitive aspects of their world view. Apparently East and West are influenced by the Zeitgeist.

55. See note 31.

56. Thich Nhat Hanh, *The Ultimate Dimension* (audio).

57. Weitsman, *Branching*, 191. The translation is modified by Suzuki Roshi who used to interpret the famous poem (put together by Shunryu Suzuki).

58. Merton quotes Professor Shin'ichi Hisamatsu in *The Way of Chuang Tzu*, 283.

59. When I talked on the telephone with Martine Batchelor about the conditions for the good and full life, she pointed out that she believes virtuous action is the most important. She went on to explain: "In Korean Zen Buddhism, virtuous action is stressed very much. We need to aspire to goodness and cultivate it. But we ought not to look for goodness as something separate from ourselves; we must find from within." Also see Martine Batchelor, where she writes: "Compassion is an essential component of the Buddhist way of life. It is at the heart of meditation because meditation is not self-absorption but, on the contrary, leads to openness and connection with others." Batchelor, *Meditation for Life*, 82.

CHAPTER 12—LIGHTHEARTEDNESS

1. This metaphor is from Hermann Hesse, *Betrachtungen über das Glück*.

2. First published in 1911, Henri Bergson wrote, "Could reality come into direct contact with sense and consciousness, could we enter into immediate communion with things and with ourselves, probably art would be useless, or rather we should all be artists, for then our soul would continuously vibrate in perfect accord with nature." From Henri Bergson, *Laughter: An Essay on the Meaning of the Comic* (London: MacMillan, 1999), 135.

3. S. Biddle and N. Mutrie, *Psychology of Physical Activity and Exercise*. (London: Springer/Tavistock/Routledge, 1991); A. Steptoe, J. Kimbell, and P. Basford, "Exercise and the Experience and Appraisal of Daily Stressors: A Naturalistic Study," *Journal of Behavioral Medicine* 21 (1996): 363–74; and R. E. Thayer, *The Biopsychology of Mood and Emotion* (New York: Oxford University Press, 1989).

4. Ratey and Hagerman, *Spark*, 38.

5. A. Bjørnebekk, A. A. Mathe, and S. Brene, "The Antidepressant Effect of Running Is Associated with Increased Hippocampal Cell Proliferation," *International Journal of Neuropsychopharmacology* 8, no. 3 (2005): 357–68.

6. Ratey and Hagerman, *Spark*.

7. Stefan Klein, *Die Glücksformel oder Wie die guten Gefühle entstehen*, 81.

8. S. M. Jaeggi, J. J. Buschkuehl, and Walter J. Perrig, "Improving Fluid Intelligence with Training on Working Memory," accessed September 27, 2011, pnas.org/content/early/2008/04/25/0801268105.abstract.

9. Linda Carstensen, PhD, a professor of psychology at Stanford University who studies the influence of age on time perception and goals, was profiled by Carlin Flora. The article explains also why older people are happier on average than previously suggested by research. Carlin Flora, "Happy Hour," *Psychology Today* (Jan/Feb 2005), 42ff.

10. "Zen," *Wikipedia*, last modified September 22, 2001, en.wikipedia.org/wiki/Zen.

11. Weitsman, *Branching*, 3.

12. Gilbert, *Upside Down Circle*, 127.

13. Daniel Kahneman, PhD, who won a Nobel prize in economics for his insights in irrationality and decision-making, has turned his attention to well-being. He is introduced by Flora, "Happy Hour," 47ff.

14. Ibid.

15. As a Buddhist, Thich Nhat Hanh believes that everything we need for happiness is already present in us (Buddha-nature). However, the "positive elements within our bodies and in our consciousness" need opportunities to get in touch with the good inside of us. He very gently directs his attention to the good in order to let it grow. In his eyes, however, the bad should never be denied. We should not blind ourselves to

who we authentically are. Yet, it is up to us what part of us we want to invite and cultivate. Thich Nhat Hanh, "Consumption/Compassion: An Interview with Thich Nhat Hanh by Kyleigh," *Journal of Holistic Lifestyle* (2001): 34.

16. Claudia Wallis, "The New Science of Happiness," *Times* (January 17, 2005): A43.

17. Watts, *The Way of Zen*, 39.

18. Eckhart Tolle, *A New Earth: Awakening to Your Life's Purpose* (New York: Plume, 2005), 8. "The first part of this truth [proposed by various religions] is the realization that the 'normal' state of mind of most human beings contains a strong element of what we might call a dysfunction or even madness." (Brackets added by me.) Although I commend Tolle for advocating successfully the need for growth, awareness, and inner tranquility with his inspiring books *The Power of Now* and *A New Earth*, I do not believe that we can disconnect from our primitive nature. However conscious we become, we will remain biologically driven creatures, and only when we can accept that fact will we develop our human potential to its fullest extent. Enlightenment must come from a place of love for our biological nature that is great enough to allow us to give it direction and add an eye of awareness to its rudimentary program.

19. Bynner, *The Way of Life*, no. 1.

20. Bergson, *Laughter*, 136.

21. Kaufmann, *Goethe's Faust*, 95.

22. Ibid., 493.

23. Ibid., 500. The soul in the Christian tradition is similar to our True Self (Buddhism) or Atman (Hinduism). It is perfect in its own nature, but needs to be transformed by living, undiscriminating love that is the grace of God.

> Grant this good soul, too, thy blessing,
> That but once herself forgot,
> Ignorant she was transgressing;
> Pardon her and spurn her not!

24. After praising the "almightly love by which all things are nursed and fashioned" (ibid., 489) and "Being" to be kind to everyone (ibid., 491), the tragedy ends with praising the all-encompassing love of Maria, the mother of Jesus, who can forgive the striving Faust. Through her (and our own) loving actions, we may get a glimpse of the indefinable, formless experience. That which is form and destructible would be a likeness of or a comparison to life, a parable. On the other hand, the indefinable, indestructible is connected with love:

> The Eternal-Feminine
> Lures to perfection.

Ibid., 503.

25. Master Lin-Chi (Japanese: Rinzai), disciple of Huang-Po (d. 850 CE), stressed many times how effort has no place in Buddhism. To him it was more about having the courage to rely solely on one's awareness. The Rinzai school, which triggers overwhelming doubt with koans, was named after him. Quote from Burton Watson, *The Zen Teachings of Master Lin-chi. A translation of the Lin-chi lu.* (New York: Columbia University Press, 1999), 52.

26. Tolle, *A New Earth*, 79.

27. Watts, *The Way of Zen*, 22.

28. Merton, *The Way of Chuang Tzu*, 23. Merton, born in France, lived in Kentucky as a Trappist monk in the Abbey of Our Lady of Gethsemani. He was a prolific writer who promoted inter-religious understanding. Although his life was cut short due to an accident when he was only fifty-three years old, he contributed greatly to making Buddhism more accessible to Westerners. See also: Thomas Merton, *Mystics and Zen Masters* (New York: Farrar, Straus, 1999) and Roger Lipsey, *Angelic Mistakes: The Art of Thomas Merton* (Boston: New Seeds, 2006).

29. Lin-Chi preached to his fellow monks: "You should stop and take a good look at yourselves. A man of old tells us that Yajnadatta thought he had lost his head and went looking for it, but once he had put a stop to his seeking mind, he found he was perfectly all right. Fellow believers, just act ordinary, don't affect some special manner." Watson, *Teachings of Master Lin-chi*, 27.

30. Ibid., 41.

31. Gilbert, *Upside Down Circle*, 145.

32. Bergson, *Laughter*, 135.

33. Merton, *Mystics and Zen Masters*, 74.

34. Watts, *The Way of Zen*, 107.

35. Merton, *Mystics and Zen Masters*, 76.

36. Watson, *Teachings of Master Lin-chi*, 87 (slightly changed quote.) Little is known of the Chinese monk P'u-hua (Japanese: Fuke), who died 860 CE. What is known can be found in the records of the Zen master Lin-chi-lu (Japanese: Rinzai). There is also a beautiful related story: when the monk felt that it was time to die, he laid himself inside a coffin. When people rushed to the coffin, they found that the body had vanished. Yet, from high in the sky they could still hear his handbell faintly, until this sound died away. Ibid., 102.

37. The flying heroes and heroines can be seen in movies such as *Crouching Tiger, Hidden Dragon; Hero;* and *House of Flying Daggers.*

38. Jalal al-Din Rumi, who lived from 1207–1273 and who was the son of a famous religious scholar (Baha al-Din), was a very influential mystic of Islam. Rumi made his contributions in the form of beautiful poetry, especially in his famous *Mathnawi* that highlights hidden aspects of Sufism and how Sufis relate to living in the world. Jalal al-Din Rumi, *The Essential Rumi, New Expanded Edition* (New York: HarperCollins, 2004), 13.

39. The great Japanese poet Basho, who lived from 1644–94, expressed himself in seventeen-syllable haiku. They are meant to be recited in one breath. Matsuo Basho, *On Love and Barley: Haiku by Basho,* Translator: Lucien Stryk (New York: Penguin Classics, 1986), 197.

40. Merton quotes professor Hisamatsu saying that the Zen view "will enable us to make a more proper attempt at a radical cure of the human predicament through the Self-awakening of that oneness which, contrary to being in estrangement from civilization, accords with, and is the source and base of civilization." Merton, *Mystics and Zen Masters,* 284.

41. Alan Watts, *The Meaning of Happiness: The Quest for Freedom of the Spirit in Modern Psychology and the Wisdom of the East* (New York: Harper & Row, 1968), 65.

42. Jack Kornfield, *The Wise Heart: A Guide to the Universal Teachings of Buddhist Psychology* (New York: Bantam, 2008), 395.

43. Ekman and Friesen have argued on behalf of the facial feedback hypothesis. They measured how people felt with and without positive facial expressions. As they found that people report feeling significantly better when they smile, as opposed to when they don't, they argued that facial expressions are not solely a function of communicating with others. They also examined various kinds of smiles, such as "felt, false and miserable smiles." P. Ekman and W. V. Friesen, "Felt, False and Miserable Smiles," *Journal of Nonverbal Behavior* 6 (1982): 238–52. In my own research I have found that depressed people tend to actively suppress the expression of a smile in that they bite their lips, push them together, or perform otherwise antagonistic movements. I have argued that a smile must fit the mood in depressed people, as otherwise they feel as if they are being untrue to themselves. In other words, the vast discrepancy between affect and mood makes depressed people uncomfortable. This can only happen if there is an instant feedback loop as described by Ekman and Friesen. Andrea F. Polard (former Andrea Floren), *Das Laecheln bei depressiven PatientInnen: Videoverhaltensanalyse von PatientInnen und Kontrollpersonen,* Diplomarbeit der Freien Universität Berlin, Institut für Psychologie, 1993.

44. The felt smile with crow's feet, as opposed to the social smile, was first described by G. B. A. Duchenne. It is therefore referred to as the "Duchenne smile." G. B. A. Duchenne, *Mechanisme de la physionomie humaine; ou analyse electrophysiologique de l'expression des passions* (Paris: Bailliere, 1862).

45. Robert R. Provine, *Laughter: A Scientific Investigation* (New York: Penguin, 2000), 124.

46. Klaus K. Klostermaier, *A Concise Encyclopedia of Hinduism* (Oxford: Oneworld Publication, 1998), 104.

47. Ibid., 52.

48. Muesse, *Great World Religions: Hinduism,* 39.

49. O'Neil, *Meister Eckhart,* 69.

50. Ibid., 69.

51. Bergson, *Laughter*, 15.

52. Ibid., 14.

53. Gilbert, *Upside Down Circle*, x.

54. Allen Klein, "Zen Humor: From Ha-Ha to Ah-Ha," accessed September 27, 2011, allenklein.com/articles/zenhumor.htm.

55. Conrad Hyers, "Humer in Zen: Comic midwifery," accessed September 27, 2011, ccbs.ntu.edu.tw/FULLTEXT/JR-PHIL/hyers1.htm.

56. The word *ryokan* means "great fool" in Japanese.

57. Watts, *The Way of Zen*, 105. Zen master Yüan-wu lived from 1063 to 1135.

58. D. T. Suzuki, *Sengai: The Zen of Ink and Paper* (Boston: Shambhala, 1999), 2.

59. Ibid., 2.

60. Ibid., 14. Kwasan lived from 891 to 960 CE.

61. Ibid., 134. Suzuki interprets the delightful calligraphy of Sengai.

62. Watts, *The Meaning of Happiness*, 186.

63. Watts's friend and collaborator, Al Chung-liang Huang, also wrote a wonderful and touching introduction to Watts and Huang, *Tao: The Watercourse Way*, ix.

64. Furlong, *Zen Effects*, 212.

CONCLUSION—A SYNTHESIS OF WESTERN AND EASTERN THOUGHT: THE THEORY OF ELASTIC CONSCIOUSNESS

1. Paulo Coelho, *Der Alchemist* (Zürich: Diogenes, 1996), 39.

2. "Much mental activity appears to occur without the exertion of substantial effort. Time-pressure is a particularly important determinant of momentary effort. Tasks that impose a heavy load on short-memory necessarily impose severe time-pressure." Danile Kahneman, *Attention and Effort* (Englewood Cliffs, NJ: Prentice-Hall, 1973), 27. So, any time-constricted activity or one in which we utilize our short-term memory—calculations—requires extra effort. Following our pursuits and people without these pressures will bring us closer to the effortlessness of the Supreme Mode. Being in the present is relaxing.

3. Miller and Stiver, *The Healing Connection*, 30ff.

4. John M. Rist, *Epicurus: An Introduction* (Cambridge, MA: Cambridge University Press, 1972), 129.

5. Henry D. Sedgwick, *The Art of Happiness: Or, The Teachings of Epicurus* (Indianapolis: Bobbs Merrill, 1933).

6. Joachim Bauer, *Warum ich fühle, was du fühlst: Intuitive Kommunikation und das Geheimnis der Spiegelneurone* (München: Wilhelm Heyne Verlag, 2005); Marco Iacoboni *Mirroring People: The New Science of How We*

Connect with Others (New York: Farrar, Straus, 2008). The latter book explains that there are specialized brain cells responsible for empathy and instant understanding.

7. "Martin Buber, perhaps the greatest Jewish philosopher of the twentieth century, believed that nothing was more important than the relationship between two people. They can be members of the same family or sometimes even complete strangers. When two individuals realize, for even just a moment, that they depend on each other, then they have come closer to God. Buber called this an I-Thou experience and imagined that the invisible lines of relation joining them to one another also join them to God." In Lawrence Kushner, *Jewish Spirituality: A Brief Introduction for Christians* (Woodstock, VT: Jewish Lights, 2001), 33.

8. D'Aquili and Newberg, *The Mystical Mind*, 95.

9. See note 3, introduction.

Happiness Resources

Please visit "Happiness Resource Page" on andreapolard.com to link directly to the recommended websites. Also see the Happiness Reference Chart on page 4.

SURVIVING

Dawkins, Richard. *The Selfish Gene.* New York: Oxford University Press, 2006. (richarddawkins.net)

Diener, Ed, and Robert Biswas-Diener. *Happiness: Unlocking the Mysteries of Psychological Wealth.* Malden, MA: Blackwell Publishing, 2008. This book contains a lot of information, including information about the importance of fulfilling basic needs. Although happiness and unhappiness can coincide, there is a point at which we become too unhappy to be happy. (diener. socialpsychology.org)

Ehrenreich, Barbara. *Nickel and Dimed: On (Not) Getting By in America.* New York: Owl Books, 2001. (barbaraehrenreich.com)

Friedman, Thomas L. *Hot, Flat, and Crowded: Why We Need a Green Revolution—And How It Can Renew America.* New York: Farrar, Straus and Giroux, 2008. (thomaslfriedman.com)

Singer, Peter. *The Life You Can Save: Acting Now to End World Poverty.* New York: Random House, 2009. (princeton.edu/~psinger/)

Wright, Robert. *Nonzero: The Logic of Human Destiny.* New York: Vintage Books, 2001. (nonzero.org)

SURVIVING WELL

Beattie, Melody. *The New Codependency: Help and Guidance for Today's Generation.* New York: Simon & Schuster, 2009. Although the concept of codependency has recently been under criticism, millions of people suffer from a compulsive urge to take care of others while unable to take care of themselves. The book is especially helpful for women and mental health care providers. (melodybeattie.com)

Diener, Ed, and Robert Biswas-Diener. *Happiness: Unlocking the Mysteries of Psychological Wealth.* Malden, MA: Blackwell Publishing, 2008. Again, this book contains a lot of useful information, including information about the importance of opportunity. (diener.socialpsychology.org)

Evans, Gail. *Play Like a Man, Win Like a Woman. What Men Know About Success That Women Need to Learn.* New York: Broadway Books, 2000. (bigspeak.com/gail-evans.html)

Friedman, Thomas L. *The World Is Flat 3.0: A Brief History of the Twenty-first Century.* New York: Picador, 2007. This book discusses building competencies that are indispensable and help us compete in the global market. (thomaslfriedman.com)

Gilbert, Daniel. *Stumbling on Happiness: Think You Know What Makes You Happy?* New York: Knopf, 2006. Gilbert reminds us of our limited cognitive ability to predict what kinds of pleasures have a positive impact on us. While pleasure is relatively unpredictable, we can use our imagination to help us stumble on happiness. (wjh.harvard.edu/~dtg/gilbertnewleftframe.htm)

Kahneman, Daniel, Ed Diener, and Norbert Schwarz. *Well-Being: The Foundation of Hedonic Psychology.* New York: Russell Sage Foundation, 1999. (diener.socialpsychology.org)

Liedloff, Jean. *The Continuum Concept: In Search of Happiness Lost.* Cambridge, MA: Perseus Books, 1985. Liedloff's book helps us to raise happy children. (continuum-concept.org)

DEFINITION OF HAPPINESS

Cantor, Nancy, and Catherine A. Sanderson. "Life Task Participation and Well-Being: The Importance of Taking Part in Daily Life," *Well-Being: The Foundation of Hedonic Psychology.* New York: Russell Sage Foundation, 1999.

The Dalai Lama, Herbert Benson, Robert F. Thurman, Howard E. Gardner, and Daniel Goldman. *MindScience: An East-West Dialogue.* Somerville, MA: Wisdom Publications, 1991. Howard E. Gardner's contribution is especially interesting as it points to a synthesis of Western and Eastern thought. Other books by Gardner include *Multiple Intelligences; Creating Minds;* and *Truth, Beauty, and Goodness Reframed.* (howardgardner.com/books/books.html)

Haidt, Jonathan. *The Happiness Hypothesis: Finding Truth in Ancient Wisdom.* New York: Basic Books, 2006. Haidt's book is a helpful intellectual analysis of ten lessons learned from ancient wisdom holding up in the light of science. Haidt's conclusion can be considered an introduction to *A Unified Theory of Happiness: An East-Meets-West Approach to Fully Loving Your Life.* (people.virginia.edu/~jdh6n/)

COMMITMENT TO HAPPINESS

Without a true commitment to happiness, it is unlikely we should go "up" that path, and we are more likely to march only on the path of survival. If we like to add happiness to our priorities, we must do so with awareness and dedication. As a constant reminder it is helpful to display a written contract with oneself or declare one's commitment publicly.

MIND-BODY FITNESS

If at all possible, avoid crash diets, and consult with a medical doctor before following advice from anybody.

Nutrition

"The Nutrition Source: Healthy Eating Plate and Healthy Eating Pyramid." (hsph.harvard.edu/nutritionsource/what-should-you-eat/pyramid/)

Boutenko, Victoria. *Green for Life*. Berkeley, CA: North Atlantic Books, 2005. (rawfamily.com)

Brazier, Brendan. *The Thrive Diet: The Whole Food Way to Lose Weight, Reduce Stress, and Stay Healthy for Life*. Cambridge, MA: Da Capo Press, 2007. (thrivediet.com)

Vegan Outreach (veganoutreach.org)

Exercise

Bakewell, Lisa. *Fitness Information for Teens: Health Tips about Exercise, Physical Well-Being, and Health Maintenance*. Detroit: Omnigraphics, 2008.

Ratey, John J., and Eric Hagerman. *Spark: The Revolutionary New Science for Exercise and the Brain*. New York: Little, Brown and Company, 2008. Outstanding information on the benefits of exercise. (youtube.com/watch?v=Bmc0ERKfjP0 and johnratey.com/newsite/index.html)

AMBITION

Bach, Richard. *Jonathan Livingston Seagull*. New York: Simon and Schuster, 1970. This is a truly timeless fiction book about the type of ambition that leads to happiness.

Csikszentmihalyi, Mihaly. *Flow: The Psychology of Optimal Experience*. New York: HarperCollins, 1990. Csikszentmihalyi explains how the pursuit of good goals can fulfill us and help us go beyond the experience of self. (brainchannels.com/thinker/mihaly.html)

Evans, Gail. *Play Like a Man, Win Like a Woman: What Men Know About Success That Women Need to Learn*. New York: Broadway Books, 2000. (bigspeak.com/gail-evans.html)

COMPETENCE

Friedman, Thomas L. *The World Is Flat 3.0: A Brief History of the Twenty-first Century*. New York: Picador, 2007. This book discusses building competencies that are indispensable and help us compete in the global market with compassion and happiness. (thomaslfriedman.com)

Gardner, Howard. *Creating Minds: An Anatomy of Creativity Seen Through the Lives of Freud, Einstein, Picasso, Stravinsky, Eliot, Graham, and Gandhi*. New York: Basic Books, 1993. Creativity is becoming increasingly important in the global market, which is why I recommend nonorganized, creative play for children. (howardgardner.com)

Maslow, Abraham H. *Toward a Psychology of Being.* 3rd ed. New York: John Wiley and Sons, 1999.

CONFIDENCE

Gardner, Howard. *Multiple Intelligences: New Horizons in Theory and Practice.* New York: Basic Books, 2006. Gardner makes a strong case for diversity in education and that each of us comes with a unique set of talents that we ought to identify and nourish. (howardgardner.com)

Harris, Russ, and Steven Hayes. *The Happiness Trap: How to Stop Struggling and Start Living.* Boston: Trumpeter Books, 2007. This book advocates strongly against the attempt to reduce ourselves to good feelings and makes a case to accept and be mindful of all feelings. (thehappinesstrap.com)

Seligman, Martin E. P. *Authentic Happiness: Using the New Positive Psychology to Realize Your Potential for Lasting Fulfillment.* New York: The Free Press, 2002. This book has made the new positive psychology famous. It stresses the importance of finding and utilizing our own internal, so-called signature strengths. (authentichappiness.com)

CONNECTION

Iacoboni, Marco. *Mirroring People: The New Science of How We Connect with Others.* New York: Picador, 2008. This book explains the specialized brain cells responsible for empathy and instant understanding.

Lerner, Harriet. *The Dance of Connection: How to Talk to Someone When You're Mad, Hurt, Scared, Frustrated, Insulted, Betrayed, or Desperate.* New York: HarperCollins, 2001. (harrietlerner.com)

Miller, Jean Baker, and Irene Pierce Stiver. *The Healing Connection: How Women form Relationships in Therapy and in Life.* Boston: Beacon Press, 1997. This book is also helpful to men.

LIGHTHEARTEDNESS

Bergson, Henri. *Laughter: An Essay on the Meaning of the Comic.* London: MacMillan, 1999. Bergson delivers the best and most helpful understanding of humor that I am aware of. (authorama.com/laughter-1.html)

Gilbert, Donald. *The Upside Down Circle: Zen Laughter.* Nevada City, CA: Blue Dolphin, 1988.

Ratey, John J., and Eric Hagerman. *Spark: The Revolutionary New Science for Exercise and the Brain.* New York: Little, Brown and Company, 2008. Outstanding information on the benefits of exercise on our happiness, especially as it relates to the experience of lightness in our body, figuratively and literally.

RELIANCE

The Dalai Lama, and Howard C. Cutler, *The Art of Happiness: A Handbook for Living*. New York: Riverhead Books, 1998.

D'Aquili, Eugene, and Andrew Newberg. *The Mystical Mind: Probing the Biology of Religious Experience*. Minneapolis: Fortress Press, 1999.

Kornfield, Jack. *The Wise Heart: A Guide to the Universal Teachings of Buddhist Psychology*. New York: Bantam, 2008. Jack Kornfield, clinical psychologist and Buddhist, offers books, classes and videos focusing on compassion and meditation. (jackkornfield.org)

Singer, Peter. *One World: The Ethics of Globalization*. New Haven, CT: Yale University Press, 2002. (princeton.edu/~psinger/)

Swimme, Brian, and Thomas Berry. *The Universe Story from the Primordial Flaring Forth to the Ecozoic Era: A Celebration of the Unfolding of the Universe*. New York: HarperCollins, 1994. (brianswimme.org)

RECEPTIVITY

Batchelor, Martine. *Meditation for Life*. Boston: Wisdom Publication, 2001. (martinebatchelor.org)

Batchelor, Stephen. *Buddhism without Beliefs: A Contemporary Guide to Awakening*. New York: Riverhead Books, 1998. (stephenbatchelor.org)

———. *The Faith to Doubt: Glimpses of Buddhist Uncertainty*. Berkeley: Parallax Press, 1990.

Shermer, Michael. *The Science of Good & Evil: Why People Cheat, Gossip, Care, Share, and Follow the Golden Rule*. New York: Times Books, 2004. (skeptic.com)

Yongey Mingyur Rinpoche. *The Joy of Living: Unlocking the Secret & Science of Happiness*. New York: Harmony Books, 2007. While the science presented in Tibetan Buddhist Yongey Mingyur Rinpoche's book stands on shaky ground, the book features a very tolerant and clear introduction to meditation.

TRANQUILITY

Daido Loori, John. *Finding the Still Point: A Beginner's Guide to Zen Meditation*. Boston: Shambhala Publications, 2007. Includes a CD of guided instructions.

Merton, Thomas. *The Way of Chuang Tzu*. New York: Penguin, 1965.

Nhat Hanh, Thich. *The Miracle of Mindfulness: An Introduction to the Practice of Meditation*. Boston: Beacon Press, 1975. Zen Buddhist monk Thich Nhat Hanh offers many books, recordings, and meditation classes in Europe and the United States. He touches people with his exemplary peacefulness. (plumvillage.org and deerparkmonastery.org)

Additional Reading List

Here is a list of other resources that offer deeper insight into some of the topics discussed in this book.

LITERATURE ABOUT HINDUISM

Daniélou, Alain. *India: A Civilization of Differences: The Ancient Tradition of Universal Tolerance.* Rochester, VT: Inner Traditions, 2003.

———. *The Myths and Gods of India.* Rochester, VT: Inner Traditions, 1991.

Dimmitt, Cornelia, and J. A. B. van Buitenen. *Classical Hindu Mythology: A Reader in the Sanskrit Purānas.* Philadelphia: Temple University Press, 1978.

Doniger O'Flaherty, Wendy. *The Rig Veda: An Anthology.* New York: Penguin Books, 1981.

Fuller, C. J. *The Camphor Flame: Popular Hinduism and Society in India.* Princeton, NJ: Princeton University Press, 1992.

Klostermaier, Klaus K. *A Concise Encyclopedia of Hinduism.* Oxford: Oneworld Publication, 1998.

Mahony, William K. *The Artful Universe: An Introduction to the Vedic Religious Imagination.* Albany, NY: State University of New York Press, 1998.

Stoler Miller, Barbara. *The Bhagavad-Gita: Krishna's Counsel in Time of War.* New York: Bantam Dell, 1986.

Radhakrishnan, Sarvepalli, and Charles A. Moore. *A Source Book in Indian Philosophy.* Princeton, NJ: Princeton University Press, 1989.

LITERATURE ABOUT BUDDHISM

Eckel, Malcolm David. *Buddhism: Origins, Beliefs, Practices, Holy Texts, Sacred Places.* New York: Oxford University Press, 2002.

Fronsdal, Gil. *The Dhammapada: A New Translation of the Buddhist Classic, with Annotations.* Boston: Shambhala Publications, 2005.

SHINTO

Hartz, Paula. *Shinto: World Religions.* 3rd ed. New York: Chelsea House, 2009.

CONFIDENCE OR COMPASSION

Patton, Kimberley C. and John S. Hawley. *Holy Tears: Weeping in the Religious Imagination.* Princeton, NJ: Princeton University Press, 2005.

JUDAISM

Gersh, Harry. *The Sacred Books of the Jews.* New York: Stein and Day, 1968.

Holtz, Barry W. *Back to the Sources: Reading Classic Jewish Texts.* New York: Simon & Schuster Paperbacks, 1984.

Kushner, Lawrence. *Jewish Spirituality: A Brief Introduction for Christians.* Woodstock, VT: Jewish Lights Publishing, 2001.

Index

About the Author

D r. Andrea F. Polard started both her meditation practice and interest in psychology when she was sixteen years old. Having endured childhood trauma, happiness was on her mind early on, as she wondered whether she and her fellow sufferers could really be happy. To find out how to reduce suffering and invite happiness, Dr. Polard enrolled in the Freie University of Berlin, Germany, where she focused her academic study on creativity and the smile, and where she received her first master's degree in clinical psychology in 1993.

When Dr. Polard immigrated to the United States, she enrolled at Ryokan College in Los Angeles where she earned her second master's degree in clinical psychology (1996) as well as her doctorate in psychology (1998). Dr. Polard's training as a psychotherapist was extensive and included psychodynamic therapies, mind-body therapy, Buddhist-oriented therapy, Zen meditation, and mindfulness practice. As she discovered happiness was indeed possible for all, she decided to share the necessary skills with others and began to write *A Unified Theory of Happiness*, a project that took her twelve years to complete.

Dr. Polard founded the Los Angeles Center for Zen Psychology, which offers Zen psychotherapy, consultations, workshops, training, and meditation groups based on both Western and Eastern thought (LosAngelesCenterForZenPsychology.com). She lives with her husband and their three children in the quiet mountains of Topanga. For more information, visit andreapolard.com.

About Sounds True

Sounds True is a multimedia publisher whose mission is to inspire and support personal transformation and spiritual awakening. Founded in 1985 and located in Boulder, Colorado, we work with many of the leading spiritual teachers, thinkers, healers, and visionary artists of our time. We strive with every title to preserve the essential "living wisdom" of the author or artist. It is our goal to create products that not only provide information to a reader or listener, but that also embody the quality of a wisdom transmission.

For those seeking genuine transformation, Sounds True is your trusted partner. At SoundsTrue.com you will find a wealth of free resources to support your journey, including exclusive weekly audio interviews, free downloads, interactive learning tools, and other special savings on all our titles.

To listen to a podcast interview with Sounds True publisher Tami Simon and author Andrea F. Polard, please visit SoundsTrue.com/bonus/UnifiedHappiness.

SOUNDS TRUE
many voices, one journey